CONTEMPORARY AMERICAN SPEECHES

A Sourcebook of Speech Forms and Principles

Fifth Edition

WIL A. LINKUGEL
University of Kansas

R. R. ALLEN
University of Wisconsin

RICHARD L. JOHANNESEN
Northern Illinois University

**KENDALL/HUNT
PUBLISHING COMPANY**
Dubuque, Iowa

B   402616   01

Contents

Preface

  This edition, like the first four editions of *Contemporary American Speeches,* is dedicated to the belief that acquisition of speaking skills is best achieved through three complementary lines of study: *theory,* from which the student may gain a basic understanding of the speech act; *example,* through which the student may evaluate precept in the light of real and varied instances of public discourse; and *practice,* in which the student may apply rhetorical principles to the creation of speeches. This book is primarily designed to contribute to the second of these lines of study, *example.*

  Teaching by example is an ancient practice. Isocrates used the study of speeches as one of his principle teaching devices. Cicero, himself an assiduous student of speeches, advocated the study of Greek and Roman speech models to all aspiring orators. Quintilian said, "It is from . . . authors worthy of our study that we must draw our stock of words, the variety of our figures and our methods of composition." Chauncey Goodrich noted that "He who would teach eloquence must do it chiefly by examples." Edmund Burke studied Demosthenes; Daniel Webster studied Burke; and Woodrow Wilson studied Webster.

  In producing a fifth edition of *Contemporary American Speeches,* we again faced the critical question of which speeches to retain and which ones to replace. As we have done with earlier editions, we approached this problem by surveying as many users of the previous editions as we could, asking them to tell us which speeches they found especially useful and which ones they felt could be discarded. We have also been guided by our own teaching experience, noting those addresses that generated much student discussion and comprehension of speech principles. We have once more decided that *contemporary* should refer to the sixties and seventies, as in the last two previous editions, and, of course, the eighties. We have selected all our speeches from that time frame. Following these guidelines, and a desire to include some new and challenging speeches on currently critical problems, we have included 23 new speeches and retained 19 from the fourth edition. Only four speeches have proven so popular that they have been used in all five editions of this volume: Martin Luther King's "Love, Law, and Civil Disobedience," Douglas

MacArthur's "Farewell to the Cadets," John F. Kennedy's "Inaugural Address," and Martin Luther King's "I Have a Dream." One other speaker, Jenkin Lloyd Jones, although his speech has been changed, has appeared in all editions, because his addresses are certain to generate classroom discussion. There are seven student speeches in this edition, at least one in each category, except for Social Cohesion.

We have also revised some of the chapter essays. Although the basic thrust and substance of each essay remains the same, we have sought to improve some of our explanations of basic concepts. Each essay develops criteria that the student may use in exploring and evaluating the speeches. The suggestions "For Further Reading" at the end of each chapter have been updated.

Our purpose in preparing headnotes for speeches in all instances has been to provide factual background concerning the speech and speaker, and to provide thought provoking suggestions and questions that hopefully will direct the student to discern vital rhetorical dimensions of each address. We significantly revised introductory headnotes for several speeches that we have retained.

Whether the teacher chooses to emphasize speech forms or speech principles, this book should prove useful. As in previous editions, we have included an Index of Rhetorical Principles which notes the passages in each speech that best illustrate the major speech principles discussed in modern speech textbooks.

This book can also serve as the core text in a course in Contemporary American Public Address. Although we have emphasized speech forms and principles rather than "name" speakers, this book nevertheless embodies typical addresses given today on some of our society's most pressing questions. The speech forms themselves assure coverage of the spectrum of contemporary public address. Knowledge, facts, values, problems, and policies have always been rhetoric's essence. At the same time, ceremonial address continues to be a vital form for social cohesion.

We again wish to acknowledge our indebtedness to the many people who have given us permission to reprint the speeches in this book. Especially important in this respect once more has been the cooperation of the managing editors of *Vital Speeches of the Day.* We are also grateful for the recommendations that have been so thoughtfully provided by colleagues, from our own and other institutions, who used this book in any or all of its first four editions.

W. A. L.
R. R. A.
R. L. J.

September 1981

Chapter 1

WHY STUDY
SPEECHES?

*Only as the constant companions of Demosthenes, Cicero, Burke,
Fox, Channing, and Webster can we hope to become orators.*

Woodrow Wilson

The primary purpose of *Contemporary American Speeches* is to present a collection of speeches for student analysis and evaluation. Just as Woodrow Wilson considered the study of speeches essential to his personal development as a speaker, we hope that this chapter will stimulate your thinking about the importance of such study in your own intellectual life.

WE STUDY SPEECHES TO INCREASE
OUR KNOWLEDGE OF HUMANITY

One of the purposes of a college education is to encourage students to ponder the nature of their own humanity. In most degree programs, students are encouraged to engage in liberal studies as a complement to the sequence of professional courses which leads to specialized careers. A professional person is, after all, a person: a lawyer is a person who practices law, a teacher is a person who teaches, a doctor is a person who practices medicine, a scientist is a person who studies the physical world in which we live. Through liberal studies, students are encouraged to develop insights regarding the potentialities and limitations of the human condition. Through such knowledge, a system of values should emerge that provides the basis for future decisions, both professional and personal.

Students may take varied paths in their efforts to understand what it means to be human. Each liberal study holds such promise—and rightfully so. Nothing thought or made or done by people is alien to the student in search of human understanding. Emerson said: "Raphael paints wisdom; Handel sings it; Phidias carves it; Shakespeare writes it; Wren builds it; Columbus sails it; Luther preaches it; Washington arms it; Watt mechanizes it." In each of these studies, students may find evidence of the creative struggle of human beings with their environment. And from each of these studies, students may gain insights into their own lives.

In the liberal arts tradition, speeches deserve to be studied because they are a unique form of human expression. No other artifact of social life reflects the same exact process. A painting encompasses the elements of thought and form; yet a speech is composed of language. A poem embraces thought, language, and form; yet a speech is conveyed by sound. Theatre makes use of thought, language, form, and sound; yet a speech is at once more urgent and real, more literal and spontaneous. A speech is a unique product of human creativity; it calls for special understanding as does a painting or a poem, a statue or a scroll.

Speeches have a quality that makes them especially deserving of study by students in search of human understanding; speeches are highly transparent. Oral rhetoric stimulates human beings in dynamic confrontation with ideas and audiences. In speeches, students will find men and women articulating the noble ideals of our civilization and making enlightened judgments on the great social, moral, and political issues of our own and other times. In speeches, students will also find men and women degrading our common humanity and concocting themes of hatred and bigotry. In speeches, the potentialities and limitations of the human condition are clearly reflected.

WE STUDY SPEECHES TO DERIVE STANDARDS FOR THE CRITICAL APPRAISAL OF PUBLIC DISCOURSE

Few will question the claim that the quality of our public dialogue is not what it might be. In lecture halls, we have grown accustomed to speakers who are dull, disorganized, and unclear. In chambers of social decisionmaking, we have come to accept as the norm underdeveloped ideas expressed in careless language and sloppy speech. And even at moments of public ceremony, we expect speeches that are trite and mundane when what is called for is an inspiring rearticulation of our social purpose and identity.

As members of audiences, we have come to demand too little of those who address us. Through the study of speeches, we may develop higher standards for the public dialogue. We may come to demand more of those who address us, both in terms of the merit of their ideas and their means of public expression.

The study of speeches offers a broad familiarity with the crucial issues of humanity. Our communion with the past, the freedom of our citizens, the quality of our private and public life, our hopes for the future—all of these are evident in the public dialogue. Through an awareness of the significant issues of our own and other times, students may come to reject trivial issues and petty thoughts as unworthy of public attention.

Through the study of speeches, students may also acquire insights regarding the habits of intellect through which responsible speakers examine, test, and temper ideas. Through such knowledge, they may appraise the worth of a speaker's critical processes. They may test the sufficiency of the speaker's proof. They may deny the specious inference and the faulty deduction. They may reject simplistic answers to complex social questions.

But the enlightened critic may not stop here. Public discourse does not exist in a social vacuum. It is not soliloquy, but purposive address seeking to impart to its hearers some knowledge or interpretation, some value or course of action. Public discourse always seeks to influence the hearer and to change his or her behavior—whether cognitive or overt. If ideas are to have social utility, they must be transformed from private conceptions into meaningful public statements. Speakers must so develop and project their thoughts that direction is given to those who listen. They must choose from a complex of elements those most likely to give energy and vitality to their ideas in a particular public context.

Through the study of speeches, students will come to realize that speakers can adapt ideas to audiences in meaningful and socially productive ways. While recognizing the shortcomings of the public intellect, they will know that speakers have made complex ideas clear. While recognizing that speakers have exploited public avarice and ignorance in achieving personal power, they will know that other speakers have fostered social excellence. While recognizing that speeches have embodied appeals to low motives and base instincts, they will know that oratory has sometimes inspired audiences to act in accord with the noble ideals of humanity.

The dimensions of rhetorical choice are numerous. In Chapter 2, you will be introduced to thirteen questions which will guide your study of the means speakers employ in rendering their ideas clear, persuasive, and memorable. As you apply these questions to speeches, you will develop an increased appreciation for the artistry which undergirds effective public communication. As you witness speakers conveying the essence of significant thoughts with skill and integrity, you will have cause to reject other speakers whose expressions are feeble, whose appeals are base, whose strategies are unethical, and whose purposes are suspect.

WE STUDY SPEECHES TO ENLARGE AND DEEPEN OUR UNDERSTANDING OF RHETORICAL THEORY

The student of speech, faced with a body of precepts set forth in a contemporary basic public speaking textbook, will often fail to assign importance to the ideas expressed. The text, it may seem, is too firm in its adherence to inviolate rules, too committed to the perpetuation of useless names and distinctions, and too verbose in the expression of common sense. Any body of principles divorced from the context that gave it being may seem drab and useless. But if these principles are viewed in their proper context, they tend to become meaningful and even intellectually stimulating.

Rhetorical theory was born of the attempt of people to systematize their observations of the purposive and dynamic public interactions of other people. In the fifth century B.C. the first body of rhetorical precepts emerged from Corax's observations of the attempts of his fellow citizens of Syracuse to give social order to a society newly emerged from tyranny. In the centuries that followed, countless other people recorded their observations of identifiable speech principles. While those who followed owed a great debt to those who preceded them, each generation of theorists sought to redefine and reconceptualize the art of speaking in a manner consistent with their own perceptions of public address as it occurred in their own cultures and in their own times.

Authors of modern public speaking textbooks must also acknowledge their debt to the great rhetorical tradition. Their task, however, is not the perpetuation of "the intellectual faults of eminent men." Rather, they seek to test and temper the principles of the art of public communication. They must blend with the old the particular insights of the new—insights gleaned from the scholarship of their own and related disciplines, insights gathered from their own judicious observation of public discourse. Building on the rhetorical philosophies of the past with a knowledge of the present, modern theorists seek to create not a memorial to the past but a structure consistent with the needs and realities of the present. Such work is vital and meaningful, not drab or devoid of intellectual stimulation.

Is it strange that what is bright with intellectual challenge in process often seems boring in product? Not really. The excitement of the intellectual search for precepts by one person is easily lost when relegated to a body of generalizations for the consumption of another. It is not that the theory is bad; it is just that theory alone, divorced from the world from which it was abstracted, is inadequate.

Would it not be best, then, for the student of speech to seek out his or her own precepts? Not really. The perceptive student, skilled in listening to popular instances of communication and afforded such great examples as Burke, Churchill, and Roosevelt, could derive his or her own theory of speech. But at what expense of time? At what expense to progress? Each student would have to begin anew the quest for order and meaning, as helplessly alone as if no one else had ever walked the same path.

While the problem is not fully solved by presenting the student with the generalizations of another's mind, concisely arranged, neither is it fully solved by presenting the student with a body of speech masterpieces, past and present, with the caution to keep "an open mind and vigilant eye." The study of a public speaking textbook is, like the study of examples of public discourse, one important element in the training of the student of public speaking. Preference for one should not lead to a discarding of the other. A public speaking textbook is a body of generalizations drawn from the author's contemplation of the long tradition of rhetorical theory, the scholarship of the day, and his or her own perceptions of human communication. It exists not to inhibit but to stimulate. Intelligent students will put the precepts of a textbook to the pragmatic test of actual public life. They will realize, as did Quintilian, that "rhetoric would be a very easy and small matter, if it could be included in one short body of rules, but rules must generally be altered to suit the nature of each individual case, the time, the occasion, and the necessity itself. . . ." By testing the generalizations of a textbook in the light of real and varied instances of public discourse, students will learn to challenge, question, and compare; and, ultimately, they will develop for themselves a theory of speech that is both comprehensive and personal.

WE STUDY SPEECHES TO DEVELOP AN APPRECIATION FOR EMINENCE IN PUBLIC ADDRESS

In 1852, Chauncey Goodrich, Professor of Rhetoric at Yale College, reviewed his teaching philosophy in the preface to his work *Select British Eloquence.* He wrote:

> My object was not only to awaken in the minds of the class that love of genuine eloquence which is the surest pledge of success, but to aid them in catching the spirit of the authors read, and, by analyzing passages selected for the purpose, to initiate the pupil in those higher principles which (whether they were conscious of it or not) have always guided the great masters of the art, till he should learn the *unwritten* rules of oratory, which operate by a kind of instinct upon the mind, and are far more important than any that are found in the books.

This passage has merit today for students who would be more than followers of blueprints. It recommends that students develop an appreciation for eminence in public address, a love of eloquence, by looking beyond textbook principles to the unwritten rules of the art. It suggests the importance of developing a sense of the rightness, or the strength, or the felicity of a thought or an expression through exposure to speeches. Such an appreciation of eminence serves to inspire students to seek in their own works only the highest level of excellence.

Students who have come to acquire this appreciation for eminence will reject trivial subjects. They will understand that a concern for significant ideas has been at the heart of great oratory since ancient times. Demosthenes spoke for the freedom of a city. Churchill spoke for the survival of a nation. Roosevelt spoke for the freedom of man. Kennedy spoke for peace in a divided world. Rhetorical eminence presupposes worthy ideas to express, ideas that merit the attention and efforts of the speaker and the concern of the audience.

But rhetorical excellence depends of eloquence of manner as well as on sublimity of matter. Given significance of ideas, great public address demands an expression that renders the idea in a striking and compelling way, giving it life and vitality. Stephen Spender once wrote a poem called *I Think Continuously of Those Who Were Truly Great*. As public speakers, students may find great inspiration from the speeches of people who surpassed the ordinary and achieved new heights in skillful and effective communication.

The dimensions of rhetorical excellence are diverse. Some speakers provide models of eminence in delivery. Billy Graham, to whom charisma is often attributed, is a model of both vocal and physical involvement and intensity. Barbara Jordan, who captured the spirit of the 1976 Democratic Convention, is known for her vocal precision and overall dynamism. Paul Harvey, with his distinctive oral style, has captivated generations of Americans via radio. Student speakers, finding inspiration in the delivery of able speakers, may seek in their own delivery the same sense of dynamism and involvement.

Students may also gain inspiration from those who use language in lively and memorable ways. The history of public discourse is rich with examples of language which illuminated thoughts in compelling ways: Roosevelt dispelled panic with the expression, "The only thing we have to fear is fear itself"; Churchill imparted strength with the expression "This was their finest hour"; Kennedy inspired dedication with the expression "Ask not what your country can do for you—ask what you can do for your country"; Martin Luther King generated hope with the expression "I have a dream." Students who are exposed to eminence in language usage may acquire an intimate sense of the rightness, appropriateness, and artistry of language that will help them to give greater force to their own ideas.

In the study of speeches, students may also find eminence in ordering ideas, marshalling supporting materials, and enlisting the emotions of audiences. Having acquired an appreciation for eloquence, students may demand more of themselves at those moments when they give public expression to their ideas.

CONCLUSION

The study of speeches can play an important role in the intellectual development of contemporary college students. Through such study we may expect to *increase our knowledge of humanity, to derive standards for the critical appraisal of public discourse, to enlarge and deepen our understanding of rhetorical theory,* and *to develop an appreciation for eminence in public address.*

For Further Reading

ON SPEECH AS A HUMANE STUDY

Linkugel, Wilmer A., and Johannesen, Richard L. "The Study of Masterpieces of Public Address." *Southern Speech Journal,* Summer 1960, pp. 289–97. Presents the rationale for the scrutiny of noted speeches in the classroom.

Nichols, Marie Hochmuth. *Rhetoric and Criticism.* Louisiana State University Press, 1963. Chapter 1 analyzes rhetoric and public address as a humane study—as a study of people making enlightened choices in a rhetorical context.

Walter, Otis. *Speaking Intelligently.* Macmillan, 1976. Chapter 1 examines the role of rhetoric as a force in the growth of civilization.

Wilson, John F., and Arnold, Carroll C. *Public Speaking as a Liberal Art.* 4th ed. Allyn and Bacon, 1978. Chapter 1 examines speech as a liberal study showing people apprehending truths about themselves and their environment and communicating them to others.

ON THE CRITICAL ANALYSIS OF SPEECHES

Auer, J. Jeffery. *Brigance's Speech Communication.* Appleton-Century-Crofts, 1967. Chapter 12 examines speech criticism from the perspective of three types of critics: scholar critics, peer critics, and citizen critics.

Bryant, Donald C., and Wallace, Karl R. *Fundamentals of Public Speaking.* 5th ed. Appleton-Century-Crofts, 1976. Chapter 22 presents a method for the study of speeches.

Cathcart, Robert. *Post Communication: Rhetorical Analysis and Evaluation.* 2nd ed. Bobbs-Merrill, 1981. A brief but very useful treatment of speech criticism for the beginning speech student.

Wilson, John F., and Arnold, Carroll C. *Public Speaking as a Liberal Art.* 4th ed. Allyn and Bacon, 1978. Chapter 11 presents a methodology for the critical appraisal of speeches.

(See also references following Chapter 2.)

ON RHETORICAL THEORY

Aristotle. *Rhetoric.* The definitive ancient treatise on the art of rhetoric.

Clark, Donald Lemen. *Rhetoric in Greco-Roman Education.* Columbia University Press, 1957. Chapter 2 explains what the ancients meant by rhetoric. Chapter 4 presents the five ancient rhetorical canons of invention, organization, style, delivery, and memory. Chapter 5 discusses how the ancients used speech models for study and emulation.

Golden, James et al., eds. *The Rhetoric of Western Thought.* 2nd ed. Kendall-Hunt Publishing Company, 1978. A collection of original and reprinted essays that trace the development of theories of rhetoric from Greco-Roman times to the present.

Wilson, John F., and Arnold, Carroll C. *Public Speaking as a Liberal Art.* 4th ed. Allyn and Bacon, 1978. Appendix A presents an overview of the historical development of rhetorical theory.

ON EMINENCE IN PUBLIC ADDRESS

Blankenship, Jane. *Public Speaking: A Rhetorical Perspective.* 2nd ed. Prentice-Hall, 1972. Chapters 6 and 7 examine both theoretical and practical matters of language style.

Bryant, Donald C. *Rhetorical Dimensions in Criticism.* Louisiana State University Press, 1973. Chapter 6 explores the concept of "eloquence" in discourse.

Longinus. "On the Sublime," in Lane Cooper, ed., *The Art of the Writer.* Cornell University Press, 1952. Chapter 4. This is a classic treatise on the nature of sublimity in discourse.

Osborn, Michael. *Orientations to Rhetorical Style.* Science Research Associates, Modcom Modules in Speech Communication, 1976. A 35 page booklet that discusses the significance, techniques, and abuses of language choices in discourse.

Wilson, John F., and Carroll C. Arnold. *Public Speaking as a Liberal Art.* 4th ed. Allyn and Bacon, 1978. Chapter 9 discusses the nature of oral and written style, resources of language, and criteria of effective style.

Chapter 2

THE ANALYSIS
OF SPEECHES

A liberally educated citizen ought ideally to be able to explain what happens when he is addressed by a speaker. He ought to be able to describe the speech he hears and to explain why and how it contributed to the results that followed. . . . None of us has achieved precision in observing and analyzing public speech, nor are we likely to achieve it soon; but we can do better than we are accustomed to.

John Wilson and Carroll Arnold

This book is a collection of speeches that exemplify the major forms and principles of public address in contemporary American society. A rationale for the study of speeches has been presented in the preceding chapter; it thus remains for us to place in perspective the underlying philosophy and the procedural patterns for the use of this book.

THE ART OF RHETORIC

Rhetoric is a term with varied and vague meanings today. Major dictionaries, reflecting the popular confusion, list numerous definitions. Among those commonly cited are the following: the speech of stereotyped politicians—empty, misleading, insincere, and high-flown; an oratorical display or exaggeration; highly figurative language, commonly called "purple patches"; the art of prose writing; and, originally, the art of oratory. *Rhetoric, oratory,* and *eloquence* all come from roots meaning *to speak.* Quintilian, the Roman schoolmaster, placed the art of rhetoric at the center of his educational system. Aristotle thought that rhetoric has the capacity to prevent the triumph of fraud and injustice, to instruct popular audiences, to help persons see both sides of an issue, and to help provide a dignified and distinctive means of self-defense.

As used in this book, *rhetoric* is the art of selecting, adapting, and communicating ideas primarily through verbal means to achieve a desired response from a specific audience. The rhetorical act involves making choices related to both the matter of communication—what subjects may be chosen, what issues they embrace, and what values they embody—and the manner of communicating perceptions in order to produce a desired effect.

It is important to the welfare of a democratic society that both of these types of choices be enlightened and ethical. Interest in the effectiveness of rhetorical techniques must not outstrip concern for their ethical use. Ethical judgments about rhetorical means employed to achieve ends or judgments of the ethics of the ends cannot be escaped. Each of us must decide for ourself the ethical balance point between our own idea in its pure form and that idea modified to achieve maximum impact on the specific audience.

In seeking to define the nature of rhetoric, theorists have identified those dimensions common to all instances of public discourse. First, there is a person with an idea and a speech purpose—the *speaker*. Governed by personal physical, intellectual, and experiential characteristics, the speaker seeks to choose, structure, and present the message so as to elicit a desired response. Next, there is the *audience*, whose members see the rhetorical context through individual lenses. They may view the speaker as expert, trustworthy, and of good will, or they may set up emotional blocks to the message because the speaker's image and reputation strike them unfavorably. They may view the speaker's thesis as interesting, wise, accurate, and of unquestionable merit, or they may erect barriers to the message because the speaker's ideas run contrary to the beliefs, attitudes, and values that their personal experiences have dictated to them. Finally, there is the *situation* in which the speech occurs: a place—a college classroom, the United States Senate, an ancient synagogue, or London's Hyde Park; a time— fourth century Athens, twentieth century Washington, before lunch or after, November 22, 1963, December 7, 1941; an occasion—a prep- school commencement, a Rotary Club meeting, a Presidential inaugural, a murder trial, a United Nations Security Council meeting, a business association luncheon, or a scientific conference.

In addition to the dimensions of speaker, audience, and situation, speech theorists have identified four variables common to the speech itself. In attempting to promote a desired response, the speaker makes choices about each of these four variables. Through the process that rhetoricians call *invention*, or the discovery and selection of the central idea and its supports, the speaker utilizes appropriate evidence, reasoning, and appeals to audience motives and values to substantiate the message. The remaining three variables relate to transmission of the idea. The speaker selects relevant patterns of *organization* to provide structure and design. Furthermore, the speaker employs impelling symbolization through *language* best suited to himself or herself, to the subject, to the audience, and to the situation. Finally, the speaker uses *delivery* to get the idea across to the audience. Whether he or she uses the impromptu, extemporaneous, manuscript, or memorized methods of delivery, the speaker employs both voice and body to reinforce the meaning and feeling embodied in the message.

Standard speech textbooks contain general principles on these dimensions and variables as they pertain to all types of speeches. By including these principles, these books seek to provide a foundation for purposive and responsible public address that you may use as a guide for your speaking behavior. We will not discuss all of these principles. Rather, we will present examples of speeches illustrating them. Additionally, the introduction to each chapter will focus on the nature of the constraints that influence the speaker's choices in adapting principles to that speech form.

THE FORMS OF SPEECHES

Since ancient times, scholars have sought to classify those social contexts that give rise to public discourse. They have done so in order to understand the nature of the rhetorical act and to formulate principles by which it might be taught. In 336 B.C. Aristotle saw men in law courts trying to secure justice concerning past actions. Accordingly, he identified one class of speeches as *forensic*. In a second instance, he witnessed men deliberating about problems and the best courses of action for their solution. He saw statesmen in the political assembly giving counsel and advice about the practicality and desirability of future policies. He saw men in legislative chambers seeking to exhort or dissuade those who could decide future action. These speeches he classified as *deliberative*. Finally, he observed men at ceremonial gatherings praising the virtuous and eulogizing the noble dead. At other times he beheld men launching vitriolic attacks against others at public gatherings. These speeches of praise and blame he labeled *epideictic*.

As Aristotle profited from appraising the speeches of his day, so too may the modern scholar of rhetoric profit from an examination of contemporary speeches. As we survey twentieth century public address, we see people in public gatherings translating technical information into popular terms; we see others describing an experience or event. At other times we see people publicly probing for definitive meanings, searching for the causes of natural and social phenomena, dispelling stereotypes, and seeking out the implications of things and events. We classify this type of speech to create understanding as *imparting knowledge*. In other situations, we see lawyers seeking decisions on the guilt or innocence of their clients, politicians asking for acceptance of what they validate as facts, and citizens arguing over the "real" cause of something. These speakers are *affirming propositions of fact*. On some occasions, we witness speakers urging adoption of new standards for human behavior, and we see drama and literary critics applying criteria to art forms to establish a judgment about their quality. When people seek to formulate or change human values or to apply standards as measurements of quality, we label their efforts *affirming propositions of value.* In some instances, we observe speakers seeking to make people vitally aware of problems that hinder personal and social fulfillment. These persons are *creating concern for problems.* In still other situations, we see persons advocating programs for the solution of perplexing problems and for the ultimate betterment of society. This effort we call *affirming propositions of policy.* Finally, we see speakers on ceremonial occasions asking for a unity of spirit or for reenergizing of effort or commitment. When a person urges increased dedication to the existing values of a group, we label that purpose *intensifying social cohesion.*

SOME GUIDELINES FOR ANALYSIS OF SPEECHES

Each of the remaining chapters in this anthology is introduced by a brief essay setting forth guidelines for analyzing the speeches which illustrate that form. At this point we will limit ourselves to suggesting some potential general dimensions and questions for use in judging speechmaking.[1]

Our suggestions are not intended as a definitive statement on speech criticism. They simply are some starting points for possible use in assessing speeches inside and outside the classroom. We do not view this set of guidelines as the only method or the "best" method of speech analysis. Other useful approaches for the criticism of speeches are described in some of the Sources for Further Reading at the end of this and subsequent chapters.

Obviously, in assessing a specific speech, each dimension or question would not be of equal importance. You might, for instance, consider reasonableness and ethicality more crucial than language and delivery. The criteria you use for evaluation should be those particularly appropriate for both the general speech form and the specific speech. Furthermore, consider how dimensions and questions may point to interaction of factors. How might a listener's value system influence her or his perception of what is reasonable? Or how might a speaker's attitude toward an audience influence that speaker's credibility or perceived ethicality?

[1]Some of the following material is adapted from the contributions of Richard L. Johannesen for *Principles and Types of Speech Communication,* Seventh Edition, by Alan H. Monroe and Douglas Ehninger, pp. 245-47, 249-57, 453-63. Copyright © 1974, 1967, 1962, 1955, 1949, 1939, 1935 by Scott, Foresman and Company.

As you analyze a particular speech, you may find that some aspects of it are so prominent and worthy of note that they "invite," indeed they "demand," your critical attention. Aspects of a speech may be noteworthy, for example, because they are so frequent, so obvious, so unique, so subtle, so probably effective, so suberbly handled, so poorly done, or so detrimental to probable effectiveness. Based on the general nature of the speech and the rhetorical aspects that invite your critical attention, you probably will select for use only some of the following dimensions or questions.

In presenting an oral or written analysis of a speech, the quality of your criticism will be improved if you discuss *both* strengths and weaknesses; criticism is not solely the making of negative judgments. In addition, quality is improved by specifying, explaining, and justifying the lines of inquiry, framework for analysis, or standards for evaluation you will utilize.

1. *To what factors in the immediate occasion or more general relevant situation does the speaker seem to be responding?*

Speechmaking is situationally motivated and a speaker makes choices of communicative ends and means in response to a set of circumstances and to a specific audience. Hence, it is well to begin an analysis of most speeches by discussing the societal milieu, the nature of the physical and ideological setting, and the probable causes that led up to the speech. How might factors in the occasion or prevailing ideological climate have influenced the speaker's purpose and/or methods? To what in particular does the speaker seem to be responding: To a problem, opportunity, lack of information, duty, challenge, ceremonial obligation, attack, issue, or routine invitation?

What is the nature and significance of the specific audience addressed by the speaker? Consider the relevance of such matters as size, age, sex, occupation, educational background, memberships in organizations, ethnic background, and knowledge of the subject of the speech. Is the primary audience the one physically present, or is it perhaps one to be exposed "second-hand" through the various mass media, or is it one "observing" a confrontation between a speaker and audience? Are there any secondary audiences intended for the message?

Sometimes the impact of a speech is influenced by such factors in the occasion as time of day, room acoustics and seating arrangement, preceding and following speeches, and audience customs and expectations. Clearly the expectations for a presidential inaugural address and for a political rally speech differ. Depending upon the role the audience expects a speaker to fulfill (such as leader, advisor, expert, lecturer, intruder, spokesperson for them or others), they may expect different evidence, appeals, proposals, language, and delivery. How adequately a speaker handles questions and answers in a forum period after the speech may influence audience perceptions of the speech.

The speech may play a role in some larger campaign of communication or in the activities of a particular social movement. Is the speaker a spokesperson in behalf of some group or other person and thus probably less free to voice entirely his or her own viewpoint? Is the speech a major effort to be supplemented by other modes of communication? Is it one in a planned series of addresses on the subject? Is the central communication thrust on this subject being carried out through other modes and channels with this speech as only a minor part of the total program? What influence might presentation via radio and/or television have on the impact of the speech?

2. What seem to be the speaker's general and specific purposes?

Typical general purposes are to entertain, to present information and increase understanding, to reinforce existing beliefs and values, to change values and beliefs, and to secure overt action. Consider whether the speaker's intent seems to be identification and agreement, shock and arousal, or confrontation and alienation. What more concrete outcome does the speaker seem to want from his or her audience? What exactly does the speaker want the audience to believe, feel, or do? Does the specific purpose seem appropriate for the subject, audience, and occasion?

Given the audience and relevant circumstances, probe whether the speaker's purposes appear realistic and achievable. Remember that countermessages from other communicators, or unexpected and uncontrollable events, may work on listener's minds to weaken the impact of the speaker's message. Remember, also, that some situations are not altered very easily through public speech. No matter what is said to some audiences, for instance, they may refuse to modify their strongly held beliefs, values, and actions. And some audiences may believe, accurately or inaccurately, that they do not possess the power, authority, skill, money, or facilities to adopt the speaker's idea.

3. How does the speaker capture and sustain audience attention and interest?

No matter how sincere the speaker's intent, no matter how sound her or his reasoning, no matter how worthwhile the message, if the audience's attention is not aroused at the outset and maintained throughout, the speaker's efforts are doomed to failure. If no one listens, belief and action cannot be influenced as the speaker hopes. In the content, language, and delivery of the speech, are such interest-factors as conflict, suspense, familiarity, novelty, humor, action, curiosity, and concreteness capitalized on? Is interest heightened through such means as narration of a story, vivid description, analogy, contrast, hypothetical and factual examples, and extended illustrations?

4. *How does the speaker strive to insure that the audience clearly understands the message as intended?*

Assess the probability that listeners will know exactly what the speaker is asking of them and concretely how to help implement that idea or proposal. Judge whether ideas are presented accurately and clearly and whether extremes of complexity and simplification are avoided. If ambiguity seems employed intentionally, what factors in the subject or occasion might account for or even justify it? How adequately does the introductory portion of the speech gain attention, challenge the audience, lead smoothly into the topic, or create goodwill for the speaker and topic? How adequately does the conclusion summarize basic ideas, convey a sense of completion, leave the listeners in an appropriate mood, or stimulate acceptance of the central belief or action sought? Consider what patterns of organization the speaker uses to foster unity and clarity: chronological, spatial, problem-solution, general-to-specific or vice versa, cause-effect, examination of alternatives, and so forth. If the speech lacks clear structure, is this apparently due to speaker ineptness or may there be some justification for it?

To promote understanding, how does the speaker utilize such devices as repetition, restatement, transitions, internal summaries, parallel phrasing, numerical "sign-posts," itemization, association with the familiar, examples and illustrations, questions and answers, statistics, and definitions. Some definitions are "objective" in the sense that they report widely accepted, noncontroversial meanings current with experts or with the public. Other definitions are "persuasive" in the sense that the speaker is asking the audience to accept her or his particular meaning as the correct or appropriate definition for a concept which is subject to challenge or controversy. How does the speaker employ audiovisual aids and vocal-physical delivery to increase understanding? If appropriate, how adequately does the speaker answer such standard questions as who, what, where, when, why, and how?

5. *To what degree might listeners perceive the speaker's proposal (idea, belief, policy) as sound and reasonable?*

Bear in mind that accepted standards of reason, logic, and soundness may vary from one audience to another, from one culture to another, or between fields of discourse (such as politics, religion, natural science, law, historiography). As a critic you may wish to apply to the message some "universal" or "traditional" tests of soundness for evidence and reasoning. But also consider whether such tests are appropriate for the specific speech situation or subject matter. Furthermore, an audience may not make a sharp distinction between so-called logical and emotional appeals. For instance, a set of statistics showing a high probability of listeners being stricken with some form of cancer during their lifetime may be perceived by them as both logical and emotional; for them it simply is a reasonable item of support.

Assess how adequately the speaker employs evidence and reasoning to demonstrate that his or her proposal actually will work, will solve the problem, will be efficient, and will not be too costly. Is the proposal feasible despite such potential limitations as minimal time, personnel, or finances? Evaluate the soundness of the factual examples, expert testimony, literal analogies, statistics, and cause-effect reasoning the speaker employs. Is the speaker's idea consistent with the relevant beliefs and attitudes of the audience? If not, is such inconsistency seemingly due to speaker ineptitude or planned to serve some persuasive function? Is there a legitimate connection between the speaker's idea or purpose and the audience's relevant needs, motives, goals, and emotions? Are listeners made to "feel" a personal stake in the outcome? Has the speaker exaggerated the connection or appealed to irrelevant needs?

What premises or fundamental beliefs are verbalized by the speaker as underpinnings for further argument? Implicitly undergirding the speaker's ideas, are there any unstated assumptions, any unspoken basic beliefs, values, premises, or stereotypes? Are such unstated assumptions probably omitted to avoid scrutiny by the audience or because the speaker and audience already share the assumption? Consider in what ways the spoken and unspoken assumptions reflect the speaker's conception of reality, truth, dependable knowledge, goodness, religion, or the essence of human nature. What might be the intended function or unintended impact of omission of an expected idea or of silence on a controversial issue?

6. *To what degree do the speaker's ideas harmonize with the audience's relevant values?*

A value, for our purposes, is defined as a conception of "The Good" or "The Desirable." Honesty, fairness, honor, efficiency, progress, economy, courage, safety, prudence, and patriotism all are examples of possible values for persons. During the 1976 presidential political campaign, Jimmy Carter overtly emphasized such values as compassion, truthfulness, belief in God, justice, love, integrity, and willingness to sacrifice. A value may function either generally, as a goal motivating our behavior, or specifically, as a standard we use to assess the acceptability of means to accomplish ends. We might, for instance, recognize that a policy or solution is efficient and economical, but reject that program for being dishonest and inhumane. Frequently dominant personal or group values are reflected in slogans or mottos: "Liberty, Equality, Fraternity"; "Duty, Honor, Country"; "Law and Order"; "Law and Order with Justice"; "Freedom Now"; "All Power to the People"; "Peace with Honor."

Values are not proved or disproved in quite the same way as "factual" matters. We measure the length of a table with a ruler to demonstrate that it is indeed one meter long. But it is difficult, if not impossible, to measure precisely degrees of beauty, courage, and honesty. And proposed measures of freedom, progress, or efficiency often themselves are controversial. As a culture or subculture develops, a given value becomes accepted as functional for that group. Naturally, the values which predominate often vary from one culture to another. One culture may hold punctuality as a basic value, for example, while another deems being on time of little importance. We develop our own individual value systems in the context of larger cultural and subcultural value systems.

Usually we *rank* the values we hold into a rough *hierarchy* so that some values to which we are committed take precedence over others. In fact, in *The New Rhetoric,* philosopher Chaim Perelman argues that a "particular audience is characterized less by values it accepts than by the way it grades them." Note also that in a specific situation several audience values may come into conflict, thus forcing a choice of one value over another in making a decision. The audience may continue to believe in both values, but temporarily set one aside in favor of the other. For instance, a speaker may advocate in a given situation adherence to honesty over efficiency, patriotism over self-concern, economy over education, or humaneness over frankness.

A warning is in order. A speaker often overtly appeals to a seemingly potent value to which the audience *says* it is committed. But do not assume that the audience always will *act* in accordance with the declared value. In a particular instance the audience may perceive some other value as more important; they may not *apply* the value appealed to and to which they in general are devoted.

In assessing the various value appeals of a speaker, consider the general approach used. Is the aim to get listeners to adopt a new value to replace an outmoded one, perhaps through a redefinition of the meaning we should have for the original value-word? Is the speaker urging acceptance of her or his value judgment of something as an accurate and appropriate judgment? In what ways does the speech function to reinforce and reenergize values already held by the audience? Is the speaker creating concern for a problem by showing that relevant audience values are being threatened or violated? Is the speaker advocating adoption of a policy or solution in part because it harmonizes with or fosters relevant audience values? By exploring such questions, you can move toward an understanding of specific techniques through which a speaker attempts to link an idea or proposal to potent audience values.

7. To what degree is the speaker perceived as a credible source on the subject?

The positive or negative perceptions that listeners have of a speaker's personal qualities play a major role in determining whether they will accept his or her information, arguments, or proposal. Ancient Greek and Roman rhetorical theorists called this concept *ethos* and identified its three major elements as good sense, good character, and good will. Contemporary communication scholars use such labels as source credibility, image, and reputation to describe audience attitude toward the speaker; they have identified expertness and trustworthiness as the two most potent dimensions of speaker credibility. Listeners assess a speaker's *expertness* by making judgments about competency, experience, and knowledge of the subject. *Trustworthiness* is a quality audiences attribute to a speaker whom they perceive as honest, dependable, sincere, fair, and similar to them in values, beliefs, and background. Researchers have identified a moderately influential dimension, often called *dynamism,* rooted in how alert, energetic, firm-minded, and interesting an audience considers a speaker. And informed observation would suggest that listeners evaluate a speaker's *good will* toward them by judging her or his friendliness, likability, and concern for them.

Ethos is variable rather than static. A speaker's credibility might vary from one audience to another, from one decade to another, or from one subject to another. Different cultures or subcultures may prize different personal qualities as constituting positive *ethos,* or an audience may perceive different qualities as relevant on different topics. The *ethos* attributed to a speaker by listeners will fluctuate during presentation of the speech as the audience judges use of evidence and reasoning, motivational appeals, language, structure, and vocal-physical delivery. Sometimes speakers directly attempt to foster positive *ethos* with an audience by overtly mentioning experiences or qualifications as marks of their expertise or by quoting or indicating associations with persons whose *ethos* with the audience already is high. A speaker's *ethos* level at the conclusion of the speech is an outcome of interaction of her or his reputation (prior audience knowledge of speaker's views, accomplishments, associations, and personality) with the audience's assessment of how well the speaker performed during the speech itself.

Although high *ethos* will not guarantee speaker success, markedly low source credibility usually thwarts a communicative effort. No matter how *actually* sound and ethical are a speaker's program, information, arguments, and appeals, if the audience *perceives* the speaker as incompetent, unethical, untrustworthy, bored, overly nervous, or aloof, then her or his message probably will have little of the desired impact.

8. *What attitudes toward his or her audience does the speaker seem to reveal?*

A speaker's attitude toward an audience reflects his or her view of the listener's personal worth and abilities as well as an indication of the speaker's orientation or stance toward the audience. First, attempt to isolate how the speaker's attitude orientation is revealed in communicative choices, strategies, and techniques. Such reflections may be inferred from verbal and nonverbal elements such as word choice, level of abstraction, types of examples, specificity of analysis, emphasis given to items, vocal pitch and quality, facial expression, and directness of eye contact.

Second, attempt to identify the attitudinal stances characteristic of all or parts of the speech. Is the attitude that you perceive probably the one perceived by the audience, the one intended by the speaker, and a sincere index of his or her "real" view? Are any of the speaker's attitudinal stances especially ethical or unethical? Our discussion later in this chapter of question #12 on ethical standards for assessing public discourse may help you consider this issue. Your efforts may be aided by considering to what degree the speech reveals one or more of the following attitude clusters: (1) respect, equality, understanding, honesty, genuineness, concern for audience welfare and improvement, sincerity, openness to new views, trust, selflessness, empathy, helpfulness, humility; (2) prudence, moderation, indifference, aloofness, unconcern, apathy, disinterest, blandness, coldness; (3) objectivity, neutrality; (4) self-aggrandizement, ego-satisfaction, personal "showing off," pretentiousness; (5) superiority, domination, exploitation for personal gain, deception, insincerity, dogmatism, coercion, facade, judgmentalism, arrogance, contempt, condescension, possessiveness, selfishness; (6) aggressiveness, abrasiveness, hostility, nonconciliation, insult, derogation, curtness; (7) inferiority, supplication, pleading, deference; (8) defensiveness, competitiveness, fear, distrust, suspicion; (9) conciliation, consensus, cooperation, identification.

Third, explore in what ways the speaker's attitude toward the audience seems to reflect personal philosophy; beliefs about human nature, society, reality, values, and ethics are some elements of such a philosophy. Does the attitude reflect optimism or pessimism toward human capabilities and potential? Does the speaker see humans as capable of reflective self-decision or only of being coerced or dominated? An attitude might indicate a belief that reality and knowledge are perceived and attained with certainty or with much relativism and uncertainty. Attitudes of cynicism, duplicity, and domination may stem from a commitment to the end justifying the means.

Fourth, probe how the speaker's attitude toward an audience relates to her or his purposes and motives. Does the attitude revealed appear to reinforce or to thwart achievement of the speaker's intended purpose? Is there any verbal and nonverbal inconsistency between the speaker's attitude and the apparent intended meaning of the speech? Does a perceived attitude of insincerity, unconcern, or superiority contradict words proclaiming sincerity, concern, or equality? Does the speaker seem to hold a particular attitude toward an audience as a *substitute* for action, as a rationale for inaction while merely verbalizing the approved and "proper" attitude?

Finally, attempt to assess the influence of the speaker's attitudinal stance on the effects or consequences of the speech. Does the attitude seem appropriate for the speaker, subject, audience, and occasion? What effects might the speaker's attitude have on the audience's beliefs, feelings, and actions? Listeners' perception of a speaker's attitude toward them may influence their estimate of expertness, trustworthiness, goodwill, and similarity to them. Attitudes of dominance, superiority, or aloofness, for example, may contribute to peoples' doubts about the speaker's sincere concern for their welfare.

9. *In what ways does the speaker's language usage contribute to clarity, interest, and persuasiveness?*

Consider whether the language is appropriate for the speaker, audience, subject, and occasion. Examine the communicative function served by stylistic resources such as repetition, restatement, rhetorical question, comparison, contrast, parallel structure, antithesis, alliteration, analogy, metaphor, imagery, personification, or narration. Do any stylistic devices seem ornamental or "added on" primarily for "showing off"? What does the speaker's language reveal about him or her personally or about the speaker's view of the audience? How do language choices compare with those the speaker reasonably might have made? What stylistic alternatives seem available to the speaker and why might the speaker have made particular choices? If the speaker's language is militant and abrasive, why might this choice have been made? If obscene words are used, what might be their intended function and actual impact?

Why might the speaker rely heavily on one particular stylistic device? If use of metaphors is a major stylistic characteristic, are they largely trite and overly familiar, or are they fresh and insightful for that particular audience? Might the audience have expected to be addressed in familiar, even stereotyped, metaphorical images? If there is a dominant or thematic metaphor woven throughout the speech, what might be its significance? What functions might be served by a speaker's heavy reliance on "god terms" and "devil terms," on value-laden concepts with intense positive or negative meanings? In what ways are names, labels, and definitions employed to channel perceptions—to direct attention toward or away from both relevant and irrelevant aspects of persons and programs? Remember, also, that public tastes in rhetorical style vary from era to era and even between different audiences in the same era. For the particular speech you are analyzing, consider what might be the most appropriate standards of stylistic judgment.

10. *In what noteworthy ways does the speaker's delivery of the speech contribute to clarity, interest, and persuasiveness?*

Do nonverbal elements of speech presentation reinforce or conflict with the speaker's verbal meaning? Does the speaker's vocal and physical delivery convey one meaning while his or her words convey another? If so, which would the audience probably believe and why? Does the manner of delivery seem appropriate for the speaker, subject, audience, and occasion? Examine the roles of loudness, vocal pitch, vocal quality, pauses, and rapidity in the presentation. How do the speaker's posture, gestures, facial expression, and eye contact help or hinder effectiveness? Are there any distracting mannerisms of vocal or bodily delivery that hinder audience attentiveness or comprehension? Explore also the communicative functions of various nonverbal cues accompanying the speech. Examine the possible intended and unintended implications of music, flags, banners, salutes, emblems, lapel pins, mode of dress, and pictures of family or revered persons.

11. *What rhetorical strategies seem noteworthy because of their frequent use, apparent function in the speech, or probable effectiveness?*

This line of inquiry obviously builds upon insights and questions from previously suggested guidelines for analysis. But such a scrutiny of concrete strategies will aid you as practitioner and critic of public discourse to see more clearly how others have approached different audiences and situations. The strategies briefly explained here are not offered as an exhaustive list but only as some possibilities. Strategies typical of discourse about values, problems, and solutions are discussed briefly in later chapters which focus on that type of speechmaking.

In the *this-or-nothing* strategy the speaker evaluates leading alternative solutions to a problem, shows in turn why each is unworkable or inappropriate, and finally presents his or her policy as the only sound remaining choice. *Visualization* involves painting a vivid word picture of the positive consequences of adopting or negative results of rejecting a proposal. Sometimes speakers use the *scapegoat* technique wherein they shift all responsibility or blame for problems or faults afflicting their own group onto the shoulders of some other person or group depicted as the embodiment of evil. As a variation of scapegoating, a *conspiracy* appeal claims that the cause of problems facing the group resides in a powerful, widespread, organized, secret effort of some other person or group.

The strategy of *persuasive definition* finds a speaker offering the audience her or his particular meaning as the correct or appropriate definition for a concept which actually is open to challenge or controversy. A speaker might employ *association* to emphasize values, beliefs, experiences mutually held with the audience and/or with persons and programs esteemed by the audience. *Disassociation* involves the speaker's repudiation of relationships with or favorable views toward undesirable people, ideas, or policies. In a strategy of *differentiation,* the speaker avoids guilt or responsibility by arguing the rationale that the action or belief under attack is different or unique from some other state of affairs which may be open to condemnation. Finally, there is a strategy of *transcendence* in which speaker and audience, or opposing groups, are to submerge, at least temporarily, differences of opinion or policy in the name of some commonly agreed upon higher value or goal: national security, political party unity, victory, humanitarianism, or national honor.

12. *As best you can determine, what were some of the effects or consequences of the speech?*

Often it is very difficult to determine exact and certain causal connections between a specific speech and later outcomes. And an effect may be the result of a number of rhetorical and nonrhetorical events. Remember, too, that a speech may have consequences never intended by a speaker; these, also, can be scrutinized. You may attempt to assess the effects of a speech by noting the impact on the immediate audience, the long-term impact on the policies and ideology of society-at-large, the impact on persons in positions of public opinion leadership, the influence on experts, and the reactions of news media reporters. You might also explore whether the speaker's aim has been achieved, whether the speaker's ideas have been verified by later historical events, or whether the audience's expectations have been met. Sometimes virtually nondetectible shifts in audience attitudes and beliefs may occur, such as from a favorable to a strongly favorable position. Finally, you may want to consider the influence of the speech on the *speaker*. Did it enhance or lower the speaker's reputation? How did the speech affect the speaker's subsequent rhetoric and actions? Did the speaker in any way become trapped by his or her own rhetoric? When speakers publicly become "locked in" to a position, later modification may be difficult.

13. What ethical judgments seem appropriate regarding the speaker's purposes, arguments, appeals, and strategies?

A speech is designed by one person (sometimes with the aid of a speechwriter or speechwriting team) to influence the lives of other persons. And a speaker makes conscious choices concerning specific ends and communicative techniques to achieve those ends. Potential ethical issues regarding means and ends seem inherent in any act of speechmaking. But how those issues are to be faced and resolved (by speaker, listener, and critic) is not clear-cut.

Traditional American textbook discussions of the ethics of public speaking, argumentation, and persuasion often include lists of standards to be applied in assessing the ethicality of an instance of discourse. What follows is Johannesen's synthesis and adaptation of a half-dozen or so typical traditional lists of ethical criteria for public discourse.[2] Such ethical criteria usually are rooted in a commitment to values deemed essential to the health and growth of our political-governmental system of representative democracy. Obviously other cultures and other governmental systems may embrace basic values that lead to quite different standards for public discourse.

Even within our own society, the following criteria are not necessarily the only or best ones possible; they are suggested as general guidelines rather than inflexible rules, and they may stimulate discussion on the complexity of judging the ethics of communication. Consider, for example, under what circumstances there may be justifiable exceptions to some of these criteria. Also bear in mind that one difficulty in applying these criteria in concrete situations

[2]For example, see the following sources: E. Christian Buehler and Wil A. Linkugel, *Speech Communication: A First Course* (Harper and Row, 1969), pp. 20–22; Robert T. Oliver, *The Psychology of Persuasive Speech,* 2nd ed. (Longmans, Green, 1957), pp. 20–34; Wayne Minnick, *The Art of Persuasion,* 2nd ed. (Houghton Mifflin, 1968), pp. 278–287; Henry Ewbank and J. Jeffrey Auer, *Discussion and Debate,* 2nd ed., (Appleton-Century-Crofts, 1951), pp. 255–258; Wayne Thompson, *The Process of Persuasion* (Harper and Row, 1975), Ch. 12; Bert E. Bradley, *Fundamentals of Speech Communication,* 3rd ed. (Wm. C. Brown Company Publishers, 1981), pp. 23–31.

stems from differing standards and meanings people may have for such key terms as: distort, falsify, rational, reasonable, conceal, misrepresent, irrelevant, and deceive.

1. Do not use false, fabricated, misrepresented, distorted, or irrelevant evidence to support arguments or claims.
2. Do not intentionally use specious, unsupported, or illogical reasoning.
3. Do not represent yourself as informed or as an "expert" on a subject when you are not.
4. Do not use irrelevant appeals to divert attention or scrutiny from the issue at hand. Among appeals that commonly serve such a purpose are: "smear" attacks on an opponent's character; appeals to hatred and bigotry; god and devil terms that cause intense but unreflective positive or negative reactions; innuendo.
5. Do not ask your audience to link your idea or proposal to emotion-laden values, motives, or goals to which it actually is not related.
6. Do not deceive your audience by concealing your real purpose, by concealing self-interest, by concealing the group you represent, or by concealing your position as an advocate of a viewpoint.
7. Do not distort, hide, or misrepresent the number, scope, intensity, or undesirable features of consequences or effects.
8. Do not use "emotional appeals" that lack a supporting basis of evidence and reasoning, or that would not be accepted if the audience had time and opportunity to examine the subject themselves.
9. Do not oversimplify complex, gradation-laden situations into simplistic two-valued, either-or, polar choices.
10. Do not pretend certainty where tentativeness and degrees of probability would be more accurate.
11. Do not advocate something in which you do not believe yourself.

We now turn to a list of some questions which we hope will stimulate your examination of various ethical issues as you assess a particular speech. To what degree should ethical standards for judging speeches be relative, flexible, and situation bound, or universal, inflexible, and absolute? Should there be different ethical standards for speechmaking in different fields such as politics, business, education, and religion? Should ethical standards for communication directed at children be higher than for messages aimed at adults? To what degree should ethical standards for public communication differ from or be similar to those appropriate for interpersonal and small group communication?

To what degree, if any, does the worthiness of the speaker's end justify the employment of communication techniques usually deemed ethically suspect? Does the sincerity of the speaker's intent release him or her from ethical responsibility for means and effects? Under what circumstances might intentional use of ambiguity be considered ethical? Should "tastefulness" and "tactfulness" be included or excluded as *ethical* criteria for assessing speeches? To what degree and for what reasons might we consider the use of "sexist" and "racist" language as unethical?

CONCLUSION

By focusing on contemporary American speeches, this book necessarily focuses on one particular kind of rhetorical practice. Speeches still form a significant portion of our communication environment, an environment constantly bombarding us with data, appeals, reasons, and judgments. Whether a speech seeks to impart knowledge and create understanding, to advocate or reinforce values and value judgments, to resolve "factual" disputes, to generate concern for problems, or to secure acceptance of solutions—that speech seeks a specific response from a specific audience. Thus such speeches inherently involve some degree of "persuasive" intent, some degree of conscious concrete influence.

As responsible citizens in a representative democracy, we are expected to develop skills in communicating our ideas and choices on matters of personal and public concern. Also we are expected to become discerning consumers of communication, to become perceptive evaluators of messages we receive. We have a social responsibility to become intelligent and ethical speakers and listeners. Part of this responsibility has been summarized forcefully by a contemporary rhetorical critic, Karlyn Kohrs Campbell: "Never has the need to understand the nature of persuasive discourses and to develop techniques and standards by which to analyze and evaluate them been more crucial. . . . In short, we shall have to become working rhetorical critics."

For Further Reading

ON THE ART OF RHETORIC
Baird, A. Craig. *Rhetoric: A Philosophical Inquiry*. Ronald Press, 1965. An overview of the nature of rhetoric.
Brockriede, Wayne. "Dimensions of the Concept of Rhetoric." *Quarterly Journal of Speech*, February 1968, pp. 1–12.

Johannesen, Richard L., ed. *Contemporary Theories of Rhetoric: Selected Readings.* Harper and Row, 1971. An anthology focusing on recent trends in rhetorical theorizing, including the works of Kenneth Burke, I. A. Richards, Richard M. Weaver, Chaim Perelman, Stephen Toulmin, and Marshall McLuhan.

Schwartz, Joseph, and Rycenga, John A., eds. *The Province of Rhetoric.* Ronald Press, 1965. A collection of essays exploring the nature, significance, development, and uses of rhetoric.

ON THE ETHICS OF RHETORIC

Jensen, J. Vernon. *Argumentation: Reasoning in Communication.* Van Nostrand, 1981. Chapter 2 suggests ethical responsibilities both to the immediate audience and to society-at-large.

Johannesen, Richard L. *Ethics in Human Communication.* Charles E. Merrill Publ. Co., 1975; reprinted Waveland Press, 1981. Explores varied perspectives, issues, and examples to foster skill in assessing degrees of ethicality.

Larson, Charles U. *Persuasion: Reception and Responsibility.* 3rd ed. Wadsworth, 1983. Includes a chapter by R. L. Johannesen on "Perspectives on Ethics in Persuasion."

Nilsen, Thomas R. *Ethics of Speech Communication.* 2nd ed. Bobbs-Merrill, 1974. Includes chapters on telling the truth, on significant choice, and on persuasion.

Sproule, J. Michael. *Argument: Language and Its Influence.* McGraw-Hill, 1980. Pages 82–84 and Chapter 8 suggest ethical guidelines and describe various contrasting codes of ethics.

ON THE FORMS OF SPEECHES

Allen, R. R., and McKerrow, Ray E. *The Pragmatics of Public Communication.* 2nd ed. Kendall/Hunt Publishing Company, 1981. Chapters 5–7 discuss informative, persuasive, and ceremonial speeches.

Culp, Ralph B. *Basic Types of Speeches.* Wm. C. Brown Company Publishers, 1968. A brief textbook on five major types of speechmaking: inquiry and explanation; persuasion and deliberation; sociality and courtesy; commemoration; counsel.

King, Robert G. *Forms of Public Address.* Bobbs-Merrill, 1969. A brief textbook surveying varied speech forms: campaign, legislative, commemorative, commencement, inaugural, keynote, after-dinner.

Walter, Otis M., and Scott, Robert L. *Thinking and Speaking.* 4th ed. Macmillan, 1979. Chapters 10–14 discuss speeches that deal with problems, causes, solutions, values, and definitions.

ON THE INVENTION OF SPEECH IDEAS

Blankenship, Jane. *Public Speaking: A Rhetorical Perspective.* 2nd ed. Prentice-Hall, 1972. Chapters 4 and 5 examine the process of invention by discussing preliminary planning and the selection of proofs.

Corbett, Edward P. J. *Classical Rhetoric for the Modern Student.* 2nd ed. Oxford University Press, 1971. Chapter 2 contains intensive discussion of the discovery of arguments.

McCroskey, James C. *An Introduction to Rhetorical Communication.* 3rd ed. Prentice-Hall, 1978. Chapter 6 offers suggestions on invention.

Wilson, John F., and Arnold, Carroll C. *Public Speaking as a Liberal Art.* 4th ed. Allyn and Bacon, 1978. Chapters 4–6 examine the basic processes of invention, including some general thought lines to aid the speaker in finding appropriate ideas and arguments.

Winterowd, W. Ross. *Contemporary Rhetoric: A Conceptual Background with Readings.* Harcourt, Brace, Jovanovich, 1975, pp. 39–162. Twelve essays focusing on invention.

ON THE CRITICAL ANALYSIS OF SPEECHES

Andrews, James R. *A Choice of Worlds: The Practice and Criticism of Public Discourse.* Harper and Row, 1973. A brief textbook presenting standards and sample analyses of public addresses.

Campbell, Karlyn Kohrs. *Critiques of Contemporary Rhetoric.* Wadsworth, 1972. Chapters 1–3 consider in some detail the process of rhetorical criticism.

Johannesen, Richard L. "Attitude of Speaker Toward Audience: A Significant Concept for Contemporary Rhetorical Theory and Criticism,"*Central States Speech Journal,* Summer 1974, 95–104.

Brock, Bernard L., and Scott, Robert L., eds. *Methods of Rhetorical Criticism: A Twentieth Century Perspective.* 2nd ed. Wayne State University Press, 1980. An anthology of essays illustrating varied approaches to the theory and practice of rhetorical criticism.

Simons, Herbert W. *Persuasion: Understanding, Practice, and Analysis.* Addison-Wesley, 1976. Chapter 14 examines how to do rhetorical criticism.

Smith, Craig R. *Orientations to Speech Criticism.* Science Research Associates, Modcom Modules in Speech Communication, 1976. A forty page booklet which explores the nature and criteria of speech criticism.

Thonssen, Lester; Baird, A. Craig; and Braden, Waldo. *Speech Criticism.* 2nd ed. Ronald Press, 1970. A revision of a "classic" textbook on speech criticism.

(See also references following Chapter 1.)

Chapter 3

SPEECHES THAT IMPART KNOWLEDGE

Because information can change society, and because the amount of information doubles every eight years, our culture, if it is to become enriched and improved by its information, needs speakers and writers to digest and assimilate information and to present it to us with clarity.

Otis M. Walter

THE NATURE AND IMPORTANCE OF SPEECHES THAT IMPART KNOWLEDGE

Americans have long valued the broad diffusion of knowledge. This value is founded on the premise that our social and political systems function most effectively when all citizens possess the knowledge that is the basis for intelligent decision making. Without affirming or denying this premise, one can note the diverse institutions that pay tribute to its worth. Our vast system of public education, the media of mass communication, and public and private agencies for information dissemination all justify their existence, at least in part, by the premise.

In contemporary America, the broad diffusion of knowledge is becoming increasingly difficult. Alvin Toffler, in his popular book *Future Shock* observes:

> Today change is so swift and relentless in the techno-societies that yesterday's truths suddenly become today's fictions, and the most highly skilled and intelligent members of society admit difficulty in keeping up with the deluge of new knowledge—even in extremely narrow fields.[1]

In response to this challenge, Otis Walter, in the quotation that headnotes this chapter, calls for a generation of communicators who can digest and assimilate the explosion of knowledge and render it useful for others who must know. As the rate of new knowledge continues to accelerate, and as

[1]Alvin Toffler, *Future Shock* (New York: Bantam Books, 1971), p. 157.

local, national, and world problems become increasingly complex, speeches that impart knowledge must continue to grow in number and significance.

Speeches that serve this function may be of different kinds. Lectures, intelligence briefings, reports of research findings, treasurers' reports, the happy chef show, and the evening TV weather report are all instances of this genre. Whenever speakers seek to create in the minds of their listeners an understanding of an event, concept, phenomenon, object, process, or relationship, they may be viewed as seeking to impart knowledge.

In certain instances, imparting knowledge is a speaker's *primary* speech purpose. A professor of history, for example, may be totally content if his students understand the major forces which contributed to the beginning of the Civil War. A computer systems engineer may be fully satisfied if installation procedures are understood by technical personnel. An accountant may be adequately rewarded if a company's executive officers understand the implications of a new federal tax regulation.

In other instances, imparting knowledge is a speaker's *ancillary* purpose. For example, a sociologist may describe an event in order that he may urge social reform. A civil rights leader may narrate a story of social injustice in order to elicit a greater commitment to social tolerance. A senator may explain a piece of legislation as a prelude to urging its adoption.

From the perspective of the audience, it is often difficult to determine the extent to which a speech imparts knowledge rather than serving some other major purpose. Audience members listening to the same speech may come away feeling informed, persuaded to a new point of view, or even inspired to recommit their lives to cherished values. But a speaker who purports to impart knowledge, whether as a primary or an ancillary purpose, should be expected to meet several fundamental criteria.

CRITERIA FOR EVALUATING SPEECHES THAT IMPART KNOWLEDGE

Four general criteria are especially important for evaluating speeches that seek to impart knowledge. Failure to satisfy any of these four will seriously restrict the speaker's communication of knowledge.

1. *Is the knowledge communicated accurately, completely, and with unity?*

Because genuine understanding by an audience is the speaker's goal when seeking to impart knowledge, an *accurate, complete,* and *unified* view of the subject must be presented. Wilson and Arnold have expressed this criterion in this way:

The speaker who undertakes to explain how a tape recorder works will err seriously if he alleges that all tape recorders use vacuum tubes for sound amplification (many use transistors), he will err in a different way if he neglects to discuss the playback systems most recorders have, and he will err in another fashion if he does not make it clear that the entire mechanical system exists to preserve sound and represent it for later examination. . . . His listeners may not reject him as a person for his error of fact, his omission, and his disregard for the total meaning of his material; but they will not understand tape recorders unless they understood them before. Why? The speaker did not put into his discourse those things that must be there if talk is to inform or teach: accuracy, completeness, unity.[2]

Given a specific body of knowledge to impart, a speaker must select those items of information that an audience must have to gain understanding. These items must then be arranged in a unified sequence and expresssed in an undistorted manner.

2. Does the speaker make the knowledge meaningful for the audience?

It is not enough that speakers know the essential components of a truth. In seeking to impart knowledge to a particular audience at a particular time, they must transform their perceptions of facts and concepts into symbols that evoke understanding in those who listen. Even a highly motivated audience may lack the substantive, linguistic, and conceptual skills essential to understanding an idea presented in its pure form. Speakers must be faithful to both the integrity of the truth that they seek to impart and to the demands of the particular audience that they address.

These demands need not be incompatible, as an example will demonstrate. Let us assume that you wish to clarify the reasoning processes of induction and deduction to an audience of laborers who have come to your campus. You know that *induction* is a method of systematic investigation that seeks to discover, analyze, and explain specific instances or facts in order to determine the existence of a general law embracing them, whereas *deduction* is a process by which a particular conclusion about an instance is drawn from the application of a general law. In appraising your audience, you recognize that, although these terms are meaningful to you, they represent an unfamiliar level of conceptual abstraction to your audience. The rhetorical problem is clear; the solution is not.

[2]John F. Wilson and Carroll C. Arnold, *Public Speaking as a Liberal Art* (Boston: Allyn and Bacon, 1964), pp. 165-66.

In 1866, Thomas Henry Huxley faced exactly the same problem. The rhetorical choices that he made in explaining these processes to a group of English workingmen in his speech entitled "The Method of Scientific Investigation" are demonstrated in the following paragraphs.

Suppose you go into a fruiterer's shop, wanting an apple—you take one up, and, on biting, you find it is sour; you look at it, and see that it is hard and green. You take another one and that too is hard, green, and sour. The shopman offers you a third; but, before biting it, you examine it, and find that it is hard and green, and you immediately say that you will not have it, as it must be sour, like those that you have already tried.

Nothing can be more simple than that, you think; but if you will take the trouble to analyze and trace out into its logical elements what has been done by the mind, you will be greatly surprised. In the first place, you have performed the operation of induction. You found that, in two experiences, hardness and greenness in apples went together with sourness. It was so in the first case and it was confirmed by the second. True, it is a very small basis, but still it is enough to make an induction from; you generalize the facts, and you expect to find sourness in apples where you get hardness and greenness. You found upon that a general law, that all hard and green apples are sour; and that, so far as it goes, is a perfect induction. Well, having got your natural law in this way, when you are offered another apple which you find is hard and green, you say, "All hard and green apples are sour; this apple is hard and green, therefore this apple is sour." That train of reasoning is what logicians call a syllogism' and has all its various parts and terms—its major premise, its minor premise, and its conclusion. And, by the help of further reasoning, which, if drawn out, would have to be exhibited in two or three other syllogisms, you arrive at your final determination. "I will not have that apple." So that, you see, you have, in the first place, established a law by induction, and reasoned out the special conclusion of the particular case.

In this instance, Huxley chose to impart only a very basic understanding of the processes of induction and deduction by showing them to be inherent in a commonplace happening familiar to the workers who comprised his audience. He chose not to treat the subtleties of form and fallacy. Did he compromise the integrity of the truth in order to win popular understanding? Most critics think not. Although he simplified these processes, he did not misrepresent them. His illustration accurately portrays their essential nature. And it is complete in the sense of comprehensively demonstrating the specific purpose of the speech: to show that "there is not one here who has not in the course of the day had occasion to set in motion a complex train of reasoning of the very same kind, though differing of course in degree, as that which a scientific man goes through in tracing the causes of natural phenomena." Finally, his speech possesses unity in providing a systematic development through which the listener may gain a clear grasp of the total meaning.

In giving meaning to the knowledge that he wished to impart, Huxley chose to move from a simple illustration to a complex generalization, to develop a common understanding of a process before attaching labels to it, and to use periodic summations of what had been discussed. Martin Luther King, in his speech reprinted in this chapter, utilized definition to amplify the various meanings of the concept of love. Other speakers have used restatement and repetition, clarity of organization, factual and hypothetical examples, synonyms and negation, comparison and contrast, analogies and statistics, description and narration, photographs and films, blackboards and diagrams, questions and answers, meaningful gestures and movement, and varied patterns of rate and pitch.

3. *Does the speaker create audience interest in the knowledge being presented?*

Because understanding is the goal of the speech designed to impart knowledge, the speaker must create in the audience a reason for concentrating on the information that is being transmitted. Creating this interest is not always easy. Often the speaker must explain technical, detailed, and abstract concepts to an apathetic audience. In seeking to do so, the speaker can capitalize on the interest factors in content, language, and delivery. *Concrete* and specific terms and illustrations have more interest value for most listeners than vague generalities or abstract concepts. *Conflict* in the form of disagreements, threats, clashes, and antagonisms capture and hold an audience's attention. *Suspense* and *curiosity* in building to a climax, anticipating a conclusion, or asking intriguing questions can be used. Description or narration focusing on activity and movement capitalizes on *action*. The new, unusual, or unexpected reflects the *novelty* factor. On the other hand, listeners are also interested in things that are "close to home" and *familiar*. When carefully and appropriately used, *humor* may increase interest while explaining or highlighting a main point.

As a study of the choices that one speaker made, let us again return to Huxley's illustration. In appraising his audience, Huxley realized that, for average English workingmen of his time, the scientific method represented an esoteric construct of little interest or significance to all but the disciples of science. By making his individual audience member "you," the chief participant in his illustration, by choosing a familiar environment as the setting, and by selecting such suspense words as "suppose" and "you will be greatly surprised" as major transitional devices, he gave to his material a sense of vitality, realism, suspense, and urgency that it did not naturally possess. Huxley chose a hypothetical illustration for this purpose; others have selected metaphors, narratives, comparisons, contrasts, real and figurative analogies, and specific examples. Thus, a speaker who is inventive need not worry about losing the audience even when an unusual or difficult subject is involved.

4. Does the speaker show the audience that the knowledge is important?

Beyond presenting knowledge that is accurate, complete, unified, meaningful, and interesting, speakers must also get their audiences to feel that they should make such knowledge a permanent part of their storehouse of data. In order to do so, speakers might clarify the relation of the knowledge to the wants and goals of their audiences. They might point out ways in which the information can be used or applied, where this new knowledge fits within the context of information already considered worthwhile by the audience, and, if appropriate, where and how the audience can obtain additional information on the subject.

Given the vast array of knowledge that may be communicated, the critic has a right to question the quality of the knowledge that the speaker chooses to impart. Student speakers often err by selecting speech topics that are trivial and lacking in real information value. Gruner, Logue, Freshley, and Huseman, in *Speech Communication in Society,* recall

> . . . a dreadful speech by a young man who spoke on and demonstrated how to use two simple types of can openers, one being the elemenary "church key" type for opening beverage cans. Disappointed by his low grade he complained, "Well, the speech *did* contain information, didn't it?" The instructor replied: "Not for this audience; I'm sure they already know how to open cans." The instructor's reply could be paraphrased: "You instructed no one."[3]

An effective speech of this form imparts knowledge that is worth having to an audience that lacks such knowledge.

[3]Charles R. Gruner, Cal M. Logue, Dwight L. Freshley, and Richard C. Huseman, *Speech Communication in Society* (Boston: Allyn and Bacon, Inc., 1972), p. 179.

CONCLUSION

Imparting knowledge is one of the primary and ancillary functions that speeches serve. When speakers try to fulfill this purpose, they must be aware of the constraints that govern their speech behavior. They must choose knowledge that is worth knowing. They must impart the knowledge with *accuracy, completeness,* and *unity.* They must be aware of the demands that varied audiences impose on the choices they make in giving *meaning, interest,* and *importance* to a body of knowledge. In other words, they must be faithful to the integrity of their perceptions of truth while adapting to the demands of their audiences.

For Further Reading

Bryant, Donald C., and Wallace, Karl R. *Fundamentals of Public Speaking.* 5th ed. Appleton-Century-Crofts, 1976. Chapters 8 and 9 explain methods of amplification and the use of visual aids, organization, and introductions and conclusions to informative speaking.

Gronbeck, Bruce E. *The Articulate Person.* Scott, Foresman, 1979. Section II on informing covers the processes of information transfer, defining, demonstrating, and explaining.

Hance, Kenneth G.; Ralph, David C.; and Wiksell, Milton J. *Principles of Speaking.* 3rd ed. Wadsworth, 1975. Chapter 16 provides an insightful discussion of the informative process and the special types of informative speaking.

Hart, Roderick P.; Friedrich, Gustav W.; and Brooks, William D. *Public Communication.* Harper and Row, 1975. Chapter 7 is devoted to reducing the complexity of information.

Netter, Gwyn. *Explanations.* McGraw-Hill, 1970. Chapters 2–6 explore the main variations of explanation used in discourse: definitional, empathetic, scientific, and ideological.

Olbricht, Thomas H. *Informative Speaking.* Scott, Foresman, 1968. A concise paperback textbook.

Rein, Irving J. *The Public Speaking Book.* Scott, Foresman, 1981. Chapters 3–5 discuss means of promoting interest, improving clarity, and making sense.

Rogge, Edward, and Ching, James C. *Advanced Public Speaking.* Holt, Rinehart and Winston, 1966. Chapters 12–14 discuss five types of speeches of exposition.

Walter, Otis M. *Speaking to Inform and Persuade.* 2nd ed. Macmillan, 1982. Chapters 2–4 present an extremely useful discussion of imparting knowledge, including selection of main ideas and use of supporting material.

THE CHALLENGES OF THE
PRESIDENCY IN THE 1980S

Roger B. Porter

Roger B. Porter, Assistant Professor of Public Policy and Management at the John F. Kennedy School of Government, Harvard University, delivered this speech on October 9, 1980 at Brigham Young University in Salt Lake City, Utah. His primary purpose was to impart knowledge about the implications for the Presidency of changes in the structure of national politics.

Speaking less than a month before a national presidential election, Professor Porter apparently assumes that a university audience will find his topic to be both timely and interesting. After making brief reference to growing dissatisfaction with and reexamination of government institutions, including the Presidency, he moves directly to a statement of purpose and to an initial partition, or preview, of his subject. Given the situation, do you think the speaker has taken sufficient time to secure audience attention and to demonstrate the importance of his subject?

Although his subject is complex, Porter uses several rhetorical resources to promote audience comprehension. He divides his speech into two main parts as signaled in the initial partition. In the first part he identifies five changes in political structure that shape the environment in which the President operates. He provides verbal "signposts" by overtly numbering each change as he comes to it. Following the last change, he provides an internal summary of the first part of the speech. The second part of the speech, while structurally more complex, is also superbly organized. Porter begins the second main point with a preview of the three subpoints to be developed. He identifies three roles that the President should play, four needs that the President has, and three strategies that the President may employ for managing his energies and resources. In developing his second part, he continues to preview and to "signpost." The speech concludes with a strong and complete summary of the points addressed.

Porter employs varied kinds and sources of information to develop his ideas: statistics, quotations, factual examples, comparison. Does such a variety of expository materials make the speech more interesting? Do the frequent quotations interfere with the coherence of the speech? Analyze the use of expository materials in paragraphs 41-48. What kinds of expository materials are employed? How effectively has the speaker developed his point that "the President must consistently use the resources of his office to educate and persuade"?

Reprinted with permission from *Vital Speeches of the Day*, January 1, 1981, pp. 172-176.

1   As the 1970's drew to a close, the U.S. Presidency became the focus of much discussion as part of a national reexamination of our institutions and destiny. This reexamination occurs at a time of much dissatisfaction. James Sundquist, a thoughtful scholar, has recently written about "The Crisis of Competence in Government," claiming that there are deep-seated trends at

work that "will make effective government even more difficult to attain in the 1980's than before." Another perceptive commentator wrote recently of the "intense dissatisfaction with the present eroding governmental system." He continued: "In 50 years of covering Washington, I have never heard, until now, such dissatisfaction with the present presidential nominating process, the choice offered, the lack of governmental responsibility, and the over-all decline of democratic accountability. America deserves a better government than it gets."

2 Our thinking and discussion of the Presidency seems to go in cycles. We become prisoners of the most recent past. We tend to react to our most recent experience—to the last man in the White House. But too close a focus on the recent past can restrict our vision and limit our perspective. Rather than concentrate on current experience or on personalities, we would do well to examine the structure of politics in the 1980's and its implications for the Presidency. In doing so, I shall first look at some trends that are changing our political landscape and then explore what these changes mean for the roles of the President, his needs, and for his conduct of the office.

3 Five trends have altered the American political landscape and will shape the environment in which the President must operate in the 1980's.

4 First, power within the Congress is more widely distributed than at any time since the early 19th century. One manifestation, the result of earnest effort by reformers to spread power more equitably, is an explosion of sub-committees. There are almost twice as many now as in Truman's time. More-over, these proliferating subcommittees exercise greater authority as Congress becomes more specialized.

5 Perhaps even more significant is the growth of congressional staffs. During the last ten years the number of personal and committee staff members in the Congress has more than tripled and the staff budget in the House of Representatives has almost quadrupled. As one representative recently ob-served: "Members are now spread so thin and staffers are so numerous that it is the staffs that often are doing the negotiation and reaching the compro-mises."

6 As committees and subcommittees have proliferated and staffs have grown, the powers of the leadership have declined. Now the House Majority Caucus—not the leadership—picks the committee and subcommittee chair-men. The House Parliamentarian no longer has the power to refer bills to a single committee selected by the Speaker. In some instances the leadership gave away key powers such as the decision to give every Democratic senator a major committee assignment and a subcommittee chairmanship. The decline of the party leadership's power has been accompanied by the rise of regional, ethnic, and subject-matter caucuses. The result is that Congress is less of an entity, while the autonomy of its individual members has been enhanced.

7   A second trend is the proliferation of highly organized interest groups. America has long been a land rich with associations. The proclivity of Americans to form in groups struck De Tocqueville in the early nineteenth century. This tendency gathered renewed strength in the 1970's with the nation's capital as its principal focus. As late as 1974 the largest share of the nation's associations were headquartered in New York City. The following year Washington overtook New York. By 1978 there were 1,800 associations headquartered in Washington with 50 new moves to Washington each year. These associations and interest groups now employ more than 40,000 persons in Washington. Over 500 corporations now have government relations offices in the nation's capital. Even states, counties, and cities are getting into the act to protect their interests.

8   But it is not just the number of interest groups and the size of their staffs that has changed. The other major movement is away from broad-based agriculture, labor, business, and ethnic groups and toward single issue groups—consumer, abortion, right to life, environmentalist, pro- and anti-SALT, pro- and anti-nuclear—that stand ready to lobby for their single issue and to reward or punish legislators.

9   Third, the growth of analytical staffs and "policy shops" in executive departments has changed the pattern of deliberations on many issues. Agencies once excluded from the process now have the analytic capacity to demand a place at the table. One senior administration official, who returned to government after more than a decade, described the change that had occurred:

In the 1960's there were a lot of people who would have liked to get into the game but just did not have the staff. They were unsupported and when you weren't supported, you couldn't carry the issue. Nobody had a group of economists to evaluate all these issues for them. The Council of Economic Advisers had a monopoly along with a few people at the Treasury. What has changed today is that every agency has an economic policy and planning group and it is not easy to tear their arguments apart. CEA cannot blow people out of the water with the depth of its analysis like it could in the 1960's. When CEA said the effect of a specific tax action on investment was such-and-such there wasn't any other agency doing its own empirical work to argue with it. But now, Treasury may say, "No, it's Y." And Labor, "It's Z." The Labor Department has turned their economic policy planning group into a mini-CEA. There is no issue that they don't regard as absolutely vital.

10 A fourth far reaching change is the character of judicial review of administrative decisions manifested in the dramatically higher number of lawsuits over executive actions and in the character of judicial decrees that result from these suits. One example will illustrate the point. Former Secretary of Health, Education, and Welfare Joseph A. Califano tells of being ordered by a federal judge to request OMB to approve an additional 1800 people to staff the Office of Civil Rights. Not only that:

> The court demanded to review the memorandum I had sent to the Director of the Office of Management and Budget asking for the additional staff. . . . During oral argument on one of the various contempt motions to which I was potentially subject, the judge even asked counsel to describe the vigor with which I presented the argument to the Director of the Office of Management and Budget during a meeting.

11 A fifth trend is the expansion of federal concerns and the enlarged scope of federal programs greatly increasing the demands on the President. The new demands arise not simply from the assumption of additional responsibilities, but also from the complexity that results from the inevitable overlap. Elliot Richardson describes the impact of interrelatedness on individual departments and agencies:

> Any increase in the number and scope of federal programs leads to a proportionally greater increase in the potential for conflict among them. As the range of federal concerns expands, program areas tend increasingly to converge and overlap. Fewer and fewer major problems still fall within the exclusive province of a single department or agency.

Thus, the President is not merely responsible for administering these arithmetically expanding programs; he is also responsible for resolving the geometrically expanding conflicts between their objectives and priorities.

12 These fundamental changes that have occurred in the U.S. political system—in the Congress, in the representation of particular interests, in the structure and capacities within the executive branch, in the judiciary, and in the scope of governmental activity—have tended to fragment power and have contributed to what might be termed an age of centrifugal political forces.

13 Barring fundamental constitutional revision, the fragmented structure of Congress and the power of organized interests are unlikely to change significantly. In such a complex environment what roles should the President play? What needs does he have? And how can he best deploy his energies and resources?

14 A primary task of presidential leadership consists in determining the hierarchy of the nation's interests. National greatness is determined as much by wisdom as by power. No writer ever laid this charge before the American nation with greater cogency than did Thomas Huxley:

> I cannot say that I am in the slightest degree impressed by your bigness, or your material resources as such. Size is not grandeur, and territory does not make a nation. The great issue, about which hangs a true sublimity and the terror of overhanging fate, is what are you going to do with all these things?

15 The President occupies a unique position in the American political system. With the exception of the Vice President, he is the only official chosen by the entire national electorate. He has a genuinely national constituency and is the focus of national political attention. Not only is his constituency unique, but his range of responsibilities knows virtually no bounds. He must be concerned with what the diplomats are doing to the nation's military strategy, and vice versa, and what defense spending and foreign commitments will cost in taxes and inflation. He has an important role in establishing priorities for what is on the national agenda. It is the President who is the focus of political leadership and administrative authority in the federal government. He has both the opportunity and the responsibility to present a vision of the direction we must move as a nation.

16 The President also has an important role as the initiator of a coherent set of broad policies, foreign and domestic, to guide the allocation of federal resources and the content of federal programs in achieving the nation's objectives. The President is once again uniquely placed to fulfill this role. It is the President from whom the Congress and the country expect initiative and direction. As Elliot Richardson observed: "The imbalance from which the Congress suffers most is a matter not of power but of capacity for coherent action—the ability to weigh competing claims, formulate a consistent strategy, and arrive at a sound consensus."

17 Finally, the President must be the driving force in mobilizing a consensus in the country behind his policies. The communications revolution has focused increased attention on the President as the single most powerful figure in an age in which television places a premium on individuals instead of institutions. In short, the President's roles are to provide a sense of direction for the country and the pattern of governmental activity, a coherent set of policies that can move the country toward those objectives, and then he must educate and persuade the country to follow.

18 If these are the President's roles, what are his needs? First, he needs help in sifting and sorting, in selecting what issues he should personally get involved in and how. The President has limited time and resources. He must focus his energies on major, not minor issues.

19 Second, the President needs help in integrating policy. He wants the parts to bear some relationship to the whole since he is uniquely accountable for the comprehensiveness and coherence of his administration's policies. Indeed, the integration of policy "is the overriding problem of policy making under conditions of diffused power."

20 Third, the President needs help in structuring his decisions. He has an interest in balancing the competing forces and interests in major areas of public policy. His decisions will be best informed if the objectives and considerations presented to him reasonably correspond to their real importance. Thus, he needs organizational arrangements that not only provide representation for all important interests, but that also do not significantly favor one perspective over another.

21 Finally, he needs help in executing, in seeing that the decisions that he makes are implemented. His success is in part tied to the cohesion of his administration. He not only must present coherent policies, but he needs a united administration—key officials who see their responsibilities in a broad setting and who understand and support his policies. The fragmented structure of the executive branch and the Congress often frustrates overall direction of policy. The President needs institutional arrangements and incentives to bring and keep together his administration team.

22 The roles for the President that I have outlined are difficult and demanding, yet they are within reach. Three principal strands of advice form the core of what I consider a wise approach to the conduct of the office. In various forms they are found in the memoirs of France's Charles de Gaulle who wrote of the need to concentrate on the issues of greatest national importance, of the necessity of delegating authority, of remaining at a distance but not in an ivory tower, of talking constantly to his people not about themselves but the greater interests of the nation.

23 First, the President must concentrate on strategic choices. He must develop an overall strategy for addressing the nation's major problems. He must avoid the temptation to become enmeshed in every issue that is pressed on him. To the extent that he gets involved in myriads of problems he will be held responsible for their outcome. He cannot respond to every need; cure every ill. To the extent that he becomes trapped in details he will squander his limited resources. In this sense he must be an economizer. He must intervene selectively. He must delegate to others. Thomas Jefferson in a letter to Edward Carrington, wrote:

"I have ever viewed the executive details as the greatest cause of evil to us, because they in fact place us as if we had no federal head, by diverting the attention of that head from great to small subjects."

24 Robert Wood, formerly Secretary of Housing and Urban Development, expressed the same idea in different words: "Confusion is created when men try to do too much at the top."

25 The pressures and the temptations are all in the other direction. As the President's clerkship functions have grown, so have his staff resources to help him perform them, and the expectations of recipients: congressmen, journalists, diplomats, bureaucrats, and advocates. Put simply, the President must not be gripped by what the historian Thomas Bailey had called "the tyranny of the trivial."

26 Second, the President must think hard and carefully about how he organizes to fulfill his roles. A president's organizational arrangements can crucially affect not only the quality of advice he receives in structuring his decisions, but also how much integrating across issues occurs, and what support there is for implementing decisions once he has made them.

27 Above all, organizationally, the President must be concerned about what staff resources he has, what they do, and how he and his staff relate to the line, operating departments and agencies.

28 Newly elected presidents during the preinauguration days almost invariably proclaim their commitment to openness in their decision making and to an enlarged role for cabinet department and agency heads. But presidential enthusiasm for closely engaging departmental officials in their policy deliberations frequently wanes. Charles Schultze, Johnson's Budget Director, remembers: "on matters of substance, Johnson hardly ever talked to Cabinet members." Indeed, White House-departmental relations are often characterized by suspicion reflecting the oft-quoted remark of Charles G. Dawes, the first Director of the Budget Bureau, that "Cabinet members are vice-presidents in charge of spending, and as such they are the natural enemies of the President."

29 Presidents surround themselves with multiple staffs that often exclude cabinet and subcabinet officials from the formulation of policy, but then expect those officials to faithfully implement the President's decisions. On occasion, Richard Nathan said of the Nixon administration, "cabinet members were completely left out of White House deliberations, as with special revenue sharing in 1971, until plans were fully formed." There will always be pressure for a centralization of authority in the White House. It is reflected in the comment of Hamilton Jordan after his appointment as White House chief of staff: "We've had too much of a democracy around here and not enough of an organization."

30 But the choice for the President is not simply between a disorderly democracy in his staffing arrangements or a highly centralized staff structure. If the President is to effectively govern, he must reach out while maintaining an orderly process.

31 He must systematically engage the resources, the expertise, and the support of line departments and agencies. An administration that includes cabinet and subcabinet officials who feel unconsulted, ignored, or excluded from major policy decisions will not present a united front to the Congress and to the country. The strength of the President's position in dealing with a fragmented Congress will importantly depend on the unity within his administration. Congressional committees inevitably attempt to drive wedges between administration witnesses representing different departments, agencies, and bureaus. An administration seen to be squabbling and in disarray is perceived by those in the Congress as a sign of presidential weakness. It is well to remember Lord Melbourne's maxim as Prime Minister when he said to his cabinet,

> "Now when we go away from here it doesn't much matter what we say as long as we all say the same thing."

32 No matter how large his personal staff, the President cannot hope to duplicate within his White House the resources and expertise that exists in the executive branch. His challenge is to harness that expertise and to cause his senior line officials to view the problems of their departments and agencies within a broader setting. This is difficult. As Richard Fenno observed twenty years ago: "The psychology of departmentalism . . . militates against the establishment of what might be called mutual responsibility—a state of mind which stresses group concerns rather than separate and particular concerns. The subjective attitude hardest to come by among Cabinet members is this sense of corporate unity and common purpose."

33 To develop and implement viable policies, the President should organize his senior officials in coherent groupings to serve as his principal advisers in broad areas of public policy. Assigning responsibility for a broad area to a single entity helps insure coordinated policies. There is a natural tendency for a president to permit and even encourage the proliferation of entities reporting directly to him. Creating a new council or cabinet-level committee reporting directly to the President demonstrates presidential concern and action both to the participants and to the public. But the more entities reporting to the President, the more specialized and narrow their outlook and mandates are likely to be. Furthermore, the more likely it is that some issues will fall through the proverbial crack since it will be difficult to pinpoint responsibility. Creating numerous specialized committees contributes to a feeling of uncertainty regarding who is responsible for what. Not least, the more groups reporting to the President, the more he must assume responsibility for fitting the pieces together. If the integration of his administration's policies concerns him, he will find himself constantly wanting to know how various problems relate to one another: how alternative energy policies would affect environmental pollution, the rate of economic growth, and inflation.

34 There are many possible ways of slicing the public policy pie. One should avoid divisions that are likely to produce consistent overlaps and jurisdictional battles. Equally important, the more closely a policy council's work is tied to a regular work flow, the more easily its members will develop a sense of collective responsibility. Moreover, to the extent that existing institutions have worked well, they should be used.

35 I have argued elsewhere that the President should have four principal channels of advice to him—the budget process and three cabinet-level interdepartmental councils responsible for national security, economic policy, and social policy. I believe this is a reasonable division of labor, given the objectives of keeping the number of entities with direct reporting relationships to the President to a minimum while not placing excessive burdens on any single institution.

36 Such councils, however, will not work well automatically. At a minimum, two conditions are absolutely essential. First, the President must demonstrate by the way he makes decisions that he relies on the policy council. Departments and agencies must perceive it as the President's vehicle. The most important sign of authority is regular access to the President through papers and meetings. The President must not permit end runs by departments or individuals but instead must insist that executive branch officials channel their advice and proposals to him through the responsible policy council. Without the President's imprimatur, officials are unlikely to take a policy council seriously, attend its meetings, devote their best resources to it, or comply with its decisions.

37 Secondly, a successful decision making process requires skillful management. Someone must be in charge—calling meetings, setting agendas, developing papers. This individual must have the confidence both of the President and of the council's members. He must exhibit two crucial qualities of an honest broker. On the one hand he must insure due process making certain that the views of interested departments and agencies are reflected fairly and faithfully. But he must also promote a genuine competition of ideas, identifying viewpoints not adequately represented or that require qualification, and sometimes augmenting the resources of one side or the other so that a balanced presentation results. He must exercise quality control while guaranteeing due process.

38 Successful brokerage at the presidential level requires certain attributes of temperament and ability as well as certain structural arrangements. The honest broker is less visible, less public than the advocate. Intellectually, the honest broker finds satisfaction in pulling the strands of a problem together or in laying out a complex issue for someone else's judgment. The advocate, by temperament, presses hard for his convictions and seeks to advance the interests of the institution and the constituency he represents.

39 His need for honest brokers will require careful judgments by the President in making his White House staff appointments. As Joseph Califano, himself a young White House assistant to Lyndon Johnson, reminds us:

> White House aides tend to be bright, mostly young, energetic and aggressive. Whether they serve in a conservative, socially laissez-faire administration or a liberal, interventionist one, their instinctive tendency will be to involve themselves in as much detail in as many matters as time permits. When they discover that most department and agency officials will follow their decisions on minor matters, they tend to become seduced by the allure of power and they revel in its exercise.

The President does not need more advocates anxious to tinker with the levers of government within his White House. He needs a select number of honest brokers, skillful in managing people and processes, with a willingness to forgo the limelight. The Brownlow Committee wisely urged the President to appoint assistants with "a passion for anonymity."

40 The system I have described would work best if the size of the councils were flexible for dealing with specific issues, but each council would have a core group of officials to provide continuity. This core group would likely develop a sense of collective responsibility for the policy area as a whole. Such a system, if those participating were prepared to make it work, would provide the President with an organizational foundation for systematic, comprehensive, and coherent policy development. The President deserves no less.

41 Third, the President must consistently use the resources of his office to educate and persuade the country in building a consensus behind his policies. Early in this century, Theodore Roosevelt hailed the Presidency as a "bully pulpit." He recognized as did the later Roosevelt, the importance of using the prestige and powers of his office to shape discussion and national debate on crucial issues, and at the same time, to build public confidence and trust in government. Skillfully articulating one's policies can help in clarifying one's own thinking and in demonstrating the depth of one's commitment to a chosen course of action.

42 Franklin Roosevelt's fireside chats not only communicated to the country what their president was doing to try to cope with the nation's problems, but they also gave his listeners a sense of hope and an attachment to him as the country's chief executive. He gladly, eagerly, accepted the role of public educator.

43 The need for the President to assume the role of mobilizing the country behind him is nowhere better illustrated than in Jimmy Carter's attempts to deal with our nation's energy problems. At the outset of his administration, President Carter publicly identified energy as his first major legislative priority.

44 Within 90 days of taking office, he went on national television in prime time to discuss the energy problem, a problem he said "that is unprecedented in our history. With the exception of preventing war, this is the greatest challenge that our country will face during our lifetime. Our decision about energy will test the character of the American people and the ability of the President and the Congress to govern this nation. This difficult effort will be the moral equivalent of war." That was on Monday evening. On Wednesday evening, April 20, he addressed a joint session of Congress again on prime time national television outlining his "National Energy Program." That Friday, he held his sixth televised news conference as President. He totally dominated the airwaves and seemingly seized the initiative on a difficult issue.

45 Admittedly, the signals that he sent the country were somewhat confusing. His Monday night address stressed the great sacrifices coping with our energy difficulties would demand. The message was simple and straightforward. On Wednesday, the President presented a long and extremely complex set of proposals. Many listeners were confused by what precisely his program was and, importantly, how it would affect them individually. By Friday, he and his senior administration officials were assuring the press and the public that the proposed rebates would mean that no segment of the society would suffer as a result of the program.

46 What is perhaps more significant, however, is what followed. In the aftermath of this public blitz was seeming presidential indifference on energy. He only addressed the nation once more during 1977, in November, seven months later. The following year, the President gave only three national addresses—his State of the Union Message in January, an address on the Panama Canal Treaty in February, and one on the Camp David accords in September. The lack of progress in legislative enactment of his energy proposals was mirrored by a relative lack of apparent presidential attention to what he had earlier referred to as an "unprecedented problem."

47 Haynes Johnson, a veteran Washington journalist, was one of a group of reporters invited by the President to the White House one early spring evening in 1978 for a general discussion. During the course of the evening the President asked how the journalists viewed his performance and what suggestions they had. Johnson hardly a retiring sort, relates that he reminded the President of what Johnson considered a "superb beginning" in putting the energy problem on the national agenda and then the almost total lack of public follow through. Carter responded crisply: "But Haynes, I laid it all out then."

48 Keeping after it is a part of political leadership. Those who the President must persuade to follow his lead rarely have undergone the total immersion in an issue that he has in developing a policy. He must do more than "lay it all out." The President must explain, and remind, and show by his persistent elevation of an issue the importance he attaches to it.

49 It is the burden of my argument that several fundamental changes have occurred in the American political system requiring a reexamination of the roles, needs, and conduct of the Presidency. The changes—in the Congress, in the representation of organized interests, in the structure and analytic capabilities within the executive branch, and in the judiciary—have reinforced the tendencies of our political processes to divide and limit power and to disperse the capacity to manage. They combine to make coherent governance more difficult than in the past.

50 The Presidency in the 1980's is filled with both great challenges but also great opportunities. There is a yearning for a sense of direction, a strategic vision of where we are going in both foreign and domestic affairs. This yearning is an opportunity for the President. In responding to it he must keep his eyes rivetted on his fundamental roles in determining the hierarchy of the nation's interests, in constructing a coherent strategy and program for achieving these objectives, and in mobilizing consensus in the country behind his policies. By focusing on major issues and strategic choices, by organizing a decision making process that lays a foundation for informed decisions while building support for those decisions within his administration, and by using the resources of his office to educate and generate support throughout the county, the President can enhance his effectiveness in filling these roles.

51 This requires restraint, wise judgment, vision, and persistence. In the difficult days ahead, the nation needs no less.

LIFESTYLE REVOLUTIONS
IN THE TELEVISION AGE

Ralph M. Baruch

On December 4, 1979, Ralph M. Baruch, Chairman of the Board and Chief Executive Officer of Viacom International, delivered this speech to the Town Hall of California in Los Angeles. The speaker sought to inform his audience about changes in the "state-of-the-communications-art" over the last few decades.

In talking about accelerating change, Mr. Baruch uses a style that is lively and dynamic; the language befits the subject. He uses vibrant language like "wildest imaginings," "presto . . . cable television was born," and "wooshed over the horizon." He uses vivid language like "this little planet will host six billion souls," "connected by earphones to a crystal set," and "squeeze radio into obsolescence." To a great extent, the high interest value of this speech may be attributed to the speaker's use of language. How many different figures of speech can be found in this address?

The introduction to this speech (paragraphs 1-9) performs most of the functions traditionally assigned to introductions in speech textbooks. What function is accomplished by each of the nine paragraphs? Unlike the introduction, which is nicely developed, the conclusion is very brief. Does the conclusion seem too hurried? How might the conclusion be strengthened?

In the body of the speech, Baruch organizes his presentation around the topics of radio, television broadcasting, and cable television. Which of these topics receives the greatest attention? What does the imbalance tell one about the speaker's primary commitment? What does the speaker think of television broadcasters? Is it important to consider speaker bias when evaluating informative speeches?

This speech is printed by permission from *Vital Speeches of the Day*, January 15, 1980, pp. 209-213.

1 Not too long ago, Walter Cronkite, the dean of American television newscasters, gave us the following quotation:

"It is a gloomy moment in the history of our country. Not in the lifetime of most men has there been so much grave and deep apprehension. Never has the future seemed so incalculable as at this time. The domestic situation is in chaos. Our dollar is weak through the world. Prices are so high as to be utterly impossible. The political cauldron seethes and bubbles with uncertainty. Russia hangs, as usual, like a cloud, dark and silent, upon the horizon; it is a solemn moment. . . . Of our troubles no man can see the end."

That quote was from an editorial that appeared in Harper's Weekly Magazine in October of 1857 . . . Over 120 years ago.

2 There is a school of thought that believes "the more things change, the more they stay the same." There is another school across the street that regards the dynamism of cultural and technological change as a very real force in shaping human destiny.

3 I got my diploma from that second school. I admit that I am addicted to the future. I see change not only as inevitable, but desirable.

4 Not that I am without qualms. Modern technology is a gigantic force that must be directed to the service of life. Our growing knowledge of this planet and the stars has unleashed power beyond our wildest imaginings. Our children take for granted miracles that would have boggled the mind of any resident visionary 100 years ago . . . 50 years ago . . . 25 years ago . . . *yesterday.*

5   More and more, it becomes evident that the key to the survival and prosperity of those curious creatures who inhabit Planet Earth . . . who dream of far-away galaxies . . . comes down to a single word . . . *communication.*

6   Before we can move forward together we must learn to talk together, and laugh together. Barriers to human communications must be overcome, be they mountains or oceans or suspicions engendered over centuries.

7   There have been many "revolutions" in this 20th Century. Political upheavals . . . revolutions in science, in transportation, even revolutions in our homes, in the way men and women relate. But there has been no more significant revolution than in the area of communications.

8   I sometimes think of the communications revolution in terms of our population explosion. Consider that it took millions of years for Earth's population to reach 250 million . . . the population of the world at the time Jesus of Nazareth was born. It took a little over 1500 years to double that count to 500 million. By 1960, the world population reached three billion and by the year 2000 it is estimated that this little planet will host six billion souls.

9   This enormous population must, by necessity, communicate better and faster. An acceleration in the state-of-the-communications-art has been clearly demonstrated over the last few decades.

10   Allow me to reminisce a moment. I remember, back in the 30's, sitting somewhere in Europe, connected by earphones to a crystal set, listening with utter amazement to an early morning short wave broadcast tell me, to my delight, that Joe Louis knocked out Max Schmeling.

11   That was in the 30's . . . not so very long ago.

12   Radio was the miracle of the 30's and 40's. Some 660 AM stations and just a handful of FM stations served the American people. The 50's brought us a new technological miracle . . . television. The impact on radio was severe . . . so severe that some predicted radio's demise . . . they told us radio would become The Shadow's shadow.

13   But what happened? Today we find 4500 AM stations and 3500 FM stations serving the nation. Radio had to change and adapt but it proved amazingly resilient. Before television: under 700 radio stations. Today, some 8000 stations. Did the frightening technology of television squeeze radio into obsolescence? Not at all! The prophets of doom and gloom were replaced by another kind of profits . . . the kind on the balance sheet.

14   Today, radio accounts for some seven percent of national advertising revenues. In years to come, as these expenditures grow, so will radio's size of the pie increase.

15   In the very near future, we shall see the advent of AM stereo radio. The AM stations will achieve technological parity with their FM brethren. In time, FM will have to develop new strategies to excel . . . and outsell their AM rivals. And so it goes. Each laboratory miracle begats another. Each new breakthrough produces new opportunity. If challenge is approached with creativity, not fear, what seems at first to be a threat can be turned into a virtue.

16 Radio is, and will be very much with us. But let us click off the radio now and turn to television.

17 In the 1950's, just about 100 television stations sent their signals in black-and-white.

18 It was early in television's history that our government regulators set limits to television's expansion. Some said they acted with fatal judgement. Others were simply delighted at the manner in which our government goofed . . . the ones with licenses already in their pockets.

19 The early generation of television sets were able to receive channels 2 to 13, which we know as the VHF band. The UHF band, channels 14 to 84, could not be tuned in by most receivers then on the market. Government regulations added to the problem, by keeping UHF an inferior signal. It wasn't until many years later that the FCC rectified some of the horrendous mistakes.

20 When, in the early 50's, the government ban on new stations was imposed, many communities were denied adequate television service.

21 When our people are within reach of something good, but can't quite grasp it, they always manifest that unique American free spirit of ingenuity. They reach out.

22 It was then that strange looking towers began appearing on mountain tops . . . towers capable of receiving more and better television signals. Those signals were carried by wire to the nearby towns and *presto* . . . cable television was born! The seeds of an exciting new communications miracle had been planted. And the flowers are just beginning to bloom.

23 But let's not move too quickly. Before we focus on the future, let's take pause to get a picture of what happened to this maverick called television. Just three decades ago this country had as many television sets as it produced triplets. Then, from a few households television burgeoned to its present 75 million American homes. Nearly half of these homes have two or more sets and 13 percent have three sets or more.

24 Are the sets being watched? You bet they are! Nielsen tells us that in 1959 the average television viewing, per home, per day, totalled four hours and 58 minutes. Ten years later, the figure was five hours and 45 minutes. This year, according to the president of ABC Television, the average American television home watches six hours and 45 minutes of television every day. Incredible as it sounds, many of us spend more time watching television than we spend on the job, or asleep.

25 That so many people turn to television for information and entertainment is obviously an overwhelming vote of confidence in an election that takes place every day and every night, all year long. It is ironic that the medium comes in for so much negative criticism when it performs such a positive service for its audience.

26 Everyone and his brother wants television to get "better", even if you could define what "better" really means. What the critics forget is that nobody wants "better" television than the industry itself. We are not in the business to make bad programs, though some might question that statement. And television has gotten better. The so-called "Golden Age" of television was made of brass compared with today's programs. Sure, television had great moments in the past. But today the programming is more diverse, consistently of much higher quality, more courageous and more innovative than ever before. News is better, sports are better done, entertainment is more varied. One problem is that there is so much good television in any given week it is harder for a single program to stand out for praise.

27 I have some advice for the chronic complainers: If you don't like a program, there is that little dial on the TV set that allows it to be turned off—use it! Broadcasters smile when the dial is turned on to their programs. When it is turned off, they go into instant depression. Television is a very democratic medium. It responds to its audience . . . to the *ratings*. When the audience takes a holiday, the programs change and fast.

28 We hear constant calls for programs that are more educational and more cultural. It is a lot easier to embrace the cause of education and culture than it is to define. Someone once said, "Those who criticize television the most would like to bring others to the levels which they themselves have not achieved." There are a host of champions for so called "better" programs for the *other fellow* to watch.

29 Broadcasters do their damndest to serve the most diverse and demanding audience in history with more and better programs. What they often fail to do is speak out in favor of television's achievements. I think broadcasters underestimate the vitality of the medium and its positive impact on the American scene. There is always room for improvement, but there is also room for pride.

30 Unfortunately, this defensive attitude among some broadcasters carries over into other areas. Those of us who spend a lot of time in Washington have seen spokesmen for the industry decry every new technology as a demon. Some leaders of the television industry oppose new technologies like prudes oppose tight jeans. Limited vision forces them to regard the emerging technologies, such as cable or subscription cable as anathema. Instead of seeing opportunity, they see devils.

31 The television establishment has done very well indeed over the years, and it will do better in the years ahead. We get a clear sense of this growing prosperity if we look at the competitive media:

32 In 1978, according to McCann Erickson, the newspaper industry attracted some thirty percent of all national advertising expenditures in this country. Television got some twenty percent.

33 If the television industry can prosper . . . which it does . . . on a twenty percent market share . . . if the television industry could survive and triumph over the loss of ten percent of its total revenues when cigarette advertising was snuffed out . . . which it did . . . imagine the leverage the industry will obtain when it gains just one or two percentage points from the competition.

34 If present trends continue, it has been estimated by a research scientist, that by the year 2000, television broadcast revenues (in terms of dollars of the late 70's) will rise from the present estimated four billion to a staggering twenty-two billion dollars.

35 By the year 2000, the American population should grow to 260 million. The largest demographic growth curve is predicted for the population segment in the 25 to 34 year age group. Those are the most desirable viewers from a television advertiser's viewpoint. It's only logical that increased advertising dollars will flow to television and that the future is very bright. You would think these kind of statistics would allow industry leaders to be a bit more receptive to the new technologies.

36 Just five years from now we will have 85 million television homes. That's a lush target for advertisers. Is it any wonder ABC paid $225 million for the 1984 Olympic Games? Do you recall when it was thought imprudent for NBC to spend over $130 million for the 1980 games? The dollars needed to support the television industry are out there. . . .

37 In the meantime, cable television has made enormous strides everywhere it is operative. Just as it took color television time to gain acceptance, it will take time for cable to flourish even further. I believe the early 1980's will be the years when cable television gives us a new communications explosion.

38 Today, there are more than 15 million cable television homes. More important, nearly half of all the homes in America can now avail themselves of cable service.

39 As the cable industry delivers alternative programming that captures more of the interest of this vast group of potential subscribers, the number of cable homes will grow even more rapidly. In a recent article, I noticed a forecast of 100 million cable homes by the year 2000.

40 At present growth rates, by 1985 we should have 30 to 35 million cable television subscriber homes. Among the cities now being cabled, or soon to be, are Houston, Nashville, Pittsburgh, Dallas, Minneapolis, St. Paul, Omaha and Boston.

41 Will the dramatic growth of cable hurt the local broadcaster? Quite the contrary. It is well known that cable-equipped homes watch more television. The cable systems help disseminate broadcast signals over a larger area. Cable viewers will watch network programs and local programs. But they will have an ever widening program choice.

42 Programming, in our business, is sometimes called *software*. That's a descriptive term, not a criticism. It's the software that attracts the viewer to the TV set. He, or she, couldn't care less how it gets there. Last year, *Newsweek Magazine* stated: "In the long run . . . the only consideration that truly counts is what sort of programming will come inside the new electronic packages." Yet something is happening with the delivery systems that is contributing enormously to the communications revolution:

43 Years ago, a science fiction writer named Arthur Clarke proposed the idea for communications satellites. As usual, reality followed imagination. By the early 1960's, what began with Sputnik beeping in Russian had given us space communications satellites with names like Echo, Telstar, Relay, Syncom, and Early Bird.

44 Telstar could only relay a signal for about 12 minutes as it wooshed over the horizon faster than a disco skater dancing to Beethoven. To my knowledge, nobody complained when satellite technology improved and gave us satellites that hang in stationary orbits 23,000 miles over the Earth. This development made continuous satellite communications possible.

45 The newly emerging cable television industry was quick to capitalize on this amazing technological breakthrough. Signals and programs could be sent, via satellite, to ground stations, and then fed into homes wired for cable service. Satellites gave cable an efficient, relatively inexpensive distribution system.

46 Regular cable service was supplemented by subscription cable, which provides, via satellite, unedited motion pictures, without commercial interruption. Subscription cable also provides specially produced attractions such as plays, concerts, sports, children's programming and other events to subscribers of this "second tier" of cable services.

47 Some members of the broadcasting fraternity saw instant doom as cable services grew. The public was told, the Congress was told that the moment pay cable reached four million subscribers it would "syphon" (that was their term anticipating the gasoline shortage) "syphon" programs and practically all major sports events from conventional over-the-air television.

48 Today, we are just about at five million pay cable subscribers. Yet, somehow, the television broadcasting industry has managed to endure and muddle through with higher profits than ever. And nobody has stolen our birthright . . . the Superbowl. In truth, the public has been the real beneficiary, enjoying services like *Showtime* and others.

49 Cable television is, at long last, providing exciting specialized services, via satellite, to its subscribers:

50 Our cable television industry has access to supplementary services offered by *Showtime* and its competitors. Additionally, signals from stations in Atlanta, New York, Los Angeles or San Francisco can be received. Cable subscribers can watch two children's networks, a specialized sports network, a Madison Square Garden network, gavel-to-gavel proceedings of the House of Representatives, an educational network, two religious networks and more. Soon we will offer a 24 hour news network, a black network . . . the horizons are as wide as the sky.

51 Estimates by Drexel Burnham Lambert, Inc. forecast that by 1985, cable revenues will reach $1 to $1.5 billion dollars. Based on the recently developing trend in cable homes to buy more than one subscription cable service, and because of new services now being developed, my own estimate is that by 1985, the figure will be closer to two billion or more in cable revenues.

52 Half of this two or more billion dollars will be earned by program suppliers like *Showtime* and its competitors. A lot of those dollars will be reinvested to develop a broader program spectrum. Incidentally, these same estimates indicate that increased cable viewing will result in no great erosion of the conventional television audience. The few percentage points lost will be more than compensated by the overall growth in the television home universe.

53 The wedding of cable and satellite technologies will produce changes far beyond new programs. They will have a deep and lasting effect on our very lifestyles. Let me give you some examples . . . or samples . . . of the future:

54 Our company, in one of our cable television systems, is installing a large number of cable-energized burglary, fire and emergency alarm systems. Cable has become a protector of life and property

55 Another of our cable systems is completing installation of an interconnected arraignment system which will save taxpayers vast sums of money in New York State by eliminating personal appearances of law enforcement officers and defendants before judges.

56 Energy conservation has become vital to America's very survival. The cable industry is experimenting with power distribution systems that could also turn appliances on and off using a cable signal from a central computer.

57 Our own company's cable division recently experimented with a law course fed via satellite from New York University to the McGeorge School of Law in California. At a time when the private college level educational structure is struggling for economic survival, wired instruction can make a major contribution to education.

58 In this great country, 134 counties are still without physicians. Two-way cable technology can help bring them medical services.

59 Cable television could well change the shopping habits of the nation. The presentation, and selection, of goods and services is now within our technological grasp. A lot of gasoline will be saved by at-home shoppers. This

emerging technology will also have enormous impact on advertising and marketing.

60 There is a good chance that, by the end of the next decade, meetings like this will be considered old fashioned. Like it or not, depending on what you did last night, cable television, satellite-interconnected video meetings will be an everyday occurrence. The convention business will, in part, go electronic.

61 Other applications of cable technology are innumerable. We could talk about the future until we reach it, but our time is limited. There are some bases we should touch before sign-off:

62 By the end of this year, the cable television industry will have about 2000 receiving Earth stations capable of obtaining a satellite signal. The television broadcast industry will have just two or three dozen Earth stations, I believe that the television industry will finally see the light and utilize satellite technology. How far is the day when the present national networks offer their affiliates not one program at a time, but via satellite, a generous "Chinese" menu of programs from which the local stations can pick up and choose depending on audience preference?

63 At some point in the 1980's, the relationship between networks and affiliated stations might well be the subject of a new structure in the making.

64 I should also mention that there are constraints implicit in current satellite technology. The maximum number of satellites assigned to use allowable broadcast frequencies will probably be limited to twenty-five. Eleven satellites are now operational. A twelfth is scheduled to be launched two days from now. There is a limit to the number of signals which can be propagated.

65 That's the bad news. The good news is that the cost of receiving dishes has declined from $100,000 just a few years ago to the present figure of $10,000–$25,000. In fact, the latest Nieman Marcus Christmas Catalog features your very own Earth station for only $36,000 plus tax.

66 Does this mean that direct satellite-to-home television is just around the corner, or cloud? I don't think so. The power required both in the sky or on the ground to make such a system practical puts direct satellite broadcasting years in the future from a cost vantage. There are also serious regulatory and political problems which must be solved.

67 When direct satellite-to-home communication was first proposed, the Soviet Union quickly suggested jamming incoming broadcasts by jamming frequencies, or, in a more neighborly mood, of sending up killer rockets or laser beams to knock out transmitting satellites.

68 A delicious sample of diplomatese can be found in the latest *United Nations General Assembly Report of the Legal Subcommittee,* which if implemented would leave us very little, if anything to put on satellites especially not news or information which could be prohibited by any of these ambiguous clauses:

I quote:

"States undertaking activities in direct television broadcasting by satellites should in all cases exclude from the television programs any material which is detrimental to the maintenance of international peace and security, which publicizes ideas of war, militarism, national and racial hatred and enmity between peoples, which is aimed at interfering in the domestic affairs of other States or which undermines the foundations of the local civilization, culture, way of life, traditions or language."

69 Again, the whole concept of satellite-to-home broadcasting brings with it enormous political and regulatory baggage.

70 We are in a period of great technological advance. We see evidence in the enormous growth of the video tape cassette market, and we will see the video disc catch on quickly. Estimates tell us that by year-end, a million video cassette players will have been sold, using different standards and vastly different formats.

71 The video-disc is about to enter the marketplace. The only thing the video-disc industry has to fear is confusion in the buyers mind. The record industry opted for incompatible standards requiring different players for different records. The video cassette industry did the same. And now potential buyers must not only be sold on the video-disc, but on which kind of video-disc . . . stylus or laser or what have you.

72 A software supplier, such as ourselves, will not worry which standard is used to reproduce the software. But we do worry about consumer confusion possibly slowing up a great technology of enormous potential in the fields of entertainment, education, and information. We hope the industry finds a way to make its products compatible for their sake, for our sake and for the sake of the buyer.

73 As these new technologies come to maturity, more and more software will be required. This will be a boon to creative communities such as the one here in Hollywood. One of the most plaguing problems has been underemployment of actors, writers, and other creative people. The new demand for product will alleviate much of that stress.

74 But a word of caution . . . a word to the unions . . . to the guilds representing this valuable creative resource: An urgent word . . . In the past, many of the unions and guilds have recognized the value of supporting new distribution methods and technologies. On the other hand, some unions did not, became greedy to what I believe was the ultimate serious detriment of their membership. Give these new technologies like pay cable the opportunity to take root and grow. My word to the union and the guilds is: Give these innovations the chance to survive their infancy before overwhelming them with demands, clauses, fees and the like. The future is golden. Constraint in the present will result in a bountiful harvest, if the plant is not cut off at the seedling stage.

75 Conversely, the timetable for the success of the electronic packages depends on the programming offered to the huge potential audience. Give us the creative skills to make the programs and we'll give you a tremendous arena in which to showcase your talents.

76 A responsive, participating audience is certain to emerge. It will be a demanding audience, more sophisticated in taste and preference than any audience before. It will challenge us to our best, and we will meet that challenge.

77 We are on the threshold of an exciting decade. Electronic technology is our bridge to the future. We must not inhibit this miracle from finding its place in the world . . . from actually changing our world for the better.

78 We must match the miracles with miracles of vision . . . miracles of service.

79 In conclusion, let me leave you with these words spoken by the late Edward R. Murrow:

"In this ever changing world in which many people, in one generation, seek to accomplish the changes of centuries, this country has a great role to fill."

Well said, Ed.
I thank you.

LOVE, LAW, AND CIVIL DISOBEDIENCE

Martin Luther King, Jr.

Dr. Martin Luther King, Jr., a Nobel Prize winner and a leader in the national nonviolent movement for Negro civil rights, delivered this address at the annual meeting of the fellowship of the Concerned, November 16, 1961. The Fellowship of the Concerned is a biracial, nondenominational organization of church women leaders that seeks to promote social and racial justice in the South. The Fellowship is affiliated with the Southern Regional Council which strives for improvement of economic, civic, and racial conditions.

Dr. King attempts to clarify the philosophy behind the nonviolent student movement for Negro civil rights to a friendly audience. To achieve this end, he enumerates the foremost characteristics of the movement and explains its rationale. Dr. King uses an unfolding organizational approach in which he states each characteristic as he begins to discuss it. This procedure can easily lead to stilted and overworked transitions. Is this true of Dr. King's address? It is also important that transitions show a clear progression of ideas. Do Dr. King's ideas progress effectively?

This speech demonstrates the important role definition may play in informative speaking. Dr. King analyzes the different meanings of the word *love* in order to make explicit in what sense the word may be applied to the participants of the movement. When to define and how to define is a question that always presents itself to the informative speaker. Was it essential for Dr. King to define the word *love* carefully? What mode of definition does he employ? Are there other terms he could profitably have defined?

Dr. King has been called a man with a very distinctive style. In which respects is style important in informative speaking? Does Dr. King's style in this speech seem more appropriate to persuasive than informative discourse?

This address points up the difficulty of placing speeches in precise, mutually exclusive categories, such as *informative* or *persuasive.* While Dr. King explains the philosophy of the nonviolent student movement to a sympathetic audience, he may still, in some instances, formulate and intensify values through his manner of explanation. Exposition may have a persuasive impact. Are there any points in the speech at which Dr. King departs from the function of imparting knowledge and becomes an open advocate?

1 Members of the Fellowship of the Concerned, of the Southern Regional Council, I need not pause to say how very delighted I am to be here today, and to have the opportunity of being a little part of this very significant gathering. I certainly want to express my personal appreciation to Mrs. Tilly and the members of the Committee, for giving me this opportunity. I would also like to express just a personal word of thanks and appreciation for your vital witness in this period of transition which we are facing in our Southland, and in the nation, and I am sure that as a result of this genuine concern, and your significant work in communities all across the South, we have a better South today and I am sure will have a better South tomorrow with your continued endeavor and I do want to express my personal gratitude and appreciation to you of the Fellowship of the Concerned for your significant work and for your forthright witness.

2 Now, I have been asked to talk about the philosophy behind the student movement. There can be no gain-saying of the fact that we confront a crisis in race relations in the United States. This crisis has been precipitated on the one hand by the determined resistance of reactionary forces in the South to the Supreme Court's decision in 1954 outlawing segregation in the public schools. And we know that at times this resistance

has risen to ominous proportions. At times we find the legislative halls of the South ringing loud with such words as interposition and nullification. And all of these forces have developed into massive resistance. But we must also say that the crisis has been precipitated on the other hand by the determination of hundreds and thousands and millions of Negro people to achieve freedom and human dignity. If the Negro stayed in his place and accepted discrimination and segregation, there would be no crisis. But the Negro has a new sense of dignity, a new self-respect, and new determination. He has reevaluated his own intrinsic worth. Now this new sense of dignity on the part of the Negro grows out of the same longing for freedom and human dignity on the part of the oppressed people all over the world; for we see it in Africa, we see it in Asia, and we see it all over the world. Now we must say that this struggle for freedom will not come to an automatic halt, for history reveals to us that once oppressed people rise up against that oppression, there is no stopping point short of full freedom. On the other hand, history reveals to us that those who oppose the movement for freedom are those who are in privileged positions who very seldom give up their privileges without strong resistance. And they very seldom do it voluntarily. So the sense of struggle will continue. The question is how will the struggle be waged.

3 Now there are three ways that oppressed people have generally dealt with their oppression. One way is the method of acquiescence, the method of surrender; that is, the individuals will somehow adjust themselves to oppression, they adjust themselves to discrimination or to segregation or colonialism or what have you. The other method that has been used in history is that of rising up against the oppressor with corroding hatred and physical violence. Now of course we know about this method in western civilization, because in a sense it has been the hallmark of its grandeur, and the inseparable twin of western materialism. But there is a weakness in this method because it ends up creating many more social problems than it solves. And I am convinced that if the Negro succumbs to the temptation of using violence in his struggle for freedom and jastice, unborn generations will be the recipients of a long and desolate night of bitterness. And our chief legacy to the future will be an endless reign of meaningless chaos.

4 But there is another way, namely the way of nonviolent resistance. This method was popularized in our generation by a little man from India, whose name was Mohandas K. Gandhi. He used this method in a magnificent way to free his people from the economic exploitation and the political domination inflicted upon them by a foreign power.

5 This has been the method used by the student movement in the South and all over the United States. And naturally whenever I talk about

the student movement I cannot be totally objective. I have to be somewhat subjective because of my great admiration for what the students have done. For in a real sense they have taken our deep groans and passionate yearnings for freedom, and filtered them in their own tender souls, and fashioned them into a creative protest which is an epic known all over our nation. As a result of their disciplined, nonviolent, yet courageous struggle, they have been able to do wonders in the South, and in our nation. But this movement does have an underlying philosophy, it has certain ideas that are attached to it, it has certain philosophical precepts. These are the things that I would like to discuss for the few moments left.

6 I would say that the first point or the first principle in the movement is the idea that means must be as pure as the end. This movement is based on the philosophy that ends and means must cohere. Now this has been one of the long struggles in history, the whole idea of means and ends. Great philosophers have grappled with it, and sometimes they have emerged with the idea, from Machiavelli on down, that the end justifies the means. There is a great system of thought in our world today, known as Communism. And I think that with all the weakness and tragedies of Communism, we find its greatest tragedy right here, that it goes under the philosophy that the end justifies the means that are used in the process. So we can read or we can hear the Lenins say that lying, deceit, or violence, that many of these things justify the ends of the classless society.

7 This is where the student movement and the nonviolent movement that is taking place in our nation would break with Communism and any other system that would argue that the end justifies the means. For in the long run, we must see that the end represents the means in process and the ideal in the making. In other words, we cannot believe, or we cannot go with the idea that the end justifies the means because the end is preexistent in the means. So the idea of nonviolent resistance, the philosophy of nonviolent resistance, is the philosophy which says that the means must be as pure as the end, that in the long run of history, immoral destructive means cannot bring about moral and constructive ends.

8 There is another thing about this philosophy, this method of nonviolence which is followed by the student movement. It says that those who adhere to or follow this philosophy must follow a consistent principle of noninjury. They must consistently refuse to inflict injury upon another. Sometimes you will read the literature of the student movement and see that, as they are getting ready for the sit-in or stand-in, they will read something like this, "if you are hit do not hit back, if you are cursed do not curse back." This is the whole idea, that the individual who is engaged in a nonviolent struggle must never inflict injury upon another. Now this has an external aspect and it has an internal one. From the external point of view it

means that the individuals involved must avoid external physical violence. So they don't have guns, they don't retaliate with physical violence. If they are hit in the process, they avoid external physical violence at every point. But it also means that they avoid internal violence of spirit. This is why the love ethic stands so high in the student movement. We have a great deal of talk about love and nonviolence in this whole thrust.

9   Now when the students talk about love, certainly they are not talking about emotional bosh, they are not talking about merely a sentimental outpouring; they're talking something much deeper, and I always have to stop and try to define the meaning of love in this context. The Greek language comes to our aid in trying to deal with this. There are three words in the Greek language for love, one is the word Eros. This is a beautiful type of love, it is an aesthetic love. Plato talks about it a great deal in his *Dialogue,* the yearning of the soul for the realm of the divine. It has come to us to be a sort of romantic love, and so in a sense we have read about it and experienced it. We've read about it in all the beauties of literature. I guess in a sense Edgar Allan Poe was talking about Eros when he talked about his beautiful Annabelle Lee, with the love surrounded by the halo of eternity. In a sense Shakespeare was talking about Eros when he said "Love is not love which alters when it alteration finds, or bends with the remover to remove; O' no! it is an ever fixed mark that looks on tempests and is never shaken, it is the star to every wandering bark." (You know I remember that because I used to quote it to this little lady when we were courting; that's Eros.) The Greek language talks about Philia which was another level of love. It is an intimate affection between personal friends, it is a reciprocal love. On this level you love because you are loved. It is friendship.

10   Then the Greek language comes out with another word which is called the Agape. Agape is more than romantic love, agape is more than friendship. Agape is understanding, creative, redemptive, good will to all men. It is an overflowing love which seeks nothing in return. Theologians would say that it is the love of God operating in the human heart. So that when one rises to love on this level, he loves men not because he likes them, not because their ways appeal to him, but he loves every man because God loves him. And he rises to the point of loving the person who does an evil deed while hating the deed that the person does. I think this is what Jesus meant when he said "love your enemies." I'm very happy that he didn't say like your enemies, because it is pretty difficult to like some people. Like is sentimental, and it is pretty difficult to like someone bombing your home; it is pretty difficult to like somebody threatening your children; it is difficult to like congressmen who spend all of their time trying to defeat civil rights. But Jesus says love them, and love is greater than like. Love is understand-

ing, redemptive, creative, good will for all men. And it is this idea, it is this whole ethic of love which is the idea standing at the basis of the student movement.

11   There is something else: that one seeks to defeat the unjust system, rather than individuals who are caught in that system. And that one goes on believing that somehow this is the important thing, to get rid of the evil system and not the individual who happens to be misguided, who happens to be misled, who was taught wrong. The thing to do is to get rid of the system and thereby create a moral balance within society.

12   Another thing that stands at the center of this movement is another idea: that suffering can be a most creative and powerful social force. Suffering has certain moral attributes involved, but it can be a powerful and creative social force. Now, it is very interesting at this point to notice that both violence and nonviolence agree that suffering can be a very powerful social force. But there is this difference: violence says that suffering can be a powerful social force by inflicting the suffering on somebody else; so this is what we do in war, this is what we do in the whole violent thrust of the violent movement. It believes that you achieve some end by inflicting suffering on another. The nonviolent say that suffering becomes a powerful social force when you willingly accept that violence on yourself, so that self-suffering stands at the center of the nonviolent movement and the individuals involved are able to suffer in a creative manner, feeling that unearned suffering is redemptive, and that suffering may serve to transform the social situation.

13   Another thing in this movement is the idea that there is within human nature an amazing potential for goodness. There is within human nature something that can respond to goodness. I know somebody's liable to say that this is an unrealistic movement if it goes on believing that all people are good. Well, I didn't say that. I think the students are realistic enough to believe that there is a strange dichotomy of disturbing dualism within human nature. Many of the great philosophers and thinkers through the ages have seen this. It caused Ovid the Latin poet to say, "I see and approve the better things of life, but the evil things I do." It caused even St. Augustine to say, "Lord, make me pure, but not yet." So that that is in human nature. Plato, centuries ago said that the human personality is like a charioteer with two headstrong horses, each wanting to go in different directions, so that within our own individual lives we see this conflict and certainly when we come to the collective life of man, we see a strange badness. But in spite of this there is something in human nature that can respond to goodness. So that man is neither innately good nor is he innately bad; he has potentialities for both. So in this sense, Carlyle was right when he said that "there are depths in man which go down to the lowest hell, and

heights which reach the highest heaven, for are not both heaven and hell made out of him, ever-lasting miracle and mystery that he is?'' Man has the capacity to be good, man has the capacity to be evil.

14 And so the nonviolent resister never lets this idea go, that there is something within human nature that can respond to goodness. So that a Jesus of Nazareth or a Mohandas Gandhi, can appeal to human beings and appeal to that element of goodness within them, and a Hitler can appeal to the element of evil within them. But we must never forget that there is something within human nature that can respond to goodness, that man is not totally depraved, to put it in theological terms, the image of God is never totally gone. And so the individuals who believe in this movement and who believe in nonviolence and our struggle in the South, somehow believe that even the worst segregationist can become an integrationist. Now sometimes it is hard to believe that this is what this movement says, and it believes it firmly, that there is something within human nature that can be changed, and this stands at the top of the whole philosophy of the student movement and the philosophy of nonviolence.

15 It says something else. It says that it is as much a moral obligation to refuse to cooperate with evil as it is to cooperate with good. Non-cooperation with evil is as much a moral obligation as the cooperation with good. So that the student movement is willing to stand up courageously on the idea of civil disobedience. Now I think this is the part of the student movement that is probably misunderstood more than anything else. And it is a difficult aspect, because on the one hand the students would say, and I would say, and all the people who believe in civil rights would say, obey the Supreme Court's decision of 1954 and at the same time, we would disobey certain laws that exist on the statutes of the South today.

16 This brings in the whole question of how can you be logically consistent when you advocate obeying some laws and disobeying other laws. Well, I think one would have to see the whole meaning of this movement at this point by seeing that the students recognize that there are two types of laws. There are just laws and there are unjust laws. And they would be the first to say obey the just laws, they would be the first to say that men and women have a moral obligation to obey just and right laws. And they would go on to say that we must see that there are unjust laws. Now the question comes into being, what is the difference, and who determines the difference, what is the difference between a just and an unjust law?

17 Well, a just law is a law that squares with a moral law. It is a law that squares with that which is right, so that any law that uplifts human personality is a just law. Whereas that law which is out of harmony with the moral is a law which does not square with the moral law of the universe. It does not square with the law of God, so for that reason it is unjust and any law that degrades the human personality is an unjust law.

18 Well, somebody says that that does not mean anything to me; first, I don't believe in these abstract things called moral laws and I'm not too religious, so I don't believe in the law of God; you have to get a little more concrete, and more practical. What do you mean when you say that a law is unjust, and a law is just? Well, I would go on to say in more concrete terms that an unjust law is a code that the majority inflicts on the minority that is not binding on itself. So that this becomes difference made legal. Another thing that we can say is that an unjust law is a code which the majority inflicts upon the minority, which that minority had no part in enacting or creating, because that minority had no right to vote in many instances, so that the legislative bodies that made these laws were not democratically elected. Who could ever say that the legislative body of Mississippi was democratically elected, or the legislative body of Alabama was democratically elected, or the legislative body even of Georgia has been democratically elected, when there are people in Terrell County and in other counties because of the color of their skin who cannot vote? They confront reprisals and threats and all of that; so that an unjust law is a law that individuals did not have a part in creating or enacting because they were denied the right to vote.

19 Now the same token of just law would be just the opposite. A just law becomes saneness made legal. It is a code that the majority, who happen to believe in that code, compel the minority, who don't believe in it, to follow, because they are willing to follow it themselves, so it is saneness made legal. Therefore the individuals who stand up on the basis of civil disobedience realize that they are following something that says that there are just laws and there are unjust laws. Now, they are not anarchists. They believe that there are laws which must be followed; they do not seek to defy the law, they do not seek to evade the law. For many individuals who would call themselves segregationists and who would hold on to segregation at any cost seek to defy the law, they seek to evade the law, and their process can lead on into anarchy. They seek in the final analysis to follow a way of uncivil disobedience, not civil disobedience. And I submit that the individual who disobeys the law, whose conscience tells him it is unjust and who is willing to accept the penalty by staying in jail until that law is altered, is expressing at the moment the very highest respect for law.

20 This is what the students have followed in their movement. Of course there is nothing new about this, they feel that they are in good company and rightly so. We go back and read the *Apology* and the *Crito,* and you see Socrates practicing civil disobedience. And to a degree academic freedom is a reality today because Socrates practiced civil disobedience. The early Christians practiced civil disobedience in a superb manner, to a point where they were willing to be thrown to the lions. They were willing to face all kinds of suffering in order to stand up for what they knew was right even though they knew it was against the laws of the Roman Empire.

21 We could come up to our own day and we see it in many instances. We must never forget that everything that Hitler did in Germany was "legal." It was illegal to aid and comfort a Jew, in the days of Hitler's Germany. But I believe that if I had the same attitude then as I have now I would publicly aid and comfort my Jewish brothers in Germany if Hitler were alive today calling this an illegal process. If I lived in South Africa today in the midst of the white supremacy law in South Africa, I would join Chief Luthuli and others in saying break these unjust laws. And even let us come up to America. Our nation in a sense came into being through a massive act of civil disobedience, for the Boston Tea Party was nothing but a massive act of civil disobedience. Those who stood up against the slave laws, the abolitionists, by and large practiced civil disobedience. So I think these students are in good company, and they feel that by practicing civil disobedience they are in line with men and women through the ages who have stood up for something that is morally right.

22 Now there are one or two other things that I want to say about this student movement, moving out of the philosophy of nonviolence, something about what it is a revolt against. On the one hand it is a revolt against the negative peace that had encompassed the South for many years. I remember when I was in Montgomery, Ala., one of the white citizens came to me one day and said—and I think he was very sincere about this—that in Montgomery for all of these years we have been such a peaceful community, we have had so much harmony in race relations and then you people have started this movement and boycott, and it has done so much to disturb race relations, and we just don't love the Negro like we used to love them, because you have destroyed the harmony and the peace that we once had in race relations. And I said to him, in the best way I could say and I tried to say it in nonviolent terms, we have never had peace in Montgomery, Ala., we have never had peace in the South. We have had a negative peace, which is merely the absence of tension; we've had a negative peace in which the Negro patiently accepted his situation and his plight, but we've never had true peace, we've never had positive peace, and what we're seeking now is to develop this positive peace. For we must come to see that peace is not merely the absence of some negative force, it is the presence of a positive force. True peace is not merely the absence of tension, but it is the presence of justice and brotherhood. I think this is what Jesus meant when he said, I come not to bring peace but a sword. Now Jesus didn't mean he came to start war, to bring a physical sword, and he didn't mean, I come not to bring positive peace. But I think what Jesus was saying in substance was this, that I come not to bring an old negative peace, which makes for stagnant passivity and deadening complacency, I come to bring something different, and whenever I come, a conflict is precipitated, between the old and the new, whenever I come a struggle takes place between justice and injustice, between the forces of light and the forces of darkness. I come not to bring a negative peace, but a positive peace, which is brotherhood, which is justice, which is the Kingdom of God.

23 And I think this is what we are seeking to do today, and this movement is a revolt against a negative peace and a struggle to bring into being a positive peace, which makes for true brotherhood, true integration, true person-to-person relationships. This movement is also revolt against what is often called tokenism. Here again many people do not understand this, they feel that in this struggle the Negro will be satisfied with tokens of integration, just a few students and a few schools here and there and a few doors open here and there. But this isn't the meaning of the movement and I think that honesty impels me to admit it everywhere I have an opportunity, that the Negro's aim is to bring about complete integration in American life. And he has come to see that token integration is little more than token democracy, which ends up with many new evasive schemes and it ends up with new discrimination, covered up with such niceties of complexity. It is very interesting to discover that the movement has thrived in many communities that had token integration. So this reveals that the movement is based on a principle that integration must become real and complete, not just token integration.

24 It is also a revolt against what I often call the myth of time. We hear this quite often, that only time can solve this problem. That if we will only be patient, and only pray—which we must do, we must be patient and we must pray—but there are those who say just do these things and wait for time, and time will solve this problem. Well the people who argue this do not themselves realize that time is neutral, that it can be used constructively or destructively. At points the people of ill will, the segregationists, have used time much more effectively than the people of good will. So individuals in the struggle must come to realize that it is necessary to aid time, that without this kind of aid, time itself will become an ally of the insurgent and primitive forces of social stagnation. Therefore, this movement is a revolt against the myth of time.

25 There is a final thing that I would like to say to you, this movement is a movement based on faith in the future. It is a movement based on a philosophy, the possibility of the future bringing into being something real and meaningful. It is a movement based on hope. I think this is very important. The students have developed a theme song for their movement, maybe you've heard it. It goes something like this "we shall overcome, deep

in my heart, I do believe, we shall overcome," and then they go on to say another verse, "we are not afraid, we are not afraid today, deep in my heart I do believe, we shall overcome." So it is out of this deep faith in the future that they are able to move out and adjourn the councils of despair, and to bring new light in the dark chambers of pessimism. I can remember the times that we've been together, I remember that night in Montgomery, Ala., when we had stayed up all night, discussing the Freedom Rides, and that morning came to see that it was necessary to go on with the Freedom Rides, that we would not in all good conscience call an end to the Freedom Rides at that point. And I remember the first group got ready to leave, to take a bus for Jackson, Miss., we all joined hands and started singing together. "We shall overcome, we shall overcome." And something within me said, now how is it that these students can sing this, they are going down to Mississippi, they are going to face hostile and jeering mobs, and yet they could sing, "We shall overcome." They may even face physical death, and yet they could sing, "We shall overcome." Most of them realized that they would be thrown into jail, and yet they could sing, "We shall overcome, we are not afraid." Then something caused me to see at that moment the real meaning of the movement. That students had faith in the future. That the movement was based on hope, that this movement had something within it that says somehow even though the arc of the moral universe is long, it bends toward justice. And I think this should be a challenge to all others who are struggling to transform the dangling discords of our Southland into a beautiful symphony of brotherhood. There is something in this student movement which says to us, that we shall overcome. Before the victory is won some may have to get scarred up, but we shall overcome. Before the victory of brotherhood is achieved, some will maybe face physical death, but we shall overcome. Before the victory is won, some will lose jobs, some will be called Communists, and reds, merely because they believe in brotherhood, some will be dismissed as dangerous rabble-rousers and agitators merely because they're standing up for what is right, but we shall overcome. That is the basis of this movement, and as I like to say, there is something in this universe that justifies Carlyle in saying no lie can live forever. We shall overcome because there is something in this universe which justifies William Cullen Bryant in saying truth crushed to earth shall rise again. We shall overcome because there is something in this universe that justifies James Russell Lowell in saying, truth forever on the scaffold, wrong forever on the throne. Yet that scaffold sways the future, and behind the dim unknown standeth God within the shadows, keeping watch above His own. With this faith in the future, with this determined struggle, we will be able to emerge from the bleak and desolate midnight of man's inhumanity to man, into the bright and glittering daybreak of freedom and justice. Thank you.

AN AMERICAN PRISONER OF WAR
IN SOUTH VIETNAM

James N. Rowe

For more than five years Major James N. Rowe was a prisoner of the Viet Cong. He was captured by the enemy when he was a Special Forces advisor in 1963 and was held prisoner in the Mekong region and the U Minh Forest. He devised a cover story about himself that kept the enemy from executing him, a fate which befell several others imprisoned with him. His cover story held up until 1968, when the enemy found out he had lied. Major Rowe thinks that they received a biographical sketch with complete information about him and his family from the Peace and Justice Loving Friends of the National Liberation Front in America. This information put him on the list for execution. But on December 31, 1968, circumstances conspired that allowed Major Rowe to escape. A heavy American air strike shook up the guards. One of the Viet Cong groups panicked when United States gunships came into the area, and Major Rowe took advantage of the confusion. He was picked up by an American helicopter pilot who almost mistook him for a member of the enemy because he was wearing the pajama-like garb of the Viet Cong. The beard that Major Rowe had grown during his imprisonment permitted the helicopter pilot to identify him as an American a second before pulling the trigger.

Major Rowe delivered this speech at the U.S. Army General Staff and Command College at Leavenworth, Kansas. The audience consisted primarily of students of the college—mostly majors and lieutenant colonels of the American Army, some Navy and Air Force personnel, and a significant number of Allied officers attending the college. [More information about Major Rowe's experiences can be found in his book, *Five Years to Freedom* (Boston: Little, Brown, 1971).]

This speech by Major Rowe is a personal narrative used to impart knowledge about Viet Cong prison camps and what an American prisoner of war lives through. In assessing the speech you will thus want to ask how well Major Rowe tells his story. Does he make effective use of suspense? Imagery? Action? Anecdotes? Is he able to organize his narrative effectively so it can easily be followed? How well does he draw knowledge with general application from his story?

Major Rowe delivered this address extemporaneously and used no notes. He has indicated that he never uses notes in telling his story. The manuscript you are about to read is a transcription of an audio-tape recording. The extemporaneous style of Major Rowe is thus very apparent. What difficulties do you encounter in reading a speech with genuine oral style? You may want to discuss the statement "Good speeches don't read well."

This speech is printed by permission of Major James N. Rowe.

1   The American prisoners of war are particularly close to those of us in the military, because the prisoners of war are members of the military. It could be any one of us, and I was one of those prisoners of war. I am Major

Nick Rowe; I spend 62 months as a prisoner of the Viet Cong in South Vietnam. The issue of the prisoners of war has come to the forefront in our nation; and in bringing this issue to the forefront, we have found that it's not that American people don't remember, or that they don't care, it's that most of the people in our country don't know. And those of us who have come out feel that we have a particular duty, because we are speaking for 1,600 men who have no voices. So this afternoon I would like to bring you some insight into the prison camps and some insight into what an American prisoner of war lives through.

2   I was a Special Forces advisor in 1963 in Phuoc Hoa. I was in a camp approximately in this area and I was captured very near there in October of 1963. Shortly after capture, I was moved down in the Mekong region; I stayed in this region until January of 1965, when I was moved into the U Minh Forest. I stayed in the U Minh Forest from January 1965 through December of 1968, when I escaped. The camp I was held in was on canal 21 and canal 6. I was approximately fourteen kilometers from our old district capital. I was that close to Americans, and yet they couldn't get to me nor could I get to them. This is the most frustrating thing about being an American prisoner in South Vietnam.

3   The conditions that an American lives under are those that are structured by his captors, and there are several new aspects of captivity. It is not the Hogan's Heroes concept that many people have, because in South Vietnam and in North Vietnam, we found that an American prisoner of war is not a military prisoner, he a political prisoner; and the Communists are dealing with American prisoners of war based on the Pavlovian theory— stimuli and response—the manipulation of human behavior. These are parameters that we have never dealt with before and are not prepared to deal with. The American prisoners find themselves being manipulated and being made more pliable by the Communists using principles that we have read about in Koestler's *Darkness at Noon,* perhaps in *1984;* these types of things that are never reality. But in prison camps in South Vietnam and in North Vietnam and in Laos, it is reality. An American prisoner of war has two main purposes for the Communists. First of all, propaganda; because in an age of ideological conflict, the most important thing is political opinion, and formation of political opinion, and this is done through propaganda. What more effective source do the Communists have for propaganda than an American prisoner of war? Through coercion, manipulation, or force, to cause that man to condemn our society, our government, our actions throughout the world; and then, as a representative of our system of government and our society, for him to confess to crimes against humanity. Think of the impact of this propaganda in either a Communist or non-Communist country when contrasted with the same propaganda coming from a Communist source.

4 The second purpose of an American prisoner of war is that when the Communists finally do decide to negotiate, what better blue chip do they have to lay down on the table than an American prisoner of war, trading American lives for political gain—this is why they take an American prisoner of war. When I was captured, there were three of us, two of us Special Forces and one MAAG advisor, who were with a strike force company when we were overrun; all three of us were wounded and were taken prisoners. The other strike force wounded were shot by the VC. And yet an American was of value. In captivity we found first of all, that we were political prisoners. We weren't military prisoners. This was typified during the initial interrogations. I was one of the first American officers captured in the Mekong Delta, and they really didn't know what to do with us. The first cadre who came in were hampered by the decided lack of ability to speak English, so they brought in a journalist-by-trade who spoke English, and used him as an interrogator. They had an S-2 who stayed across the canal from our camp in a cadre hut, and he was responsible for the interrogation. But since he couldn't speak English, he would write his questions down in Vietnamese, give them to this journalist, the interpreter, who would then translate them into English and come down to my cage. I was in the low-rent district right behind the camp, about thirty meters behind the camp, and he would come down and would sit down and ask me the questions. Anything I said he would write down verbatim. Then he would take the answers back and translate them from his Vietnamese-English dictionary back into Vietnamese to take to the S-2. Well, the first thing I discovered there was that he could deal with a large number of American prisoners, because the S-2 is in one place with the interpreter doing the legwork for him. And he got nothing for it.

5 About four to five weeks, six weeks, seven weeks, and the S-2 got upset, but he was apparently prevented from doing any more than threatening us. And when this little interpreter would come down and threaten, he would say, "I can kill you, I can torture you, I can do anything I want"; then he'd wince. So we knew he wasn't really serious; and I decided after a period of time, that since he had so much flexibility, it would be better to try and see if anything could be done to play with him, I had him come down one day, and I said, "Well, all right, Plato, I am ready to talk." We had nicknames for all of them, and he was very philosophical, so we nicknamed him Plato. I said, "All right, Plato, I am ready to talk." He beamed, pulled out extra paper and a new ballpoint pen, and sat down. I gave him four pages on the theory of laminar flow. This was to include calculus, integrated differential. I gave him pressure formulas—the weights, dams, storm gutters—the aerodynamic principles of air flow. I almost failed mechanical fluids at West Point, so it wasn't really that good anyway, but he copied it down verbatim. Everything I said he copied down, checking on spelling, and he took it back to his hut, and spent the next five days translating it from English into Vietnamese, coming down every day to check on the formulas and things like that; and I said, "Drive on, Plato, you are in good shape." Well, when he finished, he had a great volume, almost like *Khrushchev Remembers*. He took all of this great volume of paper over to the S-2. The enemy are very stoic individuals, and although I was thirty meters behind the camp, I soon heard screams from the S-2's hut. Not more than two minutes later, here came Plato scurrying down this little log walk with the S-2 right behind him. Obviously, the S-2 found out in a very short period of time what Plato had been doing, and it had erased his ability to deal with other American prisoners. Had the S-2 had the ability to deal with me as he wished, there wouldn't have been a tree high enough in the area for him to string me up to. But, I was a political prisoner, and the political cadre said no. Interrogation is secondary, indoctrination is primary. If they lose you through interrogation, they lose you for indoctrination; and so that was when we established what was of primary importance.

6   In dealing with an American prisoner of war their philosophy is that you can take any man and if you control the physical, you do not necessarily control that man; but if you can control and manipulate his mind, you will control the physical and the man. So this is what their target is, not necessarily physical torture, because they realize that indiscriminate physical torture can alienate a man, and once you have done that, he identifies you with the enemy, and you will never indoctrinate him. They will use physical torture, but they use it only to amplify the mental pressure. We found that a bruise will heal, a broken bone will heal, a wound will heal, but if they push you over the line mentally, or they break your spirit, then you are not coming back. That was the big battle. And that was what we had not been prepared for.

7   One of the first things that came up, and I will bring this up here because it is very important to members of the military, was the Code of Conduct. The Code of Conduct to me was a series of pictures in an orderly room. I had read them, I had gotten the T.I. and E. classes on Code of Conduct; it really wasn't that clear. I knew that I was supposed to give my name, my rank, my serial number, my date of birth, and then I thought I was supposed to shut up. This is the way it usually comes down to the troops. But this is a fallacy, because if you don't know the Code of Conduct when you're captured, the Communists will teach it to you. Because they teach our Code of Conduct to their cadre. And then they tell you while you're there, go ahead and follow it, but you will die if you do. They'll let you make your own decisions. What they are doing here is one of the first

steps in breaking down a man's will to resist, because generally speaking, an individual feels if he goes beyond name, rank, serial number, and date of birth, he is a traitor. I know I felt it right at first. And this is the first question that comes up in a man's mind. What about the Big Four? How long do I last? Well, you hang onto the Big Four as long as you can, but the next line says, "I will evade answering further questions to the best of my ability." It does give you credit for having basic intelligence. And this is what a man does. Fortunately, I went to West Point, and they teach you ambiguity; this is one of the things that really comes in handy. When you get a B.S. degree from West Point, that is exactly what it is. I liked English up there, and that is where they teach you to say the same thing 25 different ways. So this is what the American is doing. He is hedging, working for a way to get around, or get under, or get through. But if an individual goes in thinking, if I break from name, rank, serial number, and date of birth, I am a traitor, the first thing they are going to do is instill a guilt complex into him that will beat him into the ground. I know, because we had an individual who felt, initially, that anything beyond name, rank, serial number, and date of birth, was a violation of a punitive article of the uniform code of military justice. Now, this is where a man feels, all right, I have broken; and then they say, "Well, you have broken once, you are going to be punished, you might as well go all the way." Once they've got their finger in that crack, you're in trouble. And they teach our Code of Conduct as a punitive article, if you don't know it before you go in, find out about it now and find out exactly what it is. Because they are going to tell you and they are going to try to convince you that it is a punitive article, once you violate anything, once you go beyond name, rank, serial number, and date of birth, you have violated the Code of Conduct and you are going to be punished. Then they have their foot in the door. And they say, "Drive on, because you are going to be punished anyway. Why not get out sooner and go home?" This is the thing that a person has to be aware of. Remember that the code says, "I will make no statements disloyal to my country, its allies, or detrimental to their cause." And that's the thing that you have to remember. But as far as name, rank, serial number, and date of birth, you hold it as long as you can, but they are going to move you off of it at one point or another. They have developed all types of evasive techniques. We are training our people now, finally, to include a calculated breakdown, where you plan ahead what you are going to say, and then you dole it out a little bit at a time over an extended period, buying time to escape.

8   The other thing I used is a cover story; and in this case, I realized I wasn't the bravest person, so I decided to devise something which would allow me to say, "I don't know," rather than "I can't tell you" or "I won't tell you." So, I employed first of all the old artillery kiss formula, keep it simple, stupid. Then I built a cover story that would allow me to say, "I

don't know''; and in that cover story, I graduated from the United States Armed Forces Institute in Washington, D.C., as an engineer; I went there for four years, and gave them three years of service back. It was 1963 and I was ready to go be a civil engineer. Since I studied engineering, I was assigned to the Adjutant General. I went to Fort Belvoir afterward, and studied bridge building and house building and road building, and then I went to civilian seminars throughout the nation, again engineering subjects; finally I was assigned to a Special Forces attachment because of my outstanding capabilities as an engineer, and because they needed civil affairs project people. So this was my cover story which allowed me over the period of time to tell them, ''I don't know,'' to a great volume of things, and to hide behind it.

9   So, what they are trying to do initially is find out who is this person that they have, what are his capabilities? And they come out with a very neat form, it is entitled, ''Red Cross Index Data Card''; the first thing it says, military information: name, rank, serial number, and date of birth. And you think, great, that is what it is supposed to be. But they have a heavy dotted line; under it, it says, ''Who did you train with in the United States, what was your unit in the United States, when did you come to Vietnam, who did you come with, how did you come, when did you land, where did you serve in Vietnam, what operations did you go on?'' They want to know your educational background, your political background, your religious background; they want to know your mother, your father, your wife, your children; educational, religious, and political backgrounds for all of them; your hobbies and your sports. Then they give you four sheets of paper and they want a short biographical sketch. Now they are going to try and build a picture of this American. And they've taken American prisoners of war from Korea, from North Vietnam, and from South Vietnam. They try to fit these people into some sort of category, based on their background, the psychological category if you will, and this is column A. They've got different categories; column B is different environmental situations of the stimuli that have been applied to these different groups of Americans. In column 3, are the reactions they have gotten from them. So if they get a new man, and they can categorize him, then they just look to column 3 to find out what they want him to do, and then they come back to column 2 to find out what they have to do to him to get him to do it. This again is stimuli and response.

10   Now, in the camp, the physical conditions in South Vietnam with the Viet Cong are primitive. I was in the U Minh Forest, the camps were temporary at best. You had two to three feet of standing water during the rainy season; in the dry season it sank out, and you were hunting for drinking water. We had two meals of rice a day, and generally we got salt and nuoc mam with them. We did get infrequent fish from the guards, but

always the castoff that the guards didn't want. If we got greens, it was maybe one meal's worth every two or three months. Immediately vitamin deficiency and malnutrition were a problem. This is a thing you are going to fight the whole way through. And you are fighting on two sides. You are fighting a physical survival, and you are fighting for mental survival. The physical survival is just staying alive. We found that we had to eat a quart pan of rice each meal, two meals a day, just to stay alive. We found that if we could put down everything we had, and I think the most difficult thing initially was the nuoc mam. It is high in protein value, but the VC don't have that much money to spend on nuoc mam. You don't get Saigon nuoc mam. Theirs is called ten-meter nuoc mam. You can smell it within ten meters, and it is either repulsive or inedible, depending on how long you have been there. But this was the type of thing you are eating for nutritional value, and not for taste. So you are fighting on that side.

11   Disease, this is always present. Dysentery, beri-beri, hepatitis, jaundice, lac—which is a fungus infection, I had all those while I was in. I had about 85 percent of my body covered with lac. And you find that depending on your political attitude, there is either very little medication or no medication.

12   This is another thing which was disturbing, as if your political attitude determines whether you will get medication and what your treatment will be. And you are either reactionary or progressive, or somewhere in between. You find that it is not a military type thing, it is purely political. And again, we are not prepared for this. The Geneva Convention, international law, the VC say, we don't recognize them. The only law you are subjected to is our law. And if you ever want to go home, you are going to have to be a good POW, and it is based upon your good attitude and behavior as prisoner and your repentance of your past misdeeds. That last one is a hooker, because that is a confession. So they set up perimeters, and they set up this dirty little world that they keep you in; then they throw the mental pressure on top of this.

13   Indoctrination, this is where they take an individual's beliefs, and his faiths, and his loyalties, and they challenge them, because they have to break all of these before they can influence him. This is where thought correction comes in, because thought correction is nothing more than creating confusion and doubt in a man's mind and filling the void that follows with answers to the questions that you have created for him. If you will take a man as an island, with little bridges running to the mainland, and his faiths, his beliefs, his loyalties, his ethics, his standards, are all these little bridges that link him to something, to his place in the universe. If they can cut these, then they are going to turn that man inside himself, and they are going to make him fight himself. And that's exactly what they want him to do.

Because as soon as you compromise one of your beliefs, as soon as you compromise one of your loyalties, just to survive, then you are condemning yourself for it. That is exactly what they want. Because this is the pressure that doesn't stop. Physical torture, as soon as they stop it, you've got relief. But mental torture is something that will last 24 hours a day, and you do it to yourself.

14 One of the most vital things that came up was when men in the camp were asked, "Do you have a wife, do you have a family?" A couple of them answered, "Yes, we've got wives, we've got families." And the first thing that was asked was, "Do you think of your wife very often, do you think of your children, do you think of your family?" In an off-hand manner, we would respond, "Well, yah, we do, we are concerned, but we can't do anything about it." Then the guard would walk off. It didn't bother the individual for a couple of days, but pretty soon he started to think, and he began to wonder, "Is my wife all right, are my children all right, do they have enough money, are they sick, are they provided for?" and this was beginning to bother them, because they didn't know. Then the guard came down, and a little bit later, he would toss in another one; he would say, "How long does it take a woman in the United States to get a divorce after her husband is missing in action? Would your wife do this?" And of course, the immediate comment was, "No sweat. Not with my wife. She is going to hang in tight." Then he goes back to his cage at night, where he is by himself, and he lays there in that mosquito net, and he starts to think, and they give you plenty of time to think, and he begins to wonder, "Will she? What is it? What's the story? What's happening back there?" And he doesn't know. Next they go one step further, after he is going up the wall over these two questions, maybe a week later, he will come back, and he will say, "What is this we hear about immorality in your country? We read much about immorality. Do you know what your wife is doing?" And again, the first answer that comes out of the prisoner's mouth is what he believes, "My wife is straight, there's no problem." But then he goes back to his cage at night, and he begins to wonder: "I've been gone four years, I've been gone three years, what is happening back there?" You talk about frustration and anxiety, this is what does it to a man. This is a very subtle thumbscrew that they put on his mind, and then he tightens it down. And they don't even have to touch him. Because he doesn't know and he is in a prison camp. Now this works constantly. There is no getting away from these, and these are just everyday things.

15 Then you have the threats, and you find that anxiety comes in. When Plato said, "I can kill you, I can torture you, I can do anything I want," it really didn't mean anything. But in 1965, they moved us into the U Minh Forest and we met Mr. Hi. Mr. Hi was a political cadre, he was in charge of indoctrination, interrogation, and proselyting of the enemy troops. He was a professor of English in Saigon before he joined the Revolution. We called him Mafia, and he fitted his name. Because when Mafia said I can kill you, I can torture you, I can do anything I want, he meant it. We met him in March 1965, Captain Humbert "Rock" Vercase and I both failed the initial interrogation indoctrination, we both went to punishment camps. I stayed in a starvation camp for six months, Rocky Vercase was executed in September of 1965. That was Mafia's lesson. When he said I can kill you, I can torture you, I can do anything I want, he meant it. And that was a lesson to all the American POW's. It was an entirely new ballgame. Here was a political cadre who was in charge of our lives; he could take us and he could do anything he wanted to with us. This is a hard lesson to learn. This was the new concept beginning in 1965, and this is what exists now.

16 The threat of violence, the anticipation of violence, the anxiety that goes with it, sometimes, in fact most of the time, is far more devastating than what follows. This is what they are doing. They'll take a man and they'll threaten and then they will watch him run himself up and down the ladder worrying about what is going to happen to him. This is the thing—when they get hold of your emotions, and they can run them up and down the scale like a yoyo; then they've got you ricocheting off the wall; and this is exactly what they want. Because now they've got you fighting on both fronts. They've got you fighting to stay physically alive, and they've got you fighting to maintain your sanity. At that point you're becoming pliable. Because they're dangling this carrot in front of you that says, "Comply, and go home." And they toss in a few extras. One of the cadre told me in 1968, "Merely because the war ends is no reason for you to go home. If your attitude is not correct, you may rest here after the war." And tie that in with something he said a few months before, "We are here to tell you the truth of the situation today, and if you do not believe us, we will tell you tomorrow. And if you do not believe us tomorrow, we will tell you the day after, and the day after, until one day, if you don't die fisst, you'll believe us, and then you can go home." And so you have that carrot dangling in front of you which is "Going Home," and that is something you really want to do, because the environment is so oppressive that you want to get out of it, and yet what he is telling you is that there is no way out except our way.

17 Well, there is a way, initially, and that's escape, but that's hard. I tried three times and failed, and a fourth time it took a B-52 strike, and Cobras and light observation helicopters to get me out, which is a rotten way to do it, but it worked. But this is the only other way an American has out at the immediate time. The people in the prison camps in North Vietnam are not so fortunate. Like Bob Frishman said one time, "You know,

even if you do get out of the camp, where does a round-eye go in downtown Hanoi wearing striped pajamas?'' So this is one thing that the prisoners in North Vietnam don't even have to hope for. The prisoners in South Vietnam have this to look forward to, if they are strong enough to do it. But generally speaking, you are kept so physically weak that you can't. Yet you keep trying. So you are closed in on from all sides, and they seem to give you the only way out. But to take their way means you are going to compromise everything you believe in.

18 Now there have been individuals who have done this without really believing it, just going along to get out. The cases are very few, and I think the Communists have found that the Americans are probably the most insincere group of people they have ever come in contact with. The only thing is when a man comes out, if this has actually happened, when he finds that freedom is sometimes a hollow thing, because he has given more to get that freedom than it was worth. He's got to live with himself the rest of his life. This is one thing people have to think about. I found, for myself, that under this pressure, you find that there is a tight, hard little core inside of everybody, and it is basically faith, a person with a faith in God. This is something they can't challenge, because they don't believe in God. You find that if you can attach your belief to something far above and beyond this dirty little world they've got you in, then you have an opportunity to remove yourself from it. Their understanding of faith or of God is purely ritual and dogma. They've studied our ritual. For instance, every Christmas, they'd come down, like Mafia would come down, and he gave me a candle. He said, ''According to our policy, the Front respects the religious beliefs of the POW. Take this candle, go to your net, and burn it for Midnight Mass.'' And I said, ''Look, Mafia, I'm a Protestant, I've already had my little service, and I really don't need a candle, I don't have Midnight Mass.'' He stuck the candle out and said, ''Take it to your net and burn it, we respect your religious beliefs.'' So I took the candle, I went to my net, and I burned it, for a couple of minutes. This is what they understand about religion. But you find it's a very personal and a very simple communication between one man and his God. And that's all it requires. This is essential, because it removes you from this imprisonment. And you find, I think more importantly, that the Communists have stripped you of everything that identifies you. They strip you of your rank, your position, your money, of status, anything which allows you to identify yourself with material means, to identify yourself as a human being. They are trying to dehumanize you; you might as well be a handful of mud that they pick up off the ground. But faith in God is something that identifies you far more clearly than anything material that we have right now. Once you establish that, then you'll never lose your identity.

19 The second thing was faith in our country and faith in our government. And this they did attack very well. Initially, their Communist propaganda sources were not really effective because it was a Vietnamese writing for American consumption. When Radio Hanoi, the Radio Liberation, and all their bulletins and papers came across, they were using Webster's 1933. The words were either obsolete or obsolescent. I had to look some of them up when I got home to find out what they meant. What they are sending out is things that you will not accept because they are so far out. Like we lost 3,247 aircraft over North Vietnam, which includes five B-52's and three F-111A's. And they said one of the F-111A's was shot down by a girls' militia unit in Haiphong. So we read that and said, "Okay, fine, that's great." The next thing they came up with was that we lost more tanks and artillery than we actually had in Vietnam. Another one they came up with, two of the ones that I really liked, they said that the VC platoon in the Delta had defeated a South Korean company in hand-to-hand combat. I read through that and I sort of scratched my head on that one. The next thing they came up with was during the Tet offensive in 1968, a VC girls' militia squad in Hue, they were called the Twelve Daughters of the Perfume River, which flows through Hue, had defeated a Marine batallion. The first thing I asked the cadre was, "Well, was this hand-to-hand combat, too?" But you know, we read this, and it really didn't affect us.

20   But then, in 1966 and '67, they started dropping all their sources, and we started getting the Congressional Record, magazines, newspapers, articles from the United States. This is what really turned out to be the greatest morale-breaker in the camp. The fact that we were sitting here defending our country and our government and our system, not only against the Communist political cadre, but against individuals right within our own government. And it is difficult to defend yourself when somebody in your own government is calling you an aggressor. This is the greatest weapon that they had. I think this was the thing that was most devastating to my morale personally, because there was no way that I could contest it. This was coming from my country. How do you explain dissent to Communist cadre who have never had the right to dissent in their whole lives? It was something they couldn't understand. And yet even in this context one of the cadre said, "Very soon the people in your country will decide that your coming to Vietnam was a mistake. And at that time those of you who have died here will have died a useless death. And those who lead the Revolution in your country will be the heroes and the saviors. Why should you rot in a jungle prison camp when you can return to your home, join the Revolution, repent of your crimes, and live with your family?" And you sit there and you say, "Why?" And then you begin to evaluate; and I found that no matter how many negatives they came up with, on our side, we always had more positives than the system that they were advocating. And there was always a chance for change within our system, whereas in the

system they offered there was no chance for change. We got everything about the demonstrations, the riots, and the anti-war movement. I looked at the groups, the photographs of the college students carrying VC flags, the American flags being desecrated, and the one thing I thought of was, well, what if these people did this in Czechoslovakia, or Hungary, or Communist China? And I thought, "Thank God they are in the United States and they've got the right to do it." But it was disturbing to me, because nobody wants to die for nothing.

21 The other thing that came up was a faith in the other American POWs. You find that these are the only friends you've got. The Communist cadre are going to try to convince you that they are your friends, but you learn rapidly that all they are doing is exploiting you, they're using you as a tool. When you see an American prisoner giving up his meager ration of fish, just so another American who is sick can have a little bit more to eat, that is sacrifice. Because when you don't have anything and you give it up, or you have very little and you give it up, then you're hurting yourself, and that is true sacrifice. That's what I saw in the prison camp.

22 So those were the three things that I found were a sort of a basis for survival in this environment that's structured to break you down. The one thing they're finding out is that the American prisoners are first of all physically tougher than they ever expected. They read our society as materialistic, as being soft, as being apathetic, and yet they're finding that once they put these prisoners in this situation, and it's a battlefield just like any other, except it's more terrifying because you're fighting in the mind, they are finding that the American prisoners are hanging on. Everybody who has come out has said the same thing—there's three faiths, and these are the three things that stand strong. But the thing is, how long can these people hold up? In my camp, there were eight of us total over the five-year period. Contrary to the VC claims for humanitarian treatment, in my camp alone, out of eight of us, three died of starvation and disease, one was executed, three were released, one of whom was dying, and I escaped before I was executed. This is actuality. This is the fact contrasted with the promise.

23 Since my wife and I have been around the country, the one thing that civilians are asking is "Why doesn't the military do something for its own people? Why don't they do something to help those men?" We're starting. We just got a letter from Fort Knox the other day in Fort Campbell, and both of them are starting a concern for POW drive; the whole posts are turning out. This is the type of thing that needs to be done, because it could be any one of us, and it could be any one of the military families of men on this post. I had one individual that told me on one occasion, "Why should we do it, when we've got too much other to do, the Red Cross, the Officers' Wives' Club, the various things that we have to do?" and the only thing I could think of was "Just pray to God that your hus-

band doesn't get captured some day, and you have to ask somebody else for help.'' I think this is the saddest commentary, that the families and loved ones of these men have to go out and seek help, not only from the military community, but from the civilian community, for their husbands, and their fathers. This is to me something that needs to be changed, and it's not so much that the people don't care, it is just that most people don't know.

24   I'm thankful for the opportunity I had to come today, to perhaps enlighten you a little bit as to what does happen inside the camps. Thank you.

DAVID: AND A WHOLE LOT OF OTHER NEAT PEOPLE

Kathy Weisensel

Kathy Weisensel, a junior from Sun Prairie, Wisconsin, delivered this speech in a Fundamentals of Speech class at the University of Wisconsin-Madison in the summer of 1976. The class consisted of eighteen students representing a wide variety of interests and areas of specialization.

The particular assignment this speech was designed to fulfill emphasized message organization and the use of amplifying devices (expository materials). Does the introduction of this speech accomplish the functions normally assigned to an introduction? Is it high in interest value? What pattern and subpatterns of organization are used in the body of this speech? Are they effective? What major transitional devices are employed? Does the conclusion of this speech effectively round out the message? What amplifying devices does Ms. Weisensel use to make her message clear? Are they effective?

The purpose of this speech is to clarify the nature of mental retardation. How successful is the speaker in doing so? Ms. Weisensel's personal involvement with her subject is demonstrated in a number of passages. What effect do these personal references have on an audience for a speech that imparts knowledge?

This speech is printed by permission of Ms. Weisensel.

1   There is a problem which is shared by millions of people in the United States. It knows no barrier to age, sex, or social class. Yet, it is a problem that for years was hidden in society's darkest closet. Only recently has the closet door begun to open. That problem is mental retardation.

2   One out of thirty-three persons is born mentally retarded. It is the most widespread, permanent handicap among children. It is among the least understood handicaps of adults. In Wisconsin alone, there are 120,000 retarded people.

3 My involvement with mental retardation has been lifelong and deeply personal. For you see, David, my older brother, is mentally retarded.

4 As our family adjusted to David's problem, we became aware of a number of misconceptions which cloud the public's vision. Among these misconceptions are: that mentally retarded people are mentally ill and therefore dangerous; that mentally retarded people are ineducable; and that mentally retarded people are incapable of leading happy and productive lives. Since these misconceptions are socially harmful and painful to the retarded and their families, it is important that they be corrected.

5 How do you correct the notion that retarded people are somewhat crazy and therefore not really to be trusted? It may be helpful to start with a definition. According to Dr. E. Milo Pritchett, "Mental retardation is a condition of impaired, incomplete, or inadequate mental development. . . . Mental retardation is NOT mental illness. Mental illness is a breakdown of mental functions which were once normal. Specialized care and treatment may restore the person to normalcy. Retardation is a condition for which there is no cure."

6 But let's extend that definition with a series of contrasts. Mental retardation is always permanent; mental illness is usually temporary. Mental retardation is subnormal intelligence; mental illness is distorted intelligence. Mental retardation involves deficient cognitive abilities; mental illness involves emotional impairment of cognitive abilities. Mental retardation is manifested early; mental illness may occur anytime in life. The mentally retarded person is behaviorally stable; it is the mentally ill person who is given to erratic behavior. The extremely mentally retarded person is submissive and mute; the extremely mentally ill person may be violent and criminally dangerous. Thus retarded people are retarded, and no more. We need no longer place them in pens with the criminally insane, as was the custom in medieval societies.

7 OK, the skeptic says, so what if they aren't mentally ill—they're still ineducable. Those who favor this misconception have, in the words of Dorly D. Wang, formerly of Woods School in Pennsylvania, "one-dimensional views of the retarded." They fail to "distinguish degrees of retardation" and tend to perceive "all the retarded with one image"—and that image is of the intellectual vegetable, more appropriately planted in a cell or ward than in the school classroom. But retarded people are not all alike. Most psychologists identify three subgroups of mentally retarded people: the educable, the trainable, and the custodial.

8 The educable mentally retarded have IQ's ranging from 75 to 50. In the nation's schools, they are placed in a curriculum with a special classroom base, but are encourage to enter the curricular mainstream whenever it is possible. Most of these students share with normal students instruction in home economics, physical education, shop, and music.

9 The trainable mentally retarded's I.Q. is usually 50 to 30. In the schools, these students are not found in any normal classes. Rather, they work exclusively in special classrooms under the direction of teachers who understand their needs. In these classes they learn self-care, and they train for social and economic usefulness. Three percent of the present school population is made up of the educable and trainable mentally retarded.

10 The custodial mentally retarded have IQ's below 30. They are usually confined to institutions such as Central Colony; just across Lake Mendota from this University. These people experience little mental development. Few exceed the intellectual acuity of a normal three year old.

11 Thus, the mentally retarded are not a faceless, hopeless mass. While not all of them may profit from schooling, many will. Careful and loving teachers will eventually be rewarded by what one teacher of the retarded has called "the smile of recognition."

12 But to say that the mentally retarded person is not mentally ill and is not ineducable is not enough. It does not destroy the myth that one must be of average mentality to be socially productive and happy. In a society characterized by speed, change, competition, and progress, it is difficult for us so-called "normals" to understand that retarded people can live happily and productively in a life pattern alien to our own.

13 Bernard Posner, Deputy Executive Secretary of the President's Committee on Employment of the Handicapped, has captured society's dilemma in coming to grips with the mentally handicapped. He commented:

> . . . ours are norms in which change is a way of life. In the United States, we change jobs every five years and homes every seven years. We say that to stand still is to regress. Where do the retarded fit in, those without the capacity for constant change?
>
> . . . ours are norms of competition. We compete in school, at play, at love, at work. Where do the retarded fit in, those who can go to school, can play, can love, can work, but who cannot always come out on top in competition?
>
> . . . ours are norms of discontent. Life becomes a series of stepping-stones leading who knows where? Each of life's situations is not to be enjoyed for itself, but is to be tolerated because it leads elsewhere. Where do the retarded fit in, those who can be happy with a stay-put existence?

14 But retarded people do fit in and do lead useful and rewarding lives. A few years ago, I worked with a girl who is educably mentally retarded. Mary went to my high school and attended two normal classes— home economics and physical education. She had a driving desire to become a waitress. Her determination was evident as I tutored her in addition, subtraction, making change, and figuring sales tax. She is working today in a small restaurant—happy and self-supporting.

15   My brother David is another example. Under Wisconsin law he was entitled to school until age twenty-one, and he spent all those years in a separate special class. There he learned the basic skills of reading, writing, and mathematics. After graduation he was employed by the Madison Opportunity Center, a sheltered workshop for the retarded. He leaves home each morning on a special bus and returns each evening after eight hours of simple assembly-line work. While he is by no means self-supporting and independent, he loves his work, and he is a happy man and a neat person with whom to share a family.

16   As a final example, I give you Jeff, age 14. He is custodially mentally retarded at Central Colony. In the three years that I have worked with him, I have found him to be incredibly happy and content in his "permanent childhood." He enjoys toys, writing letters of the alphabet, and watching Sesame Street. This last summer he was especially proud to be selected as a jumper in the Special Olympics. To tell you the truth, he was chosen because he was one of the few kids in the ward who could get both feet off the floor at the same time. But Jeff doesn't know that the competition wasn't keen, and he's proud and happy.

17   While misconceptions are slow to pass away, they must surely die. Our nation's retarded are not mentally ill, totally ineducable, or incapable of happy and productive lives. I know, in a deeply personal way, the pain that these misconceptions inspire. But I also know that the world is changing. I have a deep faith that you and others of our generation will reject the senseless and destructive stereotypes of the past. As Bernard Posner has said:

. . . the young people of the world seem to be forging a new set of values. It appears to be a value system of recognizing the intrinsic worth of all humans, retarded or not . . . a value system of acceptance: of accepting life as it is, and people as they are.

18   Thank you for your acceptance.

THE FAMILY AND ITS HOME IN THE 1980S

Edward Cornish

Throughout history, people have speculated about the future. The Old Testament of the Bible contains the words of many prophets who sought to envision and describe future happenings. Throughout the generations since Biblical times, individuals have sought to foretell or predict things to come. In recent times, as the pace of society has quickened, more and more people have come to speculate, with varying degrees of rigor, about the future. The term "futurist" has often been assigned to those who engage in such prognostications.

On October 30, 1980, the President of the World Future Society, Edward Cornish, assumes the role of a futurist as he speculates about the family and its future role in society in an address to the Better Housing League of Cincinnati. In paragraph 10, the speaker provides insights into the habits of thought or inquiry employed by futurists. Given this paragraph, how would you define the term "futurist"?

In the body of his speech, Cornish offers six "scenarios" that indicate future directions the family may take in the United States. Are the six scenarios mutually exclusive? Should they be? Has the speaker overlooked a more likely alternative to the scenarios presented?

In the second part of the body, the speaker identifies two societal developments that may have strong impact on the directions families may take. Have other major developments been overlooked?

Given this example of "futurism," what value does such speculation have? What are the inherent shortcomings of "futurism"?

Speech textbook writers, when discussing informative discourse, commonly advise speakers to indicate the importance of their subjects in order to give the audience a need to listen. How does the speaker seek to assign importance to his subject? How else might the speaker have demonstrated the urgency of his subject?

This speech is reprinted with permission from *Vital Speeches of the Day,* December 1, 1980, pp. 120-124.

1   Many books and articles that discuss the family begin with a statement that seems so simple and natural that it generally gets little attention until we pause to think about it. Then we realize that the statement is packed with a portentous message for the future of our civilization.

2   The statement—expressed in different words by different writers— is this: "The family is the basic unit of society."

3   *The family is the basic unit of society.*

4   The family is where we all begin our lives . . . where we first experience ourselves and the great world around us . . . where we learn how to speak, how to feel, how to play, how to work, how to learn, how to love, how to laugh, how to cry.

5 The family is not only the basic unit of our society, it is our *future-creating* institution. It is the family that takes us as wild but weak animals and converts us, little by little, into the civilized human beings who will manage the world of tomorrow.

6 Today there is growing concern that the family—the basic element of civilization—is in trouble. Advancing technology appears to have set in motion a variety of trends, which have interacted in various ways so as to undermine the family as an institution; and since the family is the basis of our civilization, its destruction could mean the destruction of our society.

7 Despite the threat they may pose for the family, technological advances are likely to increase rather than decrease in the years immediately ahead. For example, biomedical science is beginning to make it possible to choose the sex of one's children. Will this lead to an overproduction of males, or of females, or perhaps to violent demographic swings—an oversupply of males being followed by an oversupply of females? What would this mean for the family.

8 Scientists soon may be able to control the aging process, giving human beings an indefinite lifespan. If marriage contracts continue to remain valid "until death do us part," many of us will have to face the question of whether we really want to live with the same person for, say, 500 years!

Scenarios for the Future

9 Granted the dramatic changes ahead in all aspects of civilization, any prediction for the future of the family seems almost foodhardy. But we can construct scenarios to suggest a few *possible* futures for the family.

10 A scenario provides a useful starting point for thinking seriously about the future, because it forces us out of the present by creating a plausible sequence of future events. A scenario is a kind of imaginary history of things that haven't happened—but might happen. In a sense, a scenario is a fantasy—but a fantasy that frees our thinking so we can deal with the future more realistically. A scenario shows us that we have real choices concerning what may happen in the future, and that these choices are important. By giving us glimpses of possible futures, scenarios help us to make wiser decisions concerning the future we want to achieve.

11 So let's look now at six different scenarios suggesting how the family might develop in the years ahead.

Scenario I

A Continuation of Present Trends

12 The first scenario anticipates that current trends will continue: The divorce rate will continue to rise until divorce is the "normal" way for marriage to end. The marriage and remarriage rates continue to decline, as they have in the past decade or so, leaving more and more people in the "never-married" and "divorced and not-remarried" classes. Increasingly the traditional family—husband, wife, and children—disappears. Instead we see people living by themselves or in groups of individuals unrelated by kinship or marriage. Women increasingly pursue careers and shun the role of homemakers; men perform needed household chores for themselves. Neither sex has any particular need for the other. The individual rather than the family is increasingly viewed as the "natural" unit of society; because family groupings are only brief arrangements rarely lasting more than a few years.

13 The birthrate drops further, reaching the point where the people of the United States and other advanced nations are no longer reproducing themselves and are being replaced by surplus population from the developing countries. As a result the culture of the advanced countries begins to shift in the direction of the culture of the immigrants from the developing world. For instance, the language of the United States gradually changes from English to Spanish.

14 Most people live alone. They do their own thing, unhindered by family obligations. There is a fantastic expansion of self-realization activities aimed at helping the individual to maximize his personal happiness and do his own thing. People lavish money on material objects and pleasures and travel constantly in search of excitement. Many will buy a second home and some a third, fourth, or even a fifth home.

15 So there you have one future for the family—simply a projection of what's happening, an extension of today's trends into the years ahead. Now let's go to a second scenario which might be called "a return to the status quo."

Scenario II
A Return to the Status Quo

16 The continuation of current trends seems to lead eventually to absurdities. If divorces continue to increase at the rate of recent years, there will soon be more divorces than marriages.

17 The fact that current trends cannot persist indefinitely suggests they must eventually come to a halt and even reverse direction. In fact, one can easily argue that most social trends are basically cyclical in character. This view is summed up by the French expression, *Plus ca change, plus c'est le même chose.* (The more it changes, the more it is the same thing). This second scenario envisions future life-styles that are not very different from the life-styles of today: The marriage rate moves up and down and so does the divorce rate. Economic recessions and wars push life-styles one way or the other for a few years, but eventually the trend reverses and patterns move back to where they were before.

18 People who favor this scenario can point to the cycles in customs through history: Like long skirts or short skirts, full beard or shaven face, many elements of life-styles change for a time but often come back to what they were before. If you don't like a current trend, just wait a little and soon it will reverse, because people are always, essentially, the same—always have been and always will be. So our second scenario suggests that the divorce rate, which is now very high by historical standards, will probably decline and the family will continue in the future not too different from what it is today.

19 Now let's go to a third scenario—the actual abolition of the family.

Scenario III
The Abolition of the Family

20 If the family seems to create a lot of problems for society, it may actually be abolished. So we can imagine the government making it illegal for people to marry or bear children—and imposing stiff jail sentences on any one found guilty of matrimony. Such measures might be adopted also as a means of controlling population growth; China today actually has very strict measures designed to restrict marriage among young people.

21 Other ways may be found to provide the functions that the family once offered. For example, government agencies might collect sperm and ova from suitable donors, combine them in test-tubes, and then allow the fertilized ova to gestate under careful supervision in artificial wombs that nourish and protect the baby until it is ready to eat and breathe air on its own. While the baby is developing into a child and later an adolescent and adult, he is cared for by professionals rather than by parents. The child has no family at all. Instead he is trained to think of all mankind as his family.

22 The abolition of the family could be accompanied by the elimination of sex—that is, interpersonal sex. New technology could make it possible for people to have far better orgasms through drugs or electrical stimulation of the brain. Technology also might enable people to reproduce through cloning so it will no longer be necessary for people to produce sex cells. Biologists can then start to develop people without any sexual organs at all. Long ago, James Thurber wrote a book entitled *Is Sex Necessary?* A future, civilization may prove that it is not. The creation of neuter people may lead to a far more peaceful and efficient civilization. The industriousness and unselfishness of social insects like the ant is proverbial, and much of it may arise from the fact that workers in an ant nest or beehive are neuter and therefore not distracted by sex.

23 A sexless, family-less society might develop a truly noble civilization, far more sublime than what we know today.

24 Now let's go to a fourth scenario.

Scenario IV
A Reversal

25 Our fourth scenario begins with the thought that current trends represent a radical departure from normal human behavior and they must eventually reverse: The family is therefore likely to return to what it was like in the past.

26 Reversals are hardly unknown through history: Think of the Counter-Reformation or the current resurgence of Islamic traditions in the Mideast. It is certainly conceivable that society in the future might take deliberate steps to restore the traditional family—the family of 19th-century America, for example.

27 How could this be done? For one thing, society could put more emphasis on the "sacredness" of marriage: Religion might be revitalized and called upon to help devise more impressive ceremonies to insure that couples understand what they are undertaking.

28 A second step might be the revival of community life, because of the importance of the community to the family. To strengthen communities, automobiles might be banned or heavily taxed so as to encourage people to patronize local stores and institutions.

29 A third step might be the reform of television programming. Programs that show divorce in a favorable light might be outlawed, along with TV commercials. Television commercials are, I suspect, one of the deadliest enemies of marriage and the family. In the world of television commercials, the problems of love and family living are easily solved by the swift application of the sponsor's product; but in real life, difficult and painful choices must be made between alternative goals that have both strongly desired and strongly undesired features. In our intimate relationships, we must constantly balance the claims of self against the claims of others, the realities of the present and the possibilities of the future, the longings of the heart and the cautions of the head. Television provides us with a fantasy world which leads us to attitudes that tend to destroy marriages.

30 A fourth step might be a reaffirmation of sex roles. The blurring of sex roles might come to be viewed as a horrendous mistake. Instead society might encourage parents and teachers to train boys more carefully to perform the tasks expected of husbands and girls to perforn the duties of wives. Sex-segregated institutions and groups might be encouraged as a means of protecting and strengthening marriage and the family.

31 A fifth step might be the renewal of sanctions against out-of-wedlock pregnancy. Recognition of the importance of the intact family in the emotional development of children could lead to a reversal of today's condoning sympathetic attitude toward unmarried women who bear children out of wedlock. Strong actions to prevent the birth of illegitimate children might include mandatory pregnancy tests and abortions, and sterilization for repeated offenses.

32 A sixth step might be the discouragement of sex outside marriage. Government actions might range from televised "spot announcements" on the desirability of virginity to stiff jail sentences for fornicators.

Scenario V
A Revitalization of the Family

33 A fifth scenario envisions a revitalization of the family. Instead of simply turning back the clock—restoring the family to what it once was—society might seek a new and better family, based on a clear recognition of changes in society as well as an appreciation of what the family has offered in the past and can still offer in the future.

34 A rationale for revitalizing the family rather than seeing it decline or disappear might go as follows:

35 The traditional family, based on ties of blood and marriage, is the "natural" basis of society and any departure from the natural way is risky. Not even the wisest social scientists know all the vital functions that the family fulfills in the operations of society and in the psychic life of the individual. Experience demonstrates the strong ties that can develop between a mother and the child she has carried within her body and who has suckled her breast. Similarly potent is the "pleasure bond" that develops between a man and a woman. These natural ties, part of man's biological nature, are the root of most social life. All societies everywhere and at all times that we know anything about have developed on the basis of these natural ties. Technology has given us a high standard of living but has inadvertently caused problems for the family. Now that we have a high standard of living, we can well afford to devote more attention to the family.

36 A program for revitalizing the traditional family might include:

37 1. *Matching of prospective bride and groom.* Good marriages should begin with good dating. Computerized dating services, though still in a primitive state, suggest what might be done to match up people with compatible characteristics. Only too often nowadays, people fail to make contact with potential mates with whom they could be really compatible. Instead, they find themselves dating—and even falling in love with—people whom they really have little in common with.

38 2. *Training for marriage.* Schools could provide young people with more courses in marriage and parenthood, including not only sex education but money management, child training, and dealing with interpersonal disputes. Better training could help prevent teenage pregnancy, which leads often to marital failure or to the production of children who are unlikely to receive adequate emotional support in their development.

39 3. *Stronger efforts to improve emotional development.* Many marriages fail because of the emotional immaturity of one or both of the partners. Programs could be instituted—starting perhaps in the schools—to identify people's emotional problems and assist them in overcoming them. Communities could provide psychiatric and other types of counseling to help individuals maintain good family relationships.

40 4. *Community stability.* The instability of communities due to the high mobility of the population contributes to the failure of marriages. Mothers with children need neighbors whom they can talk to and leave their children with occasionally. A variety of techniques could be used to increase community stability including, for example, fines imposed on companies that require their employes to move a long distance from one assignment to another.

41 5. *Incorporation of families.* David P. Snyder, the Life-Styles editor of THE FUTURIST, has suggested that families could be strengthened by allowing them to legally incorporate themselves. Such incorporation might provide a variety of tax and other benefits that would help to stabilize families.

42 A sixth and last scenario focuses on artificial families.

Scenario VI
Artificial Families

43 The argument for the creation of artificial families might go something like this: The traditional family has failed because it simply does not meet the needs of modern man. Permanent units based on blood relationships are simply a holdover from man's primitive past. The traditional family was never very good: There were endless problems—physical and verbal abuse, sibling rivalry, Oedipus and Electra complexes, incest, the subjugation of children, prodigal sons, adolescent rebellion, etc., etc. What is needed is something radically different.

44 Already there are a number of developments that suggest a general movement toward the creation of artificial families: Many communes and collectives have much of the character of families. Some churches have encouraged the development of artificial extended families by assigning individuals to a couple, which forms the nucleus of the artificial family. This couple adopts them as family members. The enlarged family gets together for recreational and other activities and provides mutual assistance in times of need.

45 One factor encouraging the development of artificial families is the disintegration of the natural family: Many people now find themselves without a natural family that they can really relate to. When family members are very widely scattered, the family can no longer function as the traditional family once did, and artificial families might be able to fill the void.

46 Artificial families also might allow people to play roles they cannot easily play in today's society and perhaps gain new insights into themselves.

For instance, a boy of 13 might be given the role of mother to three children, or a woman of 40 might be assigned to be the baby in a family and have no responsibilities.

Choosing a Future

47   There is no need to select one scenario as the best either from the standpoint of desirability or likelihood of realization. In fact, my guess is that each of the scenarios will be realized in some degree during the years ahead. What we do not know is what will be the dominant family forms at various periods of the future.

48   The family of the future is something that we ourselves must decide on—and since we have not yet rendered our collective decision—the future of the family remains undecided—and unpredictable. The family will be what we make it to be, by our own actions. If we want to abolish the family, we can do it. If we want to revitalize the family, we can do it. If we want to see the family slowly dissolve in a swelling tide of divorce, we can achieve that purpose too.

49   So our task really is to decide what it is we want—among those futures that are actually possible for the family.

50   The family is intimately interconnected with all aspects of our society. It's simply impossible to choose one type of family and pay no attention to such other aspects of our lives as our patterns of work, our technology, our educational system, and so on. Each family is a social system which exists within the whole congeries of other social systems which comprise the human enterprise. So to understand the family and think about its future we must look at what is happening in other areas.

51   Two areas seem to me of special importance during the 1980s: the global economic system and the communications and computer technology that is now developing. Developments in these areas may have crucial impact on the family in the next few years.

52   The first is the deterioration of the world economy. In my judgment, we may be on the verge of a global depression. If it does indeed arrive, the impact on the family could be extremely powerful. In the United States, we could see a revival of the family as relatives move back toward one another because of economic hardship. There are some signs that this may already be happening, that is, many young people find themselves unable to afford homes of their own and therefore continue to live with their parents after they become adults. The high cost of nursing homes has also made it difficult for many people to find places outside their homes for their elderly parents.

53   Economic hardship could lead to a decline in sexual permissiveness and a revival of clearly defined gender roles for men and women. Why? Simply because, during hard times, people will be willing to sacrifice a certain amount of individuality, freedom, and pleasure in order to have greater security. In the past, people depended heavily on the family to give them security; if the government fails to maintain a smoothly functioning economic system providing employment and a high living standard for most people, the family may be revived as people struggle to find a way to meet their needs for security.

54 Meanwhile, the new communications and information technology also may greatly change family life. During the 1980s, a variety of electronic technologies that very few people use today will become common items of ordinary life. For instance, today only a relatively few homes have videotape recorders or videodisc players, but by 1990, probably most homes will have this new video technology and it will open up a whole new world of education, entertainment, and information services. Increasingly, people will have large libraries of motion pictures, television shows, books, educational courses, and other materials in these new video formats.

55 At the same time, computer technology will be moving into U.S. homes in a massive way. By 1990 more than half the homes in the U.S. will probably have at least one computer or computer terminal, and people will be using computers for all kinds of things—ordering groceries, doing their income tax, learning statistics, chatting with their friends, and so on.

56 But the world economy and the new electronic technology will not, by themselves, determine the shape of tomorrow's family. What the family becomes will depend on what people decide to do, especially on the kind of families they make for themselves.

57 In conclusion, I would like to offer a few suggestions concerning what we can do to have better families and home life in the future—assuming that is what we want.

58 First and foremost, I believe we need to recognize clearly that we are responsible for the future. The future does not just happen to us. We *create* the future, both for ourselves and for others. We need to get that fact clearly in mind. We *can* create a good future for the family, if that's what we want.

59 Second, we can create a better future for the family *by thinking seriously about its future.* We need to explore the various possibilities that the family has so that we can begin to take steps to achieve for the family the future we desire for it. When we understand the possibilities of the future, we are better able to create a better future.

60 Third, we need to think about the future in very broad terms. When we start thinking about the future of the family, we must be very much aware of how the family will be impacted by developments in other areas. The family cannot be isolated from what happens in the economy, the schools, and so on.

61 Fourth, we need to support large-scale research efforts aiming at a better understanding of such broad social issues as, How can we have better family life in the future? These efforts are inherently difficult, not only because of the complexity of the issues but because they involve us in value questions, questions about what we personally believe is good or right. But research efforts in these areas can be enormously rewarding, because they can help us to understand more clearly the choices that we face.

62 The family's future is an undecided future. It is open future—a future that we must create. But as time passes, the "future" becomes the "past"—choices are made consciously or unconsciously, wisely or foolishly. If we want to revitalize the family during the next 10 years, we can do it; if we want to see the family dissolve in a rising tide of divorce, we can do it. If we want to create artificial families or abolish the natural family, we can do those things, too. The future of the family is ours to decide. But let us try to decide wisely, because the family is the basic unit of society.

THE BACKLASH PHENOMENON: THE EQUAL RIGHTS AMENDMENT

Helen B. Wolfe

The contemporary women's movement, stemming greatly from the publication of Betty Friedan's book, *The Feminine Mystique,* in 1963, gained momentum in the late sixties and peaked in the early seventies. One of the vital measures to come out of the movement is the Equal Rights Amendment, which finally passed Congress, and was presented to the states for ratification in 1972. It is this subject that gives rise to Helen Wolfe's speech, "The Backlash Phenomenon." Ms. Wolfe, General Director of the American Association of University Women, delivered the address at the Middle Atlantic Regional Conference, June, 1976. The members of the audience were all college graduates.

Wolfe begins her speech by pointing to "a shift in public attitudes from the liberal left toward the conservative right." She points to changing attitudes in education, criminal justice, and social legislation as illustrations of her contention. None of these things directly concerns the Equal Rights Amendment. What do you think the speaker is trying to achieve with this introduction? What purpose does it serve?

The bulk of the body of the speech involves a historical parallel, the Nineteenth Amendment—which gave women the right to vote—and the Equal Rights Amendment. What purpose do you think this parallel serves? Does it help clarify Wolfe's speech? Does it make her ideas more credible? Does it in any way assist her personal credibility?

In a section of her speech dealing with ERA momentum, Ms. Wolfe shows that the momentum to ratify has stopped and that, as a matter of fact, it has swung the other way as state after state is discussing rescission. She refers to this as the "backlash phenomenon." In the last part of her speech she points to four factors contributing to this backlash. Do you concur with her analysis?

Wolfe's conclusion draws again from the first woman's movement, referring specifically to a memorable date in New York State history. What purpose is served by this historical reference?

This speech is printed by permission from *Vital Speeches of the Day*, Aug. 15, 1976, pp. 669-72.

1   There has been considerable evidence in the last year that there has been a shift in public attitudes from the liberal left toward the more conservative right. This can be seen in political, economic, and social attitudes. The conservative candidates enjoyed more support in the recent Presidential primaries than did the liberal candidates.

2   In education, there has been an increasing emphasis upon career preparation rather than liberal education. This is reflected in the fact that expansion in higher education has shifted to the two-year institutions which provide vocational and technical education. Busing is an issue which cuts across both educational and social lines. Society's attitude toward busing continues to be ambivalent. After strong Civil Rights advances, it seemed that we would see a victory for integration in the schools. Opposition, however, has stiffened, and some of busing's earliest supporters are now questioning its effectiveness.

3   In the area of criminal justice, there has also been a shift to the right. There is growing support for reinstituting the death penalty. There is more emphasis upon punishment and less upon rehabilitation. In a number of cases, the Supreme Court has rendered decisions which limit the defendant's rights and expand the powers of police and prosecution. You remember the recent decisions allowing the testimony of a rape victim to become the basis for conviction of the rapist, whereas former laws required testimony from witnesses. Women considered this ruling a victory for women's rights. However, it may be as much due to the general trend to increase police and prosecution powers as due to the women's movement.

4   Social legislation reached its peak about two years ago. Since then, there has been a slowing down and a retrenchment from that high water mark. The women's movement is a part of the total social movement of our time, but there are significant differences as well. The total women's movement is much more than the Equal Rights Amendment, but the progress of ERA provides a sharper focus for consideration than any other aspect, and so I will use that as the major illustration to demonstrate the backlash occurring against the women's movement.

5   The only historical parallel available for us in American history is the 19th Amendment which gave women the right to vote. The battle for suffrage has meaning for our current dilemma. On June 4, 1919, the 19th Amendment passed Congress at 5:00 P.M. Before the month of June was

over, nine states had ratified, New York being the fifth of the nine. During that summer, five more states ratified. By the end of the year the number had grown to 22. The new year started off with a rush as five states ratified in January and another six in February, including New Jersey. In March two additional states brought the figure to 35. Only one more state was needed.

6 The final battle took place in Tennessee. Suffragettes and Anti-Suffragettes came from across the country to exert pressure. This fight was the bitterest of all, for it was also the most important. Women were against the Amendment and women were for it. Men were against it and men were for it. Threats and violence became part of the battle. The final ratification carried by a single vote. After it no longer mattered, Vermont and Connecticut ratified.

7 The momentum from Suffrage caused the Equal Rights Amendment to be introduced in Congress three years after women got the vote. But generating momentum for ERA was very difficult. Twenty-seven years after its introduction, the Senate passed ERA, but with the Hayden rider attached to it, which stated that ERA would not curtail any special rights women had under other laws. The House failed to pass the bill. Supporters of ERA resisted the Hayden rider, for its "protection" clause was a maneuver to nullify the true equality which ERA would bring. Three years later, the Senate again passed the same bill, with the same rider, and again the House resisted. The rider would have made ERA another unenforceable token measure. Seventeen years later, in 1970, the Senate considered the bill for the third time. This time two riders were attached, one to exempt women from the draft and the other to permit prayer in schools and other public buildings. Supporters of ERA were opposed to these riders and again the Senate did not act upon the measure.

8 In 1971, the House took the initiative and passed ERA in its present form, defeating efforts to bar women from the draft and not to change any other laws on the books. Six months later, on March 22, 1972, the Senate passed ERA and sent it to the states for ratification.

9 Hawaii ratified within hours. The next day three states ratified. The second day two more states ratified. The bandwagon seemed rolling when four days later yet another state ratified. Two days later it was Texas. In the next week, two more states could be counted. After nine more days it was still another state. When five more states ratified in the next two weeks, it seemed as if nothing could stop ERA. That month saw two additional states and the next month another two. The summer months had not been expected to produce anything, and so no one really noticed that the momentum had slowed. Only two more states ratified during the rest of the year. The new year, 1973, started off with a spark with eight states ratifying in

three months. And then the bandwagon was derailed. For all practical purposes, it stopped. Since March of 1973 only four additional states have ratified. The last date of a ratification was February 1975 when North Dakota was added to the plus column.

10 Our year in the sun as women was March 22, 1972 to March 22, 1973. Thirty states ratified, no state voted against ERA, and the major labor groups endorsed ERA. It is not coincidental that this same period between 1972 and 1973 produced: Title IX; the Equal Employment Opportunity Act: extension of the Equal Pay Act of 1963 to cover professional, executive, and administrative employees; and sex discrimination was added to the jurisdiction of the Civil Rights Commission. That golden year for women also saw the United Nations vote in December 1972 to proclaim the year of 1975 as International Women's Year, and the Supreme Court made two significant decisions affecting women's rights.

11 However, at the end of 1973 when Nebraska voted to rescind ERA, that signaled the fact that a new mood was in the wind. In 1974, Maine and Montana ratified ERA, but Tennessee voted to rescind. Even though rescission is illegal, this did not alter the fact that a shift in public sentiment had begun to occur. Early in 1975 North Dakota ratified, but that was the only bright spot in a difficult year. Eight states defeated ERA. Others failed to vote. New York and New Jersey defeated state ERA amendments. Rescission efforts have been mounted in two-thirds of the states which had ratified ERA. Rescission has been successfully defeated in eight of these states. It is also significant that during the last year there has not been a single significant legislative advance for women.

12 The backlash has assumed major proportions. It is not the single issue of ERA that is at stake, but all of the advances that women have made. It has been the momentum over ERA that has carried forth other legislative advances for women. If that should be lost, then the hard-won advances for women will be in jeopardy once again.

13 The 19th Amendment carried in fifteen months. Those women were never stalled for more than a few months, while we have been stalled for eighteen months. Except for the time frame, the parallels are remarkably exact. The difference is not the alleged financing of the anti-ERA movement by the insurance industry, for the anti-Suffrage movement was bank-rolled by the liquor industry. They had their Phyllis Schlafly, too, although you probably do not remember that her name then was Mrs. Wadsworth. The arguments that were used against suffrage are those same arguments used today against ERA. The only different arguments we hear are those attributable to the change in social attitudes. Suffragettes too were hurt by allies, which appeared dubious in the eyes of many people. One difference is that we have lived with suffrage for over half a century. Even the opponents of ERA would not want to have the vote taken from women, yet they recycle the arguments. The dire predictions of what would happen when women got the vote have not materialized. Are those same dire predictions so much more likely to come true today over ERA?

14 Another difference is that suffrage was a more sharply focused issue for many than is ERA. Everyone knew exactly what it meant to talk about the right to vote, even if they opposed it. Today many are confused about the ramifications of ERA. There is not the same exactitude of definition. However, this can be clarified and is not the major cause of the backlash today. The real difference is that in 1920 the United States was in an era of prosperity, with no major social problems, and had the reflected afterglow of victory from World War I. By contrast, during the period in which ERA has stalled, we have had the turmoil over Vietnam, the Watergate scandals and crisis of confidence in government, and the worst recession since the great Depression. These, I believe, are the factors which have made the difference in 1920 and 1976 for the women's movement.

15 The German philosopher Friedrich Nietzsche once wrote that the attitude of a people toward the punishment of its criminals is a reliable index of the strength of the society. A strong government and society can afford to be lenient toward its criminals. A weaker society must be more severe. This concept can be seen in the reversal of our attitudes toward crime and punishment. The complex of events associated with Watergate, the Vietnam protests, and the economic decline which set in about the same time have caused our society to perceive itself as weaker than it had once thought. Nietzsche's comment can be expanded to the range of social movements. The stronger the society, the more it feels it can challenge the traditional values of the past. The weaker society perceives itself to be, the more it tends to retreat from these potentially dangerous challenges to its traditional value system. In my judgment, this perceived weakness of society coming at a critical time for the women's movement is the ultimate cause of the backlash against women.

16 This ultimate cause, however, is not really amenable to strategy. It is only as an ultimate cause works itself out as specific factors that we can deal with it and develop strategies to meet it. I would like to suggest several of these more specific manifestations facing us today and suggest strategies to deal with them.

17 One specific reason for the backlash can be attributed to the identity crisis. Many people see ERA, and indeed the women's movement, in terms of a denial of the differences between men and women. This has been called the interchange-ability syndrome. Ruth Ashen has written that "when equality is equated with interchangeability, individuality is negated and the human person extinguished." Sixty years ago in the suffrage battle the fear was expressed that women wanted to be men and the result would be that men would be turned into women. It did not happen over suffrage, and it will not happen over ERA, but the fear lingers.

18 Many unemployed women feel that their identity as women is especially threatened by working women. If full-time homemakers perceive employed women as the ones pushing for ERA, they too can feel that working women deny the validity of their roles as homemakers. Our view of the world is bound up with our sense of identity. We cannot change our image of the world without changing our personal identity. Therefore, our value systems that support our own sense of identity filter out those messages which are contradictory to our image. We do whatever we must do to protect our sense of uniqueness as persons. For many people right now, that unfortunately means opposition to ERA.

19 We must make it clear that ERA and the women's movement does not envision the interchangeability of men and women. It is not a denial of the uniqueness of women. It is not an effort to destroy workable social models for men and women. One strategy that is important is the recognition of the validity of the role of full-time homemaker, wife, and mother. To allow a suggestion that this is not as valid a model as that of the working woman will be counterproductive. However, we must also insist that the role of the working woman is also valid. Neither is a better model than the other, and neither is contemptuous of the other.

20 ERA and the women's movement is insisting that there is a variety of role models for women today, all equally valid. A woman should be free to choose from among a variety of options. If the home is her choice, it will be by choice, not lack of opportunities for entrance into the job market.

21 The identity crisis is a subtle point, which makes it difficult to discuss and at the same time it is important in creating the backlash. The average unemployed woman would probably deny having these feelings, and the average employed woman would also probably deny it. Therefore, we do not face it together, and the backlash builds up. Only if ERA is as valid for the homemaker as it is for the working woman, and perceived as such, will it succeed.

22 A second fear that produces the backlash is economic. It is becoming evident that our society is not able to employ all of its people who want to work. Elizabeth Janeway has said "one aspect of the war between the sexes not often noted is its manipulative use of women by the State and the Establishment. Wars put women into the labor market and recessions and depressions put them out of it." With the military services having released so many people to the labor market at the same time that the defense industry is slowing down, combined with increasing inflation, and more women as heads of families, we begin to face a hard question: who is

it that is going to be unemployed? Teenagers, blacks, and women especially face this question.

23 As the competition for employment becomes keener, unemployed married women naturally become concerned about the security of their husbands' jobs. The white male feels threatened and charges reverse discrimination. If you doubt the reality of the employment backlash, review the recent decision of the Federal judge in Virginia who has ruled that affirmative action plans are illegal.

24 A third fear contributing to the backlash is that ERA and the women's movement will have an adverse effect upon the home and children and the values of our society. People fear the pace of change. People see the rising divorce rate, the increasing cynicism of the people about honesty and integrity, the increase in sexual behavior outside the bonds of traditional marriage, and a general breakdown in virtue. All of our institutions seem to be under attack—the family, the school, the church. Many people feel it is time to call a halt in these directions. ERA seems to typify these attacks on all that they believe. Our strategy must be to consider carefully the effect of the women's movement on morals and values. The excesses of some women in the movement can give credence to some of these fears. There is not the direct tie between the movement itself and the changes in values that many people fear. Most of us who favor the women's movement have the same concerns about the values of our society. We have to be more careful in spelling this out. For if people perceive ERA as another assault on all that they believe, the backlash will be fed.

25 The last factor is closely correlated with the fear about values and the home, but more specifically is related to the sense of responsibility to our families, to our jobs, to our religion, to our country. A sense of personal responsibility has been replaced by the demand for an undisciplined freedom to do our own thing. At the same time that we have lost our sense of personal responsibility, we have made greater demands upon distributive justice, and public benefits. We all want the benefits, but we no longer feel we ought to pay our dues!

26 A sense of irresponsibility is revealed in the feeling that many women have that they already have all the legal protection they need, and therefore do not want to jeopardize their favored position in society by demanding an equality that would lead to duties as well as to rights. To insist that rights must be balanced by duties is going against the total social current of our time. This is a greater issue than ERA or the women's movement. Part of the very strength of the backlash comes from this feeling.

27 November 2, 1915, was a memorable date in New York State history. That was the vote on the Suffrage Amendment to the state constitution. It was a long hard-fought battle, and that night as the returns came in, it was apparent that suffrage had lost. At the suffrage headquarters in New

York City, the women were discouraged and defeated. Suddenly, the chairwoman of the Manhattan women, Mrs. Laidlow, jumped up and said they must start their new campaign that very night. At midnight, the night suffrage was defeated' she led a parade through midtown Manhattan proclaiming the start of the 1917 campaign for state suffrage. And in 1917 it carried.

28 That was the indomitable spirit that bounced back from defeat after defeat to give us the vote in the first place. Now, though in the midst of a backlash, we must start the campaign anew. We must vigilantly guard the rights we have already won and secure the promise that lies ahead of us. Together we will emerge from the temporary darkness of the backlash and walk again in the season of light.

Chapter 4

SPEECHES THAT AFFIRM PROPOSITIONS OF FACT

Matters of fact . . . are very stubborn things.

Matthew Tindal

THE NATURE AND IMPORTANCE OF SPEECHES THAT AFFIRM PROPOSITIONS OF FACT

There are instances of discourse when a speaker tries to prove to the satisfaction of an audience that a proposition of fact is, in reality, true. While the preceding chapter was concerned with the art of interpreting established knowledge or original inquiry for the *enlightenment of an audience,* the present chapter is devoted to the principles involved in *establishing an alleged truth in order to win agreement.* Earlier, the primary task for the speaker was to help an audience understand an event, process, concept, or inquiry; in this chapter, the speaker's efforts are directed toward seeking approval of the "facts" that are presented. In the previous speech form, the speaker might publicly analyze, "What is the present state of space exploration?"; in this chapter, the speaker seeks to gain acceptance of a conclusion: "The American program of space exploration is without military significance."

The social environments that produce speeches affirming factual propositions are diverse. A district attorney may seek to establish the guilt of a labor leader charged with misuse of union funds. The president of a liberal arts college may try to convince the board of regents that faculty salaries are not equal to that of competing schools. A state legislator may attempt to prove to his or her constituency that the condition of state highways will deter expansion of the tourist industry. While in certain instances the affirmation of a proposition of fact is the sole purpose of a persuasive speech, at other times a speaker may affirm a fact as a means of affirming a value, creating concern for a problem, or gaining acceptance for a course of action. On the whole, matters of fact are more commonly argued in relation to one of those ends than they are as separate entities.

In the quotation opening this chapter, Matthew Tindal expresses an awareness that matters of fact are not self-evident. In the common vernacular, the term *fact* connotes an incontrovertible truth. Thus the novitiate to the advocate's art seeks to stifle further argument by asserting, "It's a fact"—by which it is meant, "It is uncontestable truth." But "Matters of fact . . . are very stubborn things." Were all facts self-evident, there would be no such thing as a proposition of fact because the term *proposition* implies a statement about an unsettled or controversial state of affairs.

What, then, is a proposition of fact? A proposition of fact may be defined as a statement (a sentence with assertive content) that may be affirmed or denied through tests of *existence, occurrence,* or *causality.* The fact in question may concern an individual, an event, a process, a condition, a concept, or even a policy. Whatever the fact to be judged, however, the advocate is primarily interested in gaining listener acceptance that something, was, is, or will be true. Consider these examples:

Proposition A: The Great Depression was caused by excessive speculation on the stock market.

Proposition B: The Japanese attack on Pearl Harbor was precipitated by United States failure to provide military safeguards.

Proposition C: The sighting of flying saucers are real events.

Proposition D: Marijuana smoking is harmless.

Proposition E: The nuclear family as we know it will ultimately become obsolete.

Proposition F: The absence of the player reserve clause will ultimately cause the demise of major league baseball.

Although these six propositions differ substantially in subject matter, they are all legitimate factual propositions. Propositions A and B concern matters of past causality. Propositions C and D concern matters of present existence and causality. Propositions E and F concern matters of future occurrence and future causality respectively.

Whatever the subject matter and tense of a factual proposition, its proposer is interested in gaining audience acceptance of an alleged truth. The following section identifies the criteria that are especially relevant for evaluating speeches that affirm propositions of fact.

CRITERIA FOR EVALUATING SPEECHES
THAT AFFIRM PROPOSITIONS OF FACT

Because propositions of fact treat supposedly verifiable or predictable phenomena, the tests of speeches affirming such propositions are strongly concerned with the logical sufficiency of the affirmation.

1. *Has the speaker adequately assessed the proof requirements of the factual proposition?*

Implicit in a proposition of fact is the assumption that there are reasonable criteria with which to judge the truth of alleged events, states of being, causal relationships, and so on. Proof requirements are often field dependent; that is, they differ from one area of knowledge or profession to another. For example, the affirmation of a proposition of medical fact may require that standards on the observation and clinical diagnosis of patients be met. The affirmation of a proposition of historical fact, on the other hand, may require that standards relevant to sound historical research be met. Lawyers, behavioral scientists, chemists, mathematicians, and astronomers have all devised standards by which certain types of phenomena are to be judged. When talking to a specialized group about a specialized topic, the speaker can expect that the proposition will be judged by the special proof requirements established by that profession as a modus operandi.

In the world of ordinary discourse, the criteria by which propositions of fact are judged are less well defined and less rigorous. However, even the popular proposition of fact demands that the speaker employ responsible standards of assessment. If popular speakers fail to support their assertions or if they support them with emotional appeals and shallow truisms, they will be criticized for their faulty interpretation of the responsible proof requirements of their propositions. Enlightened lay critics do not excuse the maxims and pseudo-arguments of modern mass media advertisements even though they are aware of the logical permissiveness of the American consuming public.

2. *Has the speaker offered acceptable arguments in support of the proposition of fact?*

Given that a speaker demonstrates awareness of the general proof requirements of a particular factual proposition, the next question to be raised is "Has the speaker offered relevant arguments—reasons for belief—in support of the proposition of fact?" Imagine, for example, that a district attorney seeks to affirm the proposition that "a labor leader is guilty of misusing union funds." Imagine, further, that our barrister has recognized that the particular proof demands that must be met are those of the bar rather than the public forum. We may then question whether the arguments that are selected support the conclusion that the labor leader is guilty of misusing union funds. We might expect, for example, that it would be argued that (1) the labor leader in question did spend union funds on nonunion activities, (2) legal precedence makes the misuse of union funds a criminal offense, and (3) the expenditure of the funds in question is classifiable as a misuse in light of legal precedence. Should our lawyer fail to offer any of these arguments or should irrelevant nonlegal arguments be offered in their place, we may deny that a convincing case in support of the proposition has been made.

In the world of everyday discourse, the specific argument or arguments necessary for the establishment of a factual proposition are largely dependent on the criteria of sufficiency employed by the listener/critic receiving the argument. As an enlightened critic the listener should consider the possible reasons that make the argument advanced questionable. Assume, for instance, the following argument:

Proposition (claim):   Capital punishment is not an effective deterrent to crime.

Reason (justification):   The states that have capital punishment have more serious crimes than the states that do not have capital punishment.

Will you accept this argument? What possible exceptions or reservations to this argument might you legitimately raise? Should you note that there are serious differences between the states that have capital punishment and those that do not, you are well on your way to discrediting the argument. Should you know that the capital-punishment states are highly populated urban areas, while the noncapital-punishment states are essentially rural and less populous, you may raise one important reservation to the argument. Should you know that the states with capital punishment have a higher incidence of poverty, unemployment, and racial antagonism, you may raise another serious reservation.

Thus, in evaluating an argument, the critic must ask whether there is cause to question the sufficiency of it. If there are reasonable reservations and if the speaker has failed to refute them, the argument may be denied.

3. *Has the speaker provided adequate evidence in support of arguments?*

In some fields of argument, the nature of adequate evidence is carefully specified. For example, the rules of evidence of the American bar are rather carefully specified. In the courtroom, there are rules governing the admissibility and inadmissibility of evidence. Historians, scientists, and behavioral scientists also have some clear notion of what constitutes sound evidence and what does not.

However, in the world of ordinary discourse, evidential requirements are less well known and less well defined. Perhaps the most distinctive characteristic of ordinary arguments on propositions of fact is the reliance of the speaker upon secondary information and uncontrolled, unsystematic observation. Thus, the popular speaker often bases arguments on the *testimony* of others, well-known or verifiable *specific instances,* and *statistical data.* Sometimes speakers use a *literal analogy* or describe a *cause-effect relationship.*

In using *testimony,* the speaker draws evidence from the statements of others. One interesting example of testimonial evidence occurred in the championship debate at the National College Debate Tournament at West Point in 1960. John Raser of San Diego State College sought to prove that "Eventually the public and the nation always get their way in national policy." Having stated what he hoped to prove Mr. Raser went on to say:

> Now that sounds like a strong statement, but I've got more than a few people who tell me it's true. . . . I'd first like to turn to Robert H. Jackson, the former Supreme Court Justice, who should know if anyone does. He said, in *Vital Speeches* in October, 1953, that "The practical play of the forces of politics is such that judicial power has often delayed but never permanently delayed the persistent will of substantial majorities." In other words, the majority always gets its way. Let's turn to some more support. Professor Jack W. Peltason, University of Illinois . . . [in] his book *The Federal Courts and the Political Processes,* states, "In almost every decision in which the judges have imposed a check on Congress in the name of the Constitution, in one way or another Congress eventually has done what the judges told them they could not do and should not do." . . . Let's turn to further support of this idea that judges can't really thwart national policy. James MacGregor Burns, and the same man, Jack Walter Peltason, told us that, in their joint effort, *Government by the People,* published in 1954, "Judges have no armies or police to execute their laws; they have no authority to levy taxes to support their activities. In the long run they must adapt themselves to the nature and demands of government by the people." Now what do we draw from this? Simply that the Supreme Court does not thwart national

policy because always eventually the policies which the people apparently want and always the policies which Congress endorses eventually are put into effect.

In this example, a college debater uses three pieces of testimony to support his point. In evaluating a speaker's use of testimony, the critical listener should employ some of the popular tests of testimonial evidence: (1) Was the source of the testimony in a position to observe? (2) Was the source of the testimony competent to observe? (3) Was the source of the testimony biased? (4) Was the source of the testimony qualified? (5) Was the source of the testimony consistent with other sources and with himself or herself on previous occasions? and (6) Is the testimony sufficiently recent?

In using *specific instances* as evidence, the speaker provides well-known or veritiable examples that demonstrate the truth of the proposition or of a claim leading to the proposition. An excellent example of the use of specific instances can be found in a speech delivered by Richard Nixon well before his catastrophic involvement in the Watergate affair. As vice president under Dwight Eisenhower, Nixon visited Russia, and during his stay there delivered an important "Address to the Russian People." In an effort to prove that United States efforts to assure peace had been thwarted by the Soviet government, Nixon effectively drew upon a series of specific instances.

> . . . It is possible that many of you listening to me are not aware of the positive programs the United States has proposed which were designed to contribute to peace. Let me tell you about just a few of them and what happened to them:
>
> We had a monopoly on the atomic bomb when on June 14, 1946, we submitted the Baruch plan for international control of atomic energy. What happened? It was rejected by the USSR.
>
> At the Summit Conference in Geneva on July 21, 1955, President Eisenhower made his offer of open skies aerial inspection. What happened? It was rejected by the USSR.
>
> On May 1, 1958, the United States offered an Arctic aerial inspection plan to protect both nations from surprise attack. What happened? It was rejected by the USSR.
>
> I realize that your government has indicated reasons for its rejection of each of these proposals. I do not list these proposals for the purpose of warming over past history but simply to demonstrate the initiative our government has taken to reduce tensions and to find peaceful solutions for differences between us.

An equally good example of the use of specific instances occurs in a speech by Phyllis Jones Springen on "The Dimensions of the Oppression of Women."

> An infuriating example of unequal pay for equal work concerned a New Jersey manufacturer. Their chief financial officer was a woman paid $9,000 a year. When she left, they had to pay a man $20,000 a year to do her job. When he left they hired another woman at $9,000. When she left, they hired a man at $18,000. According to the recruiter, they were all good at the job.

In evaluating specific instances used as evidence in support of factual propositions, the critic should raise such questions as these: (1) Were a sufficient number of instances presented? (2) Were the instances presented typical instances? and (3) Are there any negative instances that should be accounted for?

In using *statistical data,* the speaker draws evidence from studies that have surveyed large numbers of cases and reported data numerically. In a speech found in another chapter of this book, Charles Schalliol seeks to demonstrate that "The increasing size of our metropolitan areas is compounding our air pollution problem" by citing relevant statistics.

> Since 1940, our population has grown by 50,000,000, the use of energy has quadrupled, disposable income has increased 60%—yet—our air supply remains the same. In such a setting air pollution is a murderer. According to Edward Parkhurst, a noted health authority, death rates are "consistently higher in the central cities of 50,000 and over than in places under 10,000 and in rural areas in nonmetropolitan districts." The Census Bureau further establishes that life expectancy is three years greater in the rural states than in the urban states.

In evaluating a speaker's use of statistics, the enlightened critic asks: (1) Do these statistics come from a reliable source? (2) Are these statistics based on a reliable sample? and (3) Were these statistics accurately and completely reported? (4) Are they presented in a meaningful form?

In demonstrating a *literal analogy,* the speaker typically compares two things or instances belonging to the same category or classification (two nations, people, corporations, etc.) to show that because the two actually are similar in several major relevant elements, something known to exist in the first instance probably exists (or will exist) in the second. You might contend, for example, that because England and the United States are similar in language, general economic system, and general political system, and because so-called "socialized medicine" is working in Great Britain, it probably would work in the United States. In evaluating the soundness of a speaker's literal analogy, the critic could ask some of the standard questions: (1) Are the known elements of both actually similar enough? (2) Are the known similarities actually relevant to the issue-at-hand? (3) Are significant relevant differences ignored? (4) Does the element assumed to exist in the first instance but unknown in the second actually exist in the first? (5) Do essential points of similarity outweigh essential points of difference?

In asserting a *cause-effect relationship*, the speaker contends that one factor (or set of factors) directly contributes to the occurrence of another factor (or set of factors); in some sense the first causes (or will cause) the second. As a variation, a given effect or circumstance is described as the result of a certain cause. Sometimes use of words such as "because," "due to," or "if . . . then" can alert us to possible cause-effect arguments. Jenkin Lloyd Jones, in a speech titled "Let's Bring Back Dad: A Solid Value System," suggests a number of cause-effect relationships, including the following. At one point he describes "neo-Socialist" university professors who are "hostile" to the free enterprise business system "because they have never had any experience with it." At another point he asks concerning some Black families, "Why are our ghetto societies in such chaos? Because the man walks off when it gets tough." Jones concludes the speech by predicting a cause-effect relationship:

> . . . if enough American dads were to resolve to become partisan dads, unashamed to hold moral standards, willing to take the time to communicate values, then the chances of raising a new generation that would live in the agony of social chaos, or worse yet, lose their liberties for generations yet to come, will be substantially diminished.

To assess the soundness of any asserted cause-effect relationship, the critic could inquire: (1) Might there be multiple causes, several significant contributing and interrelated influences, rather than just the one asserted? (2) Might there be a chain or sequence of causal factors to consider, not just the asserted one as the immediate cause? (3) Is the speaker confusing a causal connection either with *chronology* (one thing simply happened after another) or with *correlation* (two things vary together in predictable ways, but *both* may be the effects of some unknown cause)? (4) Might there be additional positive or negative effects to consider other than the single effect identified? (5) Can the asserted cause-effect relationship be supported by evidence such as scientific studies, expert testimony, or other factual examples of the relationship?

CONCLUSION

In certain instances of persuasive discourse, speakers seek to prove to the satisfaction of their audiences that given propositions of fact are really true. When evaluating such speeches, the critic should consider *whether the speaker has adequately assessed the proof requirements of the factual proposition, whether acceptable arguments in support of the proposition of fact have been offered, and whether adequate evidence in support of the argument has been provided.*

For Further Reading

Berlo, David K. *The Process of Communication.* Holt, Rinehart and Winston, 1960. Pages 217–34 and 250–71 analyze reporting observations, seeking judgments, and making inferences.

Ehninger, Douglas. *Influence, Belief, and Argument.* Scott, Foresman, 1974. A brief paperback textbook presenting processes of reasoning from various types of evidence.

Freeley, Austin J. *Argumentation and Debate.* 4th ed. Wadsworth, 1976. Chapters 6–10 explore the nature of evidence, tests of evidence, and sound reasoning.

McCroskey, James C. "A Summary of Experimental Research on the Effects of Evidence in Persuasive Communications." *Quarterly Journal of Speech,* April 1969, 169–76.

Newman, Robert P., and Newman, Dale. *Evidence.* Houghton Mifflin, 1969. Presents standards of credibility for evidence and assesses sources of evidence: government, the press, pressure groups, professional scholars.

Rieke, Richard D., and Malcolm O. Sillars. *Argumentation and the Decision Making Process.* Wiley, 1975. Chapter 5 examines use of factual instances, statistics, and expert testimony and notes the field-dependent nature of some standards for sound argument.

Sproule, J. Michael. *Argument.* McGraw-Hill, 1980. Chapters 4 and 5 discuss use of factual examples, statistics, expert testimony, literal analogy, and causal argument.

Toulmin, Stephen, Richard Rieke, and Allan Janik. *An Introduction to Reasoning.* Macmillan, 1979. This book presents a framework for analyzing the soundness of arguments and stresses that criteria for sound evidence vary among fields of discourse such as law, science, the arts, and business.

Zieglmueller, George W., and Danse, Charles A. *Argumentation, Inquiry and Advocacy*. Prentice-Hall, 1975. Chapter 5 discusses "The Testing of Evidence."

DEFENSE FOR AMERICA: TRENDS AGAINST THE U.S.

Strom Thurmond

Strom Thurmond, United States Senator from South Carolina, delivered this address at the University Forum Board Series, Wichita State University, Wichita, Kansas, September 2, 1980. On this occasion Senator Thurmond developed the proposition of fact that ineffective American national defense policies are contributing to Soviet expansionism.

The first thing one notices about the speech is its's structure. It is a textbook example of speech organization. The address is clearly partitioned into four topics, the introduction leads explicitly into the body, the transitions between points clearly indicate what is to follow, and the conclusion stems directly from the body of the address. One also notes the very clear forecast of the main points of the speech Senator Thurmond makes in paragraph nine. Why is careful structuring of ideas especially important in a speech developing a proposition of fact?

A speaker has essentially three tasks in developing any proposition of fact: (1) make certain that the audience understands the first term of the proposition (the subject)—in this case "American national defense policies; (2) clarify what is meant by the second term of the proposition (the predicate)—in this instance "contributing to Soviet expansionism"; and (3) prove the validity of the predicate of the proposition—in other words, are American national defense policies really contributing to Soviet expansionistic policies?

The first three points the Senator develops for his audience at Wichita State set up the validity of the fourth and final point, Soviet expansionism. You may want to discuss the development of these three points. How does the speaker employ factual information to demonstrate the propositions of fact embedded in each point? Additionally, how does the speaker use testimony to give added credibility to each point? If you think that the testimony adds strength to a point, are there any special features about the quotations used that make them especially effective testimony? Finally, does the last point reveal how the ideas developed earlier in the speech actually contribute to Soviet expansionism?

This speech is reprinted by permission from *Vital Speeches of the Day*, October 15, 1980, pp. 5-7.

1 It was a pleasure for me to accept this invitation from the University Forum Board, as I always welcome an opportunity to speak to our young people, especially in the heartland of America in the great state of Kansas.

2 One of my more pleasant duties in the Senate has been to serve and work with your distinguished Kansas Senators, Robert Dole and Nancy Kassebaum. They are both dedicated to representing their state, and equally important, they have consistently voted for a strong national defense posture.

3 This morning I have been asked to speak to you about *national defense*. The founders of our nation set forth as one of the primary goals of our Federal government the preservation of our national security. Unfortunately, the percent of our Federal budget which has gone to defense in recent years amounts to about 23 percent, the lowest level since World War II. While we have lagged in defense spending, the Soviet Union has greatly accelerated their effort and are currently outspending the U.S. by at least 40 percent annually.

4 These trends in defense, the U.S. decline and the Soviet buildup, have become in the past several years a major political issue. The fall of our former ally, Iran, to revolutionary forces, the holding of U.S. hostages and the invasion of Afghanistan by Soviet armed forces have especially served to awaken the average American to our defense problems.

5 An Associated Press-National Broadcasting Company poll taken early this year revealed that about 63 percent of the American people now support increased defense spending. I would imagine today that the percentage is even higher, as since that poll was taken, our military leaders have warned that the U.S. has now lost the strategic nuclear advantage to the Soviet Union.

6 It is against this background that I wish to focus my remarks this morning. There is no group of Americans who should be more interested in these trends than our young people, for you are the ones who ultimately bear the burdens of armed conflict, should that day ever come.

7 Let me say at the outset that I do not believe a nuclear exchange or a head-on conflict with the Soviet Union is likely. The greater threat we face is that the Soviets will use their military power to expand their sphere of influence by denying us the support of our allies and denying us the free flow of raw materials we need for our industrial and defense growth, including the petroleum needed to run our economy.

8 My purpose this morning will be to comment briefly on four issues and then I would be pleased to answer any questions you might propound. The four subjects I would like to comment on are as follows:

9 First, *the shifting balance of power;* Second, *our defense position today;* Third, *the transfer of Western technology to Communist nations,* and Fourth, *Soviet Expansionism.*

1. *The Shifting Balance of Power*

10 In the past ten years there has been a decided shift in the balance of military power from the U.S. to the Soviet Union. After the U.S. withdrawal from Vietnam, defense spending fell drastically, as a general "reordering of priorities" took place.

11 These trends can be illustrated quite dramatically in the area of strategic military strength. In 1969 the U.S. led the Soviet Union in nearly every measure of defense systems: the numbers of land and sea-based missiles, the accuracy of these weapons, the numbers of warheads, and the megatonnage of our missile forces.

12 Now, ten years later after implementing SALT I and negotiating a follow-on SALT II Treaty, we find the Soviets have equalled or lead the U.S. in all of these categories except the number of warheads. In this final category, our defense leaders report the Soviets will be superior by 1985.

13 Our leaders, especially in the last few years, have promoted a policy of military parity with the Soviets, but while we engaged in unilateral arms restraint, the Soviets conducted a massive buildup of their strategic nuclear weapons, their Navy and their conventional forces.

14 The present Administration has especially promoted policies damaging to the maintenance of a strong U.S. defense position. President Carter has killed the B-1 bomber, delayed the MX missile deployment, refused timely development of the Navy's Trident missile, cut Navy shipbuilding programs by one-half, vetoed a nuclear aircraft carrier, cancelled the neutron warhead for NATO, closed the Minuteman missile production line, halted Minuteman modernization, withdrawn troops from Korea and relinquished the Panama Canal to a Marxist dictator—to mention a few of recent policies injurious to our defense posture.

15 It is now clear to most qualified observers that the Soviets are not interested in a position of parity, but seek *a clear military superiority*. This shift is even better perceived overseas than here in the U.S. Recently, the former Prime Minister of Great Britain, Harold MacMillan, summed up the feelings of many when he stated, "Things are as bad for the West as they could possibly be and they are getting worse."

16 In my opinion, this shifting balance of power is extremely dangerous. This Soviet buildup is far in excess of any defensive needs.

2. *Our Defense Position Today*

17 With this background on the shift of military power over the past ten years and mounting evidence of Soviet use of this power, such as in Afghanistan, I would like to now address my second point, *our defense position today*.

18 In Senate testimony this year, our military leaders have admitted that the U.S. has lost strategic nuclear superiority to the Soviets. This situation cannot be reversed until the late 1980's, even if we accelerate various strategic programs now in development.

19 This situation came about because of our idealistic foreign policies of the past ten years, our continued inability to understand the Soviet threat

and our failure to go forward with defense programs to assure—without a doubt—our military strength will be second to none.

20 For instance, our strategic strength was endangered by the cancellation of the B-1 bomber. Pilots today are flying the old B-52, a bomber older than some of the pilots. It represents technology of the 1950's, yet the Administration plans to use it into the 1990's.

21 In the area of land-based missiles, called ICBM's, the Administration has delayed the new mobile MX missile to the point that it will be 1987 before the first units can be operational. This delay took place despite the fact that improved accuracy in new Soviet missiles will enable them to destroy 90% of our Minuteman force in a first strike in the early 1980's.

22 Besides our problems in long range strategic weapons, we have allowed the numbers of ships in our Navy to fall well below that needed for protecting the sea lanes over which our exports and imports flow. The Chief of Naval Operations, Admiral Thomas Hayward, has testified that we are "trying to meet a three-ocean requirement with a one and one-half ocean Navy."

23 In the area of conventional equipment, the story is unfortunately much the same—we are behind and falling even further behind. The Soviets lead the U.S. in *tanks and armored personnel carriers, 4 to 1;* in *artillery pieces, 8 to 1;* and *in helicopters and tactical aircraft, 2 to 1.*

24 Other major problems facing the military services are the lack of sufficient numbers of missiles and spare parts to keep our planes and equipment operating. For instance, we are paying $15 million for F-14 aircraft, yet each plane has only 2 Phoenix missiles to use in wartime. We have spent $500 million to buy attack submarines, yet the numbers of torpedoes are not sufficient to allow two loads per submarine.

25 Another issue of great importance is the failure of the all-volunteer force to attract the quantity and quality of personnel to operate our military units. We have spent billions on the all-volunteer force, but if it fails, we must return to the draft.

26 On the brighter side, I can report to you today that last week Congress approved a defense bill $7 billion higher than the President requested. Congress, with wide public support, is now taking the initiative to meet many of our defense shortages.

3. *Transfer of Western Technology*

27 Moving now to my third point, I would like to comment briefly on the transfer of high technology to the Soviets through ill-advised trade policies.

28 Unfortunately, the United States has sold many high technology items which our enemies have used to their advantage. Trucks built with American technology at the Soviet Kama River truck plant were used in the invasion of Afghanistan.

29   Computers have been exported which have found use in factories that produce missile launchers. Wide body jet technology sold for commercial use has found its way into military aircraft. Ball bearing technology we have sold to the Soviets is being used to improve the accuracy of Soviet strategic missiles. This improved accuracy of Soviet missiles now threatens our own Minuteman ICBM system.

30   We are continuing to sell items to the Soviets—items such as nuclear reactor parts, transistors, test instrumentation, and advanced oil drilling materials, all of which have military as well as commercial applications. Dr. William J. Perry, Undersecretary of Defense for Research and Engineering, in testifying this year to the Senate Armed Services Committee on this subject stated that "I think we made some errors in judgment."

31   Another shocking dimension to this trade policy is the fact that the U.S. has financed the sale of some of these high technology items to the Soviets. From 1972 to 1975, during the height of the detente policy, we permitted the Soviet Union to draw official Export-Import Bank credits, guaranteed by the United States Government, at very favorable low interest rates. Now, five years after Congress put a stop to this practice, the Soviet Union still owes us approximately $447 million for these credits.

32   In addition to these official credits, the Soviet Union owes U.S. commercial banks about $815 million. The adverse effect of these loans is twofold. First, we are financing a nation which is creating problems for us throughout the world; and second, certain U.S. interests lobby for an unrealistic policy with the Soviets in order not to endanger the repayment of these loans.

33   Efforts in the Congress to reverse these policies have met with sharp Administration opposition. Many legislators have favored giving the Defense Department a veto in military related trade decisions; but to date, we have not been successful.

34   I have personally communicated with President Carter, in private conversations and by letters, on this subject, but just a few months ago he approved the sale to the Soviets of high technology oil drilling equipment. This was done despite the invasion of Afghanistan and in the face of the Soviet goal to achieve warm water ports in the rich oil-producing areas of the Middle East.

35   It makes no sense to me that the U.S. would boycott the Olympics and halt grain sales on one hand; and on the other hand, sell to the Soviets this high technology oil equipment. I totally reject this inconsistent and damaging policy to U.S. interests.

4. *Soviet Expansionism*

36   It is against this background that I would like to talk briefly about my fourth point, *Soviet expansionism.*

37 Although Soviet military strength compared to the U.S. in the 1970's was marginal, they continued their expansionist policies and with a great deal of success. For instance, their support of North Vietnam has now lead to the Communist takeover of South Vietnam, Cambodia and Laos in Indochina. The threat to Thailand and other nations of this area merely awaits the resolution of whether the pro-Chinese or pro-Soviet forces will prevail in Cambodia.

38 In Africa, they have used Cuban proxy troops and Russian-built military equipment to bring pro-Soviet forces to power in Angola, Mozambique and Ethiopia. Cuban forces have also been introduced into the Middle East in South Yemen, and last December Soviet troops were used for the first time in recent years when the invasion of Afghanistan was launched. Today the people of Afghanistan are being brutalized daily by the raw power of Soviet helicopters, tanks and guns which have destroyed entire villages to secure the Soviet puppet leader's control. Even Afghan military units have been destroyed when they attempted to revolt.

39 Closer to home, the Soviets have established air and naval bases in Cuba, conducted maneuvers with a sizable military unit there and aided Cuba in its export of revolution throughout Latin America. Nicaragua has fallen to Marxist forces, aided by Cuba and Panama; and now El Salvador and other nations are threatened.

40 Many of these events have taken place because of ineffective U.S. policies, and during a period when our U.N. Ambassador termed Cuban troops in Africa a "stabilizing force" and the Ayatollah Khomeini a man who would eventually be recognized as a "saint."

41 Thus, the question arises—if Soviet expansionism makes such gains during a period of relative parity, what will happen in the 1980's during a period of Soviet military dominance? The answer to that question might still be subject to our control if we turn our shoulder to the wheel and restore our military strength.

42 This spiral into world disorder must be ended if your generation and future generations are to enjoy periods of relative peace. This can only be accomplished by the U.S. asserting itself again, resuming its position as leader of the Free World, aiding our allies who face Communist aggression and maintaining our own military strength.

43 In addition, I would like to make one further point. A wide understanding of these issues and the problems we face is necessary if we are to deal with these questions effectively. Therefore, I urge you as individuals to study these subjects and bring the weight of your opinion to bear in your community, state and nation.

44 Finally, I would like to note that we would be well served to refer back to the greatest book ever written for advice in these perilous times. First, in the Book of Proverbs, we find this admonition—"where there is no vision, the people perish;" and second, in Luke, "when a strong man armed keepeth his place, his goods are in peace."

45 Thank you and good luck to each of you in your education, your career and your personal life.

THE REAL CAUSE OF INFLATION: GOVERNMENT SERVICES

Herbert S. Richey

Herbert S. Richey is Chairman of the Board of the Chamber of Commerce of the United States. He delivered this address to the Ohio Chamber of Commerce meeting in Columbus March 16, 1977. What political and economic predilections do you think his audience would have? Keep this in mind when you assess the probable impact of this speech.

Propositions of fact often concern causal relationships. Richey, in this case, is trying to establish the *real* cause of inflation. This obviously means he is going to try to separate the real cause from false causes. What special techniques does Herbert Richey use in trying to establish his proposition? How convincing is his argument of fact?

The opening story not only is interesting but also embodies the essence of the speaker's line of argument. Such introductions usually are quite effective. Organization and the use of definition are other factors that warrant careful attention in your analysis of this speech.

This speech is printed by permission from *Vital Speeches of the Day*, April 15, 1977, pp. 386-89.

1 I'd like to talk about modern economics today. I'm sure many of us are already familiar with that. But for those who are not, I can illustrate the theory with a story:

2 Jed is a part-time farm worker with a flair for applied economics. One day he "borrowed" a country ham from the farmer who employs him . . . without bothering to tell the farmer.

3 He went downtown and sold the ham to the grocer for $27. Then he used $20 of that money to buy $80 worth of food stamps.

4 With the food stamps he bought $48 worth of groceries. He used the remaining $32 worth of food stamps to buy back the ham.

5 Then he returned the ham to the farmer's smokehouse.

6 So the grocer made a profit, the farmer got his ham back, and Jed has $48 worth of groceries plus $7 in cash.

7 If you see no flaw in that process, then you are already familiar with modern economics.

8 On the other hand, if you suspect that someone, somewhere, has been "taken" for $80, then the rest of this speech is dedicated to you.

9 Two newspaper stories caught my eye back in February. These stories were side-by-side on the front page of the *Wall Street Journal.* One story predicted consumer fears of inflation—*fears of inflation*—will delay economic recovery. The other story said the Carter Administration puts a higher priority on economic recovery than on fighting inflation.

10 If both of these statements are true, I sincerely hope the Administration has someone who can reason from A to B. *Fighting inflation* is the best way to stimulate the economy. But the idea isn't getting the attention it deserves.

11 I get the feeling the problem of inflation has been around for so long now it's beginning to bore the policy makers. It's more fun to find new dragons to slay. Preferably photogenic dragons that interest the news media.

12 Besides, stimulating the economy usually involves giving money to the voters, whereas fighting inflation usually involves telling the voters they have to do without something. For a politician, that's not a very hard choice to make.

13 But still . . . there's that story about consumer fears of inflation. Maybe the old shell game doesn't work anymore. Maybe the politicians are deluding only themselves. Maybe the voters have grown more sophisticated than their leaders.

14 If so, it's a good time to take a new look at the cause of inflation.

15 The best definition of inflation is still the simplest: Too much money chasing too few goods.

16 The fun begins when you consider the two questions raised by that definition: *Why* is there too much money? *Why* are there too few goods? You can almost separate today's economists into various philosophical camps depending on which one of these two questions they choose to emphasize.

17 It's worthwhile to take a brief look at those philosophical camps. Their adherents chase one another through the news media like cats and dogs.

18 A few years ago the economists' Gaul was divided into three parts by Professor Karl Brunner of the University of Rochester. I'll use his terminology because it's easier than coming up with my own.

19 Professor Brunner separated economists into the eclectic, the institutionalist, and the price-theoretical schools.

20 Let's take the eclectics first.

21 The eclectics deny that inflation has any particular recurring cause. Any given inflation is caused by whatever happened to cause it, they say. For obvious reasons, this branch of economics is of use primarily to those gifted with prophetic hindsight.

22 The institutionalists are the second group. They favor a devil theory. They believe inflation is caused by the manipulations of powerful institutions; institutions such as big labor unions and big corporations. This is the "administered prices" theory. It's popular with the public because it provides clearcut villains to blame. It's popular with the politicians because the villains are not politicians.

23 The great popularizer of the institutionalist theory is John Kenneth Galbraith. In a 1970 speech to the Fabian Society in London, he proclaimed the death of Keynesian economics. Western governments can no longer manipulate their economies through fiscal and monetary policy, he said, because big labor and big business can thwart such efforts.

24 I can't resist quoting two other statements Professor Galbraith made on that occasion seven years ago, in testament to his enduring wisdom.

25 "An American coming even briefly to England," he said, "cannot but sense how much better British Socialism, as compared with American liberalism, has supported the public sector since World War II."

26 If you think that quote is rich in irony, listen to this one, from the same speech:

"There are, I've long thought, few problems in New York City which would not be solved by doubling the city budget."

27 For the record, since 1970 the budget of New York City has almost exactly doubled. I'm sure the city fathers will be glad to hear that according to Professor Galbraith, there are few problems they haven't solved.

28 I can't resist having a little fun at the expense of Professor Galbraith.

29 But fun aside, there are some very logical objections to the institutionalist hypothesis. As Professor Brunner points out, it doesn't do a very good job of explaining actual experience.

30 If wages and prices are in fact controlled by big business and big labor, then how do you account for those times when one or the other—or both—are in a slump?

31 Do you assume that their "monopoly power" has suddenly decayed? Or that they have suffered a temporary lapse of greed?

32 It just doesn't make sense. Both business and labor appear to be victims of inflation, not causes.

33 Let's leave the institutionalists and take a look at the last of Professor Brunner's classifications, the price-theoretical. This is really where the action is today.

34 Brunner subdivides price-theoretical into three groups: Monetary, Fiscal, and Keynesian.

35 The monetarist theory is the easiest of all to understand. According to the monetarists, if inflation is too much money chasing too few goods, the way to halt it is to stop creating new money faster than you can create new goods. In other words, money creation should keep pace with the growth of the economy—no more, no less. To support their theory, the monetarists can point to consistent historical correlations between general price increases and money creation.

36 The monetarist case is appealing in its logical simplicity. The biggest problem with it is this: While it *does* finger the cause of inflation, it has little to say about the *cause* of the cause—and there is where real trouble lies.

37 Central banking systems do not create excess money for the fun of it. They create it because they are under intense political and economic pressure to do so. It is the source of this pressure that should concern us, if we're going to find solutions that will work in the real world.

38 Next come the fiscalists.

39 The fiscalists believe the cause of inflation is rapid growth of government deficits. An "enlightened" fiscalist might qualify that statement to say that inflation results only from deficits incurred when an economy is booming. Lately, however, we have had both deficits and inflation when the economy was in a recession. This leaves the enlightened fiscalists with a lot to explain.

40 Finally, there are the Keynesians.

41 The Keynesians believe inflation develops when the private sector expands too rapidly. In a sense, the Keynesians are the other side of the fiscalist coin. Both groups see inflation resulting when one sector of an economy expands so rapidly that its needs outrun the available supplies of capital. There is an important clue here.

42 Let's take a closer look at the effects of a capital "shortage"—and by "capital" I mean the funds and credit that represent real wealth.

43 A relative shortage of capital bids up the price of capital. That is, interest rates go up. High interest rates squeeze some sectors of the economy sooner than others. The housing industry is especially hard hit by high interest rates.

44 The people who are hurt most by the shortage of capital raise hell about it. This pressure frequently pushes the national government into expanding the money supply; that is, into causing inflation. It's the easy way out.

45 Why is inflation the easy way out? Well, first it tends to spread around the effects of the capital shortage, so the damage is not so visible. And second, it creates an illusion of prosperity.

46 This illusion of prosperity in the early stages of an inflation has three characteristics:

> The groups that were suffering most from tight money will gain temporary relief, until interest rates go up again.
> The groups that *will* suffer most from inflation do not notice the effects for awhile.

47 Political pressure isn't the sole reason for expanding the money supply on such occasions. The authorities often feel that trouble in an important sector like housing will spread through the economy and cause a recession. So they reason like this: If we can prevent a recession by creating new money, then the economy will grow faster. If productive capacity grows enough, then the additional money won't cause inflation. "Goods" and "money" will be back in balance.

48 That is a very seductive rationalization. In fact, it's the rationalization that got us where we are today.

49 The trouble with that line of reasoning is this: The economy seldom manages to grow fast enough to catch up with the expansion of the money supply. And soon, the resulting inflation itself begins to retard growth.

50 Those early complaints caused by the initial capital shortage are like the hiss of the safety valve on a boiler. The economy is signaling that it cannot grow any faster, that the pressure is dangerously high.

51 Trying to "stimulate" the economy with new money at such times is like "fixing" your boiler by throwing more coal on the fire and shutting off the safety valve.

52 There is only one safe way to relieve the pressure on capital-short sectors on the economy: You have to reduce the demand for capital in some other sector. What you already have can be shifted around. But more cannot be created out of thin air.

53 Now we're getting very close to the true source of our economic problems. Let's review a little to clarify what comes next.

54 In the beginning I hinted that understanding would come if you could answer two questions: Why is there too much money? And, why are there too few goods?

55 I believe you can see now why there is too much money. The government creates it in a vain attempt to compensate for a capital shortage that is hampering production.

56 Why are there too few goods? Because of that capital shortage. Because the goods-producing part of the economy—the private sector—is starved for capital.

57 Now we have answered both of those key questions. And the answers lead us to a third question: Why is the private sector starved for capital?

58 The finger of suspicion points to the public sector, the government. Think of it this way: Suppose that all economic growth is caused by a magic powder which I'll call "growth stuff." Before growth can occur, this powder must be sprinkled over the place where growth is wanted—just like fertilizer.

59 This magic powder is difficult and time-consuming to make, so the supply cannot be expanded rapidly. The manufacturing facilities for the powder are all in the private sector of the economy.

60 If you controlled the supply of this powder, you could decide how the economy would grow. But you would have to make choices:

Sprinkle it evenly over both the public and the private sectors and each grows slowly.

Sprinkle it over the public sector alone and the public sector grows rapidly while the private sector stagnates.

Use it on the private sector alone and that grows while the public sector marks time.

61 Looks like six of one, half-dozen of the other, doesn't it? But there *is* a very important difference. If you use all of the growth stuff on the public sector, then the production of everything slows down in the private sector, *including the production of growth stuff itself.*

62 On the other hand, if you use most of the growth stuff on the private sector, then the production of growth stuff speeds up. Eventually you'll have more to spread around; more for the public sector, too. But it takes time.

63 You can create the illusion of a bigger supply of growth stuff by diluting the powder with an inactive ingredient. But that reduces its strength proportionately. Then you have to use more of it to get the same result. That's inflation.

64 The "growth stuff" is capital of course. And lately, we have been using more and more of the supply on the public sector, on government.

65 In 1929, federal, state, and local expenditures combined amounted to just about 10 percent of the Gross National Product. Today, combined government spending is well over a third of GNP. And that is only the visible part of the iceburg. Government regulatory activity levies enormous hidden charges on the private sector.

66   My own company produces coal, to use a familiar example. Coal has gone from $10 per ton in 1973 to $27 per ton today. The two biggest factors in that price rise have been the increased cost of the taxes we pay and the decrease in productivity due to federal regulations.

67   So the government sector of the economy has expanded enormously, both visibly and invisibly. And this expansion has diverted to the public sector resources that are also needed in the private sector.

68   Remember, what you have can be shifted around.

69   Now the private sector is in trouble, starved for capital. It needs help. There are two ways to provide that help, one real and the other illusory.

70   The real way to provide help is to shift resources—capital—growth stuff—back from the bloated public sector to the hungry private sector. Doing that requires a net reduction in total governmental expenditures. But the politicians consider this method politically impossible. And maybe it is.

71   The illusory way to provide relief for the private sector is inflation, as we have seen.

72   Inflation will be with us until most Americans realize that we are paying in three ways for all of the government services we have voted ourselves. One of these forms of payment is taxes, which everyone knows. The other two are unemployment and inflation. These last two forms of payment are much less familiar, and that's a big part of the problem.

73   We may really want and need the additional government services; or at least, some of them. That's a political question, not an economic one. But if we want them, we should be willing to face their true costs.

74   And I believe, too, that it's time to ask ourselves if many of the things we have turned to government to do could not be done with greater efficiency by the private sector. Isn't it possible that the pendulum has swung too far?

75   We have two bad habits when it comes to judging government projects. One of them is that we tend to be fascinated by the size and the drama of gargantuan government undertakings. The other of these bad habits is that we tend to look only at the *benefits* of a government program, while forgetting first to subtract the *costs*. *All* of the costs.

76   Consider the Aswan dam, in Egypt. It was built—at enormous expense—to control the flooding of the lower Nile and to produce hydroelectric power, which it does.

77   But it was the flooding of the Nile that fertilized the fields of the Egyptian farmer. Without the floods, the farmers must use chemical fertilizer. The production of chemical fertilizer uses great quantities of electricity. So a lot of the electric power from the dam is going to meet the increased need for electricity created by building the dam.

78 That's a classic example of the kind of government project that accomplishes at a high expenditure of capital a result that could have been attained by leaving well enough alone. And I hasten to add that this sophisticated level of futility can be attained—and is often attained—without the use of concrete and steel.

79 Search our own federal budget and you'll find many of these "Aswan dams"—enormously expensive attempts to accomplish at the federal level things that could be done with greater efficiency at the state, local, or private level. And things that shouldn't be done at all. But that's another speech.

80 Do we know what causes inflation? The answer is, we all do. As Pogo said, "We have met the enemy and it is us."

81 We cause inflation by believing we can vote ourselves government benefits and let the other guy pay for them.

82 Inflation is that "other guy" handing us the bill.

THE JUPITER EFFECT

Wayne Cooksey

Wayne Cooksey, a student at East Central Oklahoma State University, delivered this speech in a college oratorical contest. He develops a proposition of prediction: the possibility of our world experiencing a far reaching natural catastrophe in 1982.

To develop this prediction, Cooksey relies upon two principle sources: a book by John Gribbin and Stephen Plagemann, *The Jupiter Effect,* and the last book in the Bible, *Revelation.* The book of *Revelation* is essentially used to give added credibility to the argument of the two scientists who authored *The Jupiter Effect.* Cooksey's technique is to inform his listeners of the scientific predictions that Gribbin and Plagemann make and to provide reasonable bases for their predictions. In assessing this part of the speech you will want to determine if he cites sufficient data supporting each of the phenomena that Gribbin and Plageman predict will happen. Do you think that he manipulates this data skillfully? The second part of the speech is of course interesting in that various people from time to time have contended that the times are such that the prophecies found in *Revelations* are about to come to pass. Cooksey, however, is one of the few people who has sought to relate these predictions to scientific data. How effectively does he do this?

Propositions of prediction can of course never be demonstrated with certainty. The best the speaker can do is to create an atmosphere of plausibility. After reading this speech, would you take a vacation in San Francisco in 1982?

This speech is reprinted by permission of the Interstate Oratorical Association from *Winning Orations*, 1979, pp. 86-88.

1   Destruction, radiation, famine, death—our world's military experts have long conceded that any nuclear war, regardless of how limited, would result in irreparable damage and countless deaths. Recently, however, our scientists may have unearthed a grim new possibility—the possibility of our world experiencing a far reaching natural catastrophe!

2   In their book entitled *The Jupiter Effect,* published in 1974, authors John Gribbin, a doctor of astrophysics and a science editor for *Nature* magazine, and Stephen Plagemann, a doctor of physics and a research scientist for both the United States Geological Survey team and for NASA's Goddard Space Center, have concluded that Earth may face a devastating series of events in the fall and early winter of 1982. Each of these events by themselves would create a noticeable disturbance; however, collectively they could spell widespread destruction for our world. In order to back up this gloomy prediction, these two scientists note recent findings in such fields as solar and planetary astronomy, meteorology and geophysics.

3   The first phenomenon discussed by Gribbin and Plagemann is the Tidal Peak Date. Noting the research of Professor K. D. Wood, the November 10, 1972, issue of *Nature* magazine reported that these peak dates regularly occur every 11.08 years and are characterized by minor volcanic activity and earthquakes of varying intensities. From more extensive studies conducted by Dr. H. R. Shaw, a member of the U.S. Geological Survey team, the May 29, 1970, issue of *Science* magazine suggested that the Earth's molten inner core, like the surface oceans, is constantly in motion, and that when the movement of the inner core matches the movement of the surface oceans, a tidal peak date occurs. Each time a peak date has occurred since 1605, there has been a major earthquake recorded. The last such quake struck in the San Fernando Valley of Southern California on February 9, 1971. According to the 1976 World Almanac it registered only 6.5 on the Richter scale, but it resulted in 65 deaths, over 5,000 hospitalized injuries and more than 600 million dollars in property damages.

4   The second phenomenon discussed by Gribbin and Plagemann is the sunspot peak date. A 1965 issue of *Nature* magazine reported that these peaks regularly occur every 11.05 years. The main consequences of this particular activity include major disruptions in the world's communication systems, drastic changes in weather patterns, and earthquakes of sometimes severe intensity. In fact, in a report prepared by the National Oceanic Laboratories in 1972, it was noted that eight of the ten largest earthquakes occurring in the San Francisco Bay area, in Northern California, since 1836, have come within two years following a period of maximum solar activity. Of these eight, the most famous is the Great San Francisco Earthquake which occurred on April

18, 1906, and registered at least 8.3 on the Richter scale. This quake occurred only 30 days following a sunspot peak date. Professor Wood further claims that during these activity periods, the Earth is bombarded with massive doses of solar radiation, but so far the upper ionosphere has been able to protect the delicate world below.

5   The third and probably the most devastating phenomenon is the Grand Alignment. Gribbin and Plagemann have pointed out that normal planetary alignments regularly occur every 179 years and are characterized by volcanic activity, droughts and earthquakes! They have explained that during these times all nine planets of the solar system are simply aligned on the same side of the sun and are not scattered about the normal 360° orbital plane. In the science section of the September 4, 1974, issue of *Newsweek* magazine, however, it was noted that unlike these past planetary alignments, the 1982 Grand Alignment will, in fact, see for the first time all nine planets on a straight plane! This Grand Alignment will cause huge storms of sunspots and solar flares, drastic changes in our world's temperature and rainfall patterns, an actual slowing down of the Earth's rotation, as well as numerous earthquakes of both small and sizable proportions. Gribbin and Plagemann have further claimed that we will experience destructive changes in the upper ionosphere, a reversal of normal wind patterns and a worldwide series of volcanic eruptions triggered by what they feel will be the strongest earthquakes ever to be recorded in mankind's history.

6   Now these scientific predictions for 1982 are not solely contemporary. In fact, certain Biblical scholars, who are "commonly" referred to as premillennialists, believe that the book of the *Revelation* contains many predictions of events that are yet to be fulfilled.

7   One of the major passages supported by this group, is found in the 16th chapter and the 18th verse. For in this passage is the description of a great earthquake "such as was not since men were upon the earth." When we consider the earthquake causing potential powers in the tidal and sunspot peak dates, and the Grand Alignment, we begin to see just how this scripture could be fulfilled. Gribbin and Plagemann warn us that "Earth will already be reeling under the effects of the tidal and sunspot peak dates, as she passes through the counter-acting pull of the sun and the inner planets and the pull of the outer giants," during the Grand Alignment in 1982.

8   Another major passage supported by premillenialists, is found in the 9th chapter and the 2nd verse. For in this passage it is stated that, " . . . there arose a great smoke out of the pit, and the sun and the air was darkened." During the last planetary alignment of 1803, there were several volcanic eruptions noted in various parts of the world. These eruptions resulted in large amounts of smoke and volcanic ash that were noticed above many of the inhabited areas of the world. Gribbin and Plagemann predict that the 1982

alignment will, in fact, cause an even greater number of volcanic eruptions, releasing enough smoke and ash to actually filter out a sizable portion of the sun's light.

9 The book of the *Revelation* goes on to describe a possible drought. In the 11th chapter and the 6th verse, it was predicted that there would be ". . . power given to shut heaven, that it rain not. . . ." Both the sunspot peak activities and the planetary alignments have created drought conditions in past years. Gribbin and Plagemann have correlated information concerning recent sunspot peaks with the planetary alignment of 1803, and have predicted that the events of 1982 could create severe drought conditions. These conditions could result in shortages of both food and water. Still other key Biblical passages include: ". . . power was given (presumedly to the sun) to scorch men with a great heat. . . ." (Rev. 16:8) ". . . a third part of the trees and all green grass were burnt up. . . ." (Rev. 8:7) and "there fell . . . grievous sores upon the men. . . ."((Rev. 16:2). These scriptures are supported by the observations of Professor Wood who claims that extreme solar heat and massive doses of solar radiation, could in fact, create conditions very similar to those described in these Biblical passages.

10 Now the mere citation of a possible chain of events, of course, does not establish their actual certainty. Nowhere in either the scientific findings or Biblical scriptures is there any statement of world-ending destruction resulting from these events. But when scientific researchers and Biblical scholars come to agreement on something, something that can effect my well being, I take notice. One thing is certain, I definitely won't be taking my vacation in San Francisco in 1982.

CHEMOPHOBIA, POLITICS AND DISTORTED IMAGES

James N. Sites

James N. Sites, Vice President for Communications of Chemical Manufacturers Association, delivered this speech before the Chemical Communications Association in New York City, October 15, 1980. The address seeks to establish that the "facts" used by the news media in dealing with chemical waste problems are so distorted that they have resulted in "chemophobia."

The speaker proceeds basically by example. He cites one example after another where figures used by the news media were grossly exaggerated, and he argues that these distorted images have reflected adversely upon the chemical industry. As you assess this speech, you will want to ask if these examples effectively establish the speaker's point. Quotations are frequently used also. Again, do they make the speaker's point credible? Has the speaker, in other words, cited adequate evidence to prove his point to the average listener?

The speaker's style has a strong narrative dimension. Do you find that this use of narrative gives the speech the quality of energy and movement? What other interest factors do you find in the speech? Why is the quality of interest important to this speech?

This speech is reprinted from *Vital Speeches of the Day,* December 15, 1980, pp. 151-154.

1 A few years ago a couple of *Wall Street Journal* reporters did a remarkable study of news coverage of the anti-ballistic missile controversy, the automobile emissions debate and allegations of an oil industry energy crisis "conspiracy." They found that in such complex subject areas, press corps attitudes are frequently shaped by what they termed someone's "initial simplistic explanation." The reporters (one of whom has since become *Journal* editor) concluded that this tends to shape reporting for months to come, despite the best efforts to show it may be demonstrably *wrong.*

2 The chemical industry today finds itself up against a similar wall of frustrated communications. News reporters are being used, and the nation's news channels are being abused, by people with political axes to grind. As a result, this essential million-person industry finds itself enmeshed in a web of myths, misrepresentations, distortions and outright fabrications.

3 We—the press most of all—must recognize these for what they are. The reason is that the state of communication about our industry affects public perceptions about us—and these affect our sales, profits, research and product development capabilities, our ability to invest and expand to meet public needs.

4 Above all, public perceptions affect public policies toward us and the intensity of government regulation. In this respect, all Washington is divided into three parts: government, special interests and the news media. It's the *interaction* among these three that determines what kind of public policies will be created and how they will be implemented.

5 Unfortunately, the chemical industry has been on the losing end of this process for a long time. Such tragic incidents as Love Canal have made it almost impossible to get a balanced hearing on chemical risks and benefits—from press and politicians alike.

6 There are genuine problems involving chemicals and we're the first to admit this. However, we also know that these problems can be solved and that the nation can continue to reap the enormous benefits it derives from chemistry. What we object to in terms of communication, then, is the almost totally negative coverage you see of this industry—to the extent that a climate of chemophobia is being generated in the public domain. We run into this throughout Washington—this state of public anxiety that borders on hysteria—that then stampedes government into action that may or may not be

realistic or related to real-fact situations. Debate this year on the Administration's proposed multi-billion-dollar "superfund" legislation has directly reflected this climate.

7 The point is, though, this is hardly an accidental development. To cite some specific examples:

8 Case Number One might be called the EPA "numbers game." As CMA's vice president and technical director, Dr. Geraldine Cox, recently pointed out, the number of hazardous waste disposal sites that require remedial action is one of the largest guessing games in the country today.

9 The number most commonly used is based on the Environmental Protection Agency's Hart Study. An EPA consultant in 60 days visited 24 sites, developed partial information on 232 sites, then extrapolated to the values of 35,000 to 50,000 sites. Sheer sleight-of-hand magic!

10 The Hart report was thoroughly discredited by Rep. Bob Eckhardt's (D-Tex.) Subcommittee on Oversight and Investigation of the Interstate and Foreign Commerce Committee, which conducted extensive hearings on hazardous waste disposal last fall. The subcommittee concluded:

"The estimate of the number of sites and the degree of hazard they pose is little better than pure guesswork and thus the cleanup estimates are unreliable."

11 In an obvious effort to increase the number of sites that could be classified as hazardous, EPA Deputy Administrator Barbara Blum sent out a memorandum to regional administrators last November which states:

"All potential hazardous waste sites or incidents must be listed on the regional logs. This is true regardless of whether the initial identification of a potential site or incident comes from government sources, the media, or technically unsophisticated citizens complaints. This comprehensive approach is required to protect the integrity and usefulness of the system and to provide assurances to the public that EPA is responding to this critical problem. Some regions have adopted a policy of adding sites to their logs only after a determination has been made that a hazardous waste problem actually exists. This policy must be changed to conform to the national model."

12 In testimony in Congress, EPA's Steffen Plehn recently admitted that there are probably between 1,000 and 2,000 sites in the United States that require remedial action. That hardly tracks with the 30,000 to 50,000 that we hear about so frequently—yet EPA goes on using the larger figures.

13   Last winter, CMA asked state environmental offices what they knew about disposal sites and how many abandoned dumps were being located. Preliminary results in February from inventories then underway showed 33 states identifying 4,196 waste disposal sites. Some 431 were classified as potentially hazardous. The states found 174 "orphan" or abandoned sites where owners no longer existed or could not be identified.

14   Now, why is it important to establish a credible number of dump sites? Because this defines the size of the problem. Knowing how big the problem is should enable people to scale solutions to fit the need. But the bigger the number, the bigger the fund EPA can then ask from Congress. And that is what the numbers game is all about. . . .

15   On top of this kind of "numerology" has come a whole barrage of other myths related to Administration and environmentalist efforts to get Superfund passed this year:

—For example, the chemical industry is being continually accused of opposing or "stonewalling" legislation to clean up hazardous dump sites. Not so. The industry has been trying for over a year to get legislation passed to deal with the critical problem of *orphan* dump sites—one critical problem area not covered by existing government programs.

—Another myth is that the chemical industry is unwilling to pay its share of waste clean-up costs. False again. We have stated repeatedly that we're willing to pay a fair share of such costs—but we object strenuously to being saddled with the total bill for this society-wide problem.

—Then there's the related fallacy that chemicals somehow are the only hazardous polluter around. The fact is that this industry is only *1 of 17* that generate hazardous wastes—not to mention the government itself, the military, hospitals, etc.

—Another distortion is that the chemical industry is responsible for the so-called "midnight dumpers" you occasionally see ballyhooed on television and elsewhere. Yet as Rep. Eckhardt's Congressional survey pointed out, the 53 largest chemical companies that comprise the bulk of the industry have disposed of 94 percent of all their process wastes on their own property. And they know where over 99 percent of all their waste has gone.

16   More on the "numbers game." The Surgeon General recently put out a report on the health effects of toxic pollution. Again, even after EPA itself admits the numbers are pure guesswork, the Surgeon General picked up the same old figures and gave them renewed stature—and circulation.

17   *Time* magazine, for one, picked up the Surgeon General's report and used it in a major waste disposal story. Vividly portrayed on the cover was a man sinking into a chemical pool, normal above the ooze but a skeleton below. A dramatic boost for chemophobes!

18 Not long ago the ABC Network did an update of an hour-long TV "documentary" that was produced a year ago called "The Killing Ground." This, let me assure you, is a hair-raiser. It's downright scary.

19 But ABC's promotion for the program ran a close second. Presumably seeking to build an audience, ads appeared across the country with headlines shouting:

> "Oh, beautiful, for spacious skies, for amber waves of dioxin, chloroform, trichloroethylene, carbon tetrachloride, benzene . . ."

20 And the body copy began:

> "There are over 50,000 chemical dumpsites across America." [Heard that figure before?] "All contain" [note that word, *all*] "toxic wastes, including known cancer-causing agents and chemicals causing birth defects and death to man and the environment."

21 Pure theater! When we saw that ad, CMA President Roland sent this telegram to the top officials of ABC:

> "Statements in your network's advertisement promoting the program, "The Killing Ground: An Update," are flagrant distortions of fact and a grave disservice to public understanding in this field. I am deeply concerned that the program will further distort an already misshapen picture of the scope of the nation's hazardous waste problem"

22 Our wire took issue with the specific misrepresentations about cancer-causing agents and the 50,000 dump sites, went on to point out that EPA itself had said this figure was not valid, then ended:

> "If your program promotion can make such misrepresentations, we shudder to think what the program itself will do. We therefore urge you to correct this situation in the public's interest."

23 The result? None. No reply, not even an acknowledgment of receipt of our wire. And I guess we'll have a long wait to see any corrective communication to the nation.

24 Again, the point is that public impressions are being shaped by such distorted approaches—to the public's detriment.

25 "The Valley of the Drums" is another sad case. When that story first broke out of Louisville, Kentucky, an EPA staff person was asked on the scene to make an estimate of the number of barrels of chemicals on the site. His guess of 100,000 drums was picked up by reporting services, and that's what you've seen again and again throughout the nation. Even a normally reliable publication like the *Congressional Quarterly* used this as an illustrated cover story—further adding to the pressure for new controls on industry.

26 Well, the state of Kentucky finally counted the drums. It found 11,000 empty barrels and 5,000 full ones, with half of the full ones containing solids. So down goes the count to 2,500 barrels that could have been hazardous—*not* 100,000. We still haven't seen any news corrections of this. But we live in hope that someone somewhere someday *will* try to set this record straight.

27 Let's look at that word *cancer* again, for if there's one thing that lies at the heart of the national chemophobia scare, it's cancer. Concern over cancer in the workplace ballooned after release of a figure, still being widely quoted, by then-Secretary of Health, Education and Welfare Joseph Califano on September 11, 1978.

28 Citing a study on the incidence of cancer in the U.S. estimated to be attributable to occupational factors, prepared by the National Cancer Institute and the National Institute of Environmental Health Sciences, Califano said, "At least 20 percent of all cancer in the United States and perhaps more may be work-related."

29 Responding, Phillip H. Abelson, editor of *Science* Magazine, pointed out in an editorial on October 5, 1979, that . . .

"The report was attacked by many epidemiologists. Richard Doll, Regius Professor of Medicine at Oxford, wrote, 'I regard it as scientific nonsense.' An editorial in the British medical journal *Lancet* criticized the report, concluding with, 'It is sad to see such a fragile report under such distinguished names.' "

30 Dr. Phillip Handler, president of the National Academy of Sciences, recently set the record straight this way:

"Only one or two percent of cancers can be traced to occupational exposure in such workplaces as coal mines, asbestos mines and factories; pollutants of all sorts may contribute to—rather than cause—perhaps five percent of all cancers.

"Indeed the United States is not suffering an 'epidemic of cancer,' it is experiencing an 'epidemic of life'—in that an ever-greater fraction of the population survives to the advanced ages at which cancer has always been prevalent."

31 The *Washington Star* on September 15 carried a UPI story out of New York City quoting Dr. Michael Shimkin, professor of community medicine at the University of California at San Diego, as saying that the way we live—the general pattern of modern life—probably has more to do with cancer incidence than anything else. To avoid cancer, according to UPI, he recommends six steps:

—Do not smoke tobacco or substitutes.
—Do not drink alcohol, or at least not to excess.
—Eat sparingly, a "prudent" diet.
—Avoid unnecessary X-rays.
—Avoid excessive sun exposure.
—Avoid inappropriate drug intake.

32 Distortions on cancer figures go on, even so. Another big Washington study purporting to be authoritative came out this summer from the Toxic Substances Strategy Committee, which includes representatives of 18 federal agencies with major research or regulatory responsibilities over toxic substances. The chairman of the group, Gus Speth of the President's Council on Environmental Quality, again rested his case on that discredited 20 percent figure. And this despite all the scientific opinion that it was totally invalid.

33 When you see this pattern of questionable conclusions coming out of official sources in Washington, you begin to wonder what's going on here? You note how the studies come out in a neatly phased timetable. Recalling the appointment to top government posts of many activists from environmental organizations, you begin to wonder if certain people are using positions of public trust to advance personal biases—and trying to stampede Congress into enacting legislation like Superfund. I haven't seen many reporters asking such questions; perhaps they're missing the real story by not doing so.

34 The other day the *Washington Post,* which has consistently given heavy play to chemical stories all this year, carried a report under a Mexico City dateline headed, "Chemicals Dumped Near Puerto Rico Result in Dominican Republic Deaths." A reporter named Marlise Simons wrote:

"A mysterious discharge of highly toxic chemicals in the Caribbean off the northern coast of Puerto Rico has caused two deaths in the Dominican Republic and poisoned millions of fish in one of the world's richest fishing grounds."

35 The lurid details follow, underlining this key point:

"There is rising concern that the poisoned waters will be carried northwest toward the Bahamas and the Florida coast, where American and other fishing fleets work important fishing grounds."

36 The Associated Press looked into this story and put this follow-up report on its wire:

> "Toxic chemicals were *not* responsible for the deaths of thousands of fish in the Caribbean off the Dominican Republic, the EPA said Tuesday."

37 After providing background details, AP continued:

> "An EPA team said it could find no measurable levels of toxic chemicals in the water, and said the fish kill could not be attributable to a single or combination of industrial pollution sources.
>
> "The EPA concluded that unusually large algae blooms in the area were the likely cause of the fish kill, which it said did not reach the magnitude of 'millions,' as reported."

38 The *Post,* to its credit, does occasionally take a second look at things—as in the case of a story early this year on testing by the Du Pont Company of black employees for sickle cell traits. The implication was that this was being done by the company unilaterally. Upon learning of the fact that Du Pont was responding to these employees' request, the *Post* wrote an editorial saying:

> "As it turns out, our sources were wrong. We owe Du Pont an apology, herewith rendered."

39 Time hardly permits getting into all the mixed-up studies and reporting the nation has been subjected to on Love Canal. On Friday, a high-level report came out questioning highly publicized studies EPA had had done alleging chromosome damage and other health effects among Canal residents. A group headed by Dr. Lewis Thomas, chancellor of the Memorial Sloan-Kettering Cancer Center, said in a report to New York Governor Carey that scientific studies of the area to date have been inadequate. It said there had been no findings of acute health effects, such as clinical poisonings, and chronic effects of hazardous waste exposure, such as birth defects or cancer, have neither been established nor ruled out in a rigorously scientific manner.

40 I think the *Wall Street Journal* did the public a distinct service on June 19 when it ran a long Op Ed piece and editorial on Love Canal. This was one of the first real attempts to look behind the clouds of guilty-as-charged emotion on this issue and find out the facts. Unlike most of the news media, the *Journal* simply did what reporters normally take pride in doing: It asked penetrating questions and reported *the other side* of the controversy.

41 What the news media are finally coming to discover is that while the much-maligned Hooker Chemical Company put the *chemicals* into this waste site, it was public authority that put the *people* there. And while Hooker sealed off this site in an environmentally sound manner, it was public authority that allowed the seal to be broken, permitting release of toxic wastes into the surroundings.

42 Perhaps one should not be too hard on the press for faulty coverage of such a complex situation, or of the other involved issues concerning this high-technology industry. Dr. Etcyl Blair of the Dow Chemical Company recently said in a speech:

> "The press, which is generally not conversant with scientific matters, generally prefers the rather simplistic answer—the one it can understand over one that is complex and difficult. But the role of the press also is to seek the truth. And its problem is the same one I mentioned in the beginning—there is my truth and yours and his, and the press has a terrible time distinguishing between them. Very often it doesn't even know the right questions to ask. We need a great deal of patience with the press—the willingness to spend a lot of time with them and the willingness to risk being harpooned from time to time.
>
> "Unless we are willing to do this, the press will continue to reflect in a dominant way the thoughts and opinions of those in the scientific field who *are* willing to spend time 'educating' the representatives of the press. And I am not sure we want that."

43 This is one reason why the chemical industry has mounted the public information effort we call ChemCAP. We think that both the press and the public deserve a lot better than "initial simplistic explanations." This industry is doing some great things in managing hazardous wastes, curbing pollution, improving product safety, worker safety and transport safety—and we think people have a right to know about these constructive developments. Perverse perceptions to the contrary, here is a responsible industry responding positively to public concerns.

44 The real meaning of all this to the nation? We must recognize that chemophobia undermines not just the chemical industry and its contributions to people but, at bottom, reflects an attack on chemists and chemistry itself. It is part of an anti-science, anti-technology, anti-growth mood which, unless checked, could have devastating consequences for our nation and our future.

45 We intend to do our part to keep this from happening. We feel there is no need to make exclusionary choices between extremes. In chemicals, as elsewhere, we *can* have both progress and environmental protection. All of us—chemical workers included—are environmentalists in seeking this goal.

We all breathe the same air and drink the same water and use the same earth. The problem today may well be many of the *professional* environmentalists who staff activist organizations and many appointive government positions—and who seem to specialize in creating and magnifying issues to show what a great job they are doing.

46 As a former Washington reporter, I can attest to the fact that this fair city must surely be the one place on earth where sound travels faster than light. Here is a circus of curved mirrors and distorted images, of lights and shadows, of leaks and red herrings—where it daily becomes more difficult to separate fact from fiction. It is hardly strange, then, that reporters often get snared into transmitting to the nation some weird illusions and delusions—or, worse, of being used as pawns in a power game by people seeking to get something out of government.

47 America could probably live with Washington's myriad myths and misrepresentations except that they set the stage for unlimited government expansion at the expense of the private sector—and, eventually, of our freedoms, including freedom of the press. We would like to help prevent that.

48 What we in the chemical business would like to see is a press getting to the real facts behind problems, then reporting them in realistic perspective—so that the public and government can react rationally to situations in terms of their real dimensions and not as mountains built up out of molehills, or vice versa. In essence, we expect no more from the press than the same kind of balanced coverage of our industry that reporters themselves would expect if someone else were reporting on them.

Chapter 5

SPEECHES THAT AFFIRM PROPOSITIONS OF VALUE

Of all the ills that our . . . society is heir to, the focal one . . . is the absence of standards. We are too unsure of ourselves to assert them, to stick by them. . . . We seem to be afflicted by a widespread and eroding reluctance to take any stand on values. . . .

Barbara W. Tuchman

THE NATURE AND IMPORTANCE OF SPEECHES THAT AFFIRM PROPOSITIONS OF VALUE

Noted historian Barbara Tuchman offered the above-quoted generalization concerning American society in 1967 in a speech at the 22nd National Conference on Higher Education. Many Americans even today would agree that her judgment still largely holds true. While citizens may have grown more vocal in expressing their value preferences, dispute and uncertainty pervade the contemporary scene about what values should be basic to a healthy culture. The centrality of values to human existence and to the communication process is acknowledged by Richard M. Weaver, a rhetorical theorist and critic, and by Kenneth Boulding, a social critic and economist. In his *The Ethics of Rhetoric,* Weaver contends, "It is the nature of the conscious life of man to revolve around some concept of value. So true is this that when the concept is withdrawn, or when it is forced into conflict with another concept, the human being suffers an almost intolerable sense of being lost." Boulding, in *The Image,* argues:

. . . The value scales of any individual or organization are perhaps the most important single element determining the effect of the messages it receives on its image of the world. If a message is perceived that is neither good nor bad it may have little or no effect on the image. If it is perceived as bad or hostile to the image which is held, there will be resistance to accepting it.

In contemporary American society, values are very much in conflict. Born of the silent generation, many of today's young Americans are something less than silent in their questioning of the values assumed by their parents. Activists have questioned war as a legitimate method of resolving international disputes, poverty as a necessary consequent of a complex economic order, and civil obedience as an unquestioned obligation of responsible citizenship.

Americans of all ages have become more compellingly aware of their own values. Some have sought to translate new values into working political and economic practices. Others, threatened by the aggressiveness of protest, have reasserted their own traditional values as the appropriate way for civilized community life. Yet out of the debate stimulated by this forced reexamination of values may emerge a better society—a society born of judgment and reflection rather than passiveness and habit. The rhetoric affirming diverse value propositions hopefully would meet Richard Weaver's test of public discourse in its finer moments: ". . . Rhetoric at its truest seeks to perfect men by showing them better versions of themselves, links in that chain extending up toward the ideal. . . ."

Not all propositions of value, however, concern the crucial issues of modern social existence. While some speakers affirm propositions related to war or peace, prosperity, or poverty, and human love or bigotry, others affirm propositions of value related to artistic excellence, academic achievement, or even, via the mass media, the taste of colas and toothpastes. Propositions of value pervade all facets of human life.

Recall that in Chapter 2 we defined a value as a conception of "The Good" or "The Desirable" which functions sometimes as a goal motivating our behavior and sometimes as a standard for evaluating means to achieve ends. You may wish to reread our comments in that chapter explaining the line of critical analysis which asked: "To what degree do the speaker's ideas harmonize with the audience's relevant values?"

Sometimes speakers urge adoption of a new value, or adoption of a new perspective through redefining an old value. Some speakers aim to reinforce and reenergize audience commitment to values already held. Often speakers offer their value judgment of something (such as a book, film, play, or speech) as valid for audience belief. On occasion a speaker must defend his or her character and reputation against criticism. Such a speech of personal defense aims at refuting negative value judgments concerning the speaker's honesty, integrity, ethics, morals, and public responsibility.

Speakers also affirm values in speeches not primarily devoted to values. A speaker presenting information to enhance audience understanding will show that the information is valuable because it is relevant and useful. To generate listener perception of a situation as a problem worthy of their concern, a speaker must show that the situation threatens or violates basic relevant audience values. To secure audience acceptance of a policy as a solution to a problem, a speaker must show that the policy is consistent with or enhances central audience values. And contrary to the popular notion, "facts" do not "speak for themselves." *Humans* present and interpret matters agreed upon as factual in light of their own related values.

Whatever the particular proposition of value, the advocate seeks listener agreement that something meets or does not meet a specific value standard. Unlike the proposition of fact, which is affirmed or denied through tests of existence, occurrence, or causality, the proposition of value is affirmed through tests of *goodness* or *quality*. A value standard may be applied to an individual, an event, an object, a way of life, a process, a condition, or even to another value. Consider the following examples:

Proposition A: Modern art is rubbish.
Proposition B: Sexual chastity before marriage is an outmoded value.
Proposition C: Winston Churchill was a great man.
Proposition D: War is immoral.
Proposition E: A speaker who uses primarily emotional appeals is unethical.
Proposition F: Civil disobedience always is bad.
Proposition G: President Nixon was irresponsible in his handling of the Watergate Affair.

These propositions of value differ in subject matter being valued or devalued. However, each affirms or denies something measured against standards rooted in listener values. Like all propositions of value, those noted above include a word or words that imply a value dimension—"is rubbish," "is an outmoded value," "was a great man," "is immoral," "is unethical," "is bad," "irresponsible." Because the meanings associated with such evaluative terms are deep rooted, saturated with emotion, and wrapped in tradition, the task of the advocate seeking to affirm a proposition of value frequently is an incredibly difficult one. And equally difficult is the task of judging such speeches.

CRITERIA FOR EVALUATING SPEECHES
THAT AFFIRM PROPOSITIONS OF VALUE

1. Has the speaker demonstrated or is it assumed by the audience that he or she is a person of high credibility with respect to the proposition being advocated?

When the speaker leaves the realm of empirically verifiable fact and enters the realm of culturally-based and often abstractly-defined values, the assessment by listeners becomes increasingly dependent on their perceptions of the speaker's expertness and trustworthiness. In stressing the potency of speaker ethos, Aristotle wrote: "As a rule we trust men of probity more and more quickly about things in general, while on points outside the realm of exact knowledge, where opinion is divided, we trust them absolutely."

Listeners tend to believe statements about values and value judgments made by speakers they admire and respect. But different audiences, and cultures, value different qualities in speakers. A college professor of economics arguing that American advertising is unethical may be considered an expert by an audience of high school sophomores, a starry-eyed idealist by an audience of business people, and an extreme liberal by an audience of college Young Republicans.

Although most communication scholars agree that the speaker who is considered by an audience as highly credible has an advantage over the speaker whose ethos is low, they do not always agree on the exact factors determining speaker prestige. In *Principles of Speaking,* for example, Hance, Ralph, and Wiksell list *competence,* which "grows out of a combination of mental ability, know-how, intelligence, understanding' experience with the subject, and knowledge"; *good character,* which is "made up of honesty, integrity, sincerity, fairness, and similar qualities that meet the standards of the listeners"; and *good will,* which "consists of friendliness, likeableness, rapport, warmth, and being 'in' with the audience." In *The Art of Persuasion,* Minnick includes confidence and poise, physical energy, sincerity and conviction, mental alertness, intelligence and knowledge, fairness and justice, self-discipline, even temper and restraint, sympathy and understanding, decisiveness, dynamism, and similarity to audience values and beliefs. For further discussion of the importance of source credibility, you may want to read again in Chapter 2 the line of critical inquiry which asked: "To what degree is the speaker perceived as a highly credible source on the subject?"

Among the questions you may wish to ask about the advocate of a proposition of value are these: Is the speaker a person who embodies the qualities of character, intelligence, and experience most admired by the audience? Does the speaker's life demonstrate commitment to the value she or he advocates or applies? Does the speaker have the training and experience to qualify for making the value judgment expressed?

2. Has the speaker advanced acceptable criteria for the assessment of the proposition of value?

The criteria for assessing a proposition of value differ from those for assessing a proposition of fact. The criteria for the latter are essentially empirical or quasi-empirical, whereas those for the former are steeped in feelings and related values. For example, consider the following propositions:

Proposition of fact: Capital punishment is not an effective deterrent to crime.

Proposition of value: Capital punishment is morally bad.

In the first case, widely accepted criteria for judgment involve tests of empirical reality. Has capital punishment led to a reduction in serious crimes in states where it has been tried? Do states with capital punishment have lower rates of serious crimes than equivalent states that do not have capital punishment? Have carefully controlled, systematic studies demonstrated that potential criminals consider the consequences of their crimes before committing them? In the second instance, the criteria for judgment are rooted in earlier value commitments. Is the taking of human life, for whatever cause, contrary to values fundamental to the Judeo-Christian ethic, to human decency, or to communal life?

In attempting to gain acceptance of a proposition of value, a speaker has a number of rhetorical options available for stressing the appropriateness of his or her value criteria. The speaker can show that the value standards used or values advocated are consistent with other values already held by the audience. The speaker might show that the value advocated has produced desirable consequences in the past when adhered to; this involves using *another* value standard to demonstrate "desirability." Sometimes speakers use examples and testimony to show that "good" persons generally have accepted the advocated value and "bad" or less desirable persons have rejected it. Or the value being advocated may be *contrasted* with its undesirable opposite (disvalue) or with a less desirable value. And some speakers offer to an audience a *hierarchy* of values by verbally indicating that the value advocated or defended is *better than* other specific values. Finally, a speaker might argue that socially undesirable consequences will result from continued adherence to old, outmoded values.

Speakers need not fail when their value judgments run counter to the values of the audience. When in 1932 Franklin D. Roosevelt spoke to San Francisco's Commonwealth Club, a group of businessmen with conservative economic values, he began with a careful historical review of the values that had produced industrial America. Then he pointed out that these values had served the nation well but were no longer consistent with our best national interest. In 1886, Southerner Henry W. Grady, in an address to members of the New England Society, sought to erase their long- standing hostility toward the South by praising the spirit of Lincoln and by urging commitment to national values rather than to regional loyalties. Admittedly persuading about values is a complex task, but it is one which a perceptive and sensitive speaker can accomplish to some degree.

In evaluating a speech affirming a proposition of value, the enlightened listener must carefully consider the criteria for judgment that he or she is being asked to accept. Is the value advocated for acceptance or application clearly and exactly specified? Does the speaker demonstrate that the value is reasonable and relevant for the subject at hand? Is the value or value judgment only asserted or implied without clear and reasonable support or demonstration?

3. *Has the speaker presented a fair view of what is being evaluated?*

It should be apparent that a speaker may be eminently qualified to judge and may have acceptable criteria of judgment in mind and yet may have a distorted view of what is being judged. Propositions of value usually are emotion-laden and a speaker's bias may impair her or his ability to depict fairly the object being judged.

Propositions of value often depend on the previous acceptance or establishment of a proposition of fact. Thus the critic must consider whether the advocate has met adequate criteria for the assessment of fact that portrays what the advocate is judging. Should the speaker be interested in evaluating an event, we first must be assured that the event has been portrayed accurately. Similarly, should the speaker wish to assign a value to a work of art, a belief, an individual, an institution, an action, or another value, we should inquire about the accuracy with which the object being judged is described. Faced with an object described in two-valued, either-or, no-middle-ground terms, the critical listener must consider whether such a description is accurate and adequate for the situation.

CONCLUSION

Because values play such an important role in decisions related to individual and social well-being, the enlightened listener/critic must consider carefully the evaluative messages received each day. In assessing speeches that affirm propositions of value, the critic should consider (1) *whether the speaker is a person of high credibility with respect to the proposition being advocated,* (2) *whether the speaker has advanced acceptable criteria for the assessment of the proposition, and* (3) *whether the speaker has presented a fair view of what is being evaluated.*

Andersen, Kenneth E. *Persuasion.* 2nd ed. Allyn and Bacon, 1978. Chapter 11 probes the influence of a persuader's credibility.

Baker, Virgil L., and Eubanks, Ralph T. *Speech in Personal and Public Affairs.* McKay, 1965. Chapter 6 analyzes speech as a civilizing force in society and presents concrete suggestions for advocating values. Some of our advice has been adapted from this source.

Condon, John C., and Yousef, Fathi S. *An Introduction to Intercultural Communication.* Bobbs-Merrill, 1975. Chapters 3 and 4 examine the functioning of values in various non-American cultures and between different cultures.

Ehninger, Douglas, Alana H. Monroe, and Bruce E. Gronbeck. *Principles and Types of Speech Communication.* 8th ed. Scott, Foresman, 1978. pp. 381–384 suggest criteria for analyzing speeches of self-defense (apologia; self-justification).

Hance, Kenneth G.; Ralph, David C.; and Milton J. Wiksell. *Principles of Speaking.* 3rd ed. Wadsworth, 1975. Chapter 5 examines the nature and role of a speaker's ethos/credibility.

Harrell, Jackson; Ware, B. L.; and Linkugel, Wil A. "Failure of Apology in American Politics: Nixon on Watergate." *Speech Monographs,* November 1975, 245–61. Analyzes Nixon's first two Watergate speeches from the perspective of the bases of political authority and the theory of apology.

McEdwards, Mary G. "American Values: Circa 1920–1970." *Quarterly Journal of Speech,* April 1971, pp. 173–80. Illustrates how basic American values have remained relatively constant.

Minnick, Wayne C. *The Art of Persuasion.* 2nd ed. Houghton Mifflin, 1968, pp. 215–21. Outlines and categorizes basic American values.

Monroe, Alan, and Ehninger, Douglas. *Principles and Types of Speech Communication.* 7th ed. Scott, Foresman, 1974. Written by R. L. Johannesen, pp. 245–46 and 249–57 discuss the nature of source credibility, examine the role of value systems, and describe general value orientations of both "traditional" and "countercultural" American value stances.

Rieke, Richard D., and Sillars, Malcolm O. *Argumentation and the Decision Making Process.* Wiley, 1975, Chapter 6. After explaining the nature of values, the authors describe in detail six traditional and nontraditional American value systems.

Rokeach, Milton. *The Nature of Human Values.* Macmillan, 1970. A theoretical discussion of what values are and an empirical description of major contemporary American value commitments.

Sproule, J. Michael. *Argument.* McGraw-Hill, 1980. Chapter 6 examines the process of value judgmental argumentation.

Walter, Otis M. *Speaking Intelligently.* Macmillan, 1976, pp. 131–49, 228–30. The author focuses on the functioning of values in public discourse aimed at problem-solving.

Walter, Otis M., and Scott, Robert L. *Thinking and Speaking.* 4th ed. Macmillan, 1979. pp. 101–106 survey some contemporary American values and Chapter 14 discusses persuading about values.

Ware, B. L., and Linkugel, Wil A. "They Spoke in Defense of Themselves: On the Generic Criticism of Apologia." *Quarterly Journal of Speech.* October 1973, 273–83. Examines the rhetorical strategies and tactics available to speakers in defending their personal character against negative value judgments.

Weaver, Richard M. *The Ethics of Rhetoric.* Regnery, 1953, Chapter 9. Weaver's discussion of "ultimate terms" in the rhetoric of the era illuminates the persuasive potency of values and disvalues as they appear in the form of societal "god terms" and "devil terms."

Williams, Robin M. *American Society: A Sociological Interpretation.* 3rd ed. Knopf, 1970. Chapter 11 explains the nature of values and surveys components of the contemporary American "establishment" value system.

COMMENCEMENT ADDRESS AT DREW UNIVERSITY

Alan Alda

With only thirty-six hours prior notice, Alan Alda delivered this speech on May 19, 1979, at the 111th annual Commencement ceremonies at Drew University, a Methodist-related school in Madison, New Jersey. Alda substituted for the scheduled speaker, the Rev. Jesse Jackson, who had to cancel at the last minute due to illness. The President of the university introduced Alda as the star of the critically acclaimed television series, M*A*S*H, on which Alda portrays Captain Benjamin Franklin "Hawkeye" Pierce. Said the President, "he is also a graduate of Fordham, an army veteran, a writer, producer, at times a television critic, an impassioned supporter of good causes, including the Equal Rights Amendment, and our speaker is justly respected as one of our nation's foremost family men." Following the speech, Alda received a standing ovation and the University awarded him an honorary Doctor of Humane Letters degree.

The typical commencement speech has earned a reputation for dullness, triteness, and irrelevance. But this need not be the case. Creative and sensitive commencement speakers genuinely can praise, inspire, and challenge the graduates rather than bore them with irrelevant examples, cliché phrases, stereotyped images, and sleep-inducing platitudes. Among the expectations that an audience may hold concerning speeches honoring graduates for completion of a course of study are the following. (1) Praise for the collective and individual achievements of the class. (2) An urging to use the knowledge and skills acquired in creative, humane, socially worthy ways. (3) A plea for commitment to the values stressed by the school or to other appropriate values; sometimes these may be at odds and one or the other set of values would be stressed. (4) Description of the significant challenges, problems, or opportunities facing the graduates; sometimes this may include criticism of existing societal conditions or forces. (5) Balance between realism and idealism, between telling it like it is and envisioning how it ought to be.

This clearly is a value-oriented speech. Throughout Alda stresses the interrelation of our life-purposes and our value commitments. He examines varied difficulties we encounter in developing our personal value systems: ranking our values to clarify primary value commitments; actually living by the values to which we claim devotion; recognizing the pervasive influence of television in shaping our values. Implicit at various stages in the speech are values Alda advocates: honesty, caring, sensitivity, decency, fairness. In his conclusion, Alda explicitly lists the values to which he feels the audience should be committed.

In assessing this speech, you might consider how well he uses factual examples and narration of personal experiences to develop his main ideas. How effectively does he employ humor to capture attention or sharpen a point? Where and how well does he utilize questions for transitions or to stimulate thought? As further aid in evaluation, read again the discussion of critical guideline number six in Chapter 2: To what degree do the speaker's ideas harmonize with the audience's relevant values? Finally, you could apply the three questions explained at the beginning of this present chapter on affirming propositions of value. Has the speaker demonstrated or is it assumed by the audience that he or she is a person of high credibility with respect to the proposition being advocated? Has the speaker advanced acceptable criteria for the assessment of the proposition of value? Has the speaker presented a fair view of what is being evaluated?

This speech is reprinted by permission of Drew University.

1   Thank you, thank you very much. I am very sorry that Jesse Jackson is not well today. I hope he is getting better, but I am very grateful for this chance to spend a few minutes with you and to congratulate you on your graduation from this University, and I am sorry you didn't have better weather today. I understand the last time the Commencement exercises were held indoors was seventeen years ago when you had locusts and today you got me.

2   I was very touched by your very warm welcome and I would like in return to say something to the graduating class that will have some meaning for you. I actually hope I can say something that will set you so on fire that you will never forget it, because I remember twenty-three years ago when I was graduating from college and I was on your side of the academic footlights, I sat there and listened to some very distinguished commencement speakers

who gave us encouragement and words of wisdom and guidance and nobody could remember a damn thing anybody said. Well, I am going to tell you something that you will remember. And I'll even tell you when you'll remember it. You may not believe this as you sit there today, you know getting ready to go into your careers, but the day will come eventually, some day the day will come, when at some point in your lives, maybe it will be a year from now, or maybe ten or fifteen years from now, when you are going to look up from your work and wonder what the point of it all is. You wonder how much you are getting accomplished and how much it all means.

3   I think it is safe to say that a lot of you, maybe most of you, are going to experience this, the sentence "What's the purpose of all this?" is written in large letters over the mid-life crisis butcher shop. You can't miss it as you lug the carcass of your worldly success through the door to have it dressed and trimmed and placed in little plastic packages for people to admire. "What's the purpose of all this", you may ask yourself that next year or twenty years, but when you do, when you do think of that, at that moment you are going to remember what I am going to tell you now. This is getting good, isn't it? You thought I was just going to tell a bunch of jokes. Okay, it is this. It seems to me that your life will have meaning when you can give meaning to it, and only then, because no one else is going to give meaning to your life. There isn't a job or a title, or a degree, that has meaning in itself. The world is going to go stumbling on about without you, no matter how high your office and there isn't a liquor that will give meaning to your life, or a drug or any type of a sexual congress, either.

4   I would like to suggest to you, just in case you haven't done it lately, that this might be a very good time to find out what your values are, and then to figure out how you are going to live by them. I feel that knowing what you care about, and then devoting yourself to it, is just about the only way you are going to have a sense of purpose in your life and get through the mine field of existence and get out in one piece. Now the problem is, it can be a startling experience when you try to rank your values. Just ask yourself for a second what you feel the most important thing in the world is to you. Your family, your work, your money, your country, getting to heaven, sex, dope, alcohol—I don't need a show of hands on this, it was interesting though, thank you—or when you get the answer to that, then ask yourself how much time you actually spend on your number one value, and how much time do you spend on what you thought was number five, or number ten. What in fact is the thing you value most?

5   This may not be so easy to decide because we live in the time that seems to be split about its values, in fact it seems to be schizophrenic. For instance, if you pick up a magazine called *Psychology Today,* you'll see an article something like "White Collar Crime, It is More Widespread Than

You Think", and then you'll turn to the back of the magazine and you'll see an ad that says, "We'll Write Your Doctoral Thesis for Twenty-Five dollars". You see how our values are erroding? A doctoral thesis ought to go for at least a C note. Now who is writing the institutionalized crib notes. Scholars. I'd love to send away for an article on the ethics of scholarship and see what they send back. The question is where are their values? What do they value?

6 Unfortunately, the people we look to for leadership seem to be providing it by negative example these days. All across the country this month, commencement speakers are saying to graduating classes, we look to you for tomorrow's leaders. That's because today's leaders are all in jail. Well, I don't mean to be too hard on politicians. Politics is a very useful, very old profession—in some ways it is the oldest profession. Times have changed, politicians cannot be bought any more. That's not to say a few of them can't be rented. I think what has happened to me is that I have become disillusioned about politicians a little bit in the past couple of years because of the politicians I have met while I was campaigning for the Equal Rights Amendment. I crossed the path of some very strange legislators at that time—these are true stories I am going to tell; little thumb-nail sketches of some of the people I met. One assemblyman in a mid-western state that I campaigned in, told a woman who was lobbying for the Equal Rights Amendment that he would give her his vote, he would vote yes for the Equal Rights Amendment if she showed up in his hotel room that night. Now this was a vote for the Equal Rights Amendment. Now can you imagine a more inappropriate bargain to try to make? That's like saying you will vote yes for emancipation in exchange for a couple of good slaves. I was in a United States Senator's office in Washington one day when he was trying to get a legislator back in his home state to vote yes, and the guy he was talking to was absolutely opposed to it in principle. He just didn't believe in the amendment. However, he would change his vote and vote yes, if the senator would pay his way to Washington and arrange for his son's high school band to march in the inaugural parade. A legislator in another state was reported to be willing to change his vote if a few movie stars would call him on the phone, and another one would change his vote, if someone would buy him a trip to Washington so he could meet the president. Now the question is, "Where were these men's values?" "What did they hold as important." Anything? They didn't seem to care about whether or not it was true that the Equal Rights Amendment would help millions of men and women put food on the tables for their families and achieve a measure of dignity. All that these men seemed to care about was sex, money and power.

7 Our lives are being run right now by people with no principle whatsoever. And you find it in every field, in every business in our country. When you sell a product that you know will fall apart in a few months, when you sell the sizzle and you know there's no steak, when you take the money and

run, when you write an article or a political speech or a television show that excites and titillates, but doesn't lead to understanding and insight, when you are all style and no substance, then you might as well be tossing poison in the reservoir we all drink from. Now just think about that idea if you would. Suppose somebody came up and offered you $50 to throw a little poison in the reservoir. He says, look, it is just a little poison it won't hurt anybody, just a little bit, what would you take to throw poison in the reservoir. Would you take $50 to throw it in, just a little bit. Would you take $100, still just a little bit, how about $10,000, would you take $500,000 a year, with stock options and a Christmas bonus. The problem with everyone throwing in a little bit of poison, combines with everyone else who is doing it, and together we are tampering dangerously with a moral ecology.

8 I think it is worth examining the various ways values get accepted in our country. How are values transmitted in our country, reinforced? There may not be a more important field in the dissemination of values in our country than the entire communications industry and most strikingly television, which, of course, is my field. Networks are very sensitive to the fact that values are transmitted this way and they employ dozens of censors to prevent all of us from using language that an eight year old might have to explain to his parents you know, but the point that censors miss, I think, is that it is not so much what we say that teaches, as what we *don't* say. Even programs that attempt to make a moral point, don't always make a point that they intend to. It may be that messages get across in inverse proportion to their being made conscious, because I think when we sense we are being sold something we automatically defend against it. I think it may be the unspoken assumptions that mold an audience. Look at the way, for instance, that violence is treated on television. It is only the *quantity* that offends, there is probably more violence, at least there is no more violence on television than there is in a Shakespearean tragedy. But there is a big difference. On television you find *unfelt* violence, and in Shakespeare you tend to find *felt* violence. In Shakespeare the characters react with a human response, they speak, they fear, they hurt, they mourn. Most of the time on television, violence is dealt with by sweeping it under the rug as fast as possible, and by having people go on about their business as if nothing had happened. If I can't have less violence, I at least want a better grade of violence. There is one of the unspoken assumptions that violence can be tolerated as long as you ignore it and have no reaction to it. But that seems dangerously close to psychopathic behavior to me. I wonder if we haven't conditioned the audience over the years to accept unfelt violence as a way of life. I wonder if there is any connection between the long acceptance by our people of the Vietnam War and the thousands and thousands of deaths that we have seen over the years that were never mourned, never even paused for, except to sell shampoo for sixty seconds.

9 Maybe when you look at the whole situation, maybe our greatest problem is that we have two separate sets of value systems that we use. The one we talk about and the one that we live by. We seem to place a very high value on fairness, and on human concerns. And yet we still have widespread discrimination based on race, sex and religion. You still don't find Jews, Blacks or other minorities in any significant numbers in decision-making positions in the banking industry, for instance. You think that's an accident? I think somebody put a value on that. And you don't find women in any significant numbers in any decision-making capacities in any industry. Why? Because we place a higher value on appeasing the fragile male ego than we do on fairness and decency. Maybe what we need is a declaration of interdependence.

10 Well, it makes you wonder what we can do about it, doesn't it? I am glad you asked. I am going to tell you. Seems to me times have changed a little bit since the 60's. In those days we were all out on the streets, we were impatient, and passionate and in the depth of our caring was matched by the flamboyance of our gestures. We all demonstrated the intensity of our feelings, but it is not too clear what else we accomplished, at least not to me, and I was out there. But you have come in out of the street. They say you are thinking more about your own careers than about marching. Well if that is true, the funny thing is that it is possible you can do more to change things than one of us could in the 60's. If you could put a high value on decency, if you can put a high value on excellence, and on family, if you can love the people you share your lives with, your wives and your husbands, your children, and if you don't short change them for a few bucks, if you can love the work you do and learn the skill of it, the art of it, and love your art as poor as it may be, if you can give full measure to the people who pay you for your work, if you can try not to lie, try not to cheat, try to do good just by doing whatever you do well, then you would have made a revolution.

LIBERTY AND THE POWER OF IDEAS: FIVE IDEAS OF SOCIALISM

Lawrence W. Reed

At the Fourth Annual American Idea Seminar, Columbia, Lakes, Texas, Lawrence W. Reed delivered this speech on August 18, 1980. Reed is an Assistant Professor of Economics at Northwood Institute, a private, co-educational college which specializes in business education.

Socialism versus liberty. The battle between these opposing ideas is Reed's central focus (1, 2, 37). In reality, it is a conflict between antagonistic value systems. The differing images of the essence of human nature represent one reflection of this conflict (8, 30–31).

At the outset Reed employs factual examples to establish the significance of ideas as a force in history (3-7). Throughout the speech, he
frequently uses quotations to support or clarify an argument (2, 9, 12, 27,
31, 32, 36). In the cases where he seems to be using expert testimony, how
adequately does each use meet the standard tests for soundness of expert
testimony outlined in Chapter 4?

Embodied in the five ideas of socialism Reed discusses are at least
three values (conceptions of The Good) basic to the socialist system: laws
as the primary solutions to problems (10-14); government as the basic
provider of goods and services (15-22, 28-29); faith in government experts
to know what is best (23-27). Using cause-effect reasoning, Reed attacks
the socialist value system by showing the undesirable consequences of
adhering to those values (12-13, 19, 21-22, 26, 29). Also, he utilizes definition by synonym to underscore one of the negative effects. (12).

The "pillars of wisdom" upon which the ideal of liberty rests actually
are fundamental values (31). The assumption, not fully developed in the
speech, is that devotion to these values will lead to desirable consequences.
To what degree might Reed have strengthened the impact of his speech by
depicting these consequences in greater detail?

This speech is reprinted by permission from *Vital Speeches of the Day,*
47(October 15, 1980), pp. 19-21.

1   A belief which I stress again and again in my classes at Northwood
Institute in Midland, Michigan is the belief that *we are at war*—not a physical,
shooting war but nonetheless a war which is fully capable of becoming just
as destructive and just as costly. It is a conflict whose outcomes will be as
decisive as any military engagement ever was, for on that outcome hinges the
fate of the free society.

2   Let's understand at the outset that the battle for the preservation
and advancement of liberty is a battle not against personalities but against
opposing *ideas.* The French author Victor Hugo declared that "More powerful
than armies is an idea whose time has come." Armies conquer bodies, but
ideas capture minds. The English philosopher Carlyle put it this way many
decades ago: "But the thing a man does practically believe (and this is often
enough *without* asserting it to himself much less to others): the thing a man
does practically lay to heart, and know for certain, concerning his vital relations to this mysterious Universe, and his duty and destiny there, that is in
all cases the primary thing for him, and creatively determines all the rest."

3   In the past, ideas have had earthshaking consequences. They have
molded nothing less than the course of history.

4   After the fall of Rome and for the next thousand years, the system
of feudalism prevailed in large part because scholars, teachers, intellectuals,
educators, clergymen, and politicians propagated feudalistic ideas. The notion
of "once a serf, always a serf" kept millions of people from ever questioning
their station in life.

5 Then, under mercantilism, the widely-accepted concept that the world's wealth was fixed prompted men to take what they wanted from others in a long series of bloody wars from the War of Jenkin's Ear to the fall of Napolean.

6 The publication of Adam Smith's *The Wealth of Nations* in 1776 is a landmark in the history of the power of ideas. As Smith's message of free trade spread, political barriers to peaceful cooperation collapsed, the mercantilist era ended, and virtually the whole world decided to try free markets and political liberty for a change.

7 In arguing against freedom of the press in 1924, Lenin made the famous statement that "ideas are much more fatal than guns." To this day, ideas by themselves—just *believing* in something—can get you a prison sentence in communist lands.

8 Marx and the Marxists would have us believe that socialism is inevitable, that it will embrace the world as surely as the sun will rise in the east tomorrow. But as long as men have free will (the power to choose right from wrong), nothing that involves this human volition can ever be inevitable! Men do things because they are of the mind to do them; they are not robots programmed to carry out some preordained dictum. If socialism does come, it will come because men choose to embrace its principles!

9 Winston Churchill once said that "Socialism is the philosophy of failure, the creed of ignorance, and the gospel of envy. Its inherent trait is the equal sharing of misery." Socialism is an age-old failure, yet the socialist idea constitutes the chief threat to liberty today. So it is that believers in liberty, to be effective, must first identify and isolate the socialist notions which are taking their toll on liberty. In doing that, and then refraining from advancing those ideas, we can at the same time advance liberty. As I see it, socialism can be broken down into five ideas:

10 (1) *The Pass a Law Syndrome.* Passing laws has become a national pastime. When a problem in society is cited, the most frequent response seems to be, "Pass a law!" Business in trouble? Pass a law to give it public subsidies or restrict its freedom of action. Poverty? Pass a law to abolish it. Perhaps what America needs is a law against passing more laws.

11 Take a recent year, say, 1977. Congress enacted 223 new laws. It repealed hardly any. During that same year, the federal bureaucracy wrote 7,568 new regulations, all having the force of law.

12 James Madison in 1795 identified this syndrome as "the old trick of turning every difficulty into a reason for accumulating more force in government." His observation leads one to ask, "Just what happens when a new law goes on the books?" Almost invariably, a new law means: a) more taxes to finance its administration; b) additional government officials to regulate some heretofore unregulated aspect of life; and c) new penalties for violating the law. In brief, more laws mean more regimentation, more coercion! Let there be no doubt about what the word coercion means: force, plunder, compulsion, restraint. Synonyms for the verb form of the word are even more instructive: impel, exact, subject, conscript, extort, wring, pry, twist, dragoon, bludgeon, and squeeze!

13   When government begins to intervene in the free economy, bureaucrats and politicians spend most of their time undoing their own handiwork. To repair the damage of Provision A, they pass Provision B. Then they find that to repair Provision B, they need Provision C, and to undo C they need D, and so on until the alphabet and our freedoms are exhausted.

14   The Pass a Law Syndrome is evidence of a misplaced faith in the political process, a reliance on *force* which is anathema to the free society.

15   (2) *The Get Something for Nothing Fantasy.* Government by definition has nothing to distribute except what it first takes from people. Taxes are not donations!

16   In the Welfare State, this basic fact gets lost in the rush for special favors and giveaways. People speak of "government money" as if it were truly "free."

17   One who is thinking of accepting something from government which he could not acquire voluntarily should ask, "From whose pocket is it coming? Am I being robbed myself to pay for this benefit or is government robbing someone else *on my behalf?"* Frequently, the answer will be *both!*

18   Today, what business group, what labor union, what city, what occupation or age group is not either receiving benefits through government or at least seeking them? The obvious answer is enough to render the message of Emerson's essay on "Self Reliance" almost a dead letter in America today.

19   The end result of this "fantasy" is that everyone in society had his hands in someone else's pockets. And this corrupting notion has given us a government which is consuming nearly one-half of national income today, compared to just one-tenth at the start of this century.

20   (3) *The Pass the Buck Psychosis.* Recently a welfare recipient wrote her welfare office and demanded, "This is my sixth kid. What are *you* going to do about it?"

21   An individual is victim to the Pass the Buck Psychosis when he abandons himself as the solver of *his* problems. He might say, "My problems are really not mine at all. They are society's, and if society doesn't solve them and solve them quickly, there's going to be trouble!" I would submit to you that when individuals demand that solutions come from Washington, they are full speed ahead on a dangerous flight from responsibility.

22   Socialism thrives on the shirking of responsibility. When men lose their spirit of independence and initiative, their confidence in themselves, they become clay in the hands of tyrants and despots.

23 (4) *The Know-It-All Affliction.* Leonard Read, in *The Free Market and its Enemy,* identifies "know-it-allness" as a central feature of the socialist idea—that some men are capable of planning the lives of others.

24 The know-it-all is by nature a meddler in the affairs of others. His attitude may be expressed this way: "I know what's best for you, but I'm not content to merely *convince* you of my rightness; I'd rather *force* you to adopt my ways." The know-it-all evinces arrogance and a lack of tolerance for the great diversity among people.

25 In government, the know-it-all refrain sounds like this: "If I didn't think of it, then it can't be done, and since it can't be done, we must prevent anyone from trying."

26 A group of West Coast businessmen ran into this snag a few months back when their request to operate a barge service between the Pacific Northwest and Southern California was denied by the Interstate Commerce Commission because the agency felt the group could not operate such a service profitably!

27 The miracle of the marketplace is that when men are free to try, they can and do accomplish great things. Leonard Read's well-known admonition that there should be "no man-concocted restraints against the release of creative energy" is a powerful rejection of the Know-It-All Affliction.

28 (5) *The Envy Obsession.* Coveting the wealth and income of others has given rise to a sizable chunk of today's socialist legislation. Envy is the fuel which runs the engine of income redistribution. Surely, the many soak-the-rich schemes are rooted in envy and covetousness.

29 What happens when people are obsessed with envy? They blame those who are better off than themselves for their troubles. Society is fractured into classes and faction preys upon faction. Children are taught to despise the successful and to lust after their wealth rather than to aspire to similar achievement. Civilizations have been known to crumble under the weight of envy and the disrespect for life and property which it entails.

30 A common thread runs through these five socialist ideas. They all appeal to the darker side of man: the primitive, noncreative, slothful, dependent, demoralizing, unproductive, and destructive side of human nature. No society can long endure if its people practice such suicidal notions on a grand scale!

31 The ideal of liberty provides quite a stunning contrast. The very concept is uplifting, regenerative, motivating, creative, and dynamic! It rests, as I see it, upon these pillars of wisdom:

(1) *Self-reliance*—A man's first duty after reverence to his Creator is to refrain from becoming a burden on others.

(2) *Personal responsibility*—Every individual must recognize that he can choose between right and wrong and therefore is accountable and responsible for his actions.

(3) *Respect for life and property*—Following the teachings of the "Golden Rule" and the commandments against murdering, coveting, and stealing, make possible a peaceful society in which liberty can flourish.

(4) *Voluntary assistance to the needy*—Charity comes from the heart and material substance of a free people, not from government paternalism. When not burdened with excessive taxation and government interference, Americans have traditionally come to the aid of the needy. As de Tocqueville observed more than a century ago (paraphrasing): "America is great because America is good. When Americans cease to be good, America will cease to be great."

(5) *Limited government*—The sole function of the State should be that of a "nightwatchman"—to provide for the common defense against those, at home or abroad, who would do violence to innocent citizens. It is not the duty of government to play Robin Hood or Santa Claus.

32 Don't take my words as the final description of liberty. Listen to what these individuals have said:

Epictetus: "No man is free who is not a master of himself."

Gandhi: "Freedom is not worth having if it does not mean the freedom to make mistakes."

Dwight Eisenhower: "Only our individual faith in freedom can keep us free."

William Allen White: "Liberty is the only thing you can't have unless you give it to others."

Robert Green Ingersoll: "What light is to our eyes, what air is to the lungs, what love is to the heart, liberty is to the soul of man."

W. Somerset Maugham: "If a nation values anything more than freedom, it will lose its freedom."

Abraham Lincoln: "Those who deny freedom to others deserve it not for themselves, and under a just God, cannot long retain it."

Edward Hiles: "Freedom is not free and it must not be taken for granted. It was won through sacrifice and will be maintained only through sacrifice. It can be lost—just as surely, just as completely, and just as permanently—tax by tax, subsidy by subsidy, and regulation by regulation, as it can be lost bullet by bullet, bomb by bomb, missile by missile."

33 It's cruel irony that even as we lose our liberties, we seem to take for granted those which we have left. Whether we realize it or not, the promise of America is still the promise of liberty, for there is hardly another place on earth which men and women can still come to in rags and pull themselves up to lofty heights of accomplishment.

34 A few weeks ago, a Cuban woman, one of thousands fleeing Castro's tyranny, arrived in Florida. She had nothing but the clothes on her back in a strange, new land. A reporter inquired, as she kissed the ground, "Are you happy?"

"Oh, yes!" she exclaimed.

"Why?" asked the reporter.

Tearfully, the woman replied, "I'm free! I'm free!"

35 Now there's a soul who understands better than most Americans what liberty really is. And my guess is that she will never forget as long as she lives what it means not to have it. To her, liberty was an idea whose time was long and painfully overdue.

36 Nobel Prize winner F. A. Hayek has called attention to the power of ideas in preserving liberty: "Unless we can make the philosophic foundations of a free society once more a living intellectual issue, and its implementation a task which challenges the ingenuity and imagination of our liveliest minds, the prospects of freedom are indeed dark."

37 The verdict of this epic struggle between liberty and serfdom depends entirely upon what percolates in the hearts and minds of men and women. At the present time, the jury is still deliberating.

THE VALUE OF DISOBEDIENCE

Marvin Sacks

Marvin Sacks, a senior journalism major at Indiana University, gave this speech to his classmates in Speech Composition in April 1971. He asked his listeners to reexamine a value, that of obedience, which people ordinarily never question. Thus, to make his proposition of value acceptable, Sacks must be able to illustrate to his audience that disobedience from time to time is more desirable than obedience.

Consider what "higher values" on occasion might be used to justify disobedience. How appropriate and acceptable do you find the examples that Sacks uses? Do they in every case illustrate the points he is actually trying to make? He also relies heavily on quotations for support. Are the quotations appropriate and do you respect the person being quoted?

Near the end of the speech, Sacks refers to Martin Luther King's view concerning disobedience of unjust laws. For an extended explanation of King's view read his speech "Love, Law, and Civil Disobedience," reprinted in Chapter Three of this anthology.

This speech is printed by permission of Marvin Sacks.

1   We in this country face what may perhaps be the greatest paradox presented to a free nation: The duty to obey and to disobey. Human history began with man's act of disobedience which was at the same time the beginning of his freedom and development of his reason, according to psychoanalyst Erich Fromm.

2   In an order-filled society such as ours, the choice of whether to pledge obedience or instead, to disdainfully disobey a directive, is day-in and day-out upon us. The cause for concern involves using the proper discretion in the selection of which course of action one chooses to follow.

3   The story of man's creation makes it obvious that Adam did not use enough discretion when, in acting against his better judgment, he listened to his wife and let her word prevail. (An affliction, I might add, which not only plagued Adam, but which still is the kiss of death for married men everywhere even today.) For in being tempted by his wife and eating from the Forbidden Fruit, Adam went against the word of the Supreme Being, and consequently the earth was cursed, and even we are still answering to the charges. Henceforth, the soil only became productive as the result of hard and laborious toil, man no longer would enjoy infinite longevity—but instead return to the dust from which he was taken, woman was made to bear the pain of childbirth, and no longer were Adam and Eve like children in the Orient who in their innocence and ignorance of childhood ran about unclothed. After God drove Adam and Eve from the Garden of Eden, the world was never the same.

4   Another Bible story which evolved through the process of disobedience, though done with more discretion, tells of the thoughtful deliberation which went into Jacob's procurement of the birthright which belonged to Esau. It took care and precision, but with Rebekah's help, Jacob was able to deceive Isaac by assuming Esau's identity.

5   Disobedience, within the proper scope of circumstances, may be justified. It was not in the first illustration, but it was in the second. In most cases, obedience in a society which places emphasis on the execution of orders is the accepted norm. However, our obedience must not be blind. The set of circumstances surrounding the particular issue will determine our moral right to obey or disobey. Behavior contrary to the norm, in this case being disobedience, is regarded as constituting a deviant act until it proves justifiable.

6   Right off the bat, society gives "disobedience" a negative connotation by placing the prefix "dis"—meaning "not"—in front of the

word "obedience." Automatically, the stereotype of an obedient person takes on a good image, while that of a disobedient person is pictured as manifesting trouble, mistrust, and disrespect.

7 Yet, contradictory as it may seem, society nonetheless reserves a special admiration for those who dare to disobey and are able to get away with it. In fact, we persistently boast and brag about "someone getting away with murder," while the transgressor, himself, smilingly pats himself on the back for "getting away with it." We applaud the disobedient baseball player who in heroic defiance of the opposing team steals home plate. We laugh at Dennis the Menace's acts of disobedience, which are ultimately rewarded by Mrs. Wilson's generous portions of chocolate cake. And the disobedience that we practice on our highways is mirrored in a speedometer which reads 70 when the speed limit is 65 mph.

8 In *Love Story,* it was the son who had the nerve to disobey his powerful father that captured our hearts similar to the way that Bonnie and Clyde did by their sheer audacity in disobeying the law. Also it is the disobedient draftee with whom we have come to sympathize while perhaps not conclusively agreeing. Like rooting for an underdog, we many times tip our hats in acknowledgment of those who have flaunted obedience and merged triumphant.

9 Lt. William Calley chose obedience. A military court sentenced him to life imprisonment in reasoning that difficult though it may be, a soldier has a moral choice as well as a legal duty to question unlawful orders. English writer C.P. Snow states: "More hideous crimes have been committed in the name of obedience than have ever been committed in the name of rebellion."

10 Calley claimed that Capt. Ernest L. Medina gave orders to kill all My Lai villagers. The jury never had to agree on that charge because they agreed that even if Calley had received such an order, he was duty-bound to disobey it because it would have been patently illegal. A Harris Poll following the trial revealed that 43 percent of Americans would have "followed orders" if they had been in Calley's shoes. Forty-one percent felt that if they were a soldier in Vietnam and were ordered by superior officers to shoot men, women, and children suspected of aiding the enemy—41 percent said they would be more right to refuse orders in an act of disobedience. The other 16 percent were not sure what they would do.

11 Is it realistic to expect combat soldiers to make moral choices? Every recruit learns the Army's basic rule that instant obedience is a lifesaver in battle. Under military law, if a man refuses to follow an order, he is guilty of that offense unless he can prove that the order was illegal at his subsequent court-martial. And the defense rarely succeeds. Disobedience under the conditions of combat have even resulted in being shot on

the spot—no questions asked. However, the Calley verdict unequivocally indicated that Calley's course of action should, indeed, have been disobedience. It was expected of him, was what the jurors, in effect, proclaimed in their verdict.

12　Henry David Thoreau, in his widely-read essays on civil disobedience, defended a different kind of disobedience than in the case of Calley, but his words might hold true anywhere:

> The mass of men serve the state thus, not as men mainly, but as machines, with their bodies. . . . In most cases there is no free exercise whatever of the judgment or of the moral sense; but they put themselves on a level with wood and earth and stones; and wooden men can perhaps be manufactured that will serve the purpose as well. Such, command no more respect than men of straw or a lump of dirt. They have the same worth only as horses and dogs.

13　In a commercial and conservative society which was rapidly sprouting urban and industrial wings, Thoreau upheld the right to self-culture, to an individual life shaped by inner discipline. Some called it nonconformity. However one chose to label it, Thoreau's writing taught that a man of conscience is at liberty to follow his own convictions. He condemned blind obedience without so much as thoughtful deliberation of the alternatives on the grounds that such responsive behavior stymied individual judgment and integrity.

14　Chances are that if Thoreau had been given his choice of whether to take government or leave it, he would have left it. But it is not correct to presume that means that Thoreau would have supported violent disobedience. In fact, Mohandas Gandhi, India's wise leader and a student of Thoreau's, once was asked, "Is nonviolence a form of direct action?" Replied Gandhi, "It is not one form; it is the only form."

15　The focal problem of dealing with obedience and disobedience is defining the center of authority. If A is the recognized authority, then one is responsible to A and not to lesser authorities B, C, and D. Responsibility here is the issue which becomes paramount in the choice whether to disobey.

16　For example, Nazi Adolf Eichmann argued obedience as a defense in his trial for the perpetration of war crimes. "I only did my job," was his plea. But Eichmann assumed responsibility for his "obedient acts" which were shown to be irresponsible. Consequently, he was held liable. The 1945 Nuremberg trials held that blind obedience to orders here was wrong and that disobedience, instead, should have been pursued. The trials espoused the reasoning that the fact that an individual acts under orders should not free him from responsibility of the crimes. Punishment was imposed because acts against humanity had been committed by those who had substantial freedom of choice.

17 The story is told that a small boy crossing the street was struck by a car. When the police interrogated the victim as to why he had disobeyed the rules of traffic safety and had crossed against the light, the boy denied his disobedience. "I did not," came the smart aleck's reply. "The signal said 'Don't Walk' so I ran." Well, the point is that this kind of irresponsible disobedience cannot be justified. But responsible disobedience may not only be justified, but it may be a person's duty in some cases to disobey.

18 Former associate justice of the United States Supreme Court, Abe Fortas, brings Thoreau's ideas on civil disobedience into a contemporary light. He wrote:

> [Dr. Martin Luther King] said that many Negroes would disobey "unjust laws." These he defined as laws which a minority is compelled to observe, but which are not binding on the majority. He said that this must be done openly and peacefully, and that those who do it must accept the penalty imposed by the law.

19 Therefore, may I caution against hiding behind the shelter of obedience and then passing the buck. The price may not be worth it in the long run because it is the responsibility of our actions which speak for us and by which we are judged.

20 "There are two kinds of men who never amount to much," said Cyrus H. Curtis, journalist and publisher, "those who cannot do what they are told, and those who can do nothing else."

FOR THE WORLD TO LIVE, 'EUROPE' MUST DIE

Russell Means

In the Summer of 1980, Russell Means, a member of the Ogala Lakota tribe, addressed several thousand people during the Black Hills International Survival Gathering held on the Pine Ridge Reservation in South Dakota. This meeting was held to protest the pollution and exploitation of American Indian lands throughout the West. For most of those in his audience, Means' ethos, his level of source credibility, would be extremely high. Their perceptions of his personal qualities, such as expertness and trustworthiness, would be very positive. He co-founded the activist American Indian Movement (AIM). He has organized activist groups both in cities and on reservations. He played a major role in the protest occupation of Wounded Knee, South Dakota, in the Spring of 1973. In the course of his various activities, he has been injured, shot, and jailed. Although now he downplays his leadership role (par. 46), his audience would listen carefully to his advice because of their high esteem for him as a leader.

The central issue, according to Means, is the clash between two antagonistic value systems, between two opposite world views—the European and the traditional American Indian tribal. A revolution in value commitments is needed, and he offers a persuasive definition of what we should mean by the label "revolution" (par. 21, 23, 33-34).

An attack on the European-American value system comprises the bulk of Means' address. He pinpoints some of the values he feels are central to the European mind-set: step-by-step logical thinking (7); mechanical image of nature and humans (8); material gain (10); scientific despiritualization of nature and humans (11); and arrogant elevation of humans above other animate and inanimate things (29-30). The values of progress, development, victory, and freedom, all highly prized in the European cultural view, Means depicts as actually undesirable, as disvalues (12).

One major strategy used by Means to undermine European values is to describe the dangerous consequences of following such values (11-12, 14, 18-19, 25-26). Assess the soundness of the cause-effect reasoning he uses to make such arguments. Means contends very specifically that Marxism is only a different version of the European cultural tradition and, as such, is just as flawed as capitalism or Christianity (21-23, 27). As another rhetorical strategy he itemizes objectionable groups and individuals who embody the undesirable European values (38).

To a lesser extent, Means discusses a few of the specific values central to the traditional American Indian world view: the universe as complex and spiritual (7); "being" a good person (10); and the interrelation of all humans and facets of nature (29-31, 40). To what degree would the speech have been strengthened by a more complete discussion of the values central to the Indian world view? Might Means' audience already have understood and assumed the validity of some key values not discussed? Means mentions a few groups that seem to embody the praiseworthy tribal value system (39). The labels Means chooses heightens the stark contrast between the antagonistic value stances: "death culture" (41) versus "correct peoples" (32). Means' fundamental belief is that the strength to resist and overturn Europeanization flows from commitment to traditional American Indian tribal values (5, 34).

Reprinted with permission from *Mother Jones* magazine, December, 1980, pp. 24-38.

1   The only possible opening for a statement of this kind is that I detest writing. The process itself epitomizes the European concept of "legitimate" thinking; what is written has an importance that is denied the spoken. My culture, the Lakota culture, has an oral tradition, so I ordinarily reject writing. It is one of the white world's ways of destroying the cultures of non-European peoples, the imposing of an abstraction over the imposing of an abstraction over the spoken relationship of a people.

2 So what you read here is not what I've written. It's what I've said and someone else has written down. I will allow this because it seems that the only way to communicate with the white world is through the dead, dry leaves of a book. I don't really care whether my words reach whites or not. They have already demonstrated through their history that they cannot hear, cannot see; they can only read (of course, there are exceptions, but the exceptions only prove the rule). I'm more concerned with American Indian people, students and others, who have begun to be absorbed into the white world through universities and other institutions. But even then it's a marginal sort of concern. It's very possible to grow into a red face with a white mind; and if that's a person's individual choice, so be it, but I have no use for them. This is part of the process of cultural genocide being waged by Europeans against American Indian peoples today. My concern is with those American Indians who choose to resist this genocide, but who may be confused as to how to proceed.

3 (You notice I use the term *American Indian* rather than *Native American* or *Native indigenous people* or *Amerindian* when referring to my people. There has been some controversy about such terms, and frankly, at this point, I find it absurd. Primarily it seems that *American Indian* is being rejected as European in origin—which is true. But *all* the above terms are European in origin; the only non-European way is to speak of Lakota—or, more precisely, of Oglala, Brulé, etc.—and of the Diné, the Miccosukee and all the rest of the several hundred correct tribal names.

4 (There is also some confusion about the word *Indian,* a mistaken belief that it refers somehow to the country, India. When Columbus washed up on the beach in the Caribbean, he was not looking for a country called India. Europeans were calling that country Hindustan in 1492. Look it up on the old maps. Columbus called the tribal people he met "Indio," from the Italian *in dio,* meaning "in God.")

5 It takes a strong effort on the part of each American Indian *not* to become Europeanized. The strength for this effort can only come from the traditional ways, the traditional values that our elders retain. It must come from the hoop, the four directions, the relations; it cannot come from the pages of a book or a thousand books. No European can ever teach a Lakota to be Lakota, a Hopi to be Hopi. A master's degree in "Indian Studies" or in "education" or in anything else cannot make a person into a human being or provide knowledge into the traditional ways. It can only make you into a mental European, an outsider.

6 I should be clear about something here, because there seems to be some confusion about it. When I speak of Europeans or mental Europeans, I'm not allowing for false distinctions. I'm not saying that on the one hand there are the by-products of a few thousand years of genocidal, reactionary, European intellectual development which is bad; and on the other hand there is some new revolutionary intellectual development which is good. I'm referring here to the so-called theories of Marxism and anarchism and "leftism" in general. I don't believe these theories can be separated from the rest of the European intellectual tradition. It's really just the same old song.

7 The process began much earlier. Newton, for example, "revolutionized" physics and the so-called natural sciences by reducing the physical universe to a linear mathematical equation. Descartes did the same thing with culture. John Locke did it with politics, and Adam Smith did it with economics. Each one of these "thinkers" took a piece of the spirituality of human existence and converted it into a code, an abstraction. They picked up where Christianity ended; they "secularized" Christian religion, as the "scholars" like to say—and in doing so they made Europe more able and ready to act as an expansionist culture. Each of these intellectual revolutions served to abstract the European mentality even further, to remove the wonderful complexity and spirituality from the universe and replace it with a logical sequence: one, two, three, Answer!

8 This is what has come to be termed "efficiency" in the European mind. Whatever is mechanical is perfect; whatever seems to work at the moment—that is, proves the mechanical model to be the right one—is considered correct, even when it is clearly untrue. This is why "truth" changes so fast in the European mind; the answers which result from such a process are only stop-gaps, only temporary and must be continuously discarded in favor of new stop-gaps which support the mechanical models and keep them (the models) alive.

9 Hegel and Marx were heirs to the thinking of Newton, Descartes, Locke and Smith. Hegel finished the process of secularizing theology—and that is put in his own terms—he secularized the religious thinking through which Europe understood the universe. Then Marx put Hegel's philosophy in terms of "materialism," which is to say that Marx despiritualized Hegel's work altogether. Again, this is in Marx' own terms. And this is now seen as the future revolutionary potential of Europe. Europeans may see this as revolutionary, but American Indians see it simply as still more of that same old European conflict between *being* and *gaining*. The intellectual roots of a new Marxist form of European imperialism lie in Marx'—and his followers'—links to the tradition of Newton, Hegel and the others.

10 *Being* is a spiritual proposition. *Gaining* is a material act. Traditionally, American Indians have always attempted to *be* the best people they could. Part of that spiritual process was and is to give away wealth, to discard wealth in order *not* to gain. Material gain is an indicator of false status among traditional people, while it is "proof that the system works" to Europeans. Clearly, there are two completely opposing views at issue here, and Marxism is very far over to the other side from the American Indian view. But let's look at a major implication of this; it is not merely an intellectual debate.

11   The European materialist tradition of despiritualizing the universe is very similar to the mental process which goes into dehumanizing another person. And who seems more expert at dehumanizing other people? And why? Soldiers who have seen a lot of combat learn to do this to the enemy before going back into combat. Murderers do it before going out to commit murder. Nazi SS guards did it to concentration camp inmates. Cops do it. Corporation leaders do it to the workers they send into uranium mines and steel mills. Politicians do it to everyone in sight. And what the process has in common for each group doing the dehumanizing is that it makes it all right to kill and otherwise destroy other people. One of the Christian commandments says, "Thou shalt not kill," at least not humans, so the trick is to mentally convert the victims into nonhumans. Then you can proclaim violation of your own commandment as a virtue.

12   In terms of the despiritualization of the universe, the mental process works so that it becomes virtuous to destroy the planet. Terms like *progress* and *development* are used as cover words here, the way *victory* and *freedom* are used to justify butchery in the dehumanization process. For example, a real-estate speculator may refer to "developing" a parcel of ground by opening a gravel quarry; *development* here means total, permanent destruction, with the earth itself removed. But European logic has *gained* a few tons of gravel with which more land can be "developed" through the construction of road beds. Ultimately, the whole universe is open—in the European view—to this sort of insanity.

13   Most important here, perhaps, is the fact that Europeans feel no sense of loss in all this. After all, their philosophers have despiritualized reality, so there is no satisfaction (for them) to be gained in simply observing the wonder of a mountain or a lake or a people *in being*. No, satisfaction is measured in terms of gaining material. So the mountain becomes gravel, and the lake becomes coolant for a factory, and the people are rounded up for processing through the indoctrination mills Europeans like to call schools.

14   But each new piece of that "progress" ups the ante out in the real world. Take fuel for the industrial machine as an example. Little more than two centuries ago, nearly everyone used wood—a replenishable, natural item—as fuel for the very human needs of cooking and staying warm. Along came the Industrial Revolution and coal became the dominant fuel, as production became the social imperative for Europe. Pollution began to become a problem in the cities, and the earth was ripped open to provide coal whereas wood had always simply been gathered or harvested at no great expense to the environment. Later, oil became the major fuel, as the technology of production was perfected through a series of scientific "revolutions." Pollution increased dramatically, and nobody yet knows what the environmental costs of pumping all that oil out of the ground will really be in the long run. Now there's an "energy crisis," and uranium is becoming the dominant fuel.

15 Capitalists, at least, can be relied upon to develop uranium as fuel only at the rate at which they can show a good profit. That's their ethic, and maybe that will buy some time. Marxists, on the other hand, can be relied upon to develop uranium fuel as rapidly as possible simply because it's the most "efficient" production fuel available. That's *their* ethic, and I fail to see where it's preferable. Like I said, Marxism is right smack in the middle of the European tradition. It's the same old song.

16 There's a rule of thumb which can be applied here. You cannot judge the real nature of a European revolutionary doctrine on the basis of the changes it proposes to make within the European power structure and society. You can only judge it by the effects it will have on non-European peoples. This is because every revolution in European history has served to reinforce Europe's tendencies and abilities to export destruction to other peoples, other cultures and the environment itself. I defy anyone to point out an example where this is not true.

17 So now we, as American Indian people, are asked to believe that a "new" European revolutionary doctrine such as Marxism will reverse the negative effects of European history on us. European power relations are to be adjusted once again, and that's supposed to make things better for all of us. But what does this really mean?

18 Right now, today, we who live on the Pine Ridge Reservation are living in what white society has designated a "National Sacrifice Area." What this means is that we have a lot of uranium deposits here, and white culture (not us) needs this uranium as energy production material. The cheapest, most efficient way for industry to extract and deal with the processing of this uranium is to dump the waste by-products right here at the digging sites. Right here where we live. This waste is radioactive and will make the entire region uninhabitable forever. This is considered by industry, and by the white society that created this industry, to be an "acceptable" price to pay for energy resource development. Along the way they also plan to drain the water table under this part of South Dakota as part of the industrial process, so the region becomes doubly uninhabitable. The same sort of thing is happening down in the land of the Navajo and Hopi, up in the land of the Northern Cheyenne and Crow, and elsewhere. Thirty percent of the coal in the West and half of the uranium deposits in the U.S. have been found to lie under reservation land, so there is no way this can be called a minor issue.

19 We are resisting being turned into a National Sacrifice Area. We are resisting being turned into a national sacrifice people. The costs of this industrial process are not acceptable to us. It is genocide to dig uranium here and drain the water table—no more, no less.

20 Now let's suppose that in our resistance to extermination we begin to seek allies (we have). Let's suppose further that we were to take revolutionary Marxism at its word: that it intends nothing less than the complete overthrow of the European capitalist order which has presented this threat to our very existence. This would seem to be a natural alliance for American Indian people to enter into. After all, as the Marxists say, it is the capitalists who set us up to be a national sacrifice. This is true as far as it goes.

21 But, as I've tried to point out, this "truth is very deceptive. Revolutionary Marxism is committed to even further perpetuation and perfection of the very industrial process which is destroying us all. It offers only to "redistribute" the results—the money, maybe—of this industrialization to a wider section of the population. It offers to take wealth from the capitalists and pass it around; but in order to do so, Marxism must maintain the industrial system. Once again, the power relations within European society will have to be altered, but once again the effects upon American Indian peoples here and non-Europeans elsewhere will remain the same. This is much the same as when power was redistributed from the church to private business during the so-called bourgeois revolution. European society changed a bit, at least superficially, but its conduct toward non-Europeans continued as before. You can see what the American Revolution of 1776 did for American Indians. It's the same old song.

22 Revolutionary Marxism, like industrial society in other forms, seeks to "rationalize" all people in relation to industry—maximum industry, maximum production. It is a materialist doctrine that despises the American Indian spiritual tradition, our cultures, our lifeways. Marx himself called us "precapitalists" and "primitive." *Precapitalist* simply means that, in his view, we would eventually discover capitalism and become capitalists; we have always been economically retarded in Marxist terms. The only manner in which American Indian people could participate in a Marxist revolution would be to join the industrial system, to become factory workers, or "proletarians" as Marx called them. The man was very clear about the fact that his revolution could occur only through the struggle of the proletariat, that the existence of a massive industrial system is a precondition of a successful Marxist society.

23 I think there's a problem with language here. Christians, capitalists, Marxists. All of them have been revolutionary in their own minds, but none of them really mean revolution. What they really mean is a continuation. They do what they do in order that European culture can continue to exist and develop according to its needs.

24 So, in order for us to *really* join forces with Marxism, we American Indians would have to accept the national sacrifice of our homeland; we would have to commit cultural suicide and become industrialized and Europeanized.

25 At this point, I've got to stop and ask myself whether I'm being too harsh. Marxism has something of a history. Does this history bear out my observations? I look to the process of industrialization in the Soviet Union since 1920 and I see that these Marxists have done what it took the English Industrial Revolution 300 years to do; and the Marxists did it in 60 years. I see that the territory of the USSR used to contain a number of tribal peoples and that they have been crushed to make way for the factories. The Soviets refer to this as "The National Question," the question of whether the tribal peoples had the right to exist as peoples; and they decided the tribal peoples were an acceptable sacrifice to industrial needs. I look to China and I see the same thing. I look to Vietnam and I see Marxists imposing an industrial order and rooting out the indigenous tribal mountain people.

26 I hear a leading Soviet scientist saying that when uranium is exhausted, *then* alternatives will be found. I see the Vietnamese taking over a nuclear power plant abandoned by the U.S. military. Have they dismantled and destroyed it? No, they are using it. I see China exploding nuclear bombs, developing uranium reactors and preparing a space program in order to colonize and exploit the planets the same as the Europeans colonized and exploited this hemisphere. It's the same old song, but maybe with a faster tempo this time.

27 The statement of the Soviet scientist is very interesting. Does he know what this alternative energy source will be? No, he simply has faith. Science will find a way. I hear revolutionary Marxists saying that the destruction of the environment, pollution and radiation will all be controlled. And I see them act upon their words. Do they know *how* these things will be controlled? No, they simply have faith. Science will find a way. Industrialization is fine and necessary. How do they know this? Faith. Science will find a way. Faith of this sort has always been known in Europe as religion. Science has become the new European religion for both capitalists and Marxists; they are truly inseparable; they are part and parcel of the same culture. So, in both theory and practice, Marxism demands that non-European peoples give up their values, their traditions, their cultural existence altogether. We will all be industrialized science addicts in a Marxist society.

28 I do not believe that capitalism itself is really responsible for the situation in which American Indians have been declared a national sacrifice. No, it is the European tradition; European culture itself is responsible. Marxism is just the latest continuation of this tradition, not a solution to it. To ally with Marxism is to ally with the very same forces that declare us an acceptable cost.

29 There is another way. There is the traditional Lakota way and the ways of the other American Indian peoples. It is the way that knows that humans do not have the right to degrade Mother Earth, that there are forces beyond anything the European mind has conceived, that humans must be in harmony with *all* relations or the relations will eventually eliminate the disharmony. A lopsided emphasis on humans by humans—the Europeans' arrogance of acting as though they were beyond the nature of all related things—

can only result in a total disharmony and a readjustment which cuts arrogant humans down to size, gives them a taste of that reality beyond their grasp or control and restores the harmony. There is no need for a revolutionary theory to bring this about; it's beyond human control. The nature peoples of this planet know this and so they do not theorize about it. Theory is an abstract; our knowledge is real.

30   Distilled to its basic terms, European faith—including the new faith in science—equals a belief that man is God. Europe has always sought a Messiah, whether that be the man Jesus Christ or the man Karl Marx or the man Albert Einstein. American Indians know this to be totally absurd. Humans are the weakest of all creatures, so weak that other creatures are willing to give up their flesh that we may live. Humans are able to survive only through the exercise of rationality since they lack the abilities of other creatures to gain food through the use of fang and claw.

31   But rationality is a curse since it can cause humans to forget the natural order of things in ways other creatures do not. A wolf never forgets his or her place in the natural order. American Indians can. Europeans almost always do. We pray our thanks to the deer, our relations, for allowing us their flesh to eat; Europeans simply take the flesh for granted and consider the deer inferior. After all, Europeans consider themselves godlike in their rationalism and science. God is the Supreme Being; all else *must* be inferior.

32   All European tradition, Marxism included, has conspired to defy the natural order of all things. Mother Earth has been abused, the powers have been abused, and this cannot go on forever. No theory can alter that simple fact. Mother Earth will retaliate, the whole environment will retaliate, and the abusers will be eliminated. Things come full circle, back to where they started. *That's* revolution. And that's a prophecy of my people, of the Hopi people and of other correct peoples.

33   American Indians have been trying to explain this to Europeans for centuries. But, as I said earlier, Europeans have proven themselves unable to hear. The natural order will win out, and the offenders will die out, the way deer die when they offend the harmony by overpopulating a given region. It's only a matter of time until what Europeans call "a major catastrophe of global proportions" will occur. It is the role of American Indian peoples, the role of all natural beings, to survive. A part of our survival is to resist. We resist not to overthrow a government or to take political power, but because it is natural to resist extermination, to survive. We don't want power over white institutions; we want white institutions to disappear. *That's* revolution.

34   American Indians are still in touch with these realities—the prophecies, the traditions of our ancestors. We learn from the elders, from nature, from the powers. And when the catastrophe is over, we American Indian peoples will still be here to inhabit the hemisphere. I don't care if it's only a

handful living high in the Andes. American Indian people will survive; harmony will be reestablished. *That's* revolution.

35   At this point, perhaps I should be very clear about another matter, one which should already be clear as a result of what I've said. But confusion breeds easily these days, so I want to hammer home this point. When I use the term *European,* I'm not referring to a skin color or a particular genetic structure. What I'm referring to is a mind-set, a world view that is a product of the development of European culture. People are not genetically encoded to hold this outlook; they are *acculturated* to hold it. The same is true for American Indians or for the members of any other culture.

36   It is possible for an American Indian to share European values, a European world view. We have a term for these people; we call them "apples"—red on the outside (genetics) and white on the inside (their values). Other groups have similar terms: Blacks have their "oreos"; Hispanos have "coconuts" and so on. And, as I said before, there *are* exceptions to the white norm: people who are white on the outside, but not white inside. I'm not sure what term should be applied to them other than "human beings."

37   What I'm putting out here is not a racial proposition but a cultural proposition. Those who ultimately advocate and defend the realities of European culture and its industrialism are my enemies. Those who resist it, who struggle against it, are my allies, the allies of American Indian people. And I don't give a damn what their skin color happens to be. *Caucasian* is the white term for the white race; *European* is an outlook I oppose.

38   The Vietnamese Communists are not exactly what you might consider genetic Caucasians, but they are now functioning as mental Europeans. The same holds true for Chinese Communists, for Japanese capitalists or Bantu Catholics or Peter "MacDollar" down at the Navajo Reservation or Dickie Wilson up here at Pine Ridge. There is no racism involved in this, just an acknowledgment of the mind and spirit that make up culture.

39   In Marxist terms I suppose I'm a "cultural nationalist." I work first with my people, the traditional Lakota people, because we hold a common world view and share an immediate struggle. Beyond this, I work with other traditional American Indian peoples, again because of a certain commonality in world view and form of struggle. Beyond that, I work with anyone who has experienced the colonial oppression of Europe and who resists its cultural and industrial totality. Obviously, this includes genetic Caucasians who struggle to resist the dominant norms of European culture. The Irish and the Basques come immediately to mind, but there are many others.

40   I work primarily with my own people, with my own community. Other people who hold non-European perspectives should do the same. I believe in the slogan, "Trust your brother's vision," although I'd like to add sisters into the bargain. I trust the community and the culturally based vision

of all the races that naturally resist industrialization and human extinction. Clearly, individual whites can share in this, given only that they have reached the awareness that continuation of the industrial imperatives of Europe is not a vision, but species suicide. White is one of the sacred colors of the Lakota people—red, yellow, white and black. The four directions. The four seasons. The four periods of life and aging. The four races of humanity. Mix red, yellow, white and black together and you get brown, the color of the fifth race. This is a natural ordering of things. It therefore seems natural to me to work with all races, each with its own special meaning, identity and message.

41   But there is a peculiar behavior among most Caucasians. As soon as I become critical of Europe and its impact on other cultures, they become defensive. They begin to defend themselves. But I'm not attacking them personally; I'm attacking Europe. In personalizing my observations on Europe they are personalizing European culture, identifying themselves with it. By defending themselves in *this* context, they are ultimately defending the death culture. This is a confusion which must be overcome, and it must be overcome in a hurry. None of us have energy to waste in such false struggles.

42   Caucasians have a more positive vision to offer humanity than European culture. I believe this. But in order to attain this vision it is necessary for Caucasians to step outside European culture—alongside the rest of humanity—to see Europe for what it is and what it does.

43   To cling to capitalism and Marxism and all the other "isms" is simply to remain within European culture. There is no avoiding this basic fact. As a fact, this constitutes a choice. Understand that the choice is based on culture, not race. Understand that to choose European culture and industrialism is to choose to be my enemy. And understand that the choice is yours, not mine.

44   This leads me back to address those American Indians who are drifting through the universities, the city slums and other European institutions. If you are there to learn to resist the oppressor in accordance with your traditional ways, so be it. I don't know how you manage to combine the two, but perhaps you will succeed. But retain your sense of reality. Beware of coming to believe the white world now offers solutions to the problems it confronts us with. Beware, too, of allowing the words of native people to be twisted to the advantage of our enemies. Europe invented the practice of turning words around on themselves. You need only look to the treaties between American Indian peoples and various European governments to know that this is true. Draw your strength from who you are.

45   A culture which regularly confuses revolution with continuation, which confuses science and religion, which confuses revolt with resistance, has nothing helpful to teach you and nothing to offer you as a way of life. Europeans have long since lost all touch with reality, if ever they were in touch

with it. Feel sorry for them if you need to, but be comfortable with who you are as American Indians.

46 So, I suppose to conclude this, I should state clearly that leading anyone toward Marxism is the last thing on my mind. Marxism is as alien to my culture as capitalism and Christianity are. In fact, I can say I don't think I'm trying to lead anyone toward anything. To some extent I tried to be a "leader," in the sense that the white media like to use that term, when the American Indian Movement was a young organization. This was a result of a confusion I no longer have. You cannot be everything to everyone. I do not propose to be used in such a fashion by my enemies; I am not a leader. I *am* an Oglala Lakota patriot. That is all I want and all I need to be. And I am very comfortable with who I am.

THE WATERGATE AFFAIR

Richard M. Nixon

Early morning, June 17, 1972, five employees of the Committee to Reelect President Nixon were arrested as they attempted to burglarize the Democratic National Headquarters. High officials of the Nixon Administration, and even the President himself, quickly became involved in covering up the details of the incident. For some time, little real information concerning the incident was available. Heresay and rumor, however, were rampant. By the Spring of 1973 investigations revealed that top presidential officials participated in the cover-up. In early April, John Dean, former Presidential counsel, was dismissed, and shortly thereafter top aides, H.R. Haldeman and John Ehrlichman, resigned their positions on the President's staff. These actions were the immediate exigency that precipitated President Nixon's first Watergate apologia.

An apology is a speech of personal defense. The questioning of a person's moral nature, motives, or reputation is qualitatively different from the challenging of that individual's policies or ideas. An attack upon a person's character, upon his value as a human being, seems to demand a direct response that seeks to purify the speaker's personal image. The resulting address seeks to prove a proposition of value.

As President Nixon addressed the nation via national television on the evening of April 30, 1973, he did so against the backdrop of tradition. Socrates, Demosthenes, Martin Luther, Sir Thomas More, Edmund Burke, Sam Houston, Adlai Stevenson, and President Truman all, at one time or another, sought to purify their personal images from charges of wrongdoing. Nixon himself was no novice to this type of speaking. He had delivered his famous "Checkers" speech on national television in the 1952 election when he was charged with possessing an illegal campaign fund. Success had crowned his efforts on that occasion. Dwight Eisenhower kept Nixon on the ticket as a direct result of his apologetic appeal. But now, April 30, 1973, Richard Nixon once more faced the nation as he gave his first Watergate apologia.

Apologetic discourse commonly involves four main strategies: denial, bolstering, differentiation, and transcendence. Strategies of *denial* seek to negate alleged facts, sentiments, objects, or relationships and can easily be imagined to be important to speeches of self-defense. Denial is obviously useful to the speaker only to the extent that a negation does not constitute a known distortion of reality. When a speaker *bolsters,* he attempts to identify himself with something the audience views favorably. Bolstering thus is the obverse of denial, since it reinforces the existence of a fact, sentiment, object, or relationship. Strategies of *differentiation* are divisive in that they seek to divide the speaker from a fact, sentiment, object, or relationship. A speaker may, for example, do as Senator Edward Kennedy did in his "Chappaquiddick" speech when he sought to differentiate his erratic behavior immediately after the accident that proved fatal to Mary Jo Kopechne from that of his usual behavior when his faculties are functioning more normally. *Transcendental* strategies psychologically move the audience away from the particular charges at hand in a direction toward some more abstract, general view. When General Douglas MacArthur addressed the Congress in 1952 after President Truman relieved him of his Korean command for insubordination, he sought to move the rhetorical proposition to the larger context of American security in the Pacific. (For further elaboration of these strategies see the Ware and Linkugel citation on p. 144.)

Keep these four basic strategies in mind as you read President Nixon's first Watergate apology. What are the strategies Nixon relies upon in his attempts at personal purification? What bolstering techniques do you find? What role does differentiation play?

President Nixon's rhetoric upon this occasion achieved limited success. The Gallup Poll showed that only 30 percent of the people thought that he had "told the whole truth." Do you think it was possible for the President to be persuasive upon this occasion?

President Nixon's speech is reprinted by permission from *Vital Speeches of the Day,* May 15, 1973, pp. 450-52.

1   Good evening. I want to talk to you tonight from my heart on a subject of deep concern to every American. In recent months members of my Administration and officials of the Committee for the Reelection of the President—including some of my closest friends and most trusted aides— have been charged with involvement in what has come to be known as the Watergate affair.

2   These include charges of illegal activity during and preceding the 1972 Presidential election and charges that responsible officials participated in efforts to cover up that illegal activity.

3   The inevitable result of these charges has been to raise serious questions about the integrity of the White House itself. Tonight I wish to address those questions.

4 Last June 17 while I was in Florida trying to get a few days' rest after my visit to Moscow, I first learned from news reports of the Watergate break-in. I was appalled at this senseless, illegal action, and I was shocked to learn that employes of the reelection committee were apparently among those guilty. I immediately ordered an investigation by appropriate Government authorities.

5 On Sept. 15, as you will recall, indictments were brought against seven defendants in the case.

6 As the investigation went forward, I repeatedly asked those conducting the investigation whether there was any reason to believe that members of my Administration were in any way involved. I received repeated assurances that there were not. Because of these continuing reassurances, because I believed the reports I was getting, because I had faith in the persons from whom I was getting them, I discounted the stories in the press that appeared to implicate members of my Administration or other officials of the campaign committee.

7 Until March of this year, I remained convinced that the denials were true and that the charges of involvement by members of the White House staff were false.

8 The comments I made during this period, the comments made by my press secretary in my behalf, were based on the information provided to us at the time we made those comments.

9 However, new information then came to me which persuaded me that there was a real possibility that some of these charges were true and suggesting further that there had been an effort to conceal the facts both from the public—from you—and from me.

10 As a result, on March 21 I personally assumed the responsibility for coordinating intensive new inquiries into the matter and I personally ordered those conducting the investigations to get all the facts and to report them directly to me right here in this office.

11 I again ordered that all persons in the Government or at the reelection committee should cooperate fully with the F.B.I., the prosecutors and the grand jury.

12 I also ordered that anyone who refused to cooperate in telling the truth would be asked to resign from Government service.

13 And with ground rules adopted that would preserve the basic constitutional separation of powers between the Congress and the Presidency, I directed that members of the White House staff should appear and testify voluntarily under oath before the Senate committee which was investigating Watergate.

14 I was determined that we should get to the bottom of the matter, and that the truth should be fully brought out no matter who was involved.

15 At the same time, I was determined not to take precipitive action and to avoid if at all possible any action that would appear to reflect on innocent people.

16 I wanted to be fair, but I knew that in the final analysis the integrity of this office—public faith in the integrity of this office—would have to take priority over all personal considerations. Today, in one of the most difficult decisions of my Presidency, I accepted the resignations of two of my closest associates in the White House, Bob Haldeman and John Ehrlichman, two of the finest public servants it has been my privilege to know. I want to stress that in accepting these resignations I mean to leave no implication whatever of personal wrongdoing on their part, and I leave no implication tonight of implication on the part of others who have been charged in this matter. But in matters as sensitive as guarding the integrity of our democratic process, it is essential not only that rigorous legal and ethical standards be observed, but also that the public, you, have total confidence that they are both being observed and enforced by those in authority, and particularly by the President of the United States. They agreed with me that this move was necessary in order to restore that confidence. Because Attorney General Kleindienst, though a distinguished public servant, my personal friend for 20 years, with no personal involvement whatever in this matter, has been a close personal and professional associate of some of those who are involved in this case, he and I both felt that it was also necessary to name a new Attorney General.

17 The counsel to the President, John Dean, has also resigned.

18 As the new Attorney General, I have today named Elliott Richardson, a man of unimpeachable integrity and rigorously high principle. I have directed him to do everything necessary to insure that the Department of Justice has the confidence and the trust of every law-abiding person in this country. I have given him absolute authority to make all decisions bearing upon the prosecution of the Watergate case and related matters. I have instructed him that if he should consider it appropriate he has the authority to name a special supervising prosecutor for matters arising out of the case.

19 Whatever may appear to have been the case before, whatever improper activities may yet be discovered in connection with this whole sordid affair, I want the American people, I want you, to know beyond the shadow of a doubt that during my term as President justice will be pursued fairly, fully, and impartially, no matter who is involved.

20 This office is a sacred trust, and I am determined to be worthy of that trust!

21 Looking back at the history of this case, two questions arise:

22 How could it have happened—who is to blame?

23 Political commentators have correctly observed that during my 27 years in politics, I've always previously insisted on running my own campaigns for office. But 1972 presented a very different situation.

24 In both domestic and foreign policy, 1972 was a year of crucially important decisions, of intense negotiations, of vital new directions, particularly in working toward the goal which has been my overriding concern throughout my political career—the goal of bringing peace to America, peace to the world.

25 And that is why I decided as the 1972 campaign approached that the Presidency should come first and politics second. To the maximum extent possible, therefore, I sought to delegate campaign operations, to remove the day-to-day campaign decisions from the President's office and from the White House.

26 I also, as you recall, severely limited the number of my own campaign appearances.

27 Who then is to blame for what happened in this case?

28 For specific criminal actions by specific individuals those who committed those actions must of course bear the liability and pay the penalty. For the fact that alleged improper actions took place within the White House or within my campaign organization, the easiest course would be for me to blame those to whom I delegated the responsibility to run the campaign. But that would be a cowardly thing to do.

29 I will not place the blame on subordinates, on people whose zeal exceeded their judgment and who may have done wrong in a cause they deeply believed to be right. In any organization the man at the top must bear the responsibility.

30 That responsibility, therefore, belongs here in this office. I accept it.

31 And I pledge to you tonight from this office that I will do everything in my power to insure that the guilty are brought to justice and that such abuses are purged from our political processes in the years to come long after I have left this office.

32 Some people, quite properly appalled at the abuses that occurred, will say that Watergate demonstrates the bankruptcy of the American political system. I believe precisely the opposite is true.

33 Watergate represented a series of illegal acts and bad judgments by a number of individuals. It was the system that has brought the facts to light and that will bring those guilty to justice.

34 A system that in this case has included a determined grand jury, honest prosecutors, a courageous judge—John Sirica, and a vigorous free press.

35 It is essential that we place our faith in that system, and especially in the Judicial System.

36 It is essential that we let the judicial process go forward, respecting those safeguards that are established to protect the innocent as well as to convict the guilty.

37 It is essential that in reacting to the excesses of others, we not fall into excesses ourselves.

38 It is also essential that we not be so distracted by events such as this that we neglect the vital work before us, before this nation, before America at a time of critical importance to America and the world.

39 Since March, when I first learned that the Watergate affair might in fact be far more serious than I had been led to believe, it has claimed far too much of my time and my attention. Whatever may now transpire in the case, whatever the actions of the grand jury, whatever the outcome of any eventual trials, I must now turn my full attention—and I shall do so—once again to the larger duties of this office.

40 I owe it to this great office that I hold, and I owe it to you, to my country.

41 I know that, as Attorney General, Elliot Richardson will be both fair and he will be fearless in pursuing this case wherever it leads. I am confident that with him in charge justice will be done.

42 There is vital work to be done toward our goal of a lasting structure of peace in the world—work that cannot wait, work that I must do.

43 Tomorrow, for example, Chancellor Brandt of West Germany will visit the White House for talks that are a vital element of the Year of Europe, as 1973 has been called.

44 We are already preparing for the next Soviet-American summit meeting later this year.

45 This is also a year in which we are seeking to negotiate a mutual and balanced reduction of armed forces in Europe which will reduce our defense budget and allow us to have funds for other purposes at home so desperately needed.

46 It is the year when the United States and Soviet negotiators will seek to work out the second and even more important round of our talks on limiting nuclear arms, and of reducing the danger of a nuclear war that would destroy civilization as we know it.

47 It is a year in which we confront the difficult tasks of maintaining peace in Southeast Asia and in the potentially explosive Middle East.

48 There's also vital work to be done right here in America to insure prosperity—and that means a good job for everyone who wants to work; to control inflation that I know worries every housewife, everyone who tries to balance the family budget in America. To set in motion new and better ways of insuring progress toward a better life for all Americans.

49 When I think of this office, of what it means, I think of all the things that I want to accomplish for this nation, of all the things I want to accomplish for you.

50 On Christmas Eve, during my terrible personal ordeal of the renewed bombing of North Vietnam which, after 12 years of war, finally helped to bring America peace with honor, I sat down just before midnight. I wrote out some of my goals for my second term as President. Let me read them to you.

51 To make this country be more than ever a land of opportunity—of equal opportunity, full opportunity—for every American; to provide jobs for those who can work and generous help for those who cannot; to establish a climate of decency and civility in which each person respects the feelings and the dignity in the God-given rights of his neighbor; to make this a land in which each person can dare to dream, can live his dreams not in fear but in hope, proud of his community, proud of his country, proud of what America has meant to himself, and to the world.

52 These are great goals. I believe we can, we must work for them, we can achieve them.

53 But we cannot achieve these goals unless we dedicate ourselves to another goal. We must maintain the integrity of the White House.

54 And that integrity must be real, not transparent.

55 There can be no whitewash at the White House.

56 We must reform our political process, ridding it not only of the violations of the law but also of the ugly mob violence and other inexcusable campaign tactics that have been too often practiced and too readily accepted in the past including those that may have been a response by one-sided to the excesses or expected excesses of the other side.

57 Two wrongs do not make a right.

58 I've been in public life for more than a quarter of a century. Like any other calling, politics has good people and bad people and let me tell you the great majority in politics, in the Congress, in the Federal Government, in the state government are good people.

59 I know that it can be very easy under the intensive pressures of a campaign for even well-intentioned people to fall into shady tactics, to rationalize this on the grounds that what is at stake is of such importance to the nation that the end justifies the means.

60 And both of our great parties have been guilty of such tactics.

61 In recent years, however, the campaign excesses that have occurred on all sides have provided a sobering demonstration of how far this false doctrine can take us.

62 The lesson is clear. America in its political campaigns must not again fall into the trap of letting the end, however great that end is, justify the means.

63 I urge the leaders of both political parties, I urge citizens—all of you everywhere—to join in working toward a new set of standards, new rules and procedures to insure that future elections will be as nearly free of such abuses as they possibly can be made. This is my goal. I ask you to join in making it America's goal.

64 When I was inaugurated for a second term this past January 20, I gave each member of my Cabinet and each member of my senior White House staff a special four-year calendar with each day marked to show the number of days remaining to the Administration.

65 In the inscription on each calendar I wrote these words:

"The Presidential term which begins today consists of 1,461 days, no more, no less. Each can be a day of strengthening and renewal for America. Each can add depth and dimension to the American experience.

"If we strive together, if we make the most of the challenge and the opportunity that these days offer us, they can stand out as great days for America and great moments in the history of the world."

66 I looked at my own calendar this morning up at Camp David as I was working on this speech. It showed exactly 1,361 days remaining in my term.

67 I want these to be the best days in America's history because I love America. I deeply believe that America is the hope of the world, and I know that in the quality and wisdom of the leadership America gives lies the only hope for millions of people all over the world that they can live their lives in peace and freedom.

68 We must be worthy of that hope in every sense of the word.

69 Tonight, I ask for your prayers to help me in everything that I do throughout the days of my Presidency to be worthy of their hopes and of yours.

70 God bless America. And God bless each and every one of you.

THE PLAYBOY PHILOSOPHY—PRO

Anson Mount

Anson Mount, Manager of Public Affairs for *Playboy*, delivered this address as the affirmative of a debate with William M. Pinson, Jr., on the value of the "Playboy Philosophy." The debate occurred as part of a seminar on the topic "Toward Authentic Morality for Modern Man" that was sponsored by the Christian Life Commission of the Southern Baptist Convention. The seminar was held in the Atlanta American Motor Hotel, Atlanta, Georgia, March 16-18, 1970.

In the debate, Mount assumed the task of setting forth the *Playboy* philosophy, clearly and comprehensively, and then developing appropriate rationale in defense of it. As you study the debate, it will be useful to begin by delineating the value criteria Mount sets forth in his speech and then analyzing his method of substantiation. What role do "facts" play in this debate on a proposition of value? Does one "prove" value contentions or does one simply try to make them "acceptable" to people? Is there a difference between "proof" and "acceptability"? Try to identify the philosophical position from which the *Playboy* philosophy springs: religion, hedonism, existentialism, or what? Compare it with Pinson's philosophical position.

This speech is reprinted by permission of Anson Mount and the Christian Life Commission of the Southern Baptist Convention from the *Proceedings of the 1970 Christian Life Commission Seminar.*

1   I am sure we are all aware of the seeming incongruity of a representative of *Playboy* magazine speaking to an assemblage of representatives of the Southern Baptist Convention. I was intrigued by the invitation when it came last fall, though I was not surprised. I am grateful for your genuine and warm hospitality, and I am flattered (though again not surprised) by the implication that I would have something to say that could have meaning to you people. Both *Playboy* and the Baptists have indeed been considering many of the same issues and ethical problems; and even if we have not arrived at the same conclusions, I am impressed and gratified by your openness and willingness to listen to our views.

2   The fact that *Playboy* magazine has become so deeply involved in the discussion of current ethical and social issues, that we have become perhaps the leading editorial forum in the current reexamination of moral values, seems incredibly incongruous to some people, and it has been a bit of a surprise to us, too. We didn't plan it that way—it was a role that was thrust upon us by accidents of time and situation. And what I have to say to you today about our particular moral, ethical, and human values can be perhaps best couched in the form of a short historical narrative, the story of how *Playboy* magazine has become such a significant forum for the discussion and debate of current social issues and moral values.

3   And just in case you doubt our significance, let me remind you that *Playboy* is read by twenty million young men and women each month. And they are not just *any* twenty million; most of them are the movers and shakers and the makers of tomorrow. The majority are college educated, urban oriented, upward-striving young men who will be running this country in a few years. On any given month one half of all the men in this country between the ages of 18 and 34 read *Playboy* magazine.

4   And let us look at a few of the articles that have appeared in just the last three issues of *Playboy:* An article on the phenomenon of human genius by Robert Graves; an article about "Hunger in America" by Senator

Jacob Javits; "The Americanization of Vietnam" by David Halberstam; an examination of the personality of Jesus and his significance to current social and moral issues by Baptist theologian Harvey Cox; "The Generation Gap" by Senator George McGovern; "Sharing the Wealth" by Cesar Chavez; "Uniting the Races" by Julian Bond; articles on environment pollution and the reasons for the current student rebellions by Supreme Court Justice William O. Douglas; an examination of the emotional stresses of accelerating cultural change by Alvin Toffler; "Military Justice" by Robert Sherrill; companion articles on the natures of the revolutionary and counter-revolutionary movements in this country by Jules Segal and George Fox; a lengthy panel discussion among nine leading authorities on the drug problem—and many more.

5   I hope many of you pastors have seen fit to preach sermons on these current social and ethical issues. Certainly, we know from our audience research, our mail, and our subscription files, that tens of thousands of ordained ministers read *Playboy* religiously (if you'll pardon the expression). I would like humbly to suggest that much good sermon material can be found in the pages of our magazine.

6   But it hasn't always been so.

7   For the first few years of *Playboy's* existence, churchmen did a pretty good job of ignoring us. No leading church spokesman took notice of our presence and we were rarely if ever damned from the pulpit—at least we didn't hear about it. The only exceptions to this general rule were the occasional irate letters that came in from fundamentalist preachers. One or two of these letters would arrive each month, and occasionally one of them would find its way into our letters to the editor column. Most of these rustic epistles were remarkably alike. Aside from expressing indignation and predicting eternal torment for our souls, virtually all of our irate clerical correspondents took pains to explain the accidental circumstances under which they just happened to have come across a copy of *Playboy.*

8   It was inevitable, though, that as we became more and more successful and our circulation increased, and it became less and less possible to discount our significance by assuming that we were a broom-closet operation that would go broke any day, as our magazine became more polished and professional and as some of the country's leading corporations began to appear in our pages as advertisers, it was inevitable that churchmen would feel compelled to attempt in some way to explain the phenomena of our success and to analyze the reasons for the great rapport the younger generation felt with our magazine.

9   The first thoughtful theological critique of *Playboy* magazine was an article titled "The Lowdown on the Upbeats" in the April, 1960 issue of *Motive,* the magazine of the Methodist Student Movement. It was written

by a Methodist pastor, the Rev. Roy Larson of Evanston, Illinois. Much of the content and many of the conclusions of that article have been repeated innumerable times in other religious critiques of *Playboy* in the intervening years. This article is significant because it was here that the term "Playboy Philosophy" first appeared, a term which Mr. Hefner later picked up when he decided to write an editorial series outlining what he really did believe, rather than what his clerical critics accused him of believing.

10   The Reverend Larson said in that article, "In a sense, then, *Playboy* is more than just a handbook for a young man-about-town. It's sort of a Bible which defines his values, shapes his personality, sets his goals, dictates his choices, and governs his decisions. The Playboy Philosophy becomes, at least for a time in his life, a sort of substitute religion."

11   "First of all," continues Reverend Larson, "I'm sympathetic, very sympathetic, with *Playboy's* concern with style. As a Christian, I've always been upset by those people in the church who seem to assume that 'Blah' is more Christian than 'Style': that averageness is more Christ-like than distinctiveness. Certainly, God knows—there's nothing in the mainstream of the Christian tradition which justifies this canonization of mediocrity. . . . Secondly, speaking from what I genuinely feel is a Christian perspective, I sympathize with *Playboy's* revolt against narrow, prudish puritanism, even though I would disagree with the way this revolt is expressed." The Reverend Larson's article then went on to outline all the criticisms of *Playboy* which were later so widely popularized by Harvey Cox and which I'm sure all of you have heard a thousand times, and which I will speak about in a few minutes. But the thing that really impressed us was Reverend Larson's inference that *Playboy* had become a kind of Bible which defines the values, goals, and desires of the young men of this country. We knew about the avid readership we enjoyed among college-age men, but to read Reverend Larson's article one would get the impression that the majority of young Americans wouldn't think of buying a suit, a car, a record album, or a bottle of after-shave lotion without first consulting the pages of *Playboy* magazine. We were almost tempted to try to hire Mr. Larson as an advertising salesman.

12   This theme, that is the accusation that Playboy is a dictatorial taste maker, was repeated and amplified in surely the best known and most widely quoted criticism of Playboy magazine ever printed. The article was called "Playboy's Doctrine of Male" by Harvey Cox, a then obscure Baptist theologian. It appeared in the April 21, 1961 issue of *Christianity and Crisis*. Cox's main charge was that *Playboy* is basically antisexual because it dilutes and dissipates authentic sexuality by reducing it to an accessory and by keeping it at a safe distance. He charged that *Playboy* was interested *only*

in recreational sex and that we considered women to be playthings. He charged that since our interest in sex was only a recreational interest, authentic sexuality was ignored and that we were therefore antisexual. This was closely akin to a *Time* magazine criticism which said the Playboy Clubs are "Brothels without a second story." Our answer to this charge is simply that we feel that man's natural interest in sex is perfectly valid as an aspect of entertainment, that it is entirely normal and proper for a man to enjoy seeing a sexually attractive girl whether she is walking down the street, dancing on a stage, or whether he views her picture on a printed page, or a movie screen, or whether she is wearing a bikini, a ballroom gown, or just fingernail polish. We feel that sex as a subject of humor—and humor is certainly a major form of pleasure—is not only valid but healthy. As the Reverend Richard Hettlinger, the Chaplain at Kenyon College, said, "Playboy Clubs are hardly the only places in which people enjoy their meals more because they are served by pretty girls in reduced costumes, and many of these places are as respectable as the Bank of England. Does Harvey Cox propose to do away with chorus lines and ice shows because the girls employed in these occupations are not engaged in profound relationship with all the customers? Would Playboy Clubs be more acceptable if there *were* a second story? Provided that the girls so employed are treated as human beings and are not expected to go home with the customers after hours (which happens to be one of the strictest rules in this case) there seems to be little reason to single out Playboy Clubs as antisexual. I tend to agree with Hefner that the need to express this kind of criticism may be rooted in the uneasiness that some critics feel with sex."

13 Cox's major charge was that *Playboy* was a dictatorial taste maker, that our advice to the young on the arts of consumership are couched in words so authoritative in tone that they make a papal encyclical sound indecisive by contrast. Later critics have said that we have caused incalculable suffering because we lead young men to think and expect that all girls should look like the Playmate of the Month and that out of these unrealistic expectations much unhappiness results. Mort Sahl said, for example, that *Playboy* is raising up a whole generation of young men who think that girls fold in two places and have staples in their navels.

14 But I honestly feel that Harvey Cox's charge that we are dictatorial taste makers is especially ludicrous. I can only assume that he chose to ignore the entire American advertising industry in general and such publications as *Better Homes and Gardens, Modern Bride,* and women's magazines in particular. Compared with these publications, *Playboy* is almost indecisive in its editorial coverage of consumer tastes and trends. But what is even more interesting is Cox's apparent assumption that the young men who read *Playboy* are insulated from other influences. It is undoubt-

edly true that millions of young men look to *Playboy* for guidance in their consumer taste or for some suggestion about how to be unsquare but it seems a bit far-fetched to assume that these young men invest *Playboy* with omniscient, biblical infallibility in matters of life style, or that they are reduced to simpering slaves awaiting our fashion director's latest sartorial dicta. To accept Harvey Cox's assessment of *Playboy's* imperious influence on its readers, we would have to assume that the influence of the reader's peer group, his home, church, school, and all the other influences in his life count for nothing. One only needs to walk down Peachtree Street and look about him to know that all women don't look like *Playboy* Playmates. In short, it is ludicrous to assume that a magazine which appears once a month can totally dominate the value structures of even an unsure young man. Our advertising department would like to convince our many national advertisers that we have even half the influence on the consumer tastes of our readers for which Cox gives us credit.

15 Cox's theological criticism of *Playboy* had one very definite effect however: it set off a chain of events which radically changed *Playboy* magazine and the lives of all of us connected with it. The Cox article filled a very great void. Churchmen everywhere were becoming increasingly aware of *Playboy* and its inordinate influence with the younger generation. Many of them felt uneasy about *Playboy*, others were outwardly antagonistic. But they were too progressive or too bright to attack us merely by charging that *Playboy* was lewd. Most churchmen were too sophisticated to think that nudity is by definition obscene or that cartoons on human or sexual subjects are by definition immoral. They needed a better, more academically respectable criticism of *Playboy* than to simply charge that we were sinful. Yet the strong subsurface layer of Victorian prudery that runs throughout our culture demanded that *Playboy* be opposed and rejected. And Cox gave them their argument. It was literate, well written, and very *unprudish*. In fact, Cox applauded our fight against sexual prudery.

16 And all of a sudden articles analyzing the theological and social significance of *Playboy* magazine began to appear in dozens of church publications and theological journals. Scores of transcripts of sermons putting down *Playboy* began to arrive on my desk. Hefner got invited to appear on dozens of television talk shows. Hundreds of invitations for speaking engagements at colleges and universities poured in. And we were sort of stunned by all this. We were amazed by all these learned treatises about the meaning and significance and ultimate effect of *Playboy* magazine on twentieth century culture. The subtitle on the cover of the magazine says, "Entertainment for Men." And that was a pretty good summation of our editorial intentions. We did see our magazine as an expression of revolt against the sick Calvinist prudery that was still widespread in our culture, but other than that our principal chore was to entertain young men.

17 But after Harvey Cox's article appeared—and the dozens of other critiques that it spawned—Mr. Hefner decided that he would rather be damned for what he *really* believes than for what his critics accuse him of believing; so, he began to set down his thoughts in a series of editorials. This series, called the "Playboy Philosophy," a term which Mr. Hefner had borrowed from his critics, was a long, rambling, sometime repetitious reexamination of currently significant ethical and social issues. The series ran for about two years, during 1964 and 1965, and it was the most widely read and discussed feature in our magazine's history. It became, and still is, one of the most controversial documents of our time. Although Hefner addressed himself to an assortment of issues, it was his commentary on sex, morals, and related subjects which received most of the attention. It is impossible to reduce a quarter of a million words to a few pithy phrases, but I will attempt to summarize, at least briefly, Mr. Hefner's views as expressed in the Playboy Philosophy. Much of what Hefner said is a twentieth century version of John Stuart Mill's essay "On Liberty," including a utilitarian basis for freedom. Underlying Hefner's beliefs is a profound concern for the rights of the individual in a free society. "When I use the word 'free', I'm not referring to a society completely devoid of restrictions, of course," Hefner says, "but one in which controls are established to serve rather than suppress the common citizen: a society that is unfettered, just, rational, and humane, in which the individual and his interests are paramount."

18 Whatever critics say to the contrary, Hefner is not concerned exclusively with sexual freedom, although that aspect has had the greatest attention. In fact, his first seven installments concentrated on matters other than sex.

19 Hefner is for free enterprise. *Playboy's* emphasis on leisure and urban living, far from being merely Sybaritic, is consistent with free enterprise. The magazine motivates men by portraying the good life that is the prize for honest endeavor and hard work.

20 Hefner is for a wide arena of free expression. *"Playboy* believes that this nation is big enough, strong enough, and right enough to give free expression to the ideas and the talents of every man among us without fear of being hurt by any man's individual weaknesses or follies."

21 He is for separation of church and state. He has no quarrel with those who wish to embrace religion, but he believes that an individual has an equal right to be free *from* religion, and its influence. And the influence of religion, as he sees it, has sometimes been pervasive and noxious. By stressing self-denial and heavenly reward, it has kept man from enjoying, without guilt, the fruits of his earthly labors, and to that extent religion is incompatible with the free enterprise system. By influencing the state to enact legislation that people do not believe in and will not obey, it has contributed to a breakdown in law and order. By encouraging censorship, it has curbed free expression; by equating sin with sex, it has inspired harmful sexual repression. Indeed, it is religion not *Playboy,* that has been antisexual, he says; it is religion, not *Playboy,* that has looked upon women as a depersonalized object or possession and has continuously associated her with its antagonism toward sex.

22 Hefner says, and I quote, "In my own moral view, I think there is a justifiable place for sex outside of wedlock. It can serve as a significant source of physical and emotional pleasure: it offers a means of intimate communication between individuals and a way of establishing personal identification within a relationship and within society as a whole: it can become, at its best, a means of expressing the innermost, deepest felt longings, desires, and emotions.

23 "There was a time, not too long ago when it was assumed that sex was only moral if it was connected with procreation. Procreation I think does belong inside marriage. I think that it's important for children to have the benefit of both parents, and to be raised in a family atmosphere with the accompanying emotional security. But I think we recognize today that, thanks to technological advances, procreation and sex can be separated from one another. It's possible for sex to serve other purposes. It serves an important role in the development of the human personality, for the development of self-identity, and as a means of developing and maintaining a close, loving relationship between two human beings. And I think the suggestion that these benefits can only be possible with marriage is just unsound."

24 Let me give you a few examples of other things Hefner has said on the general subject of human sexuality: "I don't think man's sexual behavior has changed much in two thousand years. But his attitude about this behavior has changed a great deal. This thing called a sexual revolution that we're going through today is really a reexamination of our sexual activity, its moral implications, and an attempt to discard some of the hypocrisy of the past."

25 To the charge that increased sexual permissiveness is destructive because most young, unmarried people are too sexually immature to be able to handle their sex relations responsibly, Mr. Hefner said, "I think at this particular time many people in our society probably are very sexually immature, but the only way that you gain maturity in any area of activity is through experience. It's rather like, I think, what has been said about the new emerging nations in Africa: the argument that they are not really ready for political freedom. But the only way that they'll ever become ready for political freedom is to give them that freedom and allow them to grow into maturity. The same thing is true in sex. People cannot learn to exercise freedom responsibly until they get it. This is, in fact, one of the great concepts that our country was built upon. The concept of democracy is based upon the recognition that man is, by his nature, basically more good than evil. That if given the freedom of opportunity, he can find the best and most mature ways of handling his own affairs. This does not mean that we don't need civil law, even in the area of sex. But they should be rational laws. They should be rules that are designed to benefit man, to prevent one man from victimizing or exploiting another, rather than rules that are designed to reflect arbitrary religious dogma.

26 "I'm against promiscuity in the true sense of the word. Because promiscuity is not simply casual sex, it's a demeaning kind of sex: a sexual activity in which there is no real interest in the partner at all. But I don't think that commitment necessarily requires a lasting relationship. I obviously do believe that it's possible for premarital sex to be moral. I think it's possible for a sexual relationship to be a rather short term one and still be moral. I think the thing that makes a relationship moral or immoral is the quality and nature of the relationship itself, and that in turn is not necessarily dependent on the length of time that the relationship lasts.

27 "In the past, admonitions against sex outside marriage were based upon the fear of pregnancy, disease, or scandal. It is true that modern young people are increasingly free of these three fears, but under no circumstances have these considerations ceased to be important. Sometimes I think there is too little worry about them. I think we live in a period of transition right now, where we are to some extent sexually free, and yet we are simultaneously paying the price for our puritan prudery we have inherited from the past. So now it's possible for young people to be very free in their sexual activity and then pay the price in pregnancy or disease. We have gone a long way toward solving these problems scientifically, we have invented the pill and we have discovered preventions and cures for venereal disease, and yet venereal disease is blooming as never before, and we certainly haven't licked the social problem of premarital pregnancy. The problem is that we aren't applying the scientific advances we've made. And I think the reason we're not applying them is because we're so hung up with some of the old irrational taboos."

28 In one of the installments of the Playboy Philosophy Mr. Hefner wrote, "Sex is at its best an expression of love and adoration, but this is not to say that sex is or should be limited to love alone." Critics were quick to point out that when one separates sex from love, we then create quite a danger of real dehumanization and depersonalization. To this Mr. Hefner replied, "Yes, I think the danger *is* there. But I think living life is dangerous. And that can't be avoided. I don't think that any act between two people should be removed from a sense of responsible concern. I think it's quite possible, even though it's not the best kind of relationship, for a sexual relationship to be rather casual (what is sometimes called recreational sex) and for it still to be something more than just an animal act and for it to be really quite moral because, quite simply, I think I would define morality as that which serves the best interest of man. Of course, deception can enter into a sexual relationship, and that's where we have to face up to questions of morality. It's quite possible for a casual relationship to be less than casual on one side, and for there to be subterfuge or deception or lying involved in the activity, and this becomes immoral. It is immoral not because the sex act itself is immoral, but because dishonest considerations have entered into the relationship. I think it's possible for people to *use* one another, sexually or in any other area of human activity. And this I think is immoral. But the point is that people can use each other sexually within marriage as well as outside marriage. In fact, it may be easier to victimize someone sexually within marriage than outside. This is the real point. It's a matter of recognizing that it is not the issuance of a marriage license that makes sex moral.''

29 But it is on the specific subject of extramarital sex that *Playboy* magazine has been most severely criticized by many conservative churchmen. They assume, of course, that we're for it; that we are all in favor of indiscriminate free love and that we think every man ought to go out and sow his wild sperm with joyful abandon. Every time I try to pin down our critics in an effort to learn specifically where they get this nutty idea, I find that it is our cartoons and humor that give them this specific impression. I find *that* utterly fascinating. And I think this state of affairs is a far more penetrating reflection on our critics than on us. I frequently look through other magazines that print cartoons, like *The New Yorker* or *Look,* and I see many cartoons that treat reckless driving, burglary, bank robbery, wife-beating, and other forms of good clean American fun. And I'm sure that no one really gets "up tight" about these cartoons or seriously thinks the publications that print them are promoting these vices. But every time we print a cartoon kidding adultery, the conservatives go into a tailspin. I think Mr. Hefner put it most succinctly when he said, "In our cartoons, as well as in some of our fiction, we tend to make light of every area of sexuality, and we do it not as an indication of what we necessarily morally believe or don't believe, but as a decontamination of the truly pervasive puritan prudery that permeates our society. We do it in much the same way that some of the better racial comedians have made light and found the humor in some of our racial problems, and in doing so they have helped to decontaminate bigotry. We can deal with our own foibles if we first learn how to laugh at them. In much the same way, *Playboy* has been successful in putting many of our sexual problems in a better perspective. We have helped, through humor, to relate them to the total human experience by humanizing them through humor.

30   In his editorial series Mr. Hefner specifically pointed out that he felt premarital sex and extramarital sex are very different matters and should be considered separately. In marriage there is a commitment between two people that should be honored. This does not mean necessarily, however, that all forms of extramarital sex are immoral. But in the society in which we live today, in most cases extramarital sex involves deceit. It involves a basic breaking of the trust and understanding that exists between two people, and this is immoral in any human relationship.

31   It is interesting—and perhaps revealing—to notice that a large number of learned and qualified authorities have said almost exactly these same things in the intervening years, without kicking up nearly so much fuss as the Playboy Philosophy and without ruffling the fur of nearly so many churchmen. For example, only two years ago this month, a husband and wife team of Ph.D's at the State University of Pennsylvania, Doctors Rustim and Della Roy, published a book written in a rather plodding academic style called *Honest Sex*. This book summed up the thinking of a group of religious men and women who spent three years formulating their views on such things as premarital intercourse, marriage, and adultery. The thesis of the book is that physical sex is a "rightful, proper, important, and pleasurable means of communicating between two persons." Mind you—not between two married persons, not even between a man and a woman, but simply between two persons. Beyond this, they express a "Christian hope that all sexual pleasure will be taken within the context of a deep, loving relationship." And on these grounds, they attack impersonal and exploitive sex because it warps or deadens our sensibilities. The authors dismiss "the stupid focusing on marriage as life's goal" and they anticipate the ultimate dissolution of the concept that sex and marriage are inextricably and exclusively linked to each other. "The notion that no man can have good deep relationships including sexual intercourse with more than one woman at a time is patent idiocy" according to the authors, who then go on to define circumstances under which extramarital relationships are not only acceptable but virtually mandatory as manifestations of Christian love and charity. The book pleads not for more sex but for more love, and for love that fulfills the criteria of unselfishness and responsibility.

32   This book was extremely popular, enjoyed quite a large sale, and was reviewed in hundreds of magazines and newspapers. And it said almost exactly what Mr. Hefner had said on the subject of human sexuality in his Playboy Philosophy about four years earlier. Dr. Roy tells me he hasn't

received a single irate letter from a fundamentalist preacher. I can only assume that fundamentalists read *Playboy* but they don't read books.

33 I am surprised that after all these years—and after all the long and sometimes bitter criticism to which *Playboy* has been subjected—that it was only recently that a clergyman finally pinpointed the criticism to which we truly are vulnerable. It is a criticism which we acknowledge as valid. The churchman who nailed us was the Reverend Richard Hettlinger who published a book a couple of years ago titled *Living with Sex.* Incidentally, I am rather grateful for that title. Only a few years ago a preacher writing a book on this subject would have called it *Living without Sex.*

34 Anyway, the Reverend Hettlinger, after giving us high grades for our good-natured spoofing of the stiffer aspects of society and our much needed protest against prudery and Comstockery, asks: "Can the author of a work which has become the arbiter of taste and the guide of morals for millions of younger Americans avoid the responsibility of discussing the deeper levels of sexual experience to which he so evangelistically wishes to introduce his readers?" In short, Hettlinger indicts us for presenting only the pleasant, joyous, pleasurable, and happy aspects of human sexuality without giving adequate coverage to seriousness, the dark dangers, and the deeper levels of human sexual experience. He indicts us not for what we say but for what we haven't said. In all fairness, I would like to point out that some people have criticized Thomas Aquinas and John Calvin for exactly the same thing.

35 But in answer to that criticism, let me say that we feel that there has been quite enough emphasis in our culture over the past two thousand years on the dark, terrifying possibilities of sex. We've heard quite enough, thank you, about its terrors and its tyranny, about the disease and wrecked lives and tortured souls that can result from an uncommitted orgasm. All these centuries almost everything the organized church has had to say about unmarried sex has been one word: "Don't." And that's just not enough. Young people won't settle for that anymore. We have seen it as our mission to let some light and fresh air into this dark and frightening corner of human life. We have seen it as our mission to remind people that sex can, and ought to be fun; that it is a legitimate part of human experience, that it can be happy, joyous, lighthearted, and *pleasurable.* Not only that, but it ought to be.

36 Mr. Hefner put it this way in a recent interview on Chicago's Educational Television station: "I think the best argument against the Playboy Philosophy is the assumption that it is the total and only way to live. If someone lived completely isolated from society at large and read only *Playboy* and assumed that it was the sum total of human experience and that this was the only way to live, I think this would be a serious

mistake, but it's impossible to take *Playboy* out of the context of society in which it exists. We've suffered in our culture from a very real antipleasure, antiplay ethic, and *Playboy* and the Playboy Philosophy are really in response to that; they are sort of a medicine for an ill of our times. I think that if I were editing *Playboy* in a different time when puritanism were not as serious a problem as it is today, I'm sure that I would be editing *Playboy* differently and I'm sure that I would have said different things in the Playboy Philosophy.''

37 But I think there is more important work to be done. In fact, I think the Golden Age of Christianity is in the immediate future. There is a kind of unorganized underground church that seems to be rising up from a crumbling institutional church. As hierarchies weaken and denominational lines blur, I become increasingly aware of a new kind of Christianity—a new kind of priesthood. Or is it merely a rekindling of a first century priesthood? All around me, everywhere, everywhere I go, I run into carpenter's apprentices quietly doing their work. I find them in unexpected professions, sometimes wearing strange garb. Some of them are even in the ordained ministry. They are unorganized, unlisted, undefined, but they can be recognized. They are warm, they know how to *touch* people, and they have a real, joyous inner freedom. And I think something is going to come of all this; *maybe* it's the beginning of the rebirth of the church in a new and better form. If that's true, then count us in. We're with you.

38 So if you people in the church feel it is your mission to remind people of the awful terrors of sex and the horrible implications that can result from going to bed with somebody without a marriage license having been issued, then go ahead. Be our guest. It's a free country. And if you do your job half as well as we have done ours, and if you succeed in reaching the younger generation half as well as we have succeeded in doing so, and if in doing so you succeed in precipitating a total reexamination and reevaluation of moral and ethical precepts in this country, as we have, then I think you will be able to say you've done a good job. And if you do succeed in getting your message across and thereby contribute to our American atmosphere of the free exchange of ideas, then perhaps we'll all be better off for it. Who knows, you might even convince us.

39 But for right now, our religion is our love affair with life, and any man who is not in love with life doesn't have a religion worthy of the name. For us, life was made for living. If that is heresy, then make the most of it.

THE PLAYBOY PHILOSOPHY—CON

William M. Pinson, Jr.

Dr. Pinson, Associate Professor of Christian Ethics at the Southwestern Baptist Theological Seminary, Fort Worth, Texas, took the negative in the debate with Anson Mount on the "Playboy Philosophy." He attempts to analyze and refute Mount's contentions concerning the intrinsic worth of the *Playboy* philosophy and to set forth the basic differences between it and the Christian faith. You may find it especially interesting to note Dr. Pinson's approach to refutation since the subject for discussion is a proposition of value. What roles do standard means of refutation—such as exposing inconsistencies, a lack of evidence, and fallacies—play in Dr. Pinson's negative speech? What roles do values play in refuting other values?

This speech is reprinted by permission of William M. Pinson, Jr. and the Christian Life Commission of the Southern Baptist Convention from the *Proceedings of the 1970 Christian Life Commission Seminar "Toward Authentic Morality for Modern Man."*

1 In a meeting dedicated to consideration of Christian morality, why should we discuss the Playboy Philosophy? That is a legitimate question. Hundreds, perhaps even thousands, of Baptists have objected to this topic and particularly to the appearance of a representative from *Playboy* on a Baptist program. They give many reasons for this protest: It will serve only to provide added publicity to a dangerous philosophy; it will lend respectability to the publication and its publisher; it will take seriously an approach to life which does not even take itself seriously; it will consume time which should be given to more significant issues; it implies that the Bible's teachings on sex are either untrue or inadequate.

2 Such protests raise valid issues. On the other hand, there are numbers of reasons why Christians should consider the Playboy Philosophy. *Playboy* is an articulate, widely-read spokesman for a very popular way of life in America. More than six million copies of *Playboy* are sold each month (*Newsweek,* March 2, 1970, p. 71). It has many imitators. It has given birth to a number of other highly profitable enterprises including the chain of key clubs known as Playboy Clubs. It has been the subject of television shows, magazine articles, books, and discussions by theologians from all faiths. It has produced what some see as a new religion: Hugh Hefner is the Prophet; Playboy is the Book; the "Playboy Philosophy" is the Creed; the Clubs are meeting places for public celebration of the faith; the Playboy Foundation provides the charity; the rabbit is

its symbol; the bunnies are the priestesses; the god is happiness; and its way of salvation is through pleasure.

3 Anything as contrary to the Christian faith and as widely influential as the Playboy Philosophy deserves our careful attention. If we believe that *Playboy* is in error and if we care about the welfare of the millions of *Playboy* readers, we should refute its philosophy. And in order to refute it, we must know what it is saying and why people respond to its message.

4 To claim that sex is all that causes *Playboy* to sell is to misunderstand and underestimate the Playboy Philosophy. True, articles and cartoons on sex and pictures of girls are probably the magazine's basic ingredients. Take them away and the circulation would more likely nose dive than skyrocket. But other magazines stress sex and carry pictures of nude girls. Yet, they don't sell as many copies as *Playboy*. The basic conflict which Christians (at least this Christian) have with *Playboy* is over a particular life style it champions: the so-called "Playboy Philosophy." If a purchaser of *Playboy* gets beyond the looking stage and reads, he will begin to absorb that philosophy.

5 A vast segment of Hefner's philosophy is given to attacks on various subjects: puritanism, censorship, socialism, laws regulating sex, and institutional religion. Nevertheless, he does set forth his own views on life in scattered passages. This approach hardly qualifies as a philosophy; it lacks the necessary consistency, completeness, and clarity. But here is a summary of what Hefner chooses to call the Playboy Philosophy.

6 Hefner says: Happiness should be the goal of man; the major purpose of society is the promotion of individual happiness, a mental and physical state closely related to pleasure; pleasure is found through living a robust life, exercising one's abilities to gain an abundance of material possessions and luxuries, enjoying various sensual experiences, indulging freely without guilt in sexual activity within or without marriage, and operating generally according to the dictates of rational selfishness; rational selfishness indicates that a man is to prefer knowledge to ignorance, pleasure to pain, and self-gratification to self-denial; rugged individualism, democracy, the free enterprise system, and freedom make possible the successful pursuit of happiness through pleasure.

7 The Playboy Philosophy has been criticized by many persons and from many different points of view. Some of the criticism has been without reference to religion. This evaluation of the Playboy Philosophy, however, is unapologetically from a Christian perspective. A Christian evaluation is based on certain faith presuppositions: God is the ultimate authority for man. Jesus is the clearest picture of what God is like and what He wants us to be. The Bible is our best source of information about God. Without

apology, therefore, the Christian makes use of the Bible, particularly in regard to the life and teachings of Jesus, in criticizing *Playboy*.

8 A Christian evaluation should be guided by several principles. It should be honest and not twist meanings or quote out of context. It should regard those associated with *Playboy* as persons for whom we have Christian concern, not as objects to be eradicated. It should desire not so much to prove a point as to seek the improvement of persons and the quality of human life.

9 Basic to an adequate Christian approach should be the realization that there is more to sin, immorality, and obscenity than the wrong use of sex. Not all obscene words come in four letters; "nigger" has six and "war" has three. For an employer to pay near starvation wages to employees while he enjoys affluence has little to do with sex, but it is sinful nonetheless. Spreading false or misleading statements and acting on inadequate information is not sexy, but it is certainly immoral.

10 We need a more inclusive and consistent approach to morality. Many who blast *Playboy* as immoral apparently see nothing immoral in prejudice and racist segregation. Some who are outraged by dirty books and movies are unconcerned about dirty air and water. Some who campaign against nudity seem to ignore the plight of the poor who have inadequate housing and clothing. Many who protest the use of sex in the mass media are apparently untroubled by scenes depicting violence—murder, fighting, assaults, robberies, and war. Those who fight against sex education in the public schools often seem indifferent to the quality of education in schools where the children of the poor and the minorities attend. Some who condemn the exploitation of sex for profit apparently see nothing wrong in the exploitation of war for their own personal profit.

11 Of course none of these inconsistencies negates the fact that sex is an important moral issue. But from a Christian point of view, there is more to and more wrong with *Playboy* and the way of life it advocates than an approach to sex. From this perspective, then, the following objections are raised.

12 The Playboy Philosophy can be criticized for its vagueness and its inaccuracies. More important, however, many of Hefner's points, to put it mildly, are questionable interpretations of historical, psychological, and sociological data. Yet he often states them as unquestionable facts. Here are a few sweeping generalities which, though stated as fact, are disputed. Hefner says: "A free democracy stands on the belief that man is born innocent and remains so until changed by society" (Hefner, p. 22). "Those who fear and oppose the erotic in our literature and art do so because of personal repressions and feelings of frustration, inadequacy, or guilt regarding sex. They are unwilling to accept the basic sexual nature of man" (Ibid., p. 45).

"Religiously inspired sexual suppression is harmful to society" (Ibid., p. 49). "Sex exists—with and without love—and in both forms it does far more good than harm" (Ibid., p. 51).

13 Several of *Playboy's* most basic arguments rest on questionable interpretations of history. Hefner argues, for example, that the sexual problems of America are due mainly to the suppression of sex by organized religion, particularly Christianity in its puritan expression. A glance at history and at contemporary non-Christian cultures reveals that this probably would not have been the case at all. Some form of sexual restrictions have been present in societies throughout history.

14 The restrictions which have been placed on sex have not been based primarily on superstition or irrational factors, as Hefner implies. Rather, good sound reasons often existed for the restrictions: the danger of and hurt caused by pregnancy out of wedlock, the possibility of infection from disease, the damage inflicted on marriage, the likelihood of selfish exploitation of persons, the unproductive distraction from needed tasks caused by excessive sexual stimulation. Because of these and other factors, societies other than those with puritan backgrounds have had what Hefner refers to as repressive standards for sex. What standards would *Playboy* have recommended?

15 Hefner's interpretation of puritanism is in itself highly debatable. He says that puritanism was "as stultifying to the mind of man as communism, or any other totalitarian concept." It is unfair to lump all puritans together and characterize them as totalitarians with stultified minds. Somehow this description hardly does justice to John Milton, John Bunyan, Richard Baxter, or Jonathan Edwards.

16 Some of the Playboy Philosophy's interpretations of psychology are not as immune to attack as Hefner implies. One of the recurring themes in the magazine is that sexual suppression is bad. It causes all kinds of problems, according to Hefner. On the other hand, if a person ceases to suppress his sexual desires and goes against the standards of society, he feels guilty. And guilt is a very damaging, undesirable, unhealthy emotion, says *Playboy*. Damned if you don't and damned if you do is the way *Playboy* sees man's sexual dilemma. The solution *Playboy* suggests is to do away with the standards and stop suppressing sexual desire; then everyone can do what comes naturally without feeling guilty; this will make for happy, healthy people.

17 But evidence indicates that this may not be the result. The sexual revolution has been underway for some time. Many people have decided to ignore the existing standards and have entered freely into premarital sexual intercourse. Are they healthy and happy? Some evidently are not. Francis J. Braceland, as editor of the *American Journal of Psychiatry* and former president of the American Psychiatric Association, recently told a convocation on medicine and theology that premarital sexual relations resulting from exposure to the so-called "new morality" have greatly increased the number of young people in mental hospitals (*The Christian Century,* May 17, 1967, p. 644).

18 A careful look at the *Playboy* argument on sexual suppression and mental health indicates that perhaps a distinction needs to be made between *rejection* of specific sexual desires and *repression* of sexual desire in general. Any normal person rejects many desires every day—sexual and otherwise. A man may desire to steal a car, hit someone who insults him, overeat, or have sexual intercourse with another man's wife. If he admits that he has the desires and handles them by rejecting them, he is no neurotic nut. He is a disciplined human being practicing normal self-control. He is not likely to suffer any psychic damage because of his rejection of a desire to act in what some might term a natural way. On the other hand, if he represses the desire, pretends he doesn't really feel the way he does, shoves it into his subconscious, or is swept with guilt simply because he lets the thought enter his mind—then he is in for possible psychological trouble. Any harm resulting from our so-called strict standards on sex is likely due to actual repression, not to self-discipline. But Hefner seems to lump the two together.

19 It is interesting to note that Hefner's own use of statistics from the Kinsey studies calls into question his argument that America's sex problems are caused by suppression and guilt. *Playboy* cites Kinsey's statistics that 85 percent of American males and 50 percent of American females have premarital sexual intercourse, and that 50 percent of the males and at least 25 percent of the females are involved in extramarital intercourse. That doesn't sound much like a sexually suppressed society! But sometimes *Playboy* implies that the chief problems are caused not so much by suppression as by guilt created because of oppressive standards for sexual conduct. Yet, according to *Playboy,* the majority of those who were involved in premarital sex indicated that they had no regrets (Hefner, p. 51). Could it be that the increase in sex crimes, divorce, marital strife, and emotional disorder within the past few years—the time of the so-called sexual revolution—is due more to the wide-open approach to sex than to any remnants of sexual restraint left in society? That seems reasonable in light of the evidence.

20 It is obvious that much of the Playboy Philosophy is straight out of Kinsey. It is also evident that Hefner uncritically accepts not only the statistics, but also many of the conclusions of the Kinsey reports (Hefner, p. 50). In light of the vast criticism by reputable scientists of the Kinsey reports, such an approach makes Hefner's own conclusions questionable.

21 From the point of view of sociology, one of Hefner's major arguments is based on a highly questionable presupposition. Hefner argues

that since the majority of the American people are involved in premarital and extramarital sexual intercourse, we ought to change our standards to conform to the conduct. He calls for "a quest for a new code of conduct consistent with our conduct itself. . . ." (Hefner, p. 103). The kind of adjustment which Hefner calls for has been considered in the complex sociological discipline of the study of moral norms. The case Hefner makes has some support. But, as sociologist Robert Cooley Angell states, "the question of whether moral norms *should* follow modal behavior has been much discussed in all ages, and usually the answer has been negative. A positive answer would seem to imply that moral norms can make no distinctive contribution" [Robert Cooley Angell, *Free Society and Moral Crisis* (Ann Arbor: University of Michigan Press, 1958, p. 34)].

22   What Hefner's argument really says is that we ought to make our creed match our deeds instead of making our deeds match our creed. To apply this principle consistently would mean that we ought to say stealing and lying are all right because a majority of Americans have stolen and lied at some time in their lives. To follow such an approach would be to reduce moral norms to the lowest common denominator of human conduct. Christians, on the other hand, contend that moral norms should be based on the will of God rather than on the conduct of men.

23   There is really nothing startling in the discovery that people don't always abide by their moral standards. Because a standard is not lived up to does not invalidate it. Recent studies, for example, reveal that many white Americans are racists. Are we to say in light of this that it is unhealthy and hypocritical for us to work for the ideal of racial justice and equality? No! Though few live up to it, we should continue to hold high the standard of justice and love.

24   Of course, if the standard is a bad one—if lived up to it would create a sick society or harm people, then it ought to be abandoned or altered. But this is quite different than saying we simply ought to seek a new code of conduct consistent with conduct itself.

25   Many of the views of *Playboy* are unrealistic, especially those related to a man and his world. If *Playboy* were content to be merely an entertainment magazine, this might not be a serious weakness. But *Playboy* goes beyond entertainment and proposes a philosophy, a way of life. Hefner says, "*Playboy,* of course, is primarily concerned with the lighter side of life, but we have always tried to view man and his world as the sum of all their parts . . ." (Hefner, p. 13).

26   The view of modern life presented by *Playboy* is less than realistic. *Playboy* plays down problems and plays up pleasure. This is because the playboy is supposed to "see life not as a vale of tears, but as a happy time" (Ibid.). In one place the Playboy Philosophy goes so far as to

say that American free enterprise has eliminated "illiteracy, famine, and disease" (Ibid., p. 104).

27   But the real world is not like *Playboy's* world. Apathy in the face of human need, exploitation, greed, widespread racism, dishonesty, crime, violence, war—these furnish some evidence that life is not exclusively a "happy time."

28   *Playboy's* view of man does not fit reality either. According to *Playboy*, man is basically a creature guided by reason—a decidedly pre-Freudian view. He comes into the world innocent and is corrupted only by society. Who first corrupted society is not made clear. But it is clear from *Playboy* that puritanism and socialism are the main culprits today. They have resulted in censorship, moral legalism, sexual repression, the elevation of the common man, the suppression of the individual, and restriction of freedom—all of which foul people up generally. Essentially the *Playboy* answer to man's problems is a mixture of robust capitalism, rugged individualism, sexual freedom, and a rational self-interest.

29   Faith in man's capacity to act rationally in his own self-respect is central to the Playboy Philosophy. However, the fact is, men often fail to act in such a way. For example, men pollute the water and air knowing that it will make life miserable—perhaps impossible—for them and their children. Men smoke excessively knowing that, likely, their health will be damaged and their lives shortened. Men drink and drive knowing that in so doing they considerably up the risk of injury and death. Men overeat knowing that fat is folly. Men shoot heroin knowing that the horrors of addiction will result. None of these is a reasonable act. None serves a person's self-interest in the long run. Yet, millions of people do these things.

30   Why? They do them, at least in part, because they are willing to risk future pain for immediate pleasure. Such practice seems more due to irrational self-gratification than to rational self-interest. In this regard the Bible speaks of man's plight: Man is free and responsible, but he is also a victim of his irrational, selfish nature. The good he knows to do he leaves undone and the evil he knows to avoid he does (Romans 8:14-25).

31   *Playboy* does not seem to understand the seriousness of man's plight: He is trapped by his own pride and selfishness, his will and reason are crippled. To prescribe reason, self-interest, or pleasure will do no good. Man needs God. It is unrealistic to believe that man can find his way to abundant life apart from God. And the Christian believes that man finds the new life he needs through Jesus Christ.

32   The Playboy Philosophy is a form of a very old philosophy—hedonism. Hedonism had been explored by Greek philosophers and found to be inadequate long before the first century rolled around. Basically the philosophy asserts that man's actions should be determined by whatever

brings him pleasure. But the best of the hedonistic philosophers would have been appalled by the simple pleasure principle of life in the Playboy Philosophy.

33 What's wrong with the pleasure principle approach to life? Why does the person who spends his life seeking pleasure seldom, perhaps never, find what he seeks? For one thing, immediate sensual pleasure often results in future pain so intense as to make the pleasure not worth the price. Also, physical pleasure tends to require a constant upgrading of stimulation to get the same kicks. What starts out as exciting soon becomes boring. What once brought pleasure fails to produce the same results, so, new stimulations are sought. One who pursues the pleasure principle may soon find himself spending all of his time in pursuit. Or what is required to bring pleasure may begin also to bring pain. If he reduces the stimulation to avoid the pain, he find little pleasure but may face great boredom.

34 In regard to sexual relations a vicious cycle exists for people who follow the pleasure principle. If they care, they risk being hurt. If they don't care, sex often ceases to be fun. Harvey Cox states this point well:

> Sex is fun, but when it becomes nothing *but* fun, then pretty soon it is not even fun anymore. Some eminent psychiatrists have lately been reporting a neurosis that is beginning to emerge in America today. Young people come to psychiatrists not with complaints of guilt feelings arising out of a repressive Victorian background but from the fact that they have all the freedom they want now, but they aren't having fun. It's not pleasurable for them. They report that fun in sex just doesn't seem to be there, and they ask, "What's wrong?" ("The Playboy Panel: Religion and the New Morality." Reprint from *Playboy*.)

35 The pleasure philosophy, then, is self-defeating. The person who pursues pleasure frequently becomes so concerned about achieving it that he can't enjoy what pleasure he has. The picture of the playboys as seen from their letters to the editors seems to bear this out. Many don't really appear to be finding much satisfaction in life. The person who is afraid that his performance in bed won't measure up to the standards required for pleasure is hardly the picture of a man living life with a gusto.

36 *Playboy* talks more about sex than any other subject. It is an integral part of the pleasure approach to life. And much of this talk reveals what is to me an inadequate concept. Some statements appear as irresponsible oversimplifications. For example, *Playboy* seems to endorse this reply to a college student's question about premarital sex: "In sex, anything you get pleasure from is good. And that's all there is to it" (Hefner, p. 53).

37   It is not easy to determine what the Playboy Philosophy on sex is. I think that this is a fair statement of it as it has appeared in print: The Playboy Philosophy claims that any sexual practice between consenting adults in private not involving minors and not involving coercion, in which no one gets hurt, and which is in accord with rational self-interest, is permissible. *Playboy* more heartily endorses premarital heterosexual intercourse than extramarital or homosexual relations, but does not rule out the latter two.

38   I find it very difficult to understand how reason can be depended on to guide people in a relation as emotional as sexual intercourse. But *Playboy* has great faith in reason. I further doubt that any two people can know beforehand that no one "will get hurt"—whatever that phrase means. I suppose this could be possible if neither of them cared for the other, neither were part of a family, neither had venereal disease, and at least one were sterile.

39   *Playboy* also presents a narrow and restricted view of sex. In fact, some have charged the Playboy Philosophy with being antisexual. That hardly seems accurate. But it is restricted in its general approach. It misses the full power and beauty of sex by majoring on the physical aspect of sexual relations. Although Hefner professes to prefer emotion with his sex, the magazine as a whole presents a picture in the main of sex without love, emotion, or involvement.

40   Sexual intercourse is seen primarily as a function, as a performance. Sexual partners are not looked upon so much as people as coperformers. A partner's worth is related to performance, and woe to the partner who doesn't perform well. The playboys realize this all too well. One playboy in a letter to the editor complained, "I don't seem to be able to perform enough to satisfy the girls. . . . In fact, my fears about eventually being depleted take much of the pleasure out of sex for me, even when I'm performing well" (*Playboy,* December, 1969, p. 68). How sad when the beauty, wonder, and potential of sex is reduced to a physical performance.

41   Such a view misses, for one thing, the value of sex as a means of human communication through signs and touch. Sex communicates much about the roles of man and woman in general. Sexual activity can also communicate specific attitudes between two persons about each other. But meaningful communication, among other things, must be honest: In the language of sexual signal and touch, the degree of intimacy reflects the depth of feeling. Thus, the deeper the intimacy the deeper the feeling for one another should be. Otherwise, communication through sex becomes dishonest or meaningless. Sex is reduced to physical stimulations and is robbed of its distinctly human quality.

42   *Playboy* also fails to stress the impact of sex, particularly sexual intercourse, on personality. This failure may be but another revelation of

Playboy's shallow view of sex: It is so insignificant a thing that it really affects us very little other than bringing a moment of physical pleasure. Or it may be another aspect of the bias toward noninvolvement: Don't get so involved that the relation affects you. Either case is a denial of the fact that sexual intercourse does have a significant effect on personality.

43 The Bible's view of sex is far more adequate than *Playboy's*. *Playboy* declares that sex without love is acceptable. For the follower of Christ, any human relationship should be rooted in love. The Bible further reveals that sex is a gift from God and not evil in itself. However, the Bible regards sex so highly that certain standards are set in order that sex will function for man's good, not his harm. The Playboy Philosophy's approval of premarital sexual intercourse and toleration of adultery and homosexuality are in obvious conflict with the New Testament standards (Matt. 19:18; Romans 1:26; I Cor. 6:9; 13-20; 12:21; Rev. 22:15). Furthermore, sex is not a mere function of man, according to the Bible, but an essential part of his nature (Gen. 1-2; Matt. 19:4-5). The Bible declares that "the Word was made *flesh* and dwelt among us" (John 1:14) and "the *body* is the temple of the Holy Spirit" (I Cor. 6:19). The body should, therefore, be treated with great respect.

44 We need some clear thinking about sex, some insights on the issues created by a changing world. Although *Playboy* has raised many questions, it has provided no new approach. It talks more about what is permissible than about what is preferable. It lacks a clear statement of what the ideal in sex should be. *Playboy* dismisses any suggestion that sex is important enough, powerful enough, and wonderful enough to need careful discipline. The usual criticism is that such an attitude denies man's sexual nature. On the contrary, a disciplined approach is a recognition of man's sexual nature and manifests a desire to see that nature used for man's ultimate good, not his harm.

45 The *Playboy* view of sex is not only inadequate, it is also potentially destructive. "One thing that . . . the more joyous and confident revolutionaries leave out is that sex is dangerous. . . . It is a natural force, like fire; and like fire it can weld or warm or it can destroy" (Hettlinger, p. 41).

46 The *Playboy* approach can harm those who follow it. In the language of zoology, pair bonding may take place when none is intended causing emotional problems and difficulty in effecting a lasting pair bonding later. Also, some suggest that a playboy may develop a fantasy image of a female which no real woman can live up to. This could cause adjustment problems when he tries to move from the *Playboy* world into the real world [see Brooks R. Walker, *The New Immorality* (Garden City: Doubleday and Co., 1968), p. 155]. Some psychiatrists insist that serious emotional problems have resulted from a man's following the Playboy Philosophy. And, of course, pregnancy out of wedlock and venereal disease have not been eliminated by the pill and penicillin. In fact, the trend has been up in recent years both for out-of-wedlock births and for venereal disease (*New York Times,* February 9, 1970, p. 14c). Hefner notes this trend but blames it on puritanical restriction of information about venereal disease and contraception.

47 The Playboy Philosophy is also potentially destructive in that it could undermine marriage. The family remains a basic institution in American life. Unstable homes tend to produce unstable people who, in turn, contribute to an unstable society. Anything which is a threat to family life is a threat to society.

48 *Playboy* makes no plea for the abolition of marriage and family. In fact, it sometimes states that a family provides the best environment for the "conceiving and rearing of children" (Hefner, p. 176). *Playboy* also claims that its approach to life will make for happier more stable homes. The reasoning in the Playboy Philosophy is this: A play period before marriage will help a man mature and make him more suitable for family life; further, after maturing a bit he will be better qualified to determine what sort of person he will find compatible (Hefner, pp. 164, 176, 179); also, premarital sex may make for better sexual adjustment in marriage and sometimes extramarital sexual relations may help salvage a floundering marriage.

49 But why should ten or fifteen years of playboy existence prepare a man for a stable family life? Why should numerous premarital sexual experiences assist a man to practice fidelity in marriage? Isn't it more likely that just the opposite would be the case?

50 Another unresolved point in the *Playboy* plan for marriage is who will the playboy marry? If he marries the girl of his playboy dreams, she will be a fresh, frisky thing similar to the monthly center foldout. If this is the case, what is to happen ten or fifteen years later when a man's playmate is not the picture of sex she used to be? Is he justified in turning her in for a new model? And what about the girls? According to the Playboy Philosophy, shouldn't they have a chance to "play" before marriage too? But if they do, won't they be past their according-to-*Playmate* prime by the time they marry? If they don't "play," will they not, according to *Playboy,* be immature and unable to judge really what they want in a husband? The idea is simply not workable—not if it is kept within the guidelines of the Playboy Philosophy.

51 In spite of these few expressed concerns for marriage, the bulk of *Playboy* is basically antimarriage. Through stories, cartoons, and jokes the message comes through clearly: for the playboy, marriage is a trap to be avoided. Editorial comments reveal a more subtle but still obvious anti-marriage sentiment. *Playboy* indicates that marriage comes when playtime is over—a pretty depressing, forbidding picture, especially to a playboy.

52   One of the clearest insights on *Playboy's* view of marriage was in a feature called the "Playboy Coloring Book." The section ends with a picture of a pretty girl standing in front of a church. The caption reads: "She has been standing in front of the church for a long while now. Why is she wearing that funny white dress? Is she waiting for the playboy? She is going to have a long wait. Color this page completely black. Then tear it out and burn it." (*Playboy*, January, 1963, p. 78.)

53   In contrast to the *Playboy* view, the Bible sees marriage as the framework for man's most meaningful relations. The relation between husband and wife is compared to that between Christ and the Church (Eph. 5:32-33). Love and trust are basic. Unfaithfulness has no place. Thus, adultery is wrong; it violates the essence of marriage. The New Testament is very clear about this (Matt. 19:18; Mark 10:19; Luke 18:20; 1 Cor. 7). Only in an atmosphere of life commitment, love, trust, tenderness, and deep involvement—in marriage as it ought to be—can sexual relations bring the greatest satisfaction.

54   The pleasure approach to life can be destructive to human relations in general. It can degenerate easily into using people as things to gain pleasure. Man has enough temptation in this direction without needing encouragement. *Playboy,* for example, often seems to regard girls as playthings, as toys for the playboy. They can be used to bring pleasure and then discarded.

55   The differences between the Playboy Philosophy and the Christian faith are not superficial. They are basic. Some of the differences have already been mentioned: The Christian faith and the Playboy Philosophy present diverse views on the nature of man and the world, the standards for sex, the way to better life, and the guiding principles for decision making. In addition, three other basic differences stand out.

56   *1. Value of Persons:* For *Playboy* the worth of a person seems to stem more from what he *has* or what she *does* than from what he or she *is.* Women in particular are often pictured as things rather than persons. It doesn't take a Christian to spot this tendency to degrade women in the *Playboy* approach. As one girl put it, "I don't think the way to help men gain a sense of their worth is to depreciate women by dressing them as rabbits."

57   Sometimes *Playboy* is quite explicit in its view of women as toys, having value mainly because they bring pleasure to the playboy. In the "Playboy Coloring Book" the toys in the playboy's pad are the playmates. And this is what is said about the toys (girls): "These are extra playmates.

Every playboy should have several to spare. That is because variety is the spice of life. The playboy likes his life spicy. Make one of the girls a blonde. Make one of the girls a brunette. Make one of the girls a redhead. It does not matter which is which. The girls' hair colors are interchangeable. So are the girls.''

58   The Christian cannot consider a person made in God's image as a toy. One for whom Christ died has inestimable worth. An individual who is so unique that God numbers the hairs on her head must not be treated as an easily interchangeable accessory for sex play.

59   The Bible insists that all persons be treated as having worth in and for themselves regardless of physical attractiveness, mental quickness, or social grace. Likewise, the follower of Christ is not to assign superior value to any man because of his wealth or social prominence (James 2:1-4; 9; I Peter 2:17). God is no respecter of persons (Acts 10:34). Jesus again and again demonstrated the value of one person. Regardless of a person's possessions, attractiveness, social standing, or potential value to Jesus' cause, He took time to help.

60   *2. Basis of Human Relations:* Even a superficial scanning of *Playboy* and the Bible reveals basic conflict at the point of the basis of human relations. Hefner writes, ''Any doctrine is evil if it teaches that . . . self-denial is preferable to self-gratification'' (Hefner, p. 100). But, Jesus said, ''If any man will come after Me, let him deny himself, take up his cross and follow Me'' (Mark 8:34). Hefner writes, ''It is right and natural for the individual to be primarily concerned with himself.'' But the New Testament reads, ''No one should be looking out for his own interests, but for the interests of others (I Cor. 10:24), and ''We should not please ourselves. Instead, each of us should please his brother for his own good, in order to build him up in the faith. For Christ did not please Himself'' (Rom. 15:1-3 TEV). Hefner writes, ''Rational man should be expected to exercise what is termed enlightened self-interest'' (Hefner, p. 100). Jesus said, ''A new commandment I give you: love one another. As I have loved you, so you must love one another'' (John 13:34 TEV).

61   In the Playboy Philosophy love is not mentioned as the motivation for helping others. In fact, the word love is almost never used except as a synonym for sexual intercourse or romance. Love as *agape,* as a willingness to sacrifice, if need be, for the welfare of others, is not evident in the Playboy Philosophy. Hefner refers with disapproval to ''a sort of selfless interest in helping others, without doing anything to help oneself'' (Hefner, p. 14). If he is true to the Playboy Philosophy, the playboy is not likely to act to help the poor and the downtrodden of the world, not unless he sees their restlessness as in some way a threat to his own well-being.

62   Does *Playboy* really want everyone to relate to others on the basis of "enlightened self-interest"? Even if men do operate on this level much of the time, should we label it best? Is *Playboy's* increasing concern for social issues based on nothing more than enlightened self-interest?

63   A Christian is expected to love others, and love means meeting their needs even if self-sacrifice is the price. Under the impulse of love, the Christian seeks not so much to receive as to give. Other persons are neighbors to be loved, not toys to be played with for personal pleasure, not tools to be used for personal profit.

64   *3. Meaning of Life:* Happiness, *Playboy* says, should be the goal of man, it is what gives life meaning. But squeezing the juice out of the concept, *Playboy* leaves us nothing much but the pulp of pleasure. *Playboy* says: Get wealth; enjoy sensual activity; live for yourself. America has had an experiment with this way to happiness. And things haven't turned out too well. Many have discovered that life does not consist in an abundance of things, that a cause is more important than possessions. Maybe that is why Jesus has such appeal. Jesus knew who He was and what life was for. No better example of a robust, responsible nonconformist can be found. He simply refused to be crammed into anyone's mold. He refused to cower before men's opinions, harmful traditions, or military force. His actions were not based on a selfish desire to be different. They stemmed from His singular commitment to bring real life to men.

65   His rugged individualism was balanced by a deep concern for community. He created a fellowship and urged His followers to love one another.

66   Jesus demonstrated what freedom ought to be. His freedom was gained by courage and discipline. He cherished freedom not to gratify selfish desire but to help others. He promised to free us from our hang-ups, fears, and enslavements. To the degree that we become Jesus' servants (and He calls us friends!), we find freedom. And he who finds it is surprised by the joy which is his, especially as he uses his freedom to help free others.

67   Jesus was interested in man's happiness. He was no sour-faced fanatic. He enjoyed a good party. And He had a sense of humor. For Jesus, life was basically made up of worship, fellowship, and service—all done in love. And He calls us to follow Him.

68   Follow Him then. He will give you something worth dying for as well as something worth living for. He will take you on a crusade against senseless, selfish living, against exploitation, prejudice, and hate. He will lead you in a campaign for justice, human dignity, and social change. He will challenge you to new levels of love and service to others. He will show you a God who loves you and will lead you to know the thrill of worship—of realizing there is someone greater than you. In short, He will give you new life.

69 In it all you may never grow rich, own a sports car, or learn the ways of gourmet dining; these simply will not be your goals.

70 You may be ridiculed. You may grow weary. You may find there are more needs to meet than you could care for in a thousand lifetimes. But it will be an adventure. No one can tell where it will take you. But I can tell you one thing, you won't be bored. You will find meaning, freedom, and joy.

71 Others may go hopping down the bunny trail but I'll follow Him who said, "I am the way, the truth, and the life. Follow Me."

Chapter 6

SPEECHES THAT CREATE CONCERN FOR PROBLEMS

The speaker must awaken those who sleep or are indifferent; he must help others see the unnoticed danger, and understand it; he must direct us away from the false and petty problems that set us off course.

Otis M. Walter and Robert L. Scott

THE NATURE AND IMPORTANCE OF SPEECHES THAT CREATE CONCERN FOR PROBLEMS

Human existence in society gives rise to problems that threaten the perpetuation of the group and the welfare of its members. A problem might be described as a defect, difficulty, barrier, need, threat, state of dissatisfaction, or undesirable situation that people perceive as necessitating removal, rectification, or solution. The ability of groups and individuals to perceive and understand the nature and importance of the problems confronting them is one measure of a society's maturity and strength. If a society is unable to comprehend the significance of its problems, it has little chance of solving them.

Speakers often address audiences for the primary purpose of creating concern for problems. Whereas speeches advocating values are designed to develop value standards and value judgments in the minds of listeners, speeches trying to create concern for problems focus on specific social situations calling for remedial action. The mayor of a large city, for example, may seek to arouse public concern over the urban conditions that breed crime or riots. A sociologist may attempt to create concern for senior citizens on welfare. A politician may try to arouse sympathy for the plight of the American Indian.

Sometimes a speaker focuses on a problem as a prelude to advocating specific programs or policies as solutions for that problem. In any case, we face potential personal and public problems at virtually every turn: alcoholism, drug abuse, racial conflict, unemployment, suicide, pollution and abuse of the environment, violence as a way of life, discrimination against women, political deception, economic inflation, deceptive or harmful advertising, automobile accidents, and rising crime rates.

While the proposition of fact asserts that something is true or false and the proposition of value asserts that something has or lacks merit, the speech attempting to create concern for a problem asserts that specific social conditions should be perceived or defined as problems. Consider the following examples:

Proposition A: Racial unrest is Boston's most impelling community problem.

Proposition B: The unrestricted sale of firearms is cause for public alarm.

Proposition C: All parents should be concerned by the increased availability of hardcore pornography.

Proposition D: Student drug usage is a serious campus problem.

Proposition E: The depiction of violence on television programs oriented toward children merits public concern.

Proposition F: The increasing rate of traffic fatalities on Highway 12 warrants action by the state legislature.

Although the speech that creates concern for a problem usually depends on the affirmation of subsidiary propositions of fact and value, the basic purpose of such a speech is to invite attention to a problem needing solution.

CRITERIA FOR EVALUATING SPEECHES
THAT CREATE CONCERN FOR PROBLEMS

1. Has the speaker presented a compelling view of the nature of the problem?

The philosopher John Dewey emphasized the importance of this criterion when he wrote: "The essence of critical thinking is suspended judgment; and the essence of this suspense is inquiry to determine the nature of the problem before proceeding to attempts at its solution." To depict compellingly the nature of a problem, a speaker must prove that a certain state of affairs, a concrete set of circumstances, actually does exist. The nature is explained by focusing on the major elements of the problem and on its symptoms or outward manifestations.

Naturally a complete view of a problem includes a thorough exploration of the causes (the contributing influences) which combine to produce the state of affairs. Some problems are rooted in defective structures, personnel, or policies; other problems stem from inadequate goals, standards, and principles; still others derive from "outside" threats, opponents, or enemies. Remember, also, that social problems seldom are the result of a single cause. Rather, although one contributing factor may be described as the primary or the immediate cause, several contributing factors usually combine in primary-secondary and immediate-remote relationships. Finally, a compelling view often stems from describing the intensity and/or the widespread scope of the problem.

In exploring the nature of the problem, speakers may assume the role of social informant. When they do, the success of their speeches is governed, in part, by the same constraints imposed on speakers seeking to impart knowledge. They must choose those supporting materials that best demonstrate the nature of the problem: analogy and illustration, expert testimony and factual example, description, definition, and narration. Their messages are subject to the same criteria suggested in Chapter 3: Is the knowledge communicated accurately, completely, and with unity? Does the speaker make the knowledge meaningful for the audience? Does the speaker create audience interest in the knowledge presented? Has the speaker shown the audience that the knowledge is important?

In a speech called "Mingled Blood," Ralph Zimmerman, a college student and a hemophiliac, chose to use definition and description to illuminate the nature of hemophilia:

> What is this thing called hemophilia? Webster defines it as "a tendency, usually hereditary, to profuse bleeding even from slight wounds." Dr. Armand J. Quick, Professor of Biochemistry at Marquette University and a recognized world authority on this topic, defines it as "a prothrombin consumption time of 8 to 13 seconds." Normal time is 15 seconds. Now do you know what hemophilia is? . . .
> What does it really mean to be a hemophiliac? The first indication comes in early childhood when a small scratch may bleed for hours. By the time the hemophiliac reaches school age, he begins to suffer from internal bleeding into muscles, joints, the stomach, the kidneys. This latter type is far more serious, for external wounds can usually be stopped in minutes with topical thromboplastin or a pressure bandage. But internal bleeding can be checked only by changes in the blood by means of transfusion or plasma injections. If internal bleeding into a muscle or joint goes unchecked repeatedly, muscle contraction and bone deformity inevitably result.

Along with imparting knowledge about the problem, speakers also may affirm propositions of fact related to the problem. When speakers seek to prove propositions of fact in developing a compelling view of the problem, their efforts are subject to the same criteria suggested in Chapter 4: Has the speaker adequately assessed the proof requirements of the factual proposition? Has the speaker offered acceptable arguments in support of the proposition of fact? Has the speaker provided adequate evidence in support of the arguments?

2. *Has the speaker shown the significance of the problem for the specific audience?*

In addition to gaining an understanding of the nature of the problem, an audience must also be convinced that the problem has significance for them individually or collectively. Thus, value judgments must augment factual demonstrations. To demonstrate that juvenile delinquency is extensive, a factual state of affairs must be established. To demonstrate that juvenile delinquency poses a threat or is an undesirable situation, a judgment must be made in light of societal value standards. When a speaker affirms a proposition of value in showing the significance of a problem, the criteria suggested in Chapter 5 usually are relevant: Has the speaker demonstrated, or is it assumed by the audience, that he or she is a person of high credibility with respect to the proposition? Has the speaker advanced acceptable criteria for the assessment of the proposition? Has the speaker presented a fair view of what is being evaluated?

A problem is not really a problem to an audience until they perceive it as such. A situation may exist, and the audience even may know that it does, but in their eyes it remains nothing more than a lifeless fact until they view it as something that threatens or violates their interests and values. The members of an audience who have just been informed that many American Indians endure substandard economic, educational, and health conditions may greet this knowledge with indifference. Although they may accept the situation as actual, they have not perceived it as a problem for themselves, either as individuals or as members of society.

In *Personal Knowledge,* philosopher and scientist Michael Polanyi reminds us that "nothing is a problem . . . in itself; it can be a problem only if it puzzles or worries somebody." Clearly a problem is "created" for an audience through their own perceptual processes. An audience labels something as a problem only when they perceive a strong link between a situation (real or imagined) and their relevant basic values which they see as undermined or threatened by that situation. Speakers and listeners employ values as standards to "define" something as a problem.

What approaches could a speaker use to show the significance of a problem? Ralph Zimmerman concluded that for many listeners it is sufficient to show that the problem brings danger, degradation, or suffering to those who directly experience it. Thus he depicted hemophilia as a source of suffering for those afflicted by it:

> I remember the three long years when I couldn't even walk because repeated hemorrhages had twisted my ankles and knees to pretzel-like forms. I remember being pulled to school in a wagon while other boys rode their bikes, and being pushed to my table. I remember sitting in the dark empty classroom by myself during recess while the others went out in the sun to run and play. And I remember the first terrible day at the big high school when I came on crutches and built-up shoes carrying my books in a sack around my neck. . . . And how well I remember the endless pounding, squeezing pain. When you seemingly drown in your own perspiration, when your teeth ache and bombs explode back of your eyeballs; when darkness and light fuse into one hue of gray; when day becomes night and night becomes day—time stands still—and all that matters is that ugly pain.

Although the most hardened pragmatist might state that the problem is of little social importance because when Zimmerman spoke in 1955 there were only 20,000 to 40,000 hemophiliacs in the United States, most Americans, committed to the worth of the individual human, would agree with Zimmerman that "if society can keep a hemophiliac alive until after adolescence, society has saved a member."

Guided by the actual nature of the problem and by relevant standards of ethics, a speaker may choose from a variety of potential strategies to create audience concern. Here we present a few such strategies, some adapted from the writings of Otis M. Walter. To show that the problem directly or indirectly harms the audience addressed (economically, socially, morally, physically) is an approach often used. Sometimes the problem is described as a unique, immediate, and pressing one demanding speedy recognition, diagnosis, and treatment; or it is described as an important contemporary manifestation of a timeless, continuing, larger problem always faced by humanity. Awareness of the problem may be emerging only gradually in the public consciousness and an audience might be urged to be in the vanguard of citizens concerned about it. On the other hand, the audience might be asked to join large numbers of fellow citizens who already recognize the problem.

Through use of historical examples, a speaker could argue that the failure of past societies to recognize the same or a similar problem caused them harm. Often this argument is embodied in an analogy to the decline and fall of the Roman Empire. The ways in which the problem contributes to or interacts with other societal problems could be demonstrated. If the problem is now in the embryonic stage, audiences could be warned that if it is not treated it will steadily worsen and perhaps become unsolvable. On occasion a problem of concern for those affected takes on added significance when shown also to be working to the political or psychological advantage of our opponents or enemies. If the audience and the people harmed by the problem both have similar goals, values, needs, and fears, the audience could be made to feel that they might just as easily have experienced the problem themselves ("There but for the grace of God go I"). A speaker could show that the problem is acknowledged as vital by those whom the audience regards highly, such as public officials, statesmen, religious leaders, or experts on the subject.

The harmful economic, political, social, religious, or moral consequences of leaving the problem unsolved could be stressed. The problem could be shown as one of physical survival or security; or it could be shown as a problem threatening the enhancement or growth of the human spirit. A problem becomes of concern when it causes our society and its institutions to function at less than normal expected effectiveness. Sometimes the problem legitimately is described as stemming from conflict between an accepted but outmoded belief or value and existing circumstances. Finally, a speaker usually must secure audience perception of the problem as a high priority one, more crucial than most other problems faced by them or society.

CONCLUSION

In our society people often seek to generate concern about problems, both great and small. At certain times the speaker's sole purpose is to set the stage for private thought or public discussion. At other times the speaker seeks to arouse interest in a problem to prepare the audience for accepting a specific solution. In either case, the speaker must present *a compelling view of the nature of the problem* and *the reasons that it is significant for the particular audience.*

For Further Reading

Dewey, John. *How We Think.* D. C. Heath, 1910, pp. 72–74. Concisely explains the importance of understanding the nature of problems.

Jensen, J. Vernon. *Argumentation: Reasoning in Communication.* Van Nostrand, 1981. Ch. 4 suggests potential lines of argument basic to presenting the nature of a problem.

St. Onge, Keith R. *Creative Speech.* Wadsworth, 1964, pp. 203–13. Discusses in some detail the necessity and role of understanding societies problems.

Walter, Otis M., and Scott, Robert L. *Thinking and Speaking.* 4th ed. Macmillan, 1979. Chapters 10 and 11 focus on suggestions for persuading about problems and causes.

Walter, Otis M. *Speaking Intelligently.* Macmillan, 1976, Chapters 2, 3, 4 and pp. 216–21. An exploration of the nature of societal problems and causes of such problems, along with suggested strategies for persuading about problems and causes.

IS THE FREE PRESS IN AMERICA UNDER ATTACK?

Walter Cronkite

Walter Cronkite, longstanding anchorman for the CBS news, is perhaps one of the best known Americans. Even since leaving the regular news show, he still appears regularly on various CBS specials and is in great demand as a public speaker. Because he has been so favorably known to so many for so long, his personal credibility tends to be unusually high and his ideas command a good deal of attention. On the evening of January 23, 1979, during International Printing Week, Cronkite addressed an audience in New York City expressing concern for freedom of the press.

Cronkite on this occasion contended that the rights of the press have been progressively dismantled by the nation's courts, thereby encroaching upon the "public's right to know." Since a free press "is the central nervous system of a democratic society," according to Cronkite, the courts' actions should concern us all. The first question you as a student may want to deal with after reading this speech is the one that asks how much the speaker's personality affects reception of the message. Since we all are accustomed to receiving nothing but "facts" from our news commentators, is it more difficult to deal critically with this speech than it is with others? Just how important is the ethos of a speaker?

You may want to identify the various ways that Cronkite suggests the courts are infringing upon freedom of the press, thereby determining his organizational pattern as well as the key issues. In order to present a compelling view of the nature of the problem, Cronkite examines critical instances when, in his opinion, the judiciary has ruled against the press. The use of such examples as evidence in developing what is essentially a proposition of fact is integral to his case. How effectively does Cronkite employ his evidence to support his case? Is his evidence ample? Does the fact that he is a strong partisan on this topic influence you in your analysis?

At the outset, Cronkite tries to make the problem compelling through a series of strong statements about imminent dangers. Do any of these statements seem like purposeful exaggerations or do they strike you as meaningful interest generators for his listening audience? Again, in paragraph 36, Cronkite draws a comparison with Nazi Germany. Do you think this appropriate? Just how concerned is the average American about First Amendment guarantees? Does it take a rather compelling speech to make the problem graphic to people?

This speech is reprinted by permission from *Vital Speeches of the Day*, March 15, 1979, pp. 331–334.

1   I want to direct my remarks tonight to what I consider a fundamental and dangerous threat to the institution of the free press in America. It is *fundamental,* because it attacks the free flow of information, literally at its source. And it is especially *dangerous* because it comes from the one group most responsible for guarding First Amendment rights—the judiciary, led by the Supreme Court of the United States.

2   A number of court decisions in recent years, culminating most recently in rulings by the *highest* court, have had the effect of telling the press that it has no special rights, no constitutionally protected function to inform the public—and, by extension, of telling the public that it may not have any particular right to know.

3   I don't want to exaggerate the danger. I don't think anyone is going to shut down the newspapers or shut off the television networks in the *foreseeable future . . .* but I don't intend to minimize the threat, either. The right of journalists to *publish* the news is not being challenged, but our ability to *get* the news to publish is being undermined in a variety of ways and challenged at the highest levels.

4   There is no serious effort underway (that I know of) to *junk* the First Amendment. But there is a growing effort in progress to *gut* it; to make it about as meaningful as—an appendix—or a campaign promise.

5   The right of the press to protect *confidential sources* has been progressively dismantled. The police have been told they may search newsrooms without warning and with nothing more than a judicial warrant. Reporters have been stripped of their right to protect sources before grand juries or in court proceedings. And there has been a growing tendency to bar access by reporters to official, and presumably public, events, institutions and records.

6   The common theme of most of these inroads on press freedom is that journalists are not a privileged class under the law; that the First Amendment grants them no special rights or sanctions; that the rights given them are the same—no more and no less—than those granted every American citizen.

7   That theme has been spelled out in some detail by the Chief Justice of the United States.

8   Last year, in a case involving the state of Massachusetts and the National Bank of Boston, the Court ruled that a bank has as much consti-

tutional right to speak out on matters of public policy as a newspaper or an individual.

9 That seemed a simple, clear reaffirmation of First Amendment rights, and I had no trouble with it in the least.

10 But the Chief Justice wasn't satisfied. He wrote a separate, concurring opinion that shifted the emphasis and sharpened the point significantly. He turned the whole argument around. The Chief Justice wanted to make it perfectly clear that, in his opinion, the press has no rights not *afforded* a bank, or a private citizen. Even that may sound alright, until you take a closer look at what it really means. And since then, we've been given several specific examples.

11 When the Supreme Court handed down its Boston bank ruling, it also was considering a case in California where reporters had tried to exercise what they felt should be a right or privilege—access to jails and prisons for the purpose of reporting on conditions there. The case involved the Alameda County Jail, where in 1972, a federal judge had found conditions so "shocking and debasing" that they amounted to cruel and unusual punishment. When an inmate committed suicide under questionable circumstances, a San Francisco television station asked permission to visit the jail and film conditions there. The sheriff said "no," prison policy excluded the press.

12 The TV station sued, and a lower federal court ruled that the sheriff could not bar reporters altogether, and ordered him to permit limited access. The Supreme Court, however, overruled the lower court, finding that the press had no greater right of access to government facilities than the general public.

13 Explaining the majority's position. Chief Justice Burger made painfully explicit the implications of his opinion in the Boston bank case . . . as well as the Alice-In-Wonderland quality of the Court's handling of the issue. The Chief Justice drew a distinction between *gathering* news and *distributing* it.

14 Now, on several occasions, the Court had emphasized the importance of informed public opinion and a free press. But *those* cases, he explained, were concerned only with communicating information once it is *obtained*. They did not—and I quote— "remotely imply a constitutional right guaranteeing anyone access to government information beyond that open to the public generally."

15 Now that, to me, is high grade hogwash! Obviously, the general public cannot parade at will through the jails and prisons. That simply would be unmanageable. But then, the same can be said with respect to the White House and the State Department and the Capitol Building, can't it? In ruling that the press has no more right of access than the ordinary citizen, the Supreme Court has decided that the *public* has no particular right to know what goes on in public institutions, beyond that which the government chooses to reveal. And that, I submit, is an extraordinary reading of the intent of the First Amendment. Indeed, it is an extraordinary interpretation of what democracy is all about! And it could create a hole in the First Amendment big enough to drive the rest of the Constitution through.

16 Justice John Paul Stevens seemed to recognize that. In a dissenting opinion, Stevens argued that "information gathering is entitled to some measure of constitutional protection," not for the benefit of the press, "but to insure that the citizens are fully informed." And he quoted James Madison— one of those framers whose intent the Court tries to gauge in handing down interpretations of the Constitution. Madison had written: "A popular government, without popular information *or the means of acquiring it,* is but a prologue to a farce, or a tragedy; or perhaps both."

17 Now look at the effect of this in the real world. Reporters are asked to give information, names, testimony to the defense or the prosecution in a court case . . . to do their work for them, as it were. Even where a confidential source is not "burned" . . . or revealed, the *impression* is fostered that the press is part of the court system, rather than an independent entity. To people outside the law and to dissident groups on the borderline, talking to a reporter becomes tantamount to talking to a cop. They don't do it. Next time around, the courts will not be able to squeeze the reporter for information, because he won't have been given any . . . and a major channel of independent information will have dried up.

18 Critics of the press in these matters accuse reporters of trying to claim a privileged status above the rest of the citizenry. But the critics, who include many judges, and a majority of the present Supreme Court, are missing the point. We are not trying to assert *personal* privilege; we are trying to protect our ability to perform a critical social function—informing the public.

19 There are other groups in our society which have important functions to perform, and which are granted special status, or "privileges," if you will, to perform them. Policemen, doctors, lawyers, ministers come to mind. The ordinary citizen is not allowed, in most American cities, to walk around with a gun on his hip, or prescribe drugs, or argue someone else's case before a court, or protect the confidentiality of a criminal confession. None of these "special privileges" seems to cause the courts any problem, perhaps because they rarely conflict with the "special privileges" which judges assume for themselves. But let reporters assert such privilege, and a judicial howl goes up.

20 Make no mistake; where the press is denied all access, the public's right to know has been denied. It is quite as simple as that, and it sometimes is quite as deliberate as that. Over the years, for instance, there has been a growing tendency among judges to issue *"gag"* rules to protect court proceedings from prejudicial publicity. When such gags on *reporters,* themselves, were held unconstitutional, judges began barring all access to pretrial hearings and even to some trial sessions. The *purpose* of all this was to protect the right to a fair trial. The *effect* was to deny the public's right to be informed about trial proceedings—and, incidentally or not, to permit the operation of our system of justice in secrecy, locked away from public scrutiny.

21 The same issue—of free press vs. fair trial—has been the source of the most dangerous attack on the ability of the press to perform its social function. By that, I mean the rash of denials by the courts of reporters' rights to protect confidential sources. Not only does the principle of confidentiality lie at the very heart of investigative reporting, it is key to more mundane forms of reporting as well. An awful lot of what the public learns on a day-to-day basis, beyond official pronouncements and handouts, comes from un-named sources. Those sources may range from a gangster telling about an activity of organized crime, to a presidential aide talking about foreign policy. It may be a Watergate-style "deep-throat," fearful of retaliation, or the Secretary of State, who, for delicate diplomatic reasons, wants to be known only as a "senior official." Or it may be a clerk in a corrupt branch of local government. All rely on the promise of anonymity, and if they feel they cannot rely on that promise, they will have nothing to say—in the vernacular, they'll clam up.

22 Confidentiality is absolutely crucial to the process of gathering the information we report as news. But the courts have been increasingly deaf to that argument. In 1972, the Supreme Court held that the Constitution did not give reporters the right to refuse to testify before a grand jury in order to protect confidential sources. At the same time, however, the Court seemed to invite the states to give reporters that right, by statute, if they chose to do so, and enacted press "shield laws," which sought to limit the power of state courts to demand a reporter's sources, notes or testimony.

23 But in state after state, those "shields" have been tested in court, and have provided about as much protection as tissue paper. And the *state* courts have been tearing them up left and right. The most recent and noticed addition to the pile of shredded shields, of course, was the New Jersey law. *The New York Times* and reporter Myron Farber claimed protection of that shield when Farber's notes were subpoenaed by the defendant in a murder trial. The New Jersey Supreme Court, however, ruled that the shield law must give way to the Sixth Amendment rights of the accused—the right of fair trial—and the United States Supreme Court upheld that ruling.

24 Many journalists who have been concerned about the problem have been persuaded that the constitutional conflict is real . . . and that some effort to balance competing rights is required . . . (though it has seemed strange to me that so little effort is made by the judicial system to avoid these collisions. Seldom, it seems, is any effort made to find out whether the court, or the prosecution, or the defense, can get what it needs without demanding a re-porter's notes, before hauling him before a judge to snitch on his sources.)

25   That brings into focus something else that has concerned me. That is a growing tendency of government to regard itself as having rights, often in competition with rights granted the people.

26   During its last term, the Supreme Court produced a constitutional shocker, upholding a police raid on the offices of a student newspaper at Stanford University. The police had been looking for photographs they believed might contain evidence of criminal acts during a demonstration. None was found. Two lower courts found the search of the newspaper's offices illegal, because police had only a search warrant. The lower courts said a subpoena was required. A subpoena would have given the newspaper an opportunity to argue against the search in court. The Supreme Court, however, said that a search warrant, which provides for no warning, from which there is no appeal, and which is issuable in some states by a justice of the peace, was enough.

27   The decision was another serious blow against the First Amendment rights of the press. But it also tore a hole in the right of *all* Americans under the Fourth Amendment—which guarantees the right the people to be secure in their persons, houses, papers, and effects against unreasonable searches and seizures.

28   For most of our history, warrants were *limited* to searches for contraband, weapons and plunder . . . a narrow category that usually implied some guilt on the part of the owner. But now the Supreme Court has widened the category by permitting searches for more evidence, meaning information. And it has said that the homes and offices of innocent third parties . . . doctors, lawyers, clergymen, businessmen, and factory workers, as well as newspapers . . . are subject to searches with no more warning than a knock on the door and the presentation of a warrant. *We are returned by one judicial decision to the days of submission to an autocratic colonial master.*

29   The decision virtually invites conflicts between the press and police authorities and other arms of the state. Justice Stevens pointed out that it was just that sort of conflict, in which government agents might set out to grab private notes and papers, that the authors of the Fourth Amendment sought to prevent. Unfortunately, Stevens was in the dissenting minority, again.

30   Think of what might have happened if this ruling had been in effect during the Nixon administration. For one thing, the Pentagon Papers might never have seen the light of day. The White House could easily have gotten a warrant from some federal judge and seized them, early on, from *The New York Times.*

31   And what a field day the likes of Haldeman, Ehrlichman, Mitchell and Colson might have had if this decision had been in force at the time of the Watergate break-in. Who knows? With judiciously timed ransackings of the offices of *The Washington Post* and *The New York Times,* they might have uncovered enough sources and plugged enough leaks to contain that scandal sufficiently to save Richard Nixon's hold on the presidency.

32 Such scandals at the national level, fortunately, are rare. But they are less rare at the local level, and it is there that the impact of the "knock on the door decision," as it's been called, could be particularly devastating. A hypothetical example:

33 An honest minor official, or merely a disgruntled one, working in a City Hall run by a corrupt political machine, begins feeding information to the local newspaper. The information touches on a kickback scheme which can be traced all the way to the top, if the leak isn't plugged. But it is. The machine's police chief, or the machine's D.A with the flimsiest of excuses, goes to one of the *machine's* judges for a search warrant, and the paper is ransacked. While pawing through files and desk drawers, the searchers find the name of the newspaper's source on the kickback story. That honest official might be fired and threatened with prosecution on some trumped up charge if he did any more talking to the press. Or he might be intimidated in some other fashion. In some precincts, he might very well end up in the trunk of a car. In any case, the leak would be fixed. And the word would go out to other potential whistle-blowers that there is no way they can depend on remaining anonymous.

34 In this case, of course, there is no Sixth Amendment right of fair trial involved. The First and Fourth Amendments are being squeezed here, merely for the convenience of law enforcement officials.

35 It is all a very serious business, for the larger government grows, and the more complex the issues become, the greater a democracy's need for an independent press capable of monitoring the government and the performance of its public servants, After all, most of what the government does, it is doing either *for* us or *to* us. The rest it is doing in our name. Whatever, the case, we need to know.

36 You know, there was an experience shared by many of us who were in Germany at the end of the Second World War that I think is sharply relevant to this issue. People would come up to us, and with tears in their eyes they would tell us they had no idea of the horrors of Auschwitz and Buchenwald . . . they just didn't know. The curious thing was that many of them were telling the truth, or a half-truth anyway. Most probably they didn't know the full horror, or let themselves think about it if they suspected. After all, they had surrendered their civic eyes along with their national soul. They had surrendered their civic eyes along with their national soul. They had helped to dismantle their own democracy and had made no complaint when freedom of the press was abolished. They weren't informed of the gas chambers, at least most weren't.

37 But that hardly let them off the moral hook. They still shared the guilt, for they had given the Nazi's a blank check . . . and it was all done in their name.

38 And in a still functioning democracy such as ours there is no way for the people to avoid moral responsibility for the acts of their government, at every level. By definition democratic government is of the people and by the people. We are responsible for what happens in the Alameda County Jail, just as we were responsible for conditions at Attica. What government in America does, *we* do . . . you and I. It is true in our jails and prisons, just as it is true in the Capitol Building and in the White House. And it is true in our conduct of foreign policy.

39 We must demand that the press be free to give us as full and independent and up-to-date accounting of what government is doing in our name. For government operating in the dark produces things like Attica, and Watergate and Vietnam.

40 The people of a democracy must demand access for the press to their own institutions and records, and elected officials . . . for they have a critical need to know. That is particularly true today, when acts and decisions of government can affect not only the welfare of millions across the country and around the world . . . but the welfare and options of the future as well.

41 That is why the unhampered functioning of a free press is so important. Whatever the original emphasis of the First Amendment was thought to be, that, to me is its primary emphasis today . . . or should be, if it is to amount to something more than a license to blow off steam.

42 The democracy that permits its own elected or appointed officials to tell the people, in effect, that they have no right to know what goes on in public institutions, is a democracy flirting with disaster.

43 You know, whenever I read of judges telling state legislatures, as has been true in some shield law cases . . . that the law makers have no business telling the judges how to run their courts—and whenever I hear freedom of the press arguments put down as secondary not only to the rights of a defendant on trial, but to the convenience of lawyers, judges, police investigators and jail keepers—whenever I witness these displays of official arrogance, I am reminded of something attributed to the German playwright, Bertolt Brecht. Brecht, of course, was a dedicated communist, but he also was a brilliant artist with an original and independent mind. When East German workers, in 1956, rebelled against intolerably oppressive living conditions, and were put down violently, the East German government expressed its *"disappointment"* with the rebels. And Brecht, anonymously, circulated a sardonic reply that went, in part, something like this: "the government has said it is disappointed with the people. Clearly, the government should dissolve the people and elect a new one."

44   We have been told, and have told ourselves, that fundamental First and Sixth Amendment rights are in conflict and must be balanced by compromise.

45   We in the media *must* be careful with our power . . . with what privileges we manage to hang on to. We must avoid, where possible, actions which make the right of fair trial a difficult right to uphold. We must avoid unwarranted intrusions upon people's privacy. Liberty and, no less, one's reputation in the community, are terribly precious things, and they must not be dealt with lightly or endangered by capricious claims of special privilege.

46   But above all else, we must avoid aquiescing in the chipping away of First Amendment guarantees of press freedom. For the free press, after all, is the central nervous system of a democratic society. No true democracy, as we understand the term can exist without it. The press may be irresponsible at times, obstreperous, arrogant; even cruel, when innocent individuals are caught in the rip-tide of damaging publicity. But a free, unintimidated and unregulated press is democracy's early warning system against both the dangers of democracies own excesses and the approach of tyranny. And, inevitably, one of the first signs of tyranny's approach is the heavy footstep on the threshold of press freedom.

47   And when an apparent conflict between other rights is rendered inevitable by opportunistic counsel or an arrogant judiciary, then we must defend our right to inform the public. When push comes to shove, if it must, then the greater good must be found in guaranteeing the freedom of the press and the public's right to know. Now that may sound harsh. It is, in a sense, a kind of constitutional triage . . . triage being that horrible, but unfortunately necessary World War I concept for sorting out the carnage from the battlefield; the most seriously injured left to die by an overworked medical corps in order to treat those who had a better chance of surviving. But if a triage treatment of our Bill of Rights is forced upon us, I say the first priority must be the guarantor of our liberty and all our rights, the free press clause of the First Amendment.

Thank you.

TELEVISION NEWS COVERAGE

Spiro T. Agnew

Vice President Agnew delivered this speech to the Mid-West Regional Republican Committee at Des Moines, Iowa, on November 13, 1969. The address illustrates that a single speech can have great impact. The day after the speech, the New York Times reviewed it and printed the gist of it. Thousands of Americans immediately responded to the Vice President's invitation to show their concern by calling the networks and newspapers and venting their views on the media's handling of the news. The speech was both defended and denounced. CBS in seven cities received 16,000 calls, 9,000 for and 7,000 against. Television officials also responded. Dr. Frank Stanton, President of CBS, said that the Vice President's unprecedented attack on the news medium did not represent "legitimate criticism." The President of NBC, Julian Goodman, stated: "Vice President Agnew's attack on television news is an appeal to prejudice." He accused Agnew of using "his high office to criticize the way a Government-licensed news medium covers the activities of the Government itself." Agnew then challenged the three networks to carry his speech nationally and they accepted.

Ironically, the planners of the conference Agnew addressed had not even expected his appearance. Two days before convening, the Vice President called them and suggested that he speak. Quite expectedly, they agreed. The attack on the news medium, however, was unexpected. Agnew had been looking for a setting that would allow him to generate concern for what he considered to be a serious problem.

Agnew's specific purpose is to expose what he considers the problem of irresponsible television news coverage, not to offer concrete solutions to that problem. As he progresses he moves from the specific to the general, from condemnation of "instant analysis" of Administration speeches to condemnation of a general liberal network news bias. He argues that the problem should be of direct concern to American citizens because fundamental values are threatened or violated: fairness, objectivity, individual free choice, and public need for full and accurate information as a basis for decisions.

Evaluate the degree of "reasonableness" and "ethicality" of Agnew's evidence and arguments. Is the news commentator analysis really "instant" when advance copies of a President's speech typically are released to the news media at least several hours prior to delivery of a speech? How do you react to his attempt, in paragraphs 6-8, to weaken the credibility of Ambassador Harriman? Is there any contradiction between his implication (par. 9) that people now are not allowed to make up their own minds due to TV news media bias and power and his observation (par. 37) that citizens responded to a Presidential address "more warmly than did the networks"? Is there any inconsistency (par. 3 and 4) between claiming that the analysis was "instant" and yet that the analysts' "minds were made up in advance"?

Assess Agnew's choice of words to create positive and negative images. On the one hand, President Nixon "reasoned" with the people and "spent weeks" in preparation of his speech. On the other hand, a "gaggle" of provincial, parochial, privileged, "self-appointed" commentators indulged in "instant analysis and querulous criticism." And Harriman is depicted as robot-like: he "recited perfectly" after being "trotted out."

Reprinted with permission from *Vital Speeches of the Day.* December, 1, 1969, pp. 98-101.

1 Tonight I want to discuss the importance of the television news medium to the American people. No nation depends more on the intelligent judgment of its citizens. No medium has a more profound influence over public opinion. Nowhere in our system are there fewer checks on vast

power. So, nowhere should there be more conscientious responsibility exercised than by the news media. The question is, Are we demanding enough of our television news presentations? And are the men of this medium demanding enough of themselves?

2 Monday night a week ago, President Nixon delivered the most important address of his Administration, one of the most important of our decade. His subject was Vietnam. His hope was to rally the American people to see the conflict through to a lasting and just peace in the Pacific. For 32 minutes, he reasoned with a nation that has suffered almost a third of a million casualties in the longest war in its history.

3 When the President completed his address—an address, incidentally, that he spent weeks in the preparation of—his words and policies were subjected to instant analysis and querulous criticism. The audience of 70 million Americans gathered to hear the President of the United States was inherited by a small band of network commentators and self-appointed analysts, the majority of whom expressed in one way or another their hostility to what he had to say.

4 It was obvious that their minds were made up in advance. Those who recall the fumbling and groping that followed President Johnson's dramatic disclosure of his intention not to seek another term have seen these men in a genuine state of nonpreparedness. This was not it.

5 One commentator twice contradicted the President's statement about the exchange of correspondence with Ho Chi Minh. Another challenged the President's abilities as a politician. A third asserted that the President was following a Pentagon line. Others, by the expression on their faces, the tone of their questions and the sarcasm of their responses, made clear their sharp disapproval.

6 To guarantee in advance that the President's plea for national unity would be challenged, one network trotted out Averell Harriman for the occasion. Throughout the President's message, he waited in the wings. When the President concluded, Mr. Harriman recited perfectly. He attacked the Thieu Government as unrepresentative; he criticized the President's speech for various deficiencies; he twice issued a call to the Senate Foreign Relations Committee to debate Vietnam once again; he stated his belief that the Vietcong or North Vietnamese did not really want military take-over of South Vietnam; and he told a little anecdote about a "very, very responsible" fellow he had met in the North Vietnamese delegation.

7 All in all, Mr. Harriman offered a broad range of gratuitous advice challenging and contradicting the policies outlined by the President of the United States. Where the President had issued a call for unity, Mr. Harriman was encouraging the country not to listen to him.

8 A word about Mr. Harriman. For 10 months he was America's chief negotiator at the Paris peace talks—a period in which the United

States swapped some of the greatest military concessions in the history of warfare for an enemy agreement on the shape of the bargaining table. Like Coleridge's Ancient Mariner, Mr. Harriman seems to be under some heavy compulsion to justify his failure to anyone who will listen. And the networks have shown themselves willing to give him all the air time he desires.

9   Now every American has a right to disagree with the President of the United States and to express publicly that disagreement. But the President of the United States has a right to communicate directly with the people who elected him, and the people of this country have the right to make up their own minds and form their own opinions about a Presidential address without having a President's words and thoughts characterized through the prejudices of hostile critics before they can even be digested.

10   When Winston Churchill rallied public opinion to stay the course against Hitler's Germany, he didn't have to contend with a gaggle of commentators raising doubts about whether he was reading public opinion right, or whether Britain had the stamina to see the war through.

11   When President Kennedy rallied the nation in the Cuban missile crisis, his address to the people was not chewed over by a roundtable of critics who disparaged the course of action he'd asked America to follow.

12   The purpose of my remarks tonight is to focus your attention on this little group of men who not only enjoy a right of instant rebuttal to every Presidential address, but, more importantly, wield a free hand in selecting, presenting and interpreting the great issues in our nation.

13   First, let's define that power. At least 40 million Americans every night, it's estimated, watch the network news. Seven million of them view ABC, the remainder being divided between NBC and CBS.

14   According to Harris polls and other studies, for millions of Americans the networks are the sole source of national and world news. In Will Rogers' observation, what you knew was what you read in the newspaper. Today for growing millions of Americans, it's what they see and hear on their television sets.

15   Now how is this network news determined? A small group of men, numbering perhaps no more than a dozen anchormen, commentators and executive producers, settle upon the 20 minutes or so of film and commentary that's to reach the public. This selection is made from the 90 to 180 minutes that may be available. Their powers of choice are broad.

16   They decide what 40 to 50 million Americans will learn of the day's events in the nation and in the world.

17   We cannot measure this power and influence by the traditional democratic standards, for these men can create national issues overnight.

18   They can make or break by their coverage and commentary a moratorium on the war.

19   They can elevate men from obscurity to national prominence

within a week. They can reward some politicians with national exposure and ignore others.

20 For millions of Americans the network reporter who covers a continuing issue—like the ABM or civil rights—becomes, in effect, the presiding judge in a national trial by jury.

21 It must be recognized that the networks have made important contributions to the national knowledge—for news, documentaries and specials. They have often used their power constructively and creatively to awaken the public conscience to critical problems. The networks made hunger and black lung disease national issues overnight. The TV networks have done what no other medium could have done in terms of dramatizing the horrors of war. The networks have tackled our most difficult social problems with a directness and an immediacy that's the gift of their medium. They focus the nation's attention on its environmental abuses—on pollution in the Great Lakes and the threatened ecology of the Everglades.

22 But it was also the networks that elevated Stokely Carmichael and George Lincoln Rockwell from obscurity to national prominence.

23 Nor is their power confined to the substantive. A raised eyebrow, an inflection of the voice, a caustic remark dropped in the middle of a broadcast can raise doubts in a million minds about the veracity of a public official or the wisdom of a Government policy.

24 One Federal Communications Commissioner considers the powers of the networks equal to that of local state and Federal Governments all combined. Certainly it represents a concentration of power over American public opinion unknown in history.

25 Now what do Americans know of the men who wield this power? Of the men who produce and direct the network news, the nation knows practically nothing. Of the commentators, most Americans know little other than that they reflect an urbane and assured presence seemingly well-informed on every important matter.

26 We do know that to a man these commentators and producers live and work in the geographical and intellectual confines of Washington, D.C., or New York City, the latter of which James Reston terms the most unrepresentative community in the entire United States.

27 Both communities bask in their own provincialism, their own parochialism.

28 We can deduce that these men read the same newspapers. They draw their political and social views from the same sources. Worse, they talk constantly to one another, thereby providing artificial reinforcement to their shared viewpoints.

29 Do they allow their biases to influence the selection and presentation of the news? David Brinkley states objectivity is impossible to normal human behavior. Rather, he says, we should strive for fairness.

30 Another anchorman on a network news show contends, and I quote: "You can't expunge all your private convictions just because you sit in a seat like this and a camera starts to stare at you. I think your program has to reflect what your basic feelings are. I'll plead guilty to that."

31 Less than a week before the 1968 election, this same commentator charged that President Nixon's campaign commitments were no more durable than campaign balloons. He claimed that, were it not for the fear of hostile reaction, Richard Nixon would be giving into, and I quote him exactly, "his natural instinct to smash the enemy with a club or go after him with a meat axe."

32 Had this slander been made by one political candidate about another, it would have been dismissed by most commentators as a partisan attack. But this attack emanated from the privileged sanctuary of a network studio and therefore had the apparent dignity of an objective statement.

33 The American people would rightly not tolerate this concentration of power in Government.

34 Is it not fair and relevant to question its concentration in the hands of a tiny, enclosed fraternity of privileged men elected by no one and enjoying a monopoly sanctioned and licensed by Government?

35 The views of the majority of this fraternity do not—and I repeat, not—represent the views of America.

36 That is why such a great gulf existed between how the nation received the President's address and how the networks reviewed it.

37 Not only did the country receive the President's address more warmly than the networks, but so also did the Congress of the United States.

38 Yesterday, the President was notified that 300 individual Congressmen and 50 Senators of both parties had endorsed his efforts for peace.

39 As with other American institutions, perhaps it is time that the networks were made more responsive to the views of the nation and more responsible to the people they serve.

40 Now I want to make myself perfectly clear. I'm not asking for Government censorship or any other kind of censorship. I'm asking whether a form of censorship already exists when the news that 40 million Americans receive each night is determined by a handful of men responsible only to their corporate employers and is filtered through a handful of commentators who admit to their own set of biases.

41 The questions I'm raising here tonight should have been raised by others long ago. They should have been raised by those Americans who have traditionally considered the preservation of freedom of speech and freedom of the press their special provinces of responsibility.

42 They should have been raised by those Americans who share the view of the late Justice Learned Hand that right conclusions are more likely to be gathered out of a multitude of tongues than through any kind of authoritative selection.

43 Advocates for the networks have claimed a First Amendment right to the same unlimited freedoms held by the great newspapers of America.

44 (But the situations are not identical. Where *The New York Times* reaches 800,000 people, NBC reaches 20 times that number on its evening news. [The average weekday circulation of the *Times* in October was 1,012,367; the average Sunday circulation was 1,523,558.] Nor can the tremendous impact of seeing television film and hearing commentary be compared with reading the printed page.)

45 A decade ago, before the network news acquired such dominance over public opinion, Walter Lippman spoke to the issue. He said there's an essential and radical difference between television and printing. The three or four competing television stations control virtually all that can be received over the air by ordinary television sets. But besides the mass circulation dailies, there are weeklies, monthlies, out-of-town newspapers and books. If a man doesn't like his newspaper, he can read another from out of town or wait for a weekly news magazine. It's not ideal, but it's infinitely better than the situation in television.

46 There if a man doesn't like what the networks are showing, all he can do is turn them off and listen to a phonograph. Networks he stated which are few in number have a virtual monopoly of a whole media of communications.

47 The newspapers of mass circulation have no monopoly on the medium of print.

48 Now a virtual monopoly of a whole medium of communication is not something that democratic people should blindly ignore. And we are not going to cut off our television sets and listen to the phonograph just because the airways belong to the networks. They don't. They belong to the people.

49 As Justice Byron White wrote in his landmark opinion six months ago, it's the right of the viewers and listeners, not the right of the broadcasters, which is paramount.

50 Now it's argued that this power presents no danger in the hands of those who have used it responsibly. But, as to whether or not the networks have abused the power they enjoy, let us call as our first witness former Vice President Humphrey and the city of Chicago. According to Theodore White, television's intercutting of the film from the streets of Chicago with the current proceedings on the floor of the convention created the most striking and false political picture of 1968—the nomination of a man for the American Presidency by the brutality and violence of merciless police.

51 If we are to believe a recent report of the House of Represent-atives Commerce Committee, then television's presentation of the violence in the streets worked an injustice on the reputation of the Chicago police. According to the committee findings, one network in particular presented, and I quote, "a one-sided picture which in large measure exonerates the demonstrators and protesters." Film of provocations of police that was available never saw the light of day while the film of a police response which the protesters provoked was shown to millions.

52 Another network showed virtually the same scene of violence from three separate angles without making clear it was the same scene. And, while the full report is reticent in drawing conclusions, it is not a document to inspire confidence in the fairness of the network news.

53 Our knowledge of the impact of network news on the national mind is far from complete, but some early returns are available. Again, we have enough information to raise serious questions about its effect on a democratic society. Several years ago Fred Friendly, one of the pioneers of network news, wrote that its missing ingredients were conviction, con-troversy and a point of view. The networks have compensated with a vengeance.

54 And in the networks' endless pursuit of controversy, we should ask: What is the end value—to enlighten or to profit? What is the end result—to inform or to confuse? How does the ongoing exploration for more action, more excitement, more drama serve our national search for internal peace and stability.

55 Gresham's Law seems to be operating in the network news. Bad news drives out good news. The irrational is more controversial than the rational. Concurrence can no longer compete with dissent.

56 One minute of Eldridge Cleaver is worth 10 minutes of Roy Wilkins. The labor crisis settled at the negotiating table is nothing compared to the confrontation that results in a strike—or better yet, violence along the picket lines.

57 Normality has become the nemesis of the network news. Now the upshot of all this controversy is that a narrow and distorted picture of America often emerges from the televised news.

58 A single, dramatic piece of the mosaic becomes in the minds of millions the entire picture. And the American who relies upon television for his news might conclude that the majority of American students are embit-tered radicals. That the majority of black Americans feel no regard for their country. That violence and lawlessness are the rule rather than the exception on the American campus.

59 We know that none of these conclusions is true.

60 Perhaps the place to start looking for a credibility gap is not in the offices of the Government in Washington but in the studios of the networks in New York.

61 Television may have destroyed the old stereotypes, but has it not created new ones in their places?

62 What has this passionate pursuit of controversy done to the politics of progress through local compromise essential to the functioning of a democratic society?

63 The members of Congress or the Senate who follow their principles and philosophy quietly in a spirit of compromise are unknown to many Americans, while the loudest and most extreme dissenters on every issue are known to every man in the street.

64 How many marches and demonstrations would we have if the marchers did not know that the ever-faithful TV cameras would be there to record their antics for the next news show?

65 We've heard demands that Senators and Congressmen and judges make known all their financial connections so that the public will know who and what influences their decisions and their votes. Strong arguments can be made for that view.

66 But when a single commentator or producer, night after night, determines for millions of people how much of each side of a great issue they are going to see and hear, should he not first disclose his personal views on the issue as well?

67 In this search for excitement and controversy, has more than equal time gone to the minority of Americans who specialize in attacking the United States—its institutions and its citizens?

68 Tonight I've raised questions. I've made no attempt to suggest the answers. The answers must come from the media men. They are challenged to turn their critical powers on themselves, to direct their energy, their talent and their conviction toward improving the quality and objectivity of news presentation.

69 They are challenged to structure their own civic ethics to relate to the great responsibilities they hold.

70 And the people of America are challenged, too, challenged to press for responsible news presentations. The people can let the networks know that they want their news straight and objective. The people can register their complaints on bias through mail to the networks and phone calls to local stations. This is one case where the people must defend themselves; where the citizen, not the Government, must be the reformer; where the consumer can be the most effective crusader.

71 By way of conclusion, let me say that every elected leader in the United States depends on these men of the media. Whether what I've said to you tonight will be heard and seen at all by the nation is not my decision, it's not your decision, it's their decision.

72 In tomorrow's edition of *The Des Moines Register,* you'll be able to read a news story detailing what I've said tonight. Editorial comment will be reserved for the editorial page, where it belongs.

73 Should not the same wall of separation exist between news and comment on the nation's networks?

74 Now, my friends, we'd never trust such power, as I've described, over public opinion in the hands of an elected Government. It's time we questioned it in the hands of a small and unelected elite.

75 The great networks have dominated America's airwaves for decades. The people are entitled to a full accounting of their stewardship.

THE CROWN OF LIFE?

Lisa L. Golub

Lisa L. Golob, a freshman at the University of Wisconsin, delivered this speech in a public speaking course during the 1980 fall semester. Her primary purpose was to convince the audience that "the neglect of the elderly is a serious social problem."

In establishing her proposition, Ms. Golob developed three major contentions. Can you identify them? Taken collectively, do these three contentions adequately support the proposition? What kinds of evidence are employed in each of the three sections of the body? Why do differences exist in the kinds of evidence set forth in the sections?

One of the obvious strengths of this speech is its emotional impact. To what motives or emotions does the speaker appeal? On a number of occasions, the speaker's personal anger with the treatment of the elderly emerges. At what points in the manuscript are the speaker's feelings most clearly evident? How does such an expression of controlled anger influence the speaker's ethos or credibility?

Through varied and animated vocal and physical delivery, Ms. Golob communicated a sense of deep concern for society's disgraceful treatment of the aged. Through the judicious use of specific instances, she created vivid images of the elderly in anguish—images that linger in the mind's eye. At the conclusion of her speech, there was a period of profound silence engendered by the emotional intensity of the final quotation and appeal.

This speech is published by permission of Ms. Golob.

1 Old age is creeping up on you with every second that passes. Someday you too will be elderly. "So what?" you may be thinking, "That just

means being a grandma or grandpa, being respected by the young folks, and retiring to the 'good life.' "

2   Chances are it won't mean that at all. You might be a shut-in, confined to a wheelchair. But if you're blessed with good health and able to make your way out in society, you may be met by disrespect and ridicule. And your dream of the good life may be so ravaged by inflation that you are forced to add cat food to your diet because the social security check hasn't come yet, and there just . . . isn't . . . enough . . . money.

3   Does that seem hard to believe? Sadly it's not unrealistic at all. Our elderly are often forgotten, stereotyped, and disrespected. Our aged are often impoverished and ill-housed. And yes, our elderly are often physically abused by those they must depend on for care. It's no wonder gerontophobia, the fear of old age, is very common. Neglect of our elderly is a serious problem in American society.

4   The first sign of neglect is isolation. Consider family isolation. There is a woman at a nursing home I visit frequently who is a case in point. Gloria is 95 years old. She has been a resident of the Madison Convalescent Home for 13 years. Though she is confined to a wheelchair and cannot speak well due to a stroke, she is a bright and interesting woman. Each day she can be found fully dressed, make-up, and jewelry, her chair near the lobby door— waiting for a friend . . . who never comes. Where is her family?? Though she has outlived most, her remaining family lives in Florida. *Florida!* Tell me why have they left a 95 year old woman alone to die, over a thousand miles away from them? "Forgotten." Do you know that there is actually a service in California that you can call if you are near death and for $7.00 an hour they will have someone sit beside you while you die?! If you have no one. If they have forgotten.

5   Consider media induced isolation. Our aged are mocked in movies and on television where they are depicted as dirty old men, saucy rich nags, or delirious no-minds. According to Public Affairs Researcher, Irving Dickman, "true senility, or chronic organic brain syndrome, probably affects as few as 3% of all elderly."

6   Cicero once called old age ". . . the crown of life, our play's last act." Today old age is considered more a sickness than a joyous finale. This change in perception has led us to a paradox which the Catholic Bishops have expressed in this way:

(America) "is an aging nation which worships the culture, values, and appearance of youth. Instead of viewing old age as an achievement and a natural stage of life with its own merits, wisdom, and beauty, American society all too often ignores, rejects, and isolates the elderly."

Before we laugh at and accept media stereotypes of our aged, let us not forget that we are *all* going to be elderly someday—the only prerequisite is to live.

7 Consider isolation from the world of work. Older people have also faced disrespect in their jobs, or should I say the lack of their jobs due to mandatory retirement. In *Ageism—Discrimination Against Older People,* one forced retiree states it this way:

> "I don't want to fill in the time before I die. I want to use the time. I need to work . . . I want my old job back. I was good at it. To be considered unfit for the very job for which I was trained, in which I have many years of experience, is the cruelest kind of rejection. Then I am truly unfit, no good at anything."

Are we so narrow in our view of growing older that we have made true the saying, "King of the hill one day—over the hill the next."? Herman Loether, a professor at California State College, pictures job isolation in this way:

> "The man who has spent 40 years or more in the labor force, devoting a major portion of his life to his job, is suddenly handed a gold watch in recognition of his faithful service and told to go home and relax."

Maybe he doesn't want to relax! But the choice has been taken away from him. The respect for his goals, his opinion is gone.

8 Isolation—from family, by media; from work—is a major dimension of the problem. But as if loneliness were not enough, many of America's elderly live in abject poverty. Consider these facts from Public Affairs Pamphlet #575 published in 1979: Of the twenty-two million people over 65, one in every five had an income below the official poverty level. Old people, who are only 10% of the population, are 66.6% of the poor. And poverty, not poor health, has been cited as the chief source of unhappiness and worry among our aged. In that same pamphlet, pollster Louis Harris provided a summary of the economic plight of the aged when he said:

> ". . . two out of every three people with incomes below the poverty line are older citizens . . . victimized by inflation . . . desperate . . . hungry, ill-clad, in debt, and ill-housed."

According to Senator Charles H. Percy in *Growing Old in the Country of the Young,* one out of three of our elderly live in substandard housing, and three out of four of our elderly blacks live in such housing. In addition, the quality of life decreases with each increase in inflation. In Percy's book, one aged person offers this testimony:

> "I am 74 years old and living in a building 70 years old. I moved here 9 years ago and paid $90 a month for rent. Then the building was sold. The first two years, my rent was raised $4 each year. Then I got a $10 increase. Now, $20 more. I get $141 social security. Rent is $130. Plus gas, plus utilities, plus telephone. How can I eat?"

While Social Security was not designed to provide sole or adequate support, it now struggles to provide at least 90% of the total income for more than four million of our older people. The battle is being lost. The Social Security system is experiencing great stress as it tries to increase benefits and meet the needs of a rapidly graying America. And to what end? Today the average Social Security benefit still falls below the federal government's poverty line.

But perhaps worse than all of the aforementioned put together is the physical abuse that our elderly endure. According to Richard Douglass, a researcher at the University of Michigan Institute of Gerontology, physical abuse of the elderly is pervasive and serious, involving "beating, burnings, cutting or battering with fists or objects," and resulting in physical injuries ranging from "superficial wounds" (to) dislocations (to) bone fractures and many resulting fatalities." And who inflicts this abuse on our elderly? Often their own children. The adult children expect them to be "strong", and when the aged are not, they are "punished."

9   This abuse is also prevalent in our institutions. In *Growing Old in the Country of the Young,* Percy tells of a recent event in Miami where ". . . two elderly men—critically ill, homeless, penniless—were put into wheelchairs to sit in a jammed aisle of a hospital until nursing home space could be found for them. Both men died in those chairs and it was hours before anyone even noticed they were dead. One man had been sitting in his chair for three days and the other man for two. As the hospital told of the deaths of these men, ten more just like them were still sitting in that aisle."

10   Nursing homes themselves are at fault for abusing our senior citizens. Have you ever been to a nursing home where the air did not smell rancid, where the TV worked well, where the food looked *and tasted* appetizing? They are few and far between. I have personally read about and seen instances where paitients have been hit or slapped. In a recent case at Hillhaven Convalescent Home in Milwaukee a patient was forced to eat his own excrement. It's sick!

11   This directly affects your life. Because you are getting older today. Right now. Psalm 71 says "Cast me not off in the time of old age, forsake me not when my strength faileth."

12 A recent article in the *Milwaukee Journal* on aging closed with a view of a woman who visited her mother in a nursing home:

"Around the room a few more chant. 'I want to go home. I want to go home.' An ancient figure strapped in his wheelchair covers his ears with trembling, skeletal fingers and begins to sob.

My mama, as though roused from a deep sleep, begins to look around— her eyes suddenly comprehending.

'What is it, Mama? Tell me what it is.'

She looks terrified, but her voice is without emotion.

"All of my nightmares came true.' She says."

Our elderly have been greatly neglected, and I tell you, NOW is the time to care.

DO YOU THINK YOU KNOW ME?

Peggy Dersch

Peggy Dersch delivered this speech in a college oratorical contest when she was a student at Southeast Missouri State University. She was coached by Tom Harte.

This is an unusual speech and therefore this brief introductory statement will not divulge the main thrust the speaker develops. We will simply present a series of topics and questions you may want to keep in mind as you read the speech and discuss in class.

—The speech begins situationally. Why do situations tend to be effective interest-getting introductions?

—Identify key interest factors in this speech. What about the use of dialogue? Parallelisms in paragraph 5? The element of surprise? The use of examples? Direct involvement of the audience? What techniques does the speaker use to involve the audience?

—The speaker states her purpose in paragraph 6. Observe how she briefly delineates her purpose to clarify the thrust of her speech.

—Speech textbooks commonly advise speakers to show personal involvement with the topic, or, at the very least, show a relationship with the topic. How important is this in terms of establishing personal credibility?

—Has the speech affected your attitude towards the speaker's subject? Could the same results have been achieved with a different approach?

This speech is reprinted by permission of the Interstate Oratorical Association from *Winning Orations*, 1980, pp. 60-63.

1   It was winter, 1976. A news item concerning the attempted rape of an eight-year-old child was reported on WABC-TV in New York City. Following the news, the station's weather announcer, Tex Antoine, began his report by reminding viewers of what he called an ancient proverb. "Confucius once say: If rape is inevitable, relax and enjoy it!" After enough protest calls, station officials required Antoine to offer a public apology. He said simply, "I regret making the statement." And then he added, "I didn't realize the victim was a child."

2   The ignorance about rape displayed by Tex Antoine is not uncommon. In Chicago, Illinois, Gallant Greetings Corporation produced and distributed a birthday card. On the front was a disheveled woman with a wide grin across her face. The inscription read, "Birthdays are like rape." Then you open the card and the message continued. "When it's inevitable—enjoy . . . enjoy. . . ." There was a space to sign your name, and then the final phrase, "Happy Day!"

3   Jokes about rape are not difficult to find. But the truth is, rape is no laughing matter. When we consider the fact that every night of the year, in fact every 14 minutes day and night all year long a woman is forcibly raped, we realize that rape is a very serious matter.

4   But you don't have to share the ignorance of a Tex Antoine or the Gallant Corporation to be guilty of misunderstanding the nature of the crime of rape. As a matter of fact, all of us, everyone in this room, is a victim of a stereotype. We are all prejudiced against the rape victim. I know, and I intend to show you.

5   Now, let me assure you this is not just another speech on rape. In fact, let me make a few things clear about my intentions before I go any further. First of all, don't get the idea I'm out to accuse anyone of being apathetic or unconcerned. I'm not. Don't expect me to shock you with the latest probability figures showing that everyone in this room will be raped within the next ten days. I'm not. Don't think I'm trying to repulse you with brutal accounts of a victim's experience or horrifying stories of courtroom battles. I'm not.

6   My purpose is simply this: to make everyone here think more critically about how he views the crime of rape. You see, this is not a speech on rape, but on the attitudes we all have toward it: attitudes which are frequently as serious a problem as the act of rape itself.

7   Rape is an unusual crime. Some of us, like Tex Antoine, make a joke of it; others of us cry about it; and still others choose not to talk about it at all. But whatever our response to rape, one thing remains constant and it is a factor which separates rape from any other crime in the book; we see the rapist as a criminal, but we tend to see the rape victim that way too. Society attributes at least part of the blame to the victim herself. We see her, somehow, at fault.

8 I suppose there are lots of reasons for this. Some of us choose to believe that deep down women secretly want to be raped; that they ask for it. You might think this attitude is outdated but it still survives, even in our courts of law.

9 Let me give you an example. In Dane County, Wisconsin, Judge Archie Simonson let a 15-year-old boy off with only probation for raping a 16-year-old girl in the stairwell of their high school. His explanation? "I'm trying to say to women—stop teasing. . . . Whether women like it or not they are sex objects." You probably recognize this statement for the ignorance it represents. But even those who reject the notion that the victim invited the attack may still fall for the view that she didn't resist hard enough.

10 "Why didn't she fight back?" we say. "You can't hit a moving target." So common is this myth that even rape victims themselves believe it. I recently read a magazine article about one such victim; her name is Linda Rogers. She recalled: "Before the rape, I would have been surprised that a victim might feel guilty. Yet I did; not that I had invited the rape, but that I should have been able to prevent it."

11 Her feelings might be easier to understand when we examine what is currently being taught in criminology courses. For example, here's what one of the most widely used criminology textbooks, Daniel Glaser's *Adult Crime and Social Policy,* has to say: "To force a woman into intercourse is an impossible task in most cases if the female is conscious and extreme pain is not inflicted."

12 And this text is not unusual. According to Dr. Gail Wisan, professor of sociology at George Washington University, each of today's 13 most popular criminology texts, all of them published since 1970 and over half since 1975 include similar examples. Is it really any wonder that so many hold the attitudes they do? Now, of course, not everybody believes that women want to be raped or that they don't try hard enough to resist an attack. But even though we know that, we may still subconsciously feel that somehow, some way, a woman brings rape on herself.

13 Social psychologists call this the "just world hypothesis," a belief that bad things just don't happen to good people—or in other words, good women don't get raped. But whatever the logic or reasoning behind it, however you explain the tendency to view the rape victim as a criminal herself, the perception exists, and its effects are devastating. For example one rape victim called a Boston Hospital follow-up counselor and explained: "I am having problems with my family. No one wants to have anything to do with me. My grandmother doesn't want me to tell my brother and I want him to know. She says it is a shame on the family. No one is talking with me. They won't even say hello to me. Even my husband is ashamed of me."

14 And the effects can be more than just psychological. A friend of mine who worked one summer in a rape crisis center in St. Louis, Missouri, told me about Sandy, a 14-year-old girl who was raped two years ago. The only girl from a large religious family, she was considered an outcast by her parents. In their own words she had been "violated", and, therefore, was unmarriageable material. Today, at age 16, Sandy is a runaway.

15 Too often peoples' attitudes about rape and their perception of the victim do as much damage as the rapist himself. And more of us than we'd like to admit harbour these attitudes.

16 Now perhaps many of you at this point are saying to yourself, "Not me—I don't feel that way." Maybe you're right. But maybe you're wrong. Unless I'm mistaken, everyone in this room is subject to ill-conceived attitudes about rape victims. All of us, even you, are victims yourselves of a stereotype. And I think I can prove it to you.

17 Most of you have never met me before, yet even so you have been developing just in these few minutes an idea of what I'm like, so that by now you have some notion or image of me, Peggy Dersch. Now let me tell you something about myself that you don't know. At the age of 13 I was violently and forcibly raped in the home of a friend. (Don't worry, I'm not going to recount any details for you. I promise I wouldn't remember?)

18 Already your impressions of me are beginning to change aren't they? Just in these last few seconds your image of me has been altered by two words" "rape victim."

19 If you were to meet me again I'm almost sure you'd act differently than you would have ten minutes ago. And if I happened to be wearing shorts or a t-shirt you might even raise an eyebrow or sneer. Why? Because I'd be asking for trouble. You see, when a woman is labeled "rape victim," ordinary behavior is reinterpreted in sexual terms. Any attractiveness in dress or figure is held against her.

20 Is there anyone in this room who can honestly say that his impression of me has not changed just a little? Is there anyone who can honestly say he doesn't see me as a little cheapened, a little less wholesome? I've seen it happen before. I have just labeled myself rape victim, and Peggy Dersch the rape victim is different from the Peggy Dersch you knew before, isn't she?

21 I could be wrong. My point may be totally erroneous. But I can tell you this. In a survey taken in July of last year, 25% of those responding said they believed they'd be treated by their family and friends as though they were partly to blame if they were raped. Even though many said their families would be sympathetic, all of the respondents expressed a feeling that the rape victim is still considered at fault, either for having led someone on or for not having resisted more. In a word many considered her "cheapened" by the experience.

22 Now please don't misunderstand. I'm not asking you for sympathy and I'm not casting blame or trying to make you feel guilty. And I'm not saying that we haven't done a great deal already to lift the "veil of shame" around the subject of rape. But it's still there. So I only ask you to level with yourself; think for a moment whether you are truly free of the prejudice against rape victims which abounds in our society. Do you somehow look down upon me and others like me, even though you know better? Don't be surprised or ashamed if you do. The attitude is quite common. And until all of us, individually and collectively as a society, can come to grips with that attitude, we will make little progress against what may well be the most reprehensible crime of all. I ask you to consider how you would act if your sister, or daughter, or wife, or someone else you love were raped. How would you treat them? And how are you going to treat me?

THE TECHNICAL THESIS

Neil Postman

Neil Postman is professor of media ecology at New York University. He is author or coauthor of several books; for example, *Television and the Teaching of English,* 1961; *Linguistics,* 1966; *Teaching as a Subversive Activity,* 1969; *Soft Revolution,* 1971; and *Teaching as a Conserving Activity,* 1980. Professor Postman delivered this address at Seton Hall University in South Orange, New Jersey, November 9, 1978.

The first seven paragraphs of Professor Postman's speech constitute the introduction. He begins with a personal reference in the first three paragraphs to the theme for his speech and then sets forth two key examples from which the speech itself develops: HAGOTH and the IQ test. How well do these paragraphs fulfill the functions of a good speech introduction? Do they generate interest? Do they sufficiently reveal the speaker's credentials? Do they lead logically into the central thesis?

In paragraph 8 Postman states the thesis for his speech, and a brief elaboration of it. Paragraph 9 qualifies the speaker's position regarding his topic. Paragraph 10 offers a definition of the topic, and paragraphs 11 and 12 give examples illustrating the definition set forth in 10. Then paragraphs 13 and 14 explain how the problem occurs. Paragraph 15 pinpoints the problem specifically to numbers. And paragraph immediately follows with an example of the tyranny of numbers. Considerable humor is generated by the example of the judging of the Miss Universe Beauty Pageant. We think that Postman's unfolding of the topic of his speech represents model rhetorical technique. The topic has been stated, defined, clarified, pinpointed as to derivation, and exemplified with a humorous illustration.

Most of the remainder of the speech reveals the scope of the problem and how pervasive it is in our lives. Postman finds the technical thesis particularly prevalent in our schools and in the electronic media. You may want to assess his technique for giving scope to the topic and evaluate how effectively he generates concern for the problem.

Paragraph 34 pulls the speech together in terms of final implications. How effective is the ending? Would it have been better if the speaker had ended wih a summary and a final example illustrating his thesis? What makes for an effective conclusion for a speech seeking to generate concern for a problem?

This speech is reprinted by permission from *Vital Speeches of the Day,* January 1, 1979, pp. 180–185.

1 Just about five weeks ago, I received a telephone call from a man, unknown to me, who had seen some notice of tonight's lecture. In particular, he had come across a reference to its theme, Mass Communications: Culture in Crisis, and before he committed himself to attending, he wanted to know exactly what my talk would be about. Of course, I hadn't *asked* him to commit himself to attending, but I got the impression, nonetheless, that if I didn't come up with the right answer, I would have to carry on without him.

2 As it happened, my talk was not then fully conceived, or even half conceived, but I mumbled my way through an answer anyway, not wishing to lose a potential customer. Perhaps he is here tonight, perhaps he isn't. My answer couldn't have been very satisfactory. But I mention the episode because I think he was right to call me. So much has happened in America, and continues to happen, that the word *crisis,* as in *culture in crisis,* has probably lost all its meaning; certainly, all its urgency. Everything seems to be in crisis, and every lecture seems to be about one. I believe my caller merely wanted to know which of the 283 crises now available for discussion I was going to choose, since he had doubtless heard 150 of them discussed already. And even though the phrase *mass COMMUNICATION* limited the field somewhat, it could not have been of much help to him. Most of our crises have something to do with what we call the mass media, especially if we mean by that term all the technological changes that have come in such Toffleresque profusion and have led to such Kafkaesque confusion.

3 In fact, for many weeks prior to his call, and for a couple afterwards, I was nearly as unsure as my caller as to which of our present media-induced or media-amplified confusions I might give my attention to. And then, on a flight from New York to San Francisco, I chanced to locate the answer in the American Airlines magazine, which, not insignificantly, is called *American Way.* There, I saw an advertisement that struck me at once as one of those rare artifacts—of the kind archaeologists are always looking for—that reveal in capsule form the nature of a culture's most burdensome idea. It was, as I said, an advertisement, and told of a machine called HAGOTH. Anyone can buy it for $1500, making it one of the best bargains of this decade. HAGOTH has sixteen lights—eight green and eight red. If you connect HAGOTH to

your telephone, you are able to tell whether or not someone talking to you is telling the truth!

4   The way it does this is by analyzing the "stress" content of a human voice. You ask your telephone-caller some key questions, and HAGOTH will go to work in analyzing his or her replies. Red lights go on when there is much stress in the voice, green when there is little. As the ad said, "Green indicates no stress, hence truthfulness." Red, of course, means you are being deceived. HAGOTH, in other words, works exactly like an IQ test. In an IQ test, you connect a pencil to the fingers of a youth, address some key questions to him, and from his replies you can tell exactly how intelligent he is. There is a margin of error, of course, as there is in HAGOTH. But in the main the machinery of both HAGOTH and an IQ test is trusted by our citizenry: it gives us the sort of information we value in a form we respect.

5   There are several reasons why this is so. The first is that the machines themselves define what they measure. HAGOTH defines "stress" and thereby "truthfulness" and "deception" by the extent of the oscillations in a voice. Therefore, since (one assumes) it accurately measures oscillations, HAGOTH can't be wrong. It is a self-confirming system. An IQ test defines intelligence as what it measures. Therefore, your score is by definition a precise reflection of your intelligence. Simply, both HAGOTH and an IQ test define what they measure, then measure their definition. In this way we achieve what is called "clarity."

6   Second, both HAGOTH and an IQ test use numbers. Six red lights mean more lying than two red lights. A score of 136 means more intelligence than a score of 102. If you can count, it is all quite clear. HAGOTH and an IQ test provide us with what are called "objective answers." Thus, we achieve precision.

7   Third, both HAGOTH and an IQ test are simple. Philosophers may sweat the question, "What is truth?", in books that are a burden to carry, let alone read. HAGOTH bypasses all of this complexity and doubt. If you have a telephone, you have immediate access to the answer. Similarly, intelligence may be elusive to those who must rely on observing how people cope with their problems: such judgments require time and multivarious situations. The answer comes both fast and easy through an IQ test.

8   Clarity. Precision. Simplicity. Speed. This is our quest. Of course, what we are dealing with here is one of the more overbearing and dangerous teachings of our information environment. And it is this teaching that I shall take as the subject of my lecture, for there is no doubt that we have here the focal point of a serious cultural crisis. I am referring to the idea that it is only through the use of *technique* and *technicalization* that we may find out what is real, what is true and what is valuable. In its extreme form, this idea amounts to a religious conception, which I have elsewhere called "Eichmann-ism": the belief that technique is the Supreme Authority and the measure of

all things. Both HAGOTH and an IQ test are products of this belief. They do more than merely give us information. They put forward an argument which I find it useful to call "The Technical Thesis," and tonight I should like to expose this thesis to your view so that you may see it, as I do, as an intellectual snare and a cultural delusion.

9 Before proceeding, however, I must make it clear that I raise no objections against the rational use of technique to achieve human purposes. We are technical creatures, and it is in our predilection for and our ability to create techniques that we achieve high levels of clarity and efficiency. Language itself is a technique, and through it we achieve more than clarity and efficiency. We achieve humanity. Or inhumanity. For the question with language, as with other techniques, is and always has been, Who is to be the master? Will we control it, or will it control us? Thus, my argument is not against technique, without which we would be less than human: my argument is with the triumph of technique, which means technique that subordinates and even obliterates human purpose, technique that directs us to serve *its* purposes, not our own.

10 What, then, are technique and its progeny, technicalization? This is a complicated matter, which I will here try to simplify by saying that technique is a standardized method for achieving a purpose. It may be embodied in machinery or language or numbers or any sort of material that can be made to repeat itself, including, of course, human behavior. In fact, human behavior is itself the fundamental paradigm of technique, for at every level— from physiological to social—we reproduce our behaviors. We are, in a sense, clones: Our talk, our dress, our manners, our movements—these are all repetitions of previous behaviors, executed to insure predictability and control, and governed by a set of rules. The rules may not always be known to us, as is the case with those that direct our physiological processes. But they are there nonetheless. Without them, our blood would not circulate through our bodies, our cells would not regenerate themselves. It is the same with language, for the sentences we produce are not randomly created. They are governed by rules of formation and transformation which we have only recently become aware of and do not yet fully grasp. And it is the same with our social behavior, although here we know quite a bit about the nature of the rules, since we have consciously established them to serve specific purposes. For example, a classroom is an ensemble of techniques for standardizing and controlling behavior. So are a courtroom, a restaurant, and a highway. We can write down the rules that govern these situations, and even teach them in a systematic way.

11 Our artifacts and, in particular, our machinery are also governed by rules, and are designed not only to standardize *our* behavior but to standardize their own. An airplane that is so constructed that it obeys the laws of physics only occasionally is useless, as is a thermometer that responds to heat

only when it is "in the mood." We say of such machines that they are "broken," by which we mean their behavior is random, unstandardized, unreliable.

12   Thus, as I have said, we are technical creatures, and our standardized behavior and machinery—our techniques—make up most of what we call our culture. In saying this, I am saying nothing that is not obvious to everyone. But it sometimes happens that technique begins to function independently of the system it serves. It becomes autonomous, in the manner of a robot that no longer obeys its master. The "purposes" of technique somehow come to dominate a situation, and thereby become a danger to it. The robot, of course, always attacks its master first. Cancer, for example, is a "normal" physiological technique over which we have lost control. Cells regenerate themselves according to blind genetic instructions, without any coordination with the rest of the organism. The body then exists to serve the "purposes" of the process, not the other way around. In a similar way, neurosis is a linguistic technique that has become more important than our own effectiveness. When we generate sentences that produce unsatisfactory results for us, yet cannot stop doing so, then we are in the service of our sentences, not in the service of ourselves.

13   There are many names for this aberrant process by which a method for doing something becomes the reason for doing it. One of the names is *reification*. To reify a procedure or technique is to elevate it to the status of a purposeful creature, to invest it with objectives of its own. To reify is more than to put the cart before the horse, which is merely bad technique. It is to make sure that both the cart and horse get where they are going, even if the passenger does not. It is to forget that neither a cart nor a horse has any place to go, that they are the means to a human purpose.

14   But in order for reification of technique to occur certain conditions must obtain, and the most important of these is what may be called *technicalization*. Technicalization is itself a technique. It is a method of transforming a technique into an abstract, general, and precise system. To build a boat requires technique. To draw plans and a set of instructions for building a boat is technicalization. To assess the truth of another's remarks requires technique. To construct HAGOTH is technicalization. To judge someone's intelligence requires technique. To construct an IQ test is technicalization. In other words, technicalization objectifies technique. It removes technique from a specific context, separates the doer from the doing, and therefore eliminates individuality. Whereas technique is a standardized method for doing something, technicalization standardizes the standard. To technicalize is to reduce all possible techniques to one method, to convert *a* method into *the* method. Technicalization enshrines technique and renders it invariant. It is technique writ large and inviolate.

15 All cultures are products of technique. Only some are products of technicalization. Through technicalization, we can achieve prodigious scientific and industrial feats, but there is a price to pay. Paradoxically, by objectifying and sanctifying technique, we hide from ourselves what techniques are for. In a culture burdened by technicalization, we must spend most of our time learning the proper methods: learning how to read the plans, learning how to correlate the numbers, learning how to adjust the dials. There is little time to reflect on their purpose or to consider alternative methods. As a consequence, our commitment is to the integrity of our techniques, to the development of our expertise, and to the preservation of our technical definitions and directions. And therein lies the problem. We come to reify our procedures: to believe that procedure supercedes purpose, that in fact procedure is more real than purpose. For to reject a procedure is to challenge the basis on which a technicalized culture rests. Such a culture can survive purposes not achieved. What it cannot survive are procedures that are ignored.

16 It hardly needs to be said that one of the powerful devices for achieving technicalization is the use of numbers, against which mortals always seem to be defenseless. Imagine someone shouting to you on the telephone, "Help me, please! There's a fire here, my leg's broken, and I can't move. Help! Please!" Your HAGOTH would register considerable stress in the person's voice. All eight red lights would flash. Hence, the caller is deceiving you. By numerical definition. Numbers give precision to definitions, and in a technicalized culture, it is precision we want. If the caller is really in danger, so much the worse for him. The machine works. And so it does, in a sense, for in a technicalized culture, what the machine measures becomes, ultimately, the reality.

17 Everyone must have a favorite and real example of the tyranny of numbers. I have several, the most recent having occurred a couple of months ago. I and several people of reputed intelligence were together in a hotel room, watching a television program called "The Miss Universe Beauty Pageant." Now, even in a non-technicalized culture, a beauty pageant would be, it seems to me, a degrading cultural event. In this one, pure lunacy was added to the degradation by the utilization of computers to measure the measurements, so to speak, of the women involved. Each of the twelve judges was able to assign a precise number to the charm of a woman's smile, the shapeliness of her bosom, the sensuality of her walk, and even to the extent of what was called her poise. But more than this, as each judge assigned a number, a mother-computer, with legendary speed, calculated the average, which was then flashed on the upper right-hand corner of the TV screen so that the audience could know, immediately, that Miss Holland, for example, was a 6.231 on how she looked in a bathing suit, whereas Miss Finland was only a 5.827. Now, as it happened, one of the people with whom I was watching believed, as he put it, that there is no way Miss Finland is a 5.827. He estimated that she is, at a minimum, a 6.3, and maybe as high as a 7.2. Another member of our group took exception to these figures, maintaining strongly that only in a world gone mad is Miss Finland a 5.827, and that she should count herself lucky that she did not get what she deserved, which, as he figured it, was no more than a 3.8.

18 Now, the point is that here were two people whose minds had passed the point of crisis and were already in a state of rigor mortis, although they apparently didn't know it. As I left the room and headed for the hotel bar, a similar scene from my high school days came drifting back to me. Because I had received an 83 in English, I had missed by a fraction being eligible for Arista, the high school equivalent of making the Dean's List. I therefore approached my English teacher, a gentle and sensitive man by the name of Rosenbaum, and requested that he reassess my performance with a view toward elevating my grade two points. He regarded my request as reasonable and studiously examined his record book. Then he turned toward me with genuine sadness in his face and said, "I'm sorry, Neil. You're an 83. An 84 at most, but not an 85. Not this term, anyway."

19 Now, you understand, I trust, that both Rosenbaum and I were crazy. He, because he believed I was an 83 or 84 at most, and I, because I believed his belief. He had been fair. He had reviewed the numbers, which were both precise and objective. To him, my performance *was* the numbers. To me, as well. This is reification of technique, from which, several years later, I began to recover almost completely. I often wonder if Rosenbaum got better, too. The disease is not, however, so easy to overcome, because ultimately technicalization is more than a bias of culture. It is a bias of mind. Its assumptions become an interior voice which excludes alternative modes of expression.

20 What does it take for a person to believe that Miss Finland's shape is no better than a 3.8? What does it take for a teacher to believe, really believe, that a student *is* an 83 (or 84 at most)? It requires, first of all, a belief that it is possible to reduce persons or their behavior to numbers. It requires a total acceptance of the symbols and definitions of a technical system. It requires a belief that a system which supplies precision is, by that virtue, objective and hence, real. It requires, above all, a belief that the technical system can do your thinking for you—that is to say, it requires that calculation supercede judgment.

21 I remember another instance in my school career that will help me to show the power and range of the technical thesis. This time the scene was a college classroom, where I was taking a course in health. The professor was giving a lecture on the incidence of hunger throughout the world. She concluded with the remark that it can be well documented that at least six billion

children go to sleep hungry each night. Our class did not know much about these things, but we knew that there were certainly not more than three billion people on Earth—which would make her statement a logical impossibility. The point was raised. She looked startled for a moment. Checked her notes. Then said, somewhat relieved, "I know it doesn't sound right, but that's what I've got here."

22   Now, at first thought, one might say what *we* have here is just a stupid professor, or one who has merely made a mistake and is too embarrassed to acknowledge it. But there is more to it than this. Even if she were aware that her remark was preposterous, it is significant that she believed it was an acceptable excuse to refer us to the fact that the remark was suitably enshrined in her notes. Her notes were, so to speak, a closed and self-confirming system. Her defense was the equivalent of saying that eight green lights have flashed, hence the statement is true.

23   This sort of thinking, by the way, is quite common in our schools, and in fact is so well established that special names have been invented to cover "mistakes," which, in the nature of things, are not acknowledged as mistakes. I refer, for example, to the words "over-achiever" and "undera-chiever." What is an "over-achiever"? It is someone whose score on a stand-ardized IQ test is relatively low—say, a 94—but whose real-life intellectual performance is consistently high. In other words, the test can't be wrong. The student *is* a 94. He merely insists on behaving as if he were not. Perhaps there is even something perverse in him. Certainly, there is an element of perversity in the under-achiever—someone whose test score is relatively high but who does not perform well in other respects. The point is that the test score is taken as the reality. The student's behavior in various contexts is to be judged against this standard. If life contradicts a test score, so much the worse for life. Life makes mistakes. Instruments do not.

24   Schools, however, are not by any means the most dedicated pro-moters of The Technical Thesis. One may find the thesis advanced in almost every social institution, in a variety of ways and with varying degrees of ardor. The technical thesis consists of more than the tendency to reduce people to numerical abstractions. Its essence is to get people to submit themselves to the sovereignty of exclusive definitions and formal procedures. In this sense, there is no more powerful expression of the technical thesis than in the de-velopment of the State itself. For the modern state is almost pure technical-ization, consisting of nothing else than definitions, procedures, and the means of commanding obedience to them. One of the astonishing political ironies of our own time is the homage paid to large-scale technicalization by "liberals" and "humanists who, in wishing to expand human freedom, have turned consistently to the formal structure of government for assistance. The guiding principle here would seem to be: that government is best which governs most completely, and most precisely.

25 It is not enough, apparently, that government should protect against minority discrimination. Government must also insure minority equality. It is not enough that government should care for people who are ill. Government must insure that they are healthy. It is not even enough that government should protect children against child-abuse. It must also protect parents against "child responsibility" (for it is sometimes inconvenient for parents to tend their own children, in which case government should be available to provide a remedy).

26 I do not wish to argue here that any particular responsibility given to government is either good or bad. That must be the subject of another lecture by a different lecturer. Rather, I wish to point to the political danger of the technical thesis, which resides in this invariant rule: When technical organizations (that is bureaucracies) are given power to do something, they always take more of it than they actually need. Tests, computers, machines, *and* governments share this propensity. They always end up controlling more ground than one imagines had been given to them. In yielding to government the sovereignty to implement a "humane" purpose, we always sacrifice some dimension of freedom we had not intended to give. This is the technical trap to which Jacques Ellul refers in his phrase, "the political illusion," the idea that every conceivable problem of social relations may be solved by submitting it to the domain of technical control—i.e., a political solution. The precise cost is that we immerse ourselves in techniques far beyond our capacity to master them. The fact that we have been so eager to do this is a tribute to the power of the technical thesis and its fundamental presupposition: Only through objective, formal, and precise standardization can we control our lives. In other words, through machinery.

27 This thesis carries far beyond our political and social life. It ultimately forms the core of a religious conception. Consider, for example, the content of most of our popular television programs, including their commercials. These are, of course, parables, and in considering what are their meanings, we may see how deeply the technical thesis cuts, how it comes to form a modern equivalent of The Sermon on the Mount. TV commercials, especially, show this with astonishing clarity. What is the solution to each problem posed by a TV commercial? Where are we directed to seek, and what are we told we will find? The answer is that we shall find happiness through the ministrations of technology. It may be animal technology, vegetable technology, or mineral technology, but it is always technology. That is what we must commune with; that is what we must strive toward. The commercials tell us that, somewhere, there is a drug, a detergent, or a machine to deliver us from whatever shocks our flesh is heir to. Boredom, anxiety, fear, envy, sloth—there are remedies for each of these, and more. The remedies are called Scope, Comet, Cordova, Whisper Jet, Bufferin, and Pabst. They take the place of good works, piety, awe, humility, and transcendence.

28 On TV commercials, in other words, there do not really exist moral deficiencies as we customarily think of them. Nor are there intimations of the conventional roads to spiritual redemption. But there *is* Original Sin, and it consists in our having been ignorant of a technique or technology which offers happiness. We may achieve a state of grace by attending to the good news about it, which will appear every six or seven minutes. It follows from this that that person is most devout who knows of the largest array of technologies; the heretic is one who willfully ignores what is there to be used.

29 It is, of course, also part of this religion that people must think of themselves as little more than machines. Like machines, we must submit ourselves to continuous improvement. In fact, it is alleged that we exhibit a certain measure of moral weakness in resisting the opportunities to become new models. Do you think your hair is nice? It isn't. It can be made brighter and softer. Do you think you are attractive? You aren't. You can make yourself thinner or healthier. Do you think you are efficient? You are not. You can improve your productivity three-fold. What's more, you are under a moral compulsion of sorts to do so. Would the Ford Motor Company sell, in 1980, a 1979 model? How can you do the same with yourself? Like machinery, you must progress, streamline and polish yourself, present yourself as forever new.

30 All of this—technology as salvation—is what Christine Nystrom calls the "metaphysics" of the content of television, by which she means its principal assumptions about what is at the core of human failings and about how we may overcome them. This is another way of saying that television presents us with the technical thesis as a religious conception, as ultimate concern around which people organize their motivations and actions. And we find it preached not only in commercials but on what are called "programs." On action television, typically, the resolution of the struggle between good guys and bad does not recommend to us the force of a traditional moral imperative. It recommends to us the efficiency of a superior technology, technique, or technical organization. Kojak, Starsky, Hutch, Rockford, Jones, et al., are not in any clear cut terms very much morally superior to their adversaries. Not in a traditional sense, they aren't. However, according to the Technical Religion, they *are* morally superior in that their technical skills prevail. Their cars are better, their guns are better, their aim is better, their procedures are better, their organization is better.

31 What needs to be noticed is that the masters of the media have quite simply pre-empted the functions of religious leaders in articulating the moral values by which we ought to live. From this point of view, the excessive violence on TV, to which so many object, is not nearly so important an issue as is TV's replacement of the traditional moral code with the technical thesis. Even where action shows have reduced significantly their displays of violence, they still stand as celebrations of technique. "Mission: Impossible," which had relatively few instances of overt violence, was a weekly parable on the virtue, indeed, the glory, of technicalization. Its heroes were not people but techniques. Its bad guys were people whose most glaring weakness was their failure to know about or sufficiently appreciate the efficacy of sophisticated machinery. In this sense, "Mission Impossible" was the most religious program on the TV schedule. And we can be sure that its teachings were not ignored.

32   In the more benign TV programs, such as "family shows," we find no violence, but nonetheless the technical thesis is there in full force. Almost without exception, the problems which are the focus of each program are about breakdowns or misunderstandings in human relations. There rarely arise moral questions of a traditional sort. There are only questions of how to manage one's human relations. This is surely not an insignificant matter, but the point is that living is construed as a purely technical problem. One may solve the problem through amiability or increased communication or artful concealment. But the message of the parable is clear enough: the central human concern is not one's relationship to moral imperatives, but one's technique in solving the problems of relationship management. To put it simply, God is not dead. He survives as Technique.

33   It is important to say here that I am not contending that television or other electronic media have created the technical thesis. That they amplify, explicate, and celebrate it is beyond doubt. But its origins are probably to be found elsewhere. Lewis Mumford believes that the age of the "mega-machine," i.e., large-scale technicalization, began with the building of the pyramids, the first instance of the massive and systematic use of people as machines. Harold Innis suggests that technicalization began with the printing press, the first example of mass production of communications. Jacques Ellul implies that the invention of the mechanical clock was the first example of the widespread subjugation of human organization to the sovereignty of a machine, from which, he believes, we have never recovered. Ortega Y. Gasset argues that industrialization, which produced the specialist and "mass man," also produced a sort of mindless technical man. And Chaim Perelman links the origin of the technical thesis to an age-old desire to be, like God, perfect, such perfection being attainable through precision and objectivity.

34   It is not to my purpose to try to settle this question, even if I had the wit to do it. The fact is that, in our own time, the technical thesis is advanced so vigorously and on so many fronts that it has created an ecological problem, and a dangerous one. We have a generation being raised in an information environment that, on one hand, stresses visual imagery, discontinuity, immediacy, and alogicality. It is anti-historical, anti-scientific, and anti-conceptual, anti-national. On the other hand, the context within which this occurs is a kind of religious or philosophic bias toward the supreme

authority of technicalization. What this means is that as we lose confidence and competence in our ability to think and judge, we willingly transfer these functions to machines, whether they be HAGOTH, IQ tests, computers, or the State. It is no accident that so much energy is being devoted, in computer technology, to the development of "artificial intelligence," the purpose of which is to eliminate human judgment altogether. Or, if not that, to create a situation in which only a few people who are in control of the techniques have the authority to exercise human judgment. He who controls the definitions and rules of technique becomes the master, especially in a situation where people lack the intellectual ability and motivation to understand the assumptions of the technical thesis.

35 In saying all of this, I am not preparing an argument for a Luddite response. We gain nothing but chaos by banning or breaking our machines or indiscriminately disassembling our social machinery. Although at some time in the future such measures could be taken, they would be the ultimate acts of hysteria of people who live by techniques and who lack the intellectual resources to dominate them. As Ortega Y. Gasset remarks, when the masses, in despair and revolt, go searching for bread, their tendency is to destroy the bakeries. In the end, technique is not our enemy. We are. Where then do we turn to protect ourselves against ourselves?

36 The answers to this question have been given many times and with great eloquence by such people as Lewis Mumford, Jacques Ellul, Erich Fromm, Norbert Wiener, Arthur Koestler, Joseph Weizenbaum, Karl Popper, Marshall McLuhan, and Jacob Bronowski. They all tell us, first and foremost, that we may find protection in the development of our intellect and judgment, and in our continuing quest for knowledge of ourselves and our artifacts. Some of them tell us that we may find protection in the power of those traditional values which stress personal autonomy, community cohesion, family loyalty, and the primacy of human affection. And some also tell us that without a traditional basis of moral authority, we are totally disarmed. We are warned that expertise is no substitute for piety and awe, that efficiency is no substitute for sensitivity and affection, that the State is no substitute for the family, that bureaucracy is no substitute for civilized social relations, that machinery is no substitute for a sense of transcendence.

37 You may observe that all of these answers are what one might call cliches. And as I come to the close of my lecture, I must tell you that these cliches are all that stand between us and our complete immersion in the technical thesis. But cliches are more powerful than you might suppose. For a cliche is nothing less than a truth that has passed the test of time. And there is this, finally, to say about a cliche: Just at that moment when it is about to pass into the realm of complete fatuousness, it is in its nature, that the truth it embodies is rediscovered and put to work. Let us hope that our cliches will not fail us now.

TWO PAYCHECK POWER

Caroline Bird

Caroline Bird is a professional writer who is author of several prominent books on the general subject of women. *Born Female,* published in 1968, was widely acclaimed. Her recent books are: *Enterprising Women,* 1976; *What Women Want,* 1978; and *The Two Paycheck Marriage,* 1980. She delivered this address at the Second Management Training Conference, Institute for Managerial and Professional Women, Portland, Oregon, October 6, 1979.

Bird develops the theme that bosses—management—have not yet awakened to the "two paycheck" power represented by both husbands and wives working. The first part of the speech explores two points: (1) "men don't have to put up with a really lousy job any more for the sake of the wife and kids," and (2) "men and women are more alike in the way they behave on the job because they work for the same reasons." You will want to analyze how Ms. Bird develops each of these points. Are they convincing? If so, why? The second part of the address outlines how the workplace is "rigged against a balance between work and home." Bird sets forth five points in support of this thesis. The critical idea she leads to is that the workplace ought to redesign jobs around people, as they did during World War II when it was essential to utilize the available work force. Do you find that the speaker adheres strictly to her subject throughout or do you think that she strays afield from time to time on other interesting points? Try to outline the speech and see if each point sets up and leads logically into ensuing ideas.

How compelling a view of the problem does Bird convey? If you find her view compelling, try to determine what materials or ideas in her speech make it so? Does this speech alter your attitudes in any way?

This speech is reprinted by permission from *Vital Speeches of the Day,* January 15, 1980, pp. 202–205.

1 People are always asking me, What is the women's movement doing to the family? And I always answer: What family do you mean? If you mean the family that is on the logo of the Family Service Association of America, that family is gone forever. It's the one that is depicted by a breadwinning father and a homemaking mother with two little children hand in hand. Only seven percent of American families now answer to that description.

2 We have many single parents heading families, and many young couples who don't have children and aren't in a hurry to have them. And though we don't quite realize it, the most common kind of family supported by a breadwinning father is an older couple whose children are grown. The wife isn't working because she never developed the skills for a job.

3 A majority of the mothers of school-age children are not housewives, but working mothers—and more than 40 percent of the mothers of preschool children are out working too. This year, for the first time in history, a majority

of married people have the protection of a *second* paycheck coming into the house. Two-paycheck families are no longer the exception, they are the norm.

4 They are saving us from the worst hardships of inflation. And if there's to be the kind of recession that throws men out of work, the second paycheck will save us from the worst hardships of unemployment, too. Already half the unemployed men in this country have wives who are working.

5 Now all these two-paycheck couples have problems. Some are logistical: when to have a baby; how to care for the baby when both work; how to get the housework done; how to budget two paychecks. Others are power problems: which paycheck comes first; who moves if job offers lead in opposite directions (you can maximize pay or opportunity or go where the least favored spouse gets the best deal); what happens when one career pulls out ahead of the other (I happen to think the problem is worse when his career pulls out ahead of hers).

6 By and large the two-career couples are managing very nicely, thank you. They are more inventive in finding solutions than the pundits who are predicting the end of the family.

7 But they have one complaint: they are changing faster than the institutions with which they have to live.

8 It's not just the internal revenue that assumes that all wives depend on their husbands and taxes two-paycheck couples more than they would pay if they were single—so that some couples are actually discouraged from getting married. It's schools, doctors, dentists, utilities, department stores, that expect one person in the family to be available at *their* convenience. But most of all—and most damaging of all—it's the bosses who haven't changed.

9 Most of them aren't responding to the difference the second paycheck makes in the way people feel about work. First, and most visibly, men don't have to put up with a really lousy job any more for the sake of the wife and kids. Second, men and women are more alike in the way they behave on the job because they work for the same reasons.

10 The first is the biggest worry. Jobs are less important when there are two of them in the family. Two-paycheck power is doing more for the independence of workers on the job than welfare or unions have done.

11 "The decline of the work ethic" dismays me as much as it surprises them. What I hear as I travel around the country makes me painfully aware that I grew up in the Great Depression of the Thirties when people would do almost anything for a job. They might sneak a personal phone call during working hours, but they were careful to do it when they weren't disturbing their bosses. But no longer.

12 As a feminist, I am interested in the career conflicts that arise when his job takes him one place and hers another. But when I talk with young couples, I find they aren't so worried about equality. Most of the time they don't make the decision on the basis of the job at all. They go or stay where it's nicer to live. There are Californians who wouldn't go to New York for all the money in Citibank. And there are New Yorkers who won't go anywhere else. Mobil oil lost 30 percent of its workforce when it moved an operation from Manhattan to Virginia.

13 When I tell women how to buck the sexism that keeps them from promotion, they want to know whether a woman in management still has to work twice as hard as a man. I used to feel like giving them a snappy answer like, Maybe not, but what have you got to gain by proving it? Now I know that they are talking not about sex discrimination in the workplace, but about what job competition is doing to men. They are asking me whether women can use their new-found job power to cool it.

14 The picture is confusing. Two things are happening at the same time. Some people are becoming more competitive and other people are becoming more lazy. Slower growth means slower promotions, more competition for every step up the ladder. So what happens?

15 At every step more people look at their chances and count themselves out. Instead of worrying about the next promotion, they worry about the next vacation. Slower growth, second paychecks, fewer children to support, means less effort than before on the lower rungs of the ladder, withdrawal of energy from the job, retirement on the payroll. But two paychecks also mean that the surviving competitors work harder for the prizes at the top.

16 A lot of the people who are counting themselves out at lower rungs are men. And a lot of the people who are counting themselves in are the new women. Everywhere I go I meet ebullient young women who are going all out for money and power, because they've never been able to get them before. Like professional blacks, they are the true believers in the American Dream. They've bought the standard incentive system lock, stock and barrel and management ought to be thankful to promote them.

17 But the pity is that managers don't always see it that way. One reason is that the top boss may be one of the few people on the payroll who are still the sole support of their families. Because they relegated the rearing of their children to their wives, they can't understand young fathers who "act like women" in questioning transfers, overtime, schedules that interfere with family life, and the intrinsic value of the work the company wants them to do.

18 These decision-makers believe in equal opportunity for women as a matter of principle, but personally they are dismayed when the women they bring along compete "like men" for the jobs that "ought" to be attracting males.

19 And don't think this loosening up of sex roles between homemaking and breadwinning is just for the managers alone. It's happening all down the

line. Three or four years ago, for the first time, we had blue collar mothers going out to work. Even ethnic mothers are joining the exodus. Among the 5,000 couples whom we punch carded for *The Two-Paycheck Marriage,* only 27 percent of the men thought the husband of a homemaker should take a second job if money were needed. All the rest—including the socially conservative—thought the *wife* should get a job.

20 Which brings me to the second way workers are using their two-paycheck power: both men and women are demanding a better balance between work and home than either sex has ever been able to get in the past.

21 Men are beginning to rebel against the macho image that shackled their fathers to dull or demeaning jobs, just as women are rebelling against the feminine mystique that kept their mothers out of the action at home.

22 The best expression of the new androgynous values came from a high-school girl who assured me she wouldn't have any problems combining family and career. "When I get married," she said, "I'll work part time. My husband will work part time. We'll have plenty of time to do things together around the house." I felt like weeping for her. She has the perfect recipe for job and family life. An ideal setup for rearing children. But it's not going to be easy to get.

23 The system we have built is rigged against family life for men and career life for women. Employers do not provide his and her part time jobs that add up to one full time family-sized paycheck. My high-school girl will find that her husband can make so much more money than she can make that he'll be pushed into taking over the breadwinning and she will be left to do all of those things around the house by herself.

24 Consider the many ways in which the system works against sex equality at home and at work.

25 First, with a very few highly publicized exceptions, sizeable business enterprises are run by men and operated at the bench or office machine level by women. That makes the autonomy of homemaking more *interesting* than anything that most women are allowed to do at work and better paid, too. Some wives enjoy a standard of living no woman is allowed to earn for herself.

26 We've heard so much about the women in management that it is hard to explain to young women how few these really are. To make that point, I told some young women at Andover that "women just don't get to be Vice-Presidents of General Motors." Well, after I spoke, an enchanting fairy princess of a girl with long hair and a faraway look in her eyes stayed behind to tell me in private that her mother was a vice-president of General Motors. "Oh, my God," I burst out in embarrassment, "You've got to be Marina von Neumann's daughter." And she was. Female vice-presidents are that rare at G. M.

27 When I told this story to a group of personnel men a man from G. M. came up afterwards to correct me. They now have two women vice-presidents. Out of how many hundreds? If there's a third, someone is sure to charge reverse discrimination. He's sure there can't be *that* many women that good!

28 The second way that the workplace is rigged against a balance between work and home is the standard schedule. Nine to five every week day for most of us. That schedule is convenient only for men who have full time, stay-at-home wives to get their meals, take their clothes to the cleaners, mind their kids, and wait patiently at home until the plumber comes. I sometimes think the schedule remains in force because the only men for whom it really works are those who *do* have wives getting dinner.

29 Third, the unspoken rules for getting ahead still assume that the candidate for advancement is willing to go wherever and whenever the company chooses to send him. If she had a job, she's supposed to quit it, pack up the household goods the company obligingly pays for shipping, and find new quarters so that he can pay full attention to his new assignment as soon as he gets there.

30 Fourth, a candidate for management is expected to separate home and work in an arbitrary way. Kids can't understand what their parents do at business, and increasingly the work is so specialized that husbands and wives can't understand each other's business either. And the separation is physical as well. Men as well as women spend hours in their cars that they might be spending at home with their children.

31 Finally, the candidate for advancement has to put in peak effort during the late twenties and thirties, the age at which men as well as women are most heavily involved in rearing small children. This is just the time of life when two part time jobs would make better sense than either one or two intensely absorbing careers.

32 We are going through a curious period for families. We all accept now the right of a woman to decide when and whether she shall have children. Men aren't supposed to care about them, and in the first years of the women's movement they would pointedly leave the question of a family to their wives. It's her body after all, they would say. Now many women say they don't want children. But men are beginning to have second thoughts.

33 I hear curious noises. "For two years we've had an ideal, liberated marriage," a San Francisco woman of 32 told me. "We've shared the expenses, the housework, and we decided we didn't want children. But now my husband wants a baby! He's changed—but I haven't. What can I tell him?" Men like this husband are finding the work of home as mysterious and glamourous as some women find the world of the executive suite.

34   At a Vassar symposium, a recent male graduate told me that he wanted to marry a rich woman so he could stay at home and bring up children. I can only describe him as beautiful—beautiful and laid back in the new California style. If I were a rich young woman I'd take him on in a minute. Was he serious, I wondered? He might have been putting me on, I am, after all, a square old alum. He might have been snubbing my obvious work orientation a little less politely than some other students.

35   But I suspect that he really did think rearing children would be more fun than wearing a three-piece suit every day.

36   In California a few days later, I encountered just the kind of successful woman he was looking for. Her husband had been a commercial artist but he quit when he married her "to develop his talent," and hadn't done much of anything but lie around the house for years. She thought the arrangement was great at first. She was one of the rare career women with a wife. But now that she's succeeded she's wondering what she missed. Maybe she ought to have stayed at home.

37   It's the same way with all these mismatches we've named between job and family. We've thought of them as problems for women only. The fact is, of course, that they are problems for husbands as well as for wives. They are especially demoralizing obstacles for the kind of people we most need to pull us through the next twenty years. Companies which don't consider what they are doing to the home life of their employees are going to lose their best people, or worse, get less than the best they have to offer.

38   Most job incentives now assume that we're all living in the 1950's, when the top managers who set them up were young men starting out. We need to redesign jobs around the lifestyles of the 1970's. And as F. D. R. said when he asked for the first 50,000 airplanes, "The engineers can do it if they really try."

39   It's comforting to think back to World War II when we think of this future restructure, because the engineers did it. They did it by making the jobs fit people. They broke tasks up so that women could do them and blacks could do them, and people could do them part time if needed. They simplified tasks for the newcomers and made them more efficient for everyone.

40   I've been told that the telephone company is getting some of the benefit of redesigning jobs around people as they struggle to adapt outside work to women. They had trouble at first, getting women to climb poles. So they changed the way poles are climbed to adapt to the female pelvis and made it easier for bipeds of any gender. When women passed the training program but flubbed in the field, they couldn't just say to the government, "See, women can't do it." They studied what was happening and found that the training courses had never been the way that outside men learned their jobs. They had always learned them by doing, but the men who knew how weren't teaching the women apprentices. So the whole training system was revised to make older hands responsible for newcomers in the field.

41 One of these days some brilliant industrial engineer is going to discover how to conquer absenteeism and absentmindedness on the assembly lines. They can do it, according to Robert Schrank of the Ford Foundation, by installing telephones along the line so that people don't feel they are in jail when they clock in to work.

42 An immediate problem for management is the one that worried men when women were asking for suffrage. Who will wash the dishes? If women don't do the lousy, deadend jobs, how are we going to get the corporate housework done? Well, it doesn't seem impossible if you're willing to shake things up a bit.

43 Where, may I ask the managers among you, is it written that there is no other way to make your product than the way you are making it now? Your own people could probably think of half-a-dozen better ways to do it if they thought you would really listen.

44 Let me quote the reaction of Rosabeth Kanter, the Yale sociologist who looks at management with an educated outsider's eye. "The truth is that there's very little work that's inherently lousy, if it's a stepping stone, if it's temporary, if people are afforded dignity, if they have good pay, and if their ideas are heard." Five ifs. They give you a lot of room for experiment. And most of you can tick off proposals—flexitime, part time, lateral instead of vertical promotion, coeducational management training, job sharing. The engineers can do it if they really try.

45 Two of the many suggestions particularly strike my fancy. We could narrow the gap between home and work by packaging many more tasks so that they could be done at home, the way I and my husband, also a writer, arrange our lives. A great many professional workers already take home work. Lawyers write brief, copywriters write ads, executives write speeches where they can take off their shoes. Computer terminals would make it possible to package routine tasks that could be done by parents who elect to spend more time with small children. If you think they'll be interrupted—and they will— put them on piece rate.

46 My other proposal is more ambitious. Organizations have saved the career opportunities of people who have had to be away for years, provided the cause was worthy. Academics get sabbaticals. Some corporations give public service leave. In wartime, military leave freezes a patriot's career while he's fighting. Research leave is allowed in many organizations. Why not *parental* leaves for women and men who want to spend the first three years of a child's life enjoying the experience? It may not enormously improve the welfare of the child—the verdict is not yet in on that—but the experience of parenting undeniably improves the *parents*.

47 Jobs can fit people. We can do it if we really try.

"LET'S BRING BACK DAD": A SOLID VALUE SYSTEM

Jenkin Lloyd Jones

At the 79th Annual Meeting of the Ohio Chamber of Commerce, March 14, 1973, Jenkin Lloyd Jones, longtime editor and publisher of the *Tulsa Tribune*, delivered this speech to create concern for a problem. Jones is a widely sought speaker known for his conservative political critiques of contemporary American society. Also he is a respected member of the newspaper profession, having won the William Allen White Award from the American Society of Newspaper Editors in 1957.

The general problem is a degeneration of the "quality of life" in America. Jones' specific concern is with the "worst-raised generation" in American history—"middle or upper-middle class" children. To focus his concern early in the speech, and to identify the causal factor of parental irresponsibility, he uses parallel structure through a series of questions and answers. In a quotation cited toward the end of the speech, Jones summarizes three major causes: failure of the home, school, and church to teach a "sound and solid value system."

Through examples and narration of stories, Jones pinpoints the scope and nature of the problem by identifying elements which are "a job for Dad": decline in honesty; disrespect for the work ethic; pornography and sexual promiscuity; drug abuse; ignorance of the nature of business free enterprise; lack of appreciation for and willingness to defend American freedoms; and decline in self-discipline. The audience of business people Jones addresses would see the problem directly linked to their concerns because various values they cherish are being threatened or undermined. At the very least, with some certainty he could assume that the vast share of his listeners prize the work ethic (the example of Andrew Carnegie), free enterprise, and freedom from government control ("You didn't need a permit from the Health Department in those days.").

Jones attempts to weaken the credibility of liberal and countercultural heros such as Abbie Hoffman (preaches the rip-off but sues over unethical distribution of book royalties) and Norman Thomas ("bubble-head" idealist). In contrast Jones' own credibility with the audience may have been increased through various rhetorical choices. We learn that he served in the Navy in WW II and that he is a past President of the U.S. Chamber of Commerce. Indirectly he presents himself as condemning from an informed rather than uninformed position; early in his life he voted for a Socialist candidate for President and he was secretary of the University of Wisconsin Peace League. By implication he is saying that he has had personal experience with the shortcomings of liberalism and socialism.

Through the historical analogy to the decline and fall of Rome, Jones argues that America may perish just as have other nations that faced similar problems and failed to solve them. What meaning does he seem to want to convey through the twice-used Biblical allusion to reaping the whirlwind? How adequately does he refute the frequently used analogy between drinking liquor and smoking marijuana? Realizing that this speech was presented in

1973, what role does Jones apparently see for mothers, and for women generally, in transmitting the needed solid value system? Consider especially the title of the speech, his figurative analogy concerning the "man cub" and his illustration of *Mama's Bank Account*.

Reprinted with permission from *Vital Speeches of the Day*, May 15, 1973, pp. 473-76.

1   Last week on the plane from my home to Los Angeles, I found myself sitting next to an old, valued friend. Somewhere over the New Mexico desert, he blurted out, gray-faced and shaken, that his beautiful, twenty-one year old daughter, whom I have known since her birth, was caught that morning by U.S. Customs officials at the Los Angeles airport trying to smuggle in twenty-one ounces of cocaine from Lima. Everything this man and his wife had done in their adult lives was centered on this lovely child. They had given her all the "advantages." Now it was all in ashes.

2   Why do I tell you this? What does this have to do with you? Everything, gentlemen! If the next generation should, figuratively speaking, start bringing in cocaine, everything you have struggled for, everything this fine organization represents will be an exercise in futility.

3   Listen to the words of your incoming president about the responsibilities of business to the future of its community or its state. He is very right. In the old days, chambers of commerce counted the wagons coming and the wagons going out. If the outgoing overbalanced the incoming, they were in trouble. That type of chamber of commerce has no place in this modern age. Quality of life is the name of the game. And if the oncoming generation, through illusion, cannot support the quality of life, then we will be a sad generation.

4   So, for a few minutes, I want to talk a little bit about this oncoming generation. I want to talk particularly about those sons and daughters of ours who represent what we call the middle or upper-middle class. Many of these children are deprived. Sure, they got their first automobile on their sixteenth birthday. Many of them were sent to expensive schools. They had all the clothes they wanted. We gained, I suppose, a little face around the country club by telling how soon we sent them to Europe. But many of these children are deprived of the way in which life must be lived if it is not to turn to dust and ashes in their mouths.

5   I would submit, ladies and gentlemen, that the children of the so-called class which we represent is the worst-raised generation in the history of America. And who raised them? We did! Who tried to buy their love with material things for which they were not ready? We did. Who sought to gain status by seeing to it that our kid was the first kid on the block with a new gizmo? We did.

6   What generation produced a federal judiciary that has so fuzzed up the common sense definition of dirt that our youngsters are drowned in

porno? Our generation. Who produced the Hollywood that's willing to do anything for a buck and comes out with movies that would better be described as peep-shows or as visual aids in an abnormal psych class and that lards and meringues and whipped creams its hypocrisy by claiming that it is struggling toward new horizons in intellectual freedom? That's our generation. *We* sit behind the box office; we give the youngsters two bucks or two and a half to go out and see GP rated up from R and R rated up from X. I remember in my generation we were lucky to get a dime to go out and see Tom Mix and Hoot Gibson kiss their horses.

7   Who raised the most lopsided generation in human history? We did. Who collapsed when little Phyllis went into a tantrum because Mary's mother was going to let her go steady at thirteen? And who hurled little Phyllis into a premature monogamy for which she was not physically or psychologically prepared? And who is reaping the whirlwind? We are.

8   Who has retained our children, in one measure, in their swaddling clothes long after they should have been given responsibility and, in another measure, has put them under artificial and deleterious pseudosophistication which would assume that they were more adult than they are? In the state of New York, on the eve of one's twenty-first birthday, one is still supposed to be such a child that one isn't supposed to know enough not to shoot a cop. But we have decided that three years before reaching age twenty-one one knows enough to pick a president of the United States. Who created this dichotomy? We did.

9   You know, the man cub struggles to be a bear. These children are our children, and they are in our hands. They are like us; they are not measurably more or less intelligent than we are. The process of evolution is glacial. If we do not permit the man cub to stand tall, constructively, he will try to make like a bear destructively. If we do not give the man cub some reasonable responsibility at the age when he is ready, he will squeal his tires; he'll steal, and he'll smoke the joint behind the drive-in.

10   At the age of twelve Horatio Nelson was a midshipman before the mast; at the age of fourteen he was on his first voyage to the Arctic. He didn't need to hang around the drive-in; he stood tall in his own eyes. At the age of twelve Andrew Carnegie was in the cotton mills; at the age of fourteen he was a telegraph operator; at the age of sixteen he was in the railroad business; and at the age of eighteen he thought he'd give the steel business a whirl. He didn't need the drive-in.

11   Now it's true we victimize, or at least our grandfathers and great grandfathers victimized children and sent pale, wan youngsters into the sweat shop, into the textile mills, into the breaker houses of the coal mines. And they sickened, and they died; and we were sore ashamed. So we passed a lot of child labor laws, and they were overdue. But we have so far over-

done it that the kids sit around all summer on their hands because no one can think of anything good for them to do. Again, we reap the whirlwind. In an effort to protect our children from worry, we have failed to develop the mental and moral muscles which permit them to overcome the thing that makes worries.

12   I have a friend—an old shipmate in New Haven, Connecticut—whom I visited a few years after the war. He was such a good father that he should have lost his amateur standing. He had four children, aged from junior high school into high school. After I had sponged off him for dinner he said, "Now Jenk, tonight is the family board meeting." And he said, "It'll only take a few minutes, but we must get it out of the way." And I said, "The what?" And he said, "The family board meeting!" He said, "Would you like to come?" I said, "Try to keep me away."

13   The dinner dishes were all cleared away; the family sat around the table. The charts came out about the kids' savings accounts and how much had been added or drawn down in each case in the past month. The old chart came out about the mortgage on the house. They saw that another bite had been taken at it. The chart of Dad's investments on Wall Street came out, and he took quite a shellacking that previous month. Then, there was the little item of the bicycle left in the driveway. There was no screaming or incriminating, no anger. The board sat in judgment about how to replace the bicycle, and it was decided that the going rate for babysitting was a dollar and a quarter an hour and that the kids would all go out and hustle up jobs. The youngster who needed to replace the bicycle ought to be able to get a new one in about thirty-five hours of work. Everybody was very happy.

14   Then Dad said, "Now, I've got a surprise for you. You remember I went down to Cincinnati last month to the association of my professional group, and I delivered a paper down there. I didn't tell you they paid me $500.00, and so," he said, "I'm setting $200.00 of it aside for the income tax. I'm keeping a hundred; I did the work. And I'm giving Mother a hundred because she keeps the family together. Then we're cutting it down, and each one of you youngsters gets twenty-five bucks." The kids all cheered. But never after that did Dad have to explain what the income tax was. It was two hundred out of Dad's five.

15   You may remember the book, *Mama's Bank Account,* written by a girl who grew up in a poor Swedish family in San Francisco, and the old man ran a street car. He made $18.00 a week. It was a large family. They lived on the ragged edge of subsistence, but every time there was a crisis, every time there was a strike, every time there was illness, every time there were tonsils to come out, Mama would say, "Now, I'm going to bake some cookies, and you can all go down on the street corner and sell them." (You

CONTEMPORARY AMERICAN SPEECHES

didn't need a permit from the Health Department in those days.) Or, "Let's start gathering up old papers and scrap metal, and we'll sell it to the junk man; I don't want to get into my bank account. It's for a real emergency."

16   And so the kids would all get busy to get what little money they could, and the crisis would be overcome, and the bank account was not drawn upon. And after some years, they went to high school and trade school, and one of them went to college. One girl had a good job as a legal secretary. The sun began to come up, and the clouds lifted. One day, Mama dropped over with a heart attack, and then it was that Papa confessed that there wasn't any bank account; there never had been in those years. There wasn't money, but Mama had arrived at that wonderful white lie in which the children never felt total insecurity, but they felt stirred, and it was the best of both worlds.

17   Well, there is not a family in this room, blessed as most of you are, that is immune from disaster. There is not a family that may not need strong children. What have you done to raise them? Well, of course, we've sent most of them off, when they get old enough, to the universities and colleges.

18   One of the popular speakers on these campuses (and he makes a fabulous amount of money for delivering his dissertation) is Abbie Hoffman, the apostle of "Rip it off!" the apostle of "steal it; pick it up; carry it away." This louses up the hated Establishment and theoretically is supposed to bring in whatever socialist nirvana Abbie has in mind. A couple of years ago, Abbie wrote a book oddly titled, *Steal This Book,* and it was a treatise on how you break into cigarette machines, how you empty telephone coin boxes, how you jimmy up the paid gas meter.

19   The funny thing about it was that after the book was around about six months, Abbie sued his coauthor for unethical distribution of the royalties. Abbie couldn't stand to have his book stolen. And yet a lot of our children think that Abbie is camp.

20   Last month, the *New York Times* interviewed a young junior high schooler in Fairfield County, Connecticut, and he said in junior high school shoplifting is a status thing. You're out to prove you're groovy. To be caught by your parents is almost as challenging as stealing. You can come up with great explanations. Convincing your parents where you got it is part of the game.

21   Do I have to tell you what is in the future of a great economic system that has been increasingly based on trust—trust with charge accounts, trust with credit cards, trust on try it and return it if you don't like it? Do I have to tell you what is going to happen to this great structure we have been so proud of, if the next generation wants to rip it off?

22   Well, here's a job for Dad! It's time Dad sat down and explained what would happen to Junior's future if Junior became untrustworthy. You hear a lot of talk now about the work ethic being old hat, you know, the Puritan ethic and so forth. Old stuff! We're going to try something different. We're going to smell the daisies.

23   Two months ago I went down to the south island of New Zealand, and at the bottom of the mountain I picked up a young couple who had been sitting disconsolately on their packs by the side of the road. And of course, I have the bad habit of interviewing everyone. The young man turned out to be a graduate of the University of Brisbane, Australia, and he and his wife were touring around. I said, "What did you graduate in?" And he said "Biology," and I said, "You're a biologist." "No," he said, "really not." He said, "We decided to get out of the racket. We decided life is too short. We're having fun."

24   Well, after we had gone through a tunnel and driven for some miles, I said, "How do your legs feel?" He said, "Oh, fine, fine." I said, "You know why they're not aching?" He said, "What do you mean?" I said, "Because a guy involved in the rat race stopped and gave you a ride. He gave you a ride in a vehicle that was put together by people who were still involved in the rat race, and the reason why you're not clawing your way up over that crag with that heavy pack on your back is because some other joker's sweat or toil built this road, a product of the rat race." Well, they voted me a very droll fellow. *There* was a job for some Dad—a job that wasn't done.

25   You hear a lot about the new morality. I suppose the new morality is about as new as the oldest barnyard. After all, there is nothing new about tending to rationalize, letting it all hang out, and doing what comes naturally. As for ethical or religious rationalization, let's not forget that the temple prostitutes were busy twenty-three centuries ago.

26   I'm reminded of the statement of a Minnesota coed I met a couple of months ago, who said she'd come to the conclusion that sexual intercourse was just a polite social gesture, sorta like shaking hands. Here's a job for Dad. Here's a job for Dad to say, "Look Phyllis or Bill, if it's all mechanical pleasure, if this is *it,* then what happens to the first time things get tough? Why are our ghetto societies in such chaos? Because the man walks off when it gets tough. What would happen to you children if at the first moment our wedding was not all wine and roses, Mother had gone one way, and I had gone another?" Maybe Phyllis or Bill would get the idea.

27   And then we've got the drug culture. One of the commissioners last night came out with the statement that marijuana is the third most used drug in this country, first being liquor, and second tobacco. I'm getting sick

of this effort to equate cannabis with the tobacco I use, which I do not intend to give up. I'm getting sick of the idea that because Dad has a drink, Junior has a right to smoke pot. There is only one reason why Junior smokes pot, and that's to get high. And if the only reason Dad takes a drink is to get high, then Dad's in trouble.

28　But worst of all, to talk about the soft drugs or the hard drugs is to overlook the fact that even the soft drugs are an effort to ride over a perplexity, to float above it. Somebody very wisely said that most lives are destined to be neither triumphs nor tragedies but an endless series of predicaments, and our capacity to face up to and meet predicaments is the surest source of successful living. The kid who floats above them with uppers or beneath them with downers, or worse yet, takes to the needle and the spoon, or even smokes his weed, is a kid who is atrophying the capacity to meet predicaments. And what sort of a future is the youngster going to have?

29　Then, of course, you've got all these neo-Socialists, who sit at the feet of professors in our great universities, who are basically hostile to the business system because they never had any experience with it. As my professor friend at the University of Iowa said, "You would be shocked if you knew the extent of the economic illiteracy of our Letters and Science faculty." So kids read Charles Reich's *The Greening of America* in which he says, "Economic equality and social ownership of means of production are assumed."

30　I speak of these kids with a great deal of sympathy because I'm sure I'm the only ex-president of the Chamber of Commerce of the United States who cast his first vote for the Socialist candidate for president of the United States. Many years later, I found myself on a day coach between Chicago and Kansas City, and who was sitting next to me but Norman Thomas. We talked for six hours, and a kinder, more decent, more lovable bubble-head you would never meet. (That was before I'd gone behind the Iron Curtain a few times.)

31　And here is a job for Dad. A job for Dad to say, "Look Buster, do you know why under these systems, in which the means of production are arrogated by the state, there is very little freedom? Do you know why these become police states? Because in the delicate balance of the centralization of authority, you cannot have option or choice; this louses up the plan. The name of freedom is option. Across the river over there, a lot of guys have shelter; they've got three meals a day, such as they are; they have guaranteed jobs. What do *they* lack? Options. If *you* don't like the Ford, you can try the Chevrolet. If the Texaco man won't sweep out your front rug, maybe the Shell man will. This is the system by which the consumer and the customer become king; this is what we mean by free enterprise."

Maybe you'd better have a little talk with Junior before he goes off to the ivy halls.

32   Then you have a generation that has apparently decided that because of the immoralities of war in Southeast Asia, defending their country is no longer necessary, that wars are all based on misunderstanding, that if we dump our armaments into the sea, we will have universal brotherhood. They really believe this! I'm sympathetic to these kids. You're looking at the ex-secretary of the Peace League of the University of Wisconsin, circa 1932. I was sure that wars were made by munitions manufacturers. I laughed at my friend Andy who every afternoon would go down to the quadrangle and march up and down with that ridiculous Springfield rifle on his shoulder. There weren't going to be any more wars. We were going to throw all our arms away. Andy never got back from the death march on Bataan. But he and a small khaki line held, while we ex-secretaries of the Peace League were able to get around the obstacle courses and find out how to run a ship.

33   So maybe it's time for Dad to say, "Look Hank, did you ever stop to think what would happen if one of the atomic-holding powers ever got such a preponderance of conventional weapons that the other power would face the grim choice of either atomic holocaust or backdown?" And if it comes to that, if it comes to backdown, and one power gathers up all the atomic weaponry of the world, where do you think that leaves the cause of rebellion? Here's a Bastille you're not going to take with scythes and pitchforks. Here is a weapon preset and zeroed in on every great city in the world. And if this happens to be an authoritarian power, here is slavery for you and your children unto the seventh generation. You've only got to blow it once now, and you lose it all. There's a job for Dad.

34   And so we go through the rest of the catalogue of great illusions, of the situational ethics. Dr. Will Herbert described relativism as the creeping conviction that there's no such thing as truth or right but only the varying beliefs, the varying cultures, each apparently justified in its own terms, no fixed norms, but merely shifting opinions. Is your kid standing on that hill of jelly? It's amazing how many parents, frightened of being accused of being preachy, have never leveled with their young.

35   Dr. Robert E. Cavanaugh, writing in a recent issue of *Psychology Today* magazine says, "The failure of the home, the school, the church to transmit a sound and solid value system further heightens the student identity crisis. Today's student lacks a strong parental figure or a deeply indoctrinated sense of values to give him polarization."

36   In his book, *Ancient Rome, Its Rise and Fall,* Philip Van Ness Myers says, "First at the bottom, as it were, of Roman society and forming its ultimate unit was the family. The most important feature or element of

this family group was the authority of the father. It was in the atmosphere of the family that were nourished in Roman youth the virtues of obedience, deference to authority, and in the exercise of parental authority, the Roman learned how to command as well as how to obey."

37   Then what happened? Jerome Carcopino in his book, *Daily Life in Ancient Rome,* said, "By the beginning of the second century A.D., Roman fathers, having given up the habit of controlling their children, let the children govern them and took pleasure in bleeding themselves white to gratify the expensive whims of their offspring. The result was that they were succeeded by a generation of wastrels." I might point out that after the generation of wastrels came Attila, the Hun.

38   Robert Paul Smith in his little book, *"Where did you go?" "Out" "What did you do?" "Nothing,"* had this to say: "I can no longer remember the crisis which involved my son: but in essence, it had reached the point of all arguments where he was saying the hell he would and I was saying the hell he wouldn't. . . . He was two or three. His mother rushed in to say that I must Gesell him a little, or at least Spock him or treat him with a little Ilg, and I went away. . . . I found him later, ready to renew hostilities, but on his face and in his manner was much weariness, much fatigue, and a kind of desperation. I had a moment of pure illumination: I stood there and saw inside his head as clearly as if there had been a pane of glass let in his forehead. What he was saying was, 'Please, please, for Heaven's sake, somebody come and take this decision out of my hands, it's too big for me', I grabbed him and picked him up and carried him to wherever it was I thought he was supposed to go. He was little then, he hit me and bit me and wet me, he hollered bloody murder and did his level best to kill me. I remember now, it was to his bed he was supposed to go. I got him there, and dumped him in, put the crib side up. He was in his cage, and he had been put there by his keeper, and he went to sleep as happy as ever I saw him. There were rules. Nobody was going to leave him out in the middle of nowhere trying to figure out what he was supposed to do, when he was too young to know what to do."

39   Another writer says, "Children need and want discipline. Every time they misbehave, they are saying help me; show me how far I can go; don't let me hurt myself."

40   Well, ladies and gentlemen, the era of family tyrants is past, and good riddance. I'm glad the woodshed has been taken down and the strap is no longer involved. There was much brutality in the old system. Today, Dad must be a leader, not a drill instructor, but he must not err in the other direction and try to become just a chum. Bill Buckley says, "What ten-year old wants a forty-year old friend?" I've seen dads trying so hard to be Boy

Scouts that I've wondered when they're going to get their Second Class badges.

41 Dad must be awesome if he's going to preserve what he's been working for all these years. The dad who comes home drunk from the bar or country club may be a little frightening, but he'll never be awesome. The dad who boasts about how he outwitted the Highway Patrol or cheated on this income tax will have a hard time making any mileage. Dad must be an awesome thing. Dad must be something to push against, not a feather pillow.

42 If enough American dads, seeing what we are seeing around us now—the wreckage of a misguided and largely miserable group of youngsters—if enough American dads were to resolve to become partisan dads, unashamed to hold moral standards, willing to take the time to communicate values, then the chances of raising a new generation that would live in the agony of social chaos, or worse yet, lose their liberties for generations yet to come, will be substantially diminished.

43 Last year, up on the Russian River in central California, I watched a father osprey at the top of a dead tree teaching his chick how to fish. The father osprey would take off and dive like a plummet into the river in which the whiting were running, come up with a fish, and fly back to the limb, and then the chick would take off and describe a couple of clumsy cartwheels in the air and hit the water with a splash, and less often come up with a fish. And do you know what? I didn't hear that chick say to his father, I didn't hear him say, "Look Dad, you're irrelevant."

44 Dad was the way of life; Dad was the secret of survival. And if that's good for the osprey nest, then for the sake of our nation and its oncoming generations, let's bring back Dad!

Chapter 7

SPEECHES THAT AFFIRM PROPOSITIONS OF POLICY

> *. . . I have suspected for some time that the key division of this society, given the awesome rate of change and what it has done to tradition and values, is not a classic ideological or economic split, but how people react to change. Whether they welcome it, merely accept it, or, as in many cases, feel deeply threatened by it.*
>
> David Halberstam

THE NATURE AND IMPORTANCE OF SPEECHES THAT AFFIRM PROPOSITIONS OF POLICY

Whenever people have been free to choose their personal or collective destinies, speakers have arisen to advocate courses of action. When a President of the United States stands before a television camera to encourage popular approval of a Supreme Court ruling, he or she is proposing a course of action. When a legislator stands at the rostrum of a state senate to recommend adoption of a new taxation program, he or she is advocating a policy. When a social reformer urges the abolition of capital punishment, a union official the rejection of a contract, a theologian an end to doctrinal conflict, or politicians a vote in their behalf, they all are engaged in the affirmation of policies.

Listeners and speakers would benefit from holding a *process view,* rather than a static view, of life. Such a view assumes that change, process, and coping with change are normal rather than exceptional phenomena. There is no "status quo," no static existing state of affairs, to defend. Present policies and programs always evolve, modify, and change to some degree. The choice is not between change and nonchange. The choices center on how to manage the speed, degree, and direction of inevitable change. Solutions and policies never are entirely permanent. No sooner has a program been instituted than the conditions which necessitated it have altered somewhat and new conditions have arisen, thus at least partly rendering the program obsolete.

Although a society's problems have been clearly illuminated, that society will not grow and prosper unless effective courses of action are advocated and undertaken. Some critics of contemporary American society argue that advocates today too seldom conceive and present effective policies. The blunt evaluation in 1951 by William G. Carleton, a professor of political science, still seems remarkably applicable to much public discourse today:

> American speeches . . . for the most part have ceased seriously to examine fundamental policy, to discuss first principles, to isolate and analyze all the possibilities and alternative courses with respect to a given policy. . . . The result is that speeches today are rarely intellectually comprehensive or cogently analytical.

One reason for this shortcoming is the complexity of propositions of policy. The call to take action or change policy is made up of a number of intermediate claims involving all of the intellectual and rhetorical operations identified in the preceding chapters. For example, a speaker who is trying to demonstrate that "It is necessary for the federal government to subsidize the higher education of superior students" might first affirm the proposition of fact that "Many qualified high school graduates are unable to attend college for financial reasons," the proposition of value that "The development of the nation's intellectual resources is socially desirable," and the problem-centered claim that "The loss of intellectual resources constitutes a significant contemporary social and economic problem."

Speakers try to win acceptance of facts and values and create concern for problems on the basis that they are *true, good,* or *significant.* Speakers advocate policies in the belief that they are *necessary* and/or *desirable.* You might note that in the phrasing of propositions of policy, the term *should* (meaning it is necessary or desirable that) appears with great frequency.

Although many persuaders urge *adoption* of a new policy or course of action, in *Perspectives on Persuasion,* Wallace Fotheringham suggests other important categories of action that speakers may seek. In addition to adoption, speakers may defend *continuance* of an existing policy, urge *discontinuance* of an existing policy, or seek *deterrence* by arguing against adoption of a proposed policy. Sometimes speakers urge retention of the basic principles or structure of an existing policy along with *revision* of means and mechanisms of implementing that policy.

All of the following assertions may be classified as propositions of policy:

Proposition A: The negative income tax should be adopted.
Proposition B: The United States should continue its support of the United Nations.

Proposition C: The use of marijuana should be decriminalized.

Proposition D: Federal regulation of the print mass media should not be adopted.

If speakers have been intellectually shallow in affirming propositions of policy, at least a portion of the blame must rest with their audiences who place too few demands on the speakers' rhetorical behaviors.

CRITERIA FOR EVALUATING SPEECHES THAT AFFIRM PROPOSITIONS OF POLICY

Although propositions of policy may call for continuance, discontinuance, deterrence, and revision in addition to adoption, the criteria that follow are written for the speech seeking adoption. The criteria can be made applicable to the other kinds of propositions of policy through modest rephrasing.

1. *Has the speaker demonstrated or is it readily apparent that a need exists for a fundamental change in policy?*

Because programs for action are responses to problems, the critic first should consider whether a legitimate problem exists. Among the subquestions the evaluator will wish to consider are the following:

Are there circumstances that may legitimately be viewed as a problem?

Is the present policy to blame for such problems?

Is the problem sufficiently severe to require a change in policy, or may it be met through repairs, adjustments, or improvements in the present program?

In establishing a need for a fundamental change in policy, the speaker may affirm a series of propositions related to facts, values, and problems, each of which may be tested by the listener against criteria developed in earlier chapters.

2. *Has the speaker provided a sufficient view of the nature of the new policy or program?*

If a speech affirming a proposition of policy is to have maximum impact, the audience must know exactly what is to be done and how to do it. A sound, well-rounded policy usually encompasses not only the basic principles to guide the course of action but also the specific steps, procedures, or machinery for implementing that policy.

When the speaker describes the nature of a policy, he or she is essentially an imparter of knowledge and should be assessed by the same criteria outlined in Chapter 3: Has the speaker presented an accurate, complete, and unified view of the policy? Has the speaker made the policy meaningful to the audience? Has the speaker explained the policy in a sufficiently interesting way? Has the speaker shown the audience that the knowledge is important?

3. *Has the speaker demonstrated that the new policy will remedy the problem?*

If the speaker is to be successful, the audience must believe that the policy will solve the problem and that it realistically can be put into operation. Among the questions that the listener should raise are the following:

Can the policy be put into effect?
Is the policy enforceable once it has been instituted?
Will the policy alleviate the specific problem or problems described by the speaker (by removing the basic causes, or by speedily treating symptoms of a problem the causes of which are unknown)?

In response to such questions, a speaker will affirm one or more propositions of fact by advancing varied arguments. Speakers may argue that the proposed course of action has worked effectively elsewhere in similar situations; that analogous policies have succeeded in remedying similar problems; that experts attest to its ability to solve the problem. The best expert testimony is that which supports the specific program advocated, not just the general principle of the policy. Through word pictures and descriptions the audience should vividly visualize the desirable consequences which will follow if the solution is adopted, and the undesirable consequences which will occur if it is not adopted.

4. *Has the speaker demonstrated that the new policy is advantageous?*

In addition to showing that the policy will alleviate the problem, the speaker should demonstrate that the policy will produce significant additional benefits and should indicate clearly how the advantages will outweigh any possible disadvantages. A speaker who advocates federal economic aid for public education could show that this policy would not only ease the immediate shortages of facilities and equipment but also would have the additional benefit of helping to equalize educational opportunity throughout the nation. The speaker might stress that the possible remote defect of federal interference in local educational matters is far outweighed by definite immediate advantages and benefits. To demonstrate such benefits, the speaker should employ appropriate examples, statistics, analogies, and expert testimony.

Because people characteristically resist new courses of action in favor of traditional policies, the speaker often will find it wise to recognize in advance and deprecate relevant major policies and arguments that run counter to the proposed policy. Beyond providing adequate reasons for adopting the proposed policy, the speaker frequently must refute alternative programs and opposing arguments. An advocate might directly refute opposing arguments with evidence and reasoning; or show that the arguments, while true in general, really are irrelevant to the specific proposal at hand; or show that the arguments have only minimal validity and are outweighed by other considerations.

People also judge the advantageousness of policies on the basis of personal values and goals. An audience of business people may judge a program partly by the effect it will have on corporate profits. An audience of clergy may judge a policy by its consistency with spiritual values. An audience of minority-group members may judge a proposal by the contribution it will make to equality of opportunity. An audience of laborers may judge a program by its effect on their wages. No matter who composes the audience, the speaker advancing propositions of policy must recognize the influence that listener values, wants, and goals exert on their evaluation of courses of action. An advantageous policy not only removes the causes of a problem but also harmonizes with such values as efficiency, speed, economy, fairness, humaneness, and legality.

In evaluating speeches affirming propositions of policy, the listener could ask such questions as these:

Does the policy have significant additional benefits?
Do the advantages of the policy outweigh its disadvantages?
Does the policy have greater comparative advantages than other relevant policies?
Can the policy be experimented with on a limited basis before full-scale adoption is undertaken?
Is the policy consistent with relevant personal and societal values?

In responding to these questions, the capable speaker will affirm a cluster of evaluative and factual propositions. Such propositions may, in turn, be evaluated in terms of the criteria proposed in earlier chapters.

Although the advocate may sometimes find it wise to fulfill each of the four major criteria in detail, at other times he or she may deem it unnecessary to meet all of them. Speakers may neglect to elaborate on the need or problem because they know the audience already shares their concern for it. A detailed statement of policy may be avoided because the speaker believes it sufficient to show that a general course of action is in some ways superior to one currently pursued. A persuader may avoid mentioning the negative effects of a proposal because its defects are not major. An arguer may pose a theoretical ideal and demonstrate the superiority of the proposal in light of that ideal. Concerning the appropriateness and ethicality of such choices of emphasis as just described, a critical listener may reach judgments differing from the speaker's. But whatever the constraints imposed by audience, setting, and subject, the speaker affirming a proposition of policy must demonstrate to the audience that the proposed course of action is necessary, desirable, and beneficial.

CONCLUSION

In a free society people often assemble to consider courses of future action. In evaluating such speeches, the listener/critic may raise numerous questions that cluster around the following four criteria. *Has the speaker demonstrated, or is it readily apparent, that a need exists for a fundamental change in policy? Has the speaker provided a sufficient view of the nature of the new policy or program? Has the speaker demonstrated that the new policy will remedy the problem? Has the speaker demonstrated that the new policy is advantageous?*

For Further Reading

Carleton, William G. "Effective Speech in a Democracy." *Vital Speeches of the Day,* June 15, 1951, pp. 540–44.

Ehninger, Douglas, Alan Monroe, and Bruce E. Gronbeck. *Principles and Types of Speech Communication.* 8th ed. Scott, Foresman, 1978. Chapter 9 explains the nature and uses of the "motivated sequence" structure (attention, need, satisfaction, visualization, action) that is especially useful in speeches advocating policies.

Ewbank, Henry L., and Auer, Jeffrey J. *Discussion and Debate.* 2nd ed. Appleton-Century-Crofts, 1951, pp. 53–56, 180–92. Discusses John Dewey's pattern of reflective thinking about problems and selecting the best solution.

Fotheringham, Wallace C. *Perspectives on Persuasion.* Allyn and Bacon, 1966. Chapters 3 and 11 examine the major goals of persuasive discourse and some undesirable action responses by audiences.

Jensen, J. Vernon. *Argumentation: Reasoning in Communication.* Van Nostrand, 1981. Chapter 5 explains potential lines of argument basic to presenting solutions, policies, and programs.

Leys, Wayne A. R. *Ethics for Policy Decisions.* Prentice-Hall, 1952. Chapters 1, 12, and 22. Pages 189–92 list the critical questions relevant to policy decisions developed in 10 major systems of ethics.

Minnick, Wayne C. *The Art of Persuasion.* 2nd ed. Houghton Mifflin, 1968, pp. 208–26. Discusses winning audience belief and action through appeals to their wants and values.

Monroe, Alan H., and Ehninger, Douglas. *Principles and Types of Speech Communication.* 7th ed. Scott, Foresman, 1974. Chapter 13 explains the nature and uses of the "motivated sequence" structure (attention, need, satisfaction, visualization, action) which is especially useful in speeches advocating policies.

Newman, Robert P., and Newman, Dale. *Evidence.* Houghton Mifflin, 1969. Chapters 1–3 present guidelines for analyzing propositions of policy.

Rogers, Everett M., and Shoemaker, F. Floyd. *Communication of Innovations.* 2nd ed. Free Press, 1971, pp. 19–23. A description of characteristics of innovations, as perceived by receivers of communication about those innovations, which contribute to the rate of adoption.

Walter, Otis M., and Scott, Robert L. *Thinking and Speaking.* 4th ed. Macmillan, 1979. Chapter 12 presents suggestions for persuading about solutions to problems.

Walter, Otis M. *Speaking Intelligently.* Macmillan, 1976. Chapters 1 and 5 and pp. 222–24. The author stresses the necessity of high-quality problem-solving for societal survival and growth and suggests strategies for persuading about solutions and policies.

SPACE EXPLORATION

James A. Michener

What's a nice author like you doing in a place like this? This question must have occurred to James Michener, author of such best selling novels as *Bridges at Toko-Ri, Sayonara, Hawaii, The Covenant,* and *Centennial,* as he prepared to address the U.S. Senate Subcommittee on Science, Technology, and Space in Washington, D.C. on 1 February 1979. An author, even a Pulitzer Prize winning author, is not an expert on space.

In choosing to speak in favor of space exploration to a Senate Subcommittee, James Michener is well aware of his lack of technical competence. As he begins his speech, he raises the question of his competence and offers a plausible defense of his right to testify: he has, for years, "been studying the rise and fall of nations and in so doing . . . [has] reached certain conclusions governing that process." The remainder of his lengthy introduction (paragraphs 2-15) is devoted to an historical discussion in support of the notion that nations must seize great opportunities if they are to continue to grow and prosper. What impact is the historical discussion likely to have on his audience's perception of his credibility?

In urging a continuation of our policy of space exploration, Michener advances three lines of argument: non-military advantages are to be gained from a space program, military advantages are to be gained from a space program, and spiritual advantages are to be gained from a space program. Do these three lines of argument offer compelling justification for the proposition that the United States should continue its policy of space exploration? What counterarguments might be advanced?

In developing his third argument, Michener alleges that space is the primary challenge of our age and that a retreat from that challenge would signal national decline. How convincing do you find this argument?

In concluding his address, Michener again refers to his competence. After reading and studying the speech, what credibility do you assign to Michener as a spokesman for space exploration?

This speech is reprinted by permission from *Vital Speeches of the Day*, July 15, 1979, pp. 578-581.

1   The only justification for allowing me to appear before your Committee is that for some years I have been studying the rise and fall of nations and in so doing have reached certain conclusions governing that process.

2   There seem to be great tides which operate in the history of civilization, and nations are prudent if they estimate the force of those tides, their genesis and the extent to which they can be utilized. A nation which guesses wrong on all its estimates is apt to be in serious trouble if not on the brink of decline. Toward the middle of the Fifteenth Century the minds of sensible men were filled with speculations about the nature of their world and, although not much solid evidence was available, clever minds could piece together the fragments and achieve quite remarkable deductions.

3   Prince Henry the Navigator of Portugal occupies a curious place in history. He never captained one of his ships; he never sailed on any voyage of exploration; in fact, he stayed at home devouring old books, new rumors and future guesses, and from this melange constructed a view of the world that was extraordinarily accurate, even though he died some thirty years before Portuguese explorers brought proof of his theories.

4   Christopher Columbus had very little solid data to work with, but he had clever intuitions and a powerful capacity to piece together odd bits of

information, leading him to conclusions that resulted in the effective discovery of America.

5 Nations at that time faced problems comparable to those faced by individuals like Columbus, Vasco da Gama and Sebastian Cabot. They had to decide whether they wanted to participate in the exploration of the world and, if so, to what degree of commitment. Those like Portugal and Spain, who made early and fast decisions, gained empires of fantastic richness. Others, like disoriented Germany and Italy, who did not perceive the possibilities, suffered grave disadvantages and never caught up. England and France were very tardy, but in the end the first made a stunning recovery; the latter never did.

6 I am not primarily interested in either the exploits of a few daring captains or the economic advantages of the nations they represented. The more lasting effect was on the spirit of the times, that wonderful enlarging of the human consciousness when it realized that the old definitions no longer applied, when it knew that the world consisted of a great deal more than Europe. To have missed the explorations was regrettable, but to have missed this spiritual awakening would have been disastrous. France and Sweden are excellent examples of nations which did little of the manual work but which reaped the intellectual rewards of the period.

7 One might almost argue that Portugal and Spain dragged home the raw material for France and Sweden to codify and digest, proving that any nation can participate in the great swing of civilization according to its peculiar capabilities. Portugal provided daring sea captains. England provided able administrators. And France provided the philosophers. Those which provided nothing lost an entire cycle of historical experience from which they never fully recovered.

8 Nor do I think that the rewards resulting from participation in a great cycle need be permanent, reaching down to all generations. I am quite content if my nation gains enlightenment or riches or advantages of other kinds for a respectable period. It can't be the hullabaloo of a single day or week, nor the celebration without foundation of some accidental accomplishment with little subsequent meaning. But if a nation responds to a challenge, succeeds in its effort, garners the rewards for a sensible period, and then loses the commanding position, I think no harm has been done. The nation has gleaned from that experience about all that it was destined to achieve, and a great good has been accomplished because then the nation is prepared psychologically to tackle the next big problem when it comes along. And it surely will, for the life of any nation since the beginning of history has been a record of how it confronted the great challenges that inevitably came its way.

9 It may be unfortunate that I started these remarks with Portugal and its navigational and colonizing victories, as if they were the only kind that mattered. Actually, I would place them in second position, somewhat down the line in the scale of historical values. It is triumphs in the world of ideas and concepts that loom largest in my thinking, and I would like to stipulate several to give you a clue to my thinking. Today we are witnessing in the Near East the phenomenal vitality of the ideas promulgated some thirteen hundred years ago by Muhammad; these ideas have always been far more powerful than the empire put together by Portugal. The entire civilized world is indebted to the miracles that occurred in England during Elizabeth's reign and that of James I: I mean the extraordinary combination of Shakespeare's plays and the new translation of the Bible into English. These works fixed the English language as a tool of great beauty, great potential, and I often think of the Bible in its King James translation when someone tells me that no committee ever accomplishes anything. Two of the greatest documents of our language were written by committees—our English Bible and our American Constitution. The trick, it seems, is to assemble the right committee.

10   I would place in this pantheon of great ideas Sigmund Freud's analysis of human behavior and Karl Marx's dissection of production and distribution. For any nation to have missed the significance of these powerful movements was to have missed the meaning of contemporary history.

11   Certainly the world was changed by that cascade of brilliant industrial inventions produced by England in the late 1700s and early 1800s. We live today on the consequences of that industrial revolution. And I would include our own nation's enviable capacity to finance, organize, and manage large industrial corporations.

12   Finally, of course, the historian must think of the impact of Christ's teachings two thousand years ago. They had a far greater importance than any mere exploration or conquest or empire.

13   But history is a grand mix of concepts, actions, organizings, and commitments which determines the extent to which any nation can achieve a good life for its citizens, and I believe without question that if a nation misses the great movements of its time it misses the foundations on which it can build for the future.

14   One word of caution, I am not here speaking of either fad or fashion. I am not extolling the attractive ephemeral. And I am certainly not sponsoring the idea that was so fashionable in the 1930s—that German Nazism represented "the wave of the future." Anyone who subscribed to that idea had a very limited view of what the future of the human race could be, and few fashionable ideas have ever crumbled so fast and so disastrously. The senate of any nation is obligated to discern the merely fashionable when it offers itself and reject it.

15   Suppose that all I have said is true, which would be a miracle equal to those we've been discussing. Where does that leave the United States in

relation to its space program? I am competent to comment on only three aspects, leaving the more technical details to others.

16 *Are there non-military advantages to be gained from a space program?* The high technical requirements for success in space are so fundamental that spin-off rewards are almost automatic. Radio, television, medical instrumentation, miniaturizing, watches, new food processes, communications, health advances and improvement in clothing are some of the few advantages which I myself have gained because of the space program, and I am speaking only of small items which can be comprehended and used by the individual.

17 If one considers the larger items, like intercontinental communications satellites, the mapping of weather patterns, the analysis of soils and forests, the exploration for minerals including oil, the management of fisheries and the like, the potential rewards are multiplied many times.

18 And the nature of human intelligence is such that no one today can even guess the limits of either the personal items or the industrial which might accrue from the basic scientific work that has to be done in a space program. I have followed our past space adventures about as carefully as an uninstructed layman could, and I have a rather imaginative mind, but I anticipated almost none of these significant by-products and I doubt if any of us in this room today could predict where the next contributions will be made.

19 I have heard one impressive argument against what I am saying now. A man of some probity said, "If we had applied our scientific brains to these problems, we could have solved them all at one-tenth the cost." He is right. Had the Congress twenty years ago set aside a substantial budget, and had it authorized the assembling of a body of top scientists, and had it provided them with spacious laboratories and told them, "Devise a computerized navigational instrument that will operate regardless of where in space it is stationed," this could surely have been done. But neither Congress nor the human mind works that way. It is only when great felt needs spur the imagination that certain accomplishments become possible. As a project by itself, few of the bonuses cited above would have materialized; as part of a national effort with a clearly defined goal, they all came into being—and others like them will follow.

20 *Are there military advantages to be gained from a space program?* I would be terrified today if only Russian and Chinese vehicles were orbiting in space. Their military advantage would be so tremendous that we might almost suffer as a nation a kind of psychological shock from which we might never recover. For we would certainly be at their mercy.

21 I fear that the potentials of space warfare have even yet not been impressed upon the American public. We do not realize the overwhelming advantage a nation would enjoy if it alone commandeered space, if it alone could direct by radio beam when and where an object or its cargo was to be brought down to earth. Any nation which allowed its enemies such a superiority would be doomed.

22 But if all nations have the capacity to utilize space defensively, then the peril is diminished and reasonable arrangements can be worked out. But only through parity can this be done.

23 Therefore, the United States must have a sensible space program, whether it wants one or not. To fail to keep up with new developments in this field would be disastrous, and any administration which permitted a lag should be condemned. We must know what the capabilities of space are, and we must retain our proficiency in using them.

24 I think we have done a fairly good job in this area so far, and I would suppose that from our strength we would be able to deal intelligently with those other nations who have attained or will attain a comparable capacity. This is the great unknown ocean of the universe, and we in 1979 are as obligated to probe it and use it and participate in its control as the nations of Europe were obligated to explore their terrestrial oceans in 1479.

25 The future and the safety of those nations depended upon their mastery of the seas; ours depends in shocking measure to our cautious control of space, and if we abandon it to others we condemn ourselves.

26 *Are there spiritual advantages to be gained from a space program?* The spirit of man, and the resolve of a nation, are tenuous things, to be fortified by the strangest experiences or destroyed by the most unanticipated accidents. Outward events influence them but inner resolves usually determine outcomes. A novelist sees men and women destroy themselves because the will to survive has been lost; the historian watches nations go down because of fatal wrong choices which sap the national energy. Usually the tragedy occurs when inner convictions are lost, or when a sense of general frustration or waning purpose prevails.

27 It is extremely difficult to keep a human life or the life of a nation moving forward with enough energy and commitment to lift it into the next cycle of experience. My own life has been spent chronicling the rise and fall of human systems, and I am convinced that we are all terribly vulnerable.

28 I do not for a moment believe that the spiritual well-being of our nation depends primarily upon a successful space program. There are, as William James said, moral equivalents to war, moral substitutes for any charismatic national experience. I am sure we could as a nation attain great spiritual reassurance from rebuilding our cities or distributing our farm produce better. And my experience in the arts has taught me to be suspicious of late fashions or high styles. Space progams are stylish today and run the risk of being abused.

29 But I also believe that there are moments in history when challenges occur of such a compelling nature that to miss them is to miss the whole meaning of an epoch. Space is such a challenge. It is the kind of challenge William Shakespeare sensed nearly four hundred years ago when he wrote:

There is a tide in the affairs of men,
Which, taken at the flood, leads on to fortune;
Omitted, all the voyage of their life
Is bound in shallows and in miseries.
On such a full sea are we now afloat,
And we must take the current when it serves,
Or lose our ventures.

We risk great peril if we kill off this spirit of adventure, for we cannot predict how and in what seemingly unrelated fields it will manifest itself. A nation which loses its forward thrust is in danger, and one of the most effective ways to retain that thrust is to keep exploring possibilities. The sense of exploration is intimately bound up with human resolve, and for a nation to believe that it is still committed to forward motion is to ensure its continuance.

    30   I doubt if there is a woman or man in this room who honestly believes that the United States could ever fall backward, as other nations have within our lifetime. Intuitively we feel that we are exempt. Yet for us to think so is to fly in the face of all history, for many nations at their apex were inwardly doomed because their will power had begun to falter, and soon their vulnerability became evident to all. Enemies do not destroy nations; time and loss of will bring them down.

    31   Therefore we should be most careful about retreating from the specific challenge of our age. We should be reluctant to turn our back upon the frontier of this epoch. Space is indifferent to what we do; it has no feeling, no design, no interest in whether we grapple with it or not. But we cannot be indifferent to space, because the grand slow march of our intelligence has brought us, in our generation, to a point from which we can explore and understand and utilize it. To turn back now would be to deny our history, our capabilities.

    32   Each era of history progresses to a point at which it is eligible to wrestle with the great problem of that period. For the ancient Greeks it was the organization of society; for the Romans it was the organization of empire; for the Medievalists the spelling out of their relationship to God; for the men of the Fifteenth and Sixteenth Centuries the mastery of the oceans; and for us it is the determination of how mankind can live in harmony on this finite globe while establishing relationships to infinite space.

    33   I was not overly impressed when men walked upon the moon because I knew it to be out there at a specific distance with specific characteristics, and I supposed that we had enough intelligence to devise the necessary machinery to get us there and back. But when we sent an unmanned object hurtling into distance space, and when it began sending back signals—a chain of numbers to be exact—which could be reassembled here on earth to provide us with a photograph of the surface of Mars, I was struck dumb with wonder. And when computers began adjusting the chain of numbers, augmenting some, diminishing others, so that the photographs became always more clear and defined, I realized that we could accomplish almost anything there in the farthest reaches of space.

34 My life changed completely on the day I saw those Mars photographs, for I had participated in that miracle. My tax dollars had helped pay for the project. The universities that I supported had provided the brains to arm the cameras. And the government that I helped nourish had organized the expedition. I saw the universe in a new light, and myself and my nation in a new set of responsibilities. My spirit was enlarged and my willingness to work on the future projects fortified.

35 No one can predict what aspect of space will invigorate a given individual, and there must have been millions of Americans who did not even know Mars had been photographed.

36 But we do know that in previous periods when great explorations were made, they reverberated throughout society. Dante and Shakespeare and Milton responded to the events of their day. Scientists were urged to new discoveries. And nations modified their practices.

37 All the thoughts of men are interlocked, and success in one area produces unforeseen successes in others. It is for this reason that a nation like ours is obligated to pursue its adventure in space. I am not competent to say how much money should be spent. I am not competent to advise on how the program should be administered. But I am convinced that it must be done.

RELIGION AND POLITICS: A COMMITMENT TO A PLURALISTIC SOCIETY

Patricia Roberts Harris

In 1980, Americans became increasingly aware of the existence of a young organization—The Moral Majority. The avowed purpose of the organization was to influence the American political process in favor of "pro-Christian" viewpoints. The rapid growth and prosperity of The Moral Majority and similar groups caused alarm among those committed to a pluralistic society. As a spokeswoman for the pluralistic viewpoint, Patricia Roberts

Harris, United States Secretary of Health and Human Services, addressed the American Whig-Cliosophic Society in Princeton, New Jersey on September 23, 1980.

Ms. Harris begins her address by reviewing our heritage of religious freedom as articulated by Thomas Jefferson and George Mason. She then describes three recent events that stand in stark contrast to our heritage of religious tolerance. These three specific instances dramatically illustrate the growing political involvement and intolerance of fundamentalist religious organizations. Are three specific instances sufficient support for the claim that this phenomenon is pervasive?

Harris continues by noting that she is not claiming that all "born again" Christians are either right-wing or political activitists. Still, she views with alarm the poll data that between 35 and 60 million Americans are "born again" Christians. Does this seem inconsistent?

This speech illustrates the difficulty of categorizing speeches by form. In paragraph 20, the speaker indicates that she wishes to discuss the threat posed by religious activism. If this is her major intent, the speech can be viewed as affirming the existence of a problem: the moral absolutism movement poses a serious threat to the American democratic process. The speaker advances this proposition by arguing that the movement is exclusionary, intolerant, and potentially dangerous. However, the second part of the body of the speech involves a striking reaffirmation of the American policy of religious pluralism. If this is the speaker's major intent, the speech can be viewed as affirming (or reaffirming) a policy: as Americans we must recommit ourselves to the policy of religious pluralism. Or, perhaps we might best conclude that this speech both affirms the existence of a problem and reaffirms commitment to a policy in the light of that threat.

The structure of this speech is perplexing. The introduction appears to end with a partial initial partition in paragraph 21. If this is true, why do you think the speaker chooses to spend so much time in getting to the point? What other observations should be made about the organization of this speech?

This speech is reprinted by permission from *Vital Speeches of the Day*, November 1, 1980, pp. 50–53.

1   In recent weeks newspaper columns and the television airwaves have been filled with the allegedly new phenomenon of the entry of American Evangelicals into the elective political process. The news-cum-entertainment program (or is it the other way around) "60 Minutes" this week gave us the unedifying spectacle of overt threats to targeted political figures because they failed to agree with the political position of putative religious leaders on several issues.

2   That "Sixty Minutes" has reported the phenomenon confirms its reality and, indeed, its pervasiveness. What we need to remember is that this invasion of the political process by those purporting to act in the name of religion is neither new nor a matter for entertainment.

3   Two hundred and one years ago, in 1779, Thomas Jefferson condemned such activity by religious leaders, saying in the preamble to a bill on religious freedom which he had introduced in the Virginia legislature:

"Our civil rights have no dependence on our religious opinions, any more than our opinions in physics and geometry; therefore, the proscribing of any citizen as unworthy of the public confidence by laying upon him an incapacity of being called to office of public trust . . . unless he profess or renounce this or that religious opinion, is depriving him injuriously of those privileges and advantages to which he has a natural right."

4   Thomas Jefferson was born into a society acutely aware of the danger of an official relationship between religious and political institutions. Requirements of religious orthodoxy had caused churning of the political life of England from which the early settlers derived so much of their political perception. Every school-boy and girl is taught that the pilgrims came to Plymouth seeking religious freedom. Few understand how little there was for those who refused to accept the orthodoxy of the dominant protestants who led the Massachusetts Bay colony.

5   Anne Hutchinson's belief that God's love is communicated immediately to the regenerate and that this love serves as a guide to action without mediation of the clergy, was considered politically subversive and she was banished from the Massachusetts Bay colony by John Cotton.

6   Thus our founding fathers had early and significant experience with the demand of religious leaders and their flocks for acceptance of a particular theology, and the insistence that political punishment would result from failure to accept the orthodox religious opinion.

7   The result was the adoption of George Mason's eloquent provision for religious freedom in the first Virginia Bill of Rights adopted in 1776, which was the forerunner of the first amendment to the constitution of the United States. His provision read:

"That religion, or the duty which we owe to our creator, and the manner of discharging it, can be directed only by reason and conviction, not by force or violence; and therefore all men are equally entitled to the free exercise of religion, according the dictates of conscience; and that it is the mutual duty of all to practice christian forebearance, love and charity towards each other."

8   George Mason would undoubtedly be appalled today—two hundred and four years after Virginia adopted this statement of tolerance—to discover the following:

—An organization called "The Moral Majority"—founded just a little over a year ago by a fundamentalist minister from Virginia—has 400,000 members nationwide and is forming political action committees in all 50 states to distribute $1.5 million to political candidates who it determines favor a "pro-christian" viewpoint.

—During last spring's "Washington for Jesus" rally, a number of participants visited the office of a southern senator and they informed him that he scored only 23 percent in a "morality rating" prepared by Christian Voice, a political committee organized by right wing Californians. They demanded that he fall on his knees and pray for forgiveness. When he refused, he was targeted for defeat in the fall elections.

—Evangelical leaders and conservative politicians gathered last month in Dallas for two days of oratory and political activism strategy sessions. At that meeting in Dallas, the New York *Times* quoted one leader as saying:

"It is interesting at great political rallies how you have a protestant to pray, a catholic to pray, and then you have a Jew to pray. With all due respect to those dear people, my friends, God Almighty does not hear the prayer of the Jew."

He has refused to withdraw the statement.

9 There is none of the "christian forebearance, love, and charity towards each other" urged by George Mason in these three examples.

10 These three reports do illustrate the nature of the growing involvement of fundamentalist religious organizations in the political process. Furthermore, the preponderance of this involvement is on the right, rather than the left, side of the political spectrum.

11 Now before going any further in my examination of this phenomenon and its danger to previously accepted political values, let me make several important points.

12 First of all, I do not intend to become involved in any discussion of the personal religious beliefs of any individuals or groups. The freedom to hold religious convictions and to worship freely is fundamental to both the constitution and the very soul of this nation. I do not propose to talk about religion per se, but only about the nature of religious participation in the secular, partisan political process.

13 Second, I do not imply that all "born again" Christians reflect a right-wing, or even conservative, political outlook. Any number of evangelical Christians—President Carter, Senator Mark Hatfield and former Senator Harold Hughes, for example, hold decidedly different views. The vast majority of such individuals believe in and practice toleration of opposing views and vote as most of us vote—on the basis of deeply felt beliefs about priorities and goals, parties and candidates—and their votes are therefore widely distributed all across the politic   ~~ctrum.

14 Nor do I imply that all evangelical Christians want their churches or other religious organizations to participate in a direct and particular way in political campaigns.

15 There is evidence, however, that significant numbers of evangelical Christian organizations are moving toward intense involvement in elective politics and that they have become a major factor in energizing right-wing politics in our country.

16 The terms "born again" and "evangelical" have been popularly applied to individuals who attest to having had a personal religious experience which has changed their lives. A large number of these individuals, in addition to experiencing a personal conversion, also hold to a stricter or more "fundamental" interpretation of the scripture.

17 The American religious tradition is a rich and varied one, and the distinction between the evangelical and more "establishment" religious experience is as old as the country. What is significant about the trend today is that the number of "born again" Christians seems to be steadily on the rise. Public opinion polls have tried to measure the number of Americans in that category and, although they do not agree on a number, they variously estimate it to be between 35 and 60 million.

18 In the last few years we have seen evidence of the trend in large rallies like the one held in Washington last May. We have also seen rapid growth in the so-called "Christian oriented" media—several hundred television and radio outlets which are now devoted primarily to religious programming.

19 The growing activism of such religious groups can also be seen in the political arena. At the session of fundamentalist leaders in Dallas last month, one evangelist said, "Not voting is a sin against Almighty God," and he urged his audience to "crawl out from under those padded pews." According to one newspaper account, "attentions swung widely from theology and scripture to instruction on how to organize without violating tax laws, the practicality of registering a congregation to vote during the Sunday service, and the importance of keeping a 'moral score card' on the voting records of elected representatives."

20 I have no quarrel with the right of individuals and groups—no matter what their political positions—to become involved in the political process. I have sought such involvement all my life. At the same time, however, there are aspects and implications of these particular efforts which pose a serious threat to the American democratic process, and tonight I want to discuss my reasons for believing this to be the case.

21 My chief concern is that fundamentalist politics as practiced at this time is at best exclusionary, and at worst a dangerous, intolerant and polarizing influence in our political system.

22   At the recent Dallas conference, speaker after speaker denounced "perverts, radicals, leftists, communists, liberals and humanists" who presumably have taken over the country and are actively seeking its destruction. This kind of overt "us against them" appeal—the "God-fearing" against the "heathen"—has roots in virtually every generation in American history. At various times it has made victims of catholics, immigrants, Jews, blacks, Indians, and countless others who failed to fit into neat patterns of acceptability. In my judgment, at least, there are under-currents of many of the same prejudices in much of the new right rhetoric today.

23   One slightly more subtle example of exclusionary practices is the so-called "Christian yellow pages"—a telephone directory, similar to the one in popular use, that lists only "born again" merchants and exhorts Christians to restrict their business to those establishments.

24   George Will—a columnist, a graduate of Princeton and a man few regard as a radical, a leftist or even a humanist—described such an appeal as "an act of aggression against a pluralistic society." He added "discrimination condoned—indeed, incited—in commerce will not be confined to commerce."

25   Although the majority of the people of the country classify themselves as Christian, the nation has consistently, painfully, and with great success moved from intolerance to toleration of both political and religious dissent.

26   We Americans have, in this century, truly come to agree with Voltaire that we may "disagree with what you say, but we will fight to the death for your right to say it" because we recognize the value of both political dissenters and of non-Christian traditions. Our democracy has functioned because, as a rule, we have sought out common ground—shared values and beliefs, rather than an orthodoxy espoused by any particular group. The end result may not have pleased everyone, but it has offered to each individual a reasonable measure of freedom in which to exercise his or her civil and human rights.

27   That consensus orientation is profoundly threatened by those who advocate a "Christian crusade" or who want our leadership narrowed to include only "pro-Christian" public officials.

28   In this particular campaign, fundamentalist organizations seek to identify "pro-Christian" candidates with a measuring stick of very specific issues. More often than not, the connection between Christian scripture and such concerns is mystifying.

29   I am sure that I need not remind this audience of the positions fundamentalist groups have taken on our most pressing and most controversial social issues.

30   In a time of rapid and often disconcerting change in social and moral values, right wing political operatives are working hard to cultivate votes among the distressed. Direct scriptural guidance is cited in determining the "Christian position" on such issues as equal rights for women, gun control, abortion, sex education in schools and pornography. I grant the existence of profound moral issues in the debate on the legality of funding of abortion, but I can find only a political basis for being opposed to gun control.

31 Earlier, I mentioned a senator's meeting with a group who rated him "poor" on a moral score card. His so-called "morality rating" took into account his positions on such issues as recognition of Taiwan as the legitimate Chinese government, prayer in the public schools, a balanced budget, sanctions against the former Rhodesian government, and creation of the Federal Department of Education.

32 A 1978 candidate for Congress in Virginia, himself an evangelical minister, saw a direct biblical admonition against welfare programs, called the income tax "unscriptural" and declared that "the free market is the Biblical approach to economics."

33 A senator who was defeated in 1978, largely because of his vote in support of the Panama Canal treaties, said an astonishing number of letters from his constituents admonished him "as a Christian" to vote against ratification.

34 In sheer exasperation, another former senator, Harold Hughes—a Christian evangelist himself—said recently, "I have searched the scriptures diligently and I have not found one word in them on Jesus Christ's position on the Panama Canal. To say you've got to believe this or that in the political arena or you are not a Christian is absolute blasphemy."

35 Whether you agree or disagree with the position fundamentalist organizations have taken on these issues is beside the point. What is important are the underlying premises which serve as the basis for their views: that this is a "Christian" and not a pluralistic society; that the nation must achieve its "Christian" destiny by adhering to a specific set of positions derived from scripture as interpreted by a particular theological school, and that the imposition of those beliefs on the nation as a whole is not only permissible, but desirable.

36 The consequences of the demand for orthodoxy enforced by the political process are found throughout history—from Socrates to the victims of the Ayatollah Khomeini. For those who assert that their restrictive interpretations are essential to the well-being of this country, I would remind them that the theory that the world was round was denied by certain theologians as little as fifty years before "Columbus sailed the ocean blue." If we could speak to Galileo about whether the "Christian" position on Copernican theory and his own work on astronomy was in the best interest of that genius or the world he served, he might well suggest that if the fundamentalism of his time had prevailed, its modern U.S. proponents would live in Europe, and Indians

would still own this land. The association of church and state, the identity of interest of Aristotelian professors who disagreed with Galileo's ideas, and their ability to end his freedom and halt his work, are some of the inevitable consequences of the achievement of the kind of identity of theology and public policy that our political evangelicals appear to seek today.

37 We have conveniently forgotten that Scopes was convicted of violating the law when he taught the theory of evolution, which some fundamentalists still oppose. That conviction was in this century.

38 On one issue which the radical right refuses to leave alone—prayer in the school—the lack of respect for difference, and the insistence upon using government to achieve particular Christian theological ends, is most blatant and most intolerant. That Jews, Moslems, Buddhists or non-believers must have the time and nature of their relationship with the deity determined by the state runs counter to George Mason's Virginia Bill of Rights and to the Bill of Rights of the Constitution. Such a position is blatantly intolerant of both of the religious and non-believers, and takes us back to days of religious inquisitions that I thought we had rejected in this country with the adoption of our Bill of Rights.

39 The damage such viewpoints do by excluding large numbers of people from full participation in the nation's present and future is difficult to assess, but the problem of exclusion is exacerbated by the righteous fervor with which these political fundamentalists approach the debate.

40 This is especially painful for other Christians who do not share a right wing viewpoint.

41 Public officials today regularly encounter citizens who tell them how "real Christians" would vote or act—or how "real Christians" will repay an errant representative for his sins. This offends me because I care about what my Jewish and Buddhist and Bahai brothers and sisters believe about an issue, and I want to be sure that what I do is as broadly acceptable to their ethical system as I can make it.

42 Republican senator Mark Hatfield wrote: "During my opposition to the Vietnam war, the religious segment of the radical right attacked not only my patriotism, but the authenticity of my personal Christian faith."

43 When the argument is so presented, there is no room for discussion of the issues. Politics—that crucible of ambiguities and compromises, choices and alternatives—degenerates into a raw power struggle in which one side impugns the other's religious sincerity and the judgment of how to act is based on numbers of votes, and not the validity of the idea. To argue that there is a single "Christian" viewpoint, or even a religious point of view on every issue in foreign and domestic policy, is to say no debate is necessary or desirable— that all that is required is unquestioning obedience of "God's will"—as revealed to a single individual or group. I thought that was what the last four hundred years had rejected.

44 That kind of moral absolutism is alien to the best of the American experience, and it is sobering to note that one country in which such a totalitarian interpretation of "God's will" is today practiced in Iran. In that nation the rich variety of Islamic culture has been trampled by religious zealots who profess to know the one truth and who are willing to impose their narrow interpretation of Moslem principles on the entire nation.

45 Our own country has been nurtured and sustained in a more tolerant atmosphere. Even in the darkest days of the Civil War, Abraham Lincoln reminded the country that both north and south pray to the same God, and when he invoked the diety he understood that we see the right only "as God gives us to see the right."

46 That spirit of humility and tolerance which so characterized Lincoln is much needed today. The absolute certainty with which some individuals approach the political battle—and the arrogance with which they propose a crusade to "re-Christianize" America—is dangerous for our democracy. I am beginning to fear that we could have an Ayatolloh Khomeini in this country, but that he will not have a beard, but he will have a television program.

47 I would argue that the politicization of evangelical Christianity is bad for religion. As Paul Tillich reminded us, "Doubt is not the opposite of faith; it is an element of faith." Those who measure their piety and the piety of others with "moral score cards" are the modern day Pharisees, and they do themselves, as well as their nation, no service. We may find that equating religious position with particular political positions will lead to rejection of both. The founding fathers of this nation were religious men, and they did not seek to divorce religious, moral and ethical beliefs from the practice of politics. They knew that such beliefs are the foundation on which political philosophies are based. But at the same time, they pointedly chose to separate church and state because they did not want one particular group, or one particular point of view, to dominate all the others. They knew the result of failure to separate church and state could be excommunication from the polity as well as excommunication from the church, as happened to both Galileo and Ann Hutchinson.

48 Our society—infinitely more pluralistic today than was the America of 1789—needs to re-examine that premise and reaffirm our commitment to that principle.

49 Pluralism requires political discipline on the part of the majority. Any majority has the power in a democracy to eliminate the minority or to eliminate the expression of the ideas of the minority. It is the essence of democracy that the majority protects, respects and listens to its minorities.

50 Neither political nor religious absolutism is consistent with the United States democratic assumption that unfettered debate may lead to a change of mind on issue.

51 It is ironic that the political absolutism with which we are faced today finds its center of support in protestant groups. That very name is a reminder that these denominations grew out of a protest against religious absolutism.

52 Reinhold Niebuhr reminded us that "we must never confuse our fragmentary apprehension of the truth with the truth itself." Our political system rests on our having the humility to remember that fact, and act accordingly.

53 None of us knows a single truth which closes the debate and dictates our actions in the political world, but in a democracy we can work together in the search for truth and in doing so create the just and humane society which all of us seek.

54 Although the first amendment directs itself to the Congress in its prohibition of the establishment of religion, the history out of which it came, and the intent with which it was adopted, were clearly part of the movement of this country to a toleration of differences and encouragement of dissent. That these two concerns must live side by side with the right of the majority to make decisions if no consensus can be reached, and no compromise adopted, does not say that the majority has the right to refuse to seek consensus and compromise.

55 There is hope that for all the attention garnered by the religious absolutists in this campaign, the people of this nation have understood and accepted the admonition of religious freedom of George Mason and Thomas Jefferson. In Boston last week, voters backed candidates denounced from the pulpit of their church.

56 The Des Moines, Iowa *Register* reported on September 14 that a new Iowa poll showed the Iowans overwhelmingly disapprove of religious leaders urging their followers to vote for specific candidates, and only four percent of those polled said they would be persuaded to vote for a candidate if their religious leader asked them to do so.

57 Before we become too optimistic about these results, it should be pointed out that four percent would be enough to determine a close election.

58 The solution, of course, is for the majority that supports rationality and consensus to go to the polls, vote their informed consensus and, in so doing, again overwhelm the forces of bigotry and polarization.

59 If they stay home, absolutism will win, and we may be required to begin again the battle for humanism, rationality and the democratic spirit which we thought had been won with the Declaration of Independence and the Bill of Rights of the United States Constitution.

THE NEW CHIMAERAS

Russell E. Walker

Russell Walker, a student at Murray State University, represented his university and the state of Kentucky at the 106th Annual Contest of the Interstate Oratorical Association. The contest was hosted by William Jewell College in Liberty, Missouri on May 3-4, 1979. Mr. Walker survived preliminary and semi-final rounds and participated as a finalist.

In this speech, Walker endorses National Institute of Health guidelines on DNA research and urges the extension of these guidelines to all private firms. He also proposes that access to gene modifying chemicals be restricted. Prior to discussing policy, Walker discusses the nature of recombinant DNA research, the promise that such research holds, and the dangers of recombinant DNA research. How effectively does this discussion prepare the listener for the policy portion of the speech?

In introducing his speech (paragraphs 1 and 2), Walker uses many of the introductory devices advocated in speech textbooks. He captures the attention of his audience by using a hypothetical illustration. He provides background material. He stresses the importance of his subject. And, in the final sentence of the introduction, he provides an initial partition to guide the listener through the remainder of the speech. In his conclusion, Walker refers back to the hypothetical illustration that was used as attention material in the introduction. By so doing, he provides psychological closure for his listeners.

This speech is reprinted with permission from *Winning Orations*, 1979, pp. 37-39.

1   The creature was called the Chimaera, and an awesome sight it must have been—with the head of a lion, the body of a goat, and a wickedly fanged serpent for a tail. It prowled through the stories of ancient Greek mythology, breathing fire, devouring heroes, and generally causing trouble. The Chimaera was finally killed by an archer named Bellerophon, and thanks to him, we don't have to worry about the beast today. However, modern science is now on the verge of raising up a whole host of new Chimaeras in our midst—each potentially more deadly than the mythical monster. These latter-day composites don't breathe fire, and they're so small they can only be seen under a microscope. They are genetically engineered bacteria, and their creators are researchers in recombinant DNA.

2   In the relatively short time since its inception, the study of recombinant DNA has been much publicized but little understood. The researchers in this field are tinkering with the basic molecule of life itself, and their work holds tremendous promise and tremendous risks. To gain the benefits while avoiding the dangers, we must fully recognize the nature and possible consequences of DNA research, the inadequacies in present attempts to regulate it, and the changes in regulation needed to protect us all.

3 The foundation of recombinant DNA research is the molecule deoxyribonucleic acid—DNA. DNA is the chemical carrier of the genetic code. Its molecules, arranged into genes and chromosomes in all living cells, carry an encoded blueprint of the structure of a particular organism. Every time an amoeba divides, a flower buds, or a human reproduces, the cells of the new organism are built according to the plans written in the DNA. Change the DNA pattern, and you change the characteristics of that form of life.

4 Recently, scientists have learned to do just that—and today, such genetic modification has become the fastest-growing field of biological research.

5 Some of the tremendous promise of this research is already being realized. In September of last year, scientists at the City of Hope National Medical Center announced that they had successfully altered bacteria genes to make the bacteria produce human insulin.

6 Researchers say the outlook for the future is even more optimistic. Writing in *Science Digest,* January 1978, Nicholas Wade forecast the development of revolutionary crop strains that need no fertilizers, micro-organisms to convert sunlight directly into usable energy, and cures for hundreds of human genetic defects and diseases, possibly including cancer. No wonder Nobel Laureate Dr. Peter B. Medawar has called DNA work "the greatest achievement of science in the twentieth century."

7 Unfortunately, hand in hand with the promises come the perils. The danger of recombinant DNA research lies in scientists' inability to relate a specific gene to a specific characteristic of an organism without trial-and-error experimentation. This produces whole batches of bugs with unpredictable properties. It's a strange kind of genetic Russian roulette; so far these misses have been harmless, but it's not hard to imagine experimental bacteria that would be deadly. Researchers could easily make diseases immune to all known antibiotics, or fast-multiplying germs that cause rather than cure cancer. Synthetic epidemics—modern-day plagues—could ravage our society.

8 The escape of even the intentional products of gene research could be disastrous. For example, one genetically engineered bacterium feeds on oil. Properly controlled, it could one day be used to devour ocean oil spills; uncontained, it would quite happily munch away on the oil in your car's brakes and steering, or the lubricants in the controls of a jetliner. Both our machines and our people are vulnerable to these products of recombinant DNA.

9 This, then, is the dilemma presented by gene research. The potential benefits are so great that the work must proceed; yet the chances for an irremediable disaster demand regulations to prevent catastrophe. We must control the risks without stifling the research.

10 The dilemma was partially resolved in July of 1976 when officials at the National Institute of Health drew up guidelines for DNA research that were soon applied to all studies performed under Federal grants. The rules are aimed at ensuring that laboratory organisms cannot escape into the outside world.

11   They have been praised by both environmentalists and scientists engaged in gene research as neither too lenient nor too restrictive. Typical are the comments of Roy Curtiss of the University of Alabama medical school. Dr. Curtiss was one of the first to warn the scientific community about the dangers of recombinant DNA; but he terms experiments conducted under the NIH rules "not risky" and says they offer "no danger whatsoever to any human being . . . (or) to nonhuman organisms in the biosphere."

12   The NIH guidelines, then, would seem to be the perfect solution; and they are ideal, as far as they go. However, present rules are limited in two crucial areas, each of which invites disaster.

13   First, the regulations do not apply to industrial research. They are binding only on federally funded work. This means U.S. industrial firms and drug companies, the same wonderful people that brought us toxic chemical spills and thalidomide, are free to conduct unrestricted forays into gene manipulation. Already, at least nine private companies are working in the field, with dozens more preparing to enter. Their safety records in more conventional areas are not reassuring. For example, Abott Labs, one of the firms already engaged in genetic engineering recently pleaded guilty to a sixty-count Federal indictment involving the sale of contaminated intraveneous fluids linked with over 150 blood poisonings. Eli Lilly, a drug company now tooling up for gene research, is being sued for over 70 million dollars for administering the cancer-causing drug DES to 1100 women without their knowledge or consent. Such practices carry over into industrial work with DNA. A report at the December 1977, meeting of the NIH disclosed that Miles Laboratories is already supporting research deemed unsafe under the NIH guidelines.

14   As bad as it is to give carte blanche to industry profiteers, it would be even worse to give the same power to virtually anyone. Yet this is precisely what we are doing, for present Federal rules do not restrict access to the material for DNA alteration. Nicholas Wade reports in *Science Digest* that the critical chemicals can be purchased by mail for a few dollars, and that the basic technique is, in his words, "extremely easy to perform." Susan Wright recently predicted in *Environment* magazine that, as more information about genetic research becomes publicized, soon even high school students will be able to tinker with genes. Picture the amateur "basement bomber" chemist brewing his own little crop of home-grown pathogens. Worse, picture the terrorist who finds atomic bomb construction too complicated, busily making biological weapons. Are these the people we want tinkering with the basic substance of life?

15   We must correct these inadequacies in the regulations immediately, before we are overrun by hordes of Brave New Bugs spewing from some

industrial lab—or from some radical's basement workshop. The essential changes are twofold.

16 First, all private firms engaged in genetic research must be licensed and required to conform to the NIH regulations. Industrial labs must be inspected regularly to ensure their compliance, and their licenses revoked if they fail to observe the guidelines.

17 Second, we must restrict access to the gene modifying chemicals. The two substances in question—called restriction endonucleases and DNA ligases—are essential for DNA manipulation and are used for nothing else. It must be made illegal to buy or sell these chemicals without authorization.

18 By enacting these provisions, we need not choose between gaining the benefits of genetic research and avoiding the evils of genetic disasters. We can have the synthetic hormones, the miracle plant strains, even the oil-slick-devouring microbes—without taking needless chances with deadly new forms of life.

19 In Greek mythology, the only solution to the problem of the Chimaera was to kill the beast outright. Today, with the problem of recombinant DNA, we have a better option. We can—in fact we must—regulate but not eliminate genetic engineering. Only thus can we safely harness our scientific new Chimaeras.

THE STATE OF THE NATION'S ECONOMY

Ronald Reagan

On February 5, in the first month of his Presidency, Ronald Reagan delivered this televised address to the American people from the White House. The speech was intended to win popular support for the "economic package" the President was sending to Congress. The importance of the speech was underscored by Budget Director Stockman's observation that the President would have to generate a million messages to Congress from the people if the proposals were to win Congressional sanction.

The President begins his speech with a jumble of statistics in support of his allegation that "we are in the worst economic mess since the Great Depression." He then personalizes the audit by discussing the impact of inflation on the worth of the dollar, the dream of home ownership, and the cost of an automobile. Moving next to the cause of our economic problems, he places the blame squarely on government policy: big spending, deficit financing, punitive taxing, and excessive regulation. He then reviews, in very general terms, his economic program. He concludes by urging cooperation, determination, and selflessness.

The text is heavily punctuated by statistics. How important are these statistics to the President's description of the problem? How is the problem "brought home" to the American people? Two charts depict the effects of the proposed economic policy. Are charts helpful in enabling a mass audience to vizualize the intended effects of a policy? The President uses the word "we" with great frequency. What effect does this have on a listener? In reviewing President Reagan's address, *Newsweek* observes "his speech was an effective piece of exhortation, combining his earnest performing skills with a text that bristled with persuasive examples." Do you agree with this assessment?

This speech is printed by permission from *Vital Speeches of the Day*, March 1, 1981, pp. 290-293.

1   I am speaking to you tonight to give you a report on the state of our nation's economy. I regret to say that we are in the worst economic mess since the Great Depression. A few days ago I was presented with a report I had asked for—a comprehensive audit if you will of our economic conditions. You won't like it, I didn't like it, but we have to face the truth and then go to work to turn things around. And make no mistake about it, we can turn them around.

2   I'm not going to subject you to the jumble of charts, figures, and economic jargon of that audit but rather will try to explain where we are, how we got there, and how we can get back.

3   First, however, let me just give a few "attention getters" from the audit. The Federal budget is out of control and we face runaway deficits of almost $80 billion for this budget year that ends Sept. 30. That deficit is larger than the entire Federal budget in 1957, and so is the almost $80 billion we will pay in interest this year on the national debt.

4   Twenty years ago in 1960 our Federal Government payroll was less than $13 billion. Today it is $75 billion. During these 20 years, our population has only increased by 23.3 percent. The Federal budget has gone up 528 percent.

5   We have just had two years of back-to-back double digit inflation— 13.3 percent in 1979, 12.4 percent last year. The last time this happened was in World War I.

6   In 1960 mortgage interest rates averaged about 6 percent. They are two and a half times as high now, 15.4 percent. The percentage of your earnings the Federal Government took in taxes in 1960 has almost doubled. And finally there are seven million Americans caught up in the personal indignity and human tragedy of unemployment. If they stood in a line— allowing three feet for each person—the line would reach from the coast of Maine to California.

7   Well, so much for the audit itself. Let me try to put this in personal terms. Here is a dollar such as you earned, spent or saved in 1960. Here is a quarter, a dime and a penny—37 cents. Thirty-six cents is what this 1960 dollar is worth today. And if the present inflation rate should continue three

more years, that dollar of 1960 will be worth a quarter. What incentive is there to save? And if we don't save we are short of the investment capital needed for business and industry expansion. Workers in Japan and West Germany save several times the percentage of their income than Americans do.

8 What has happened to that American dream of owning a home? Only 10 years ago a family could buy a home and the monthly payment averaged little more than a quarter—27 cents out of each dollar earned. Today it takes 42 cents out of every dollar of income. So, fewer than one out of 11 families can afford to buy their first new home.

9 Regulations adopted by Government with the best of intentions have added $666 to the cost of an automobile. It is estimated that altogether regulations of every kind, on shopkeepers, farmers, and major industries, add $100 billion to the cost of the goods and services we buy. And then another $20 billion is spent by Government handling the paperwork created by those regulations.

10 I'm sure you are getting the idea that the audit presented to me found Government policies of the last few decades responsible for our economic troubles. We forgot or just overlooked the fact that Government—any Government—has a built-in tendency to grow. We all had a hand in looking to Government for benefits, as if Government had some sources of revenue other than our earnings. Many if not most of the things we thought of, or that Government offered to us, seemed attractive.

11 In the years following the second world war it was easy (for a while at least) to overlook the price tag. Our income more than doubled in the 25 years after the war. We increased our take-home pay in those 25 years by more than we had amassed in all the preceding 150 years put together. Yes, there was some inflation, 1 or 1½ percent a year, that didn't bother us. But if we look back at those golden years we recall that even then voices had been raised warning that inflation, like radioactivity, was cumulative and that once started it could get out of control. Some Government programs seemed so worthwhile that borrowing to fund them didn't bother us.

12 By 1960 our national debt stood at $284 billion. Congress in 1971 decided to put a ceiling of $400 billion on our ability to borrow. Today the debt is $934 billion. So-called temporary increases or extensions in the debt ceiling have been allowed 21 times in these 10 years, and now I have been forced to ask for another increase in the debt ceiling or the Government will be unable to function past the middle of February, and I've only been here 16 days. Before we reach the day when we can reduce the debt ceiling we may, in spite of our best efforts, see a national debt in excess of a trillion dollars. This is a figure literally beyond our comprehension.

13 We know now that inflation results from all that deficit spending. Government has only two ways of getting money other than raising taxes. It can go into the money market and borrow, competing with its own citizens and driving up interest rates, which it has done, or it can print money, and it's done that. Both methods are inflationary.

14 We're victims of language; the very word "inflation" leads us to think of it as high prices. Then, of course, we resent the person who puts on the price tags, forgetting that he or she is also a victim of inflation. Inflation is not just high prices; it is a reduction in the value of our money. When the money supply is increased but the goods and services available for buying are not, we have too much money chasing too few goods.

15 Wars are usually accompanied by inflation. Everyone is working or fighting, but production is of weapons and munitions, not things we can buy and use.

16 One way out would be to raise taxes so that Government need not borrow or print money. But in all these years of Government growth, we've reached—indeed surpassed—the limit of our people's tolerance or ability to bear an increase in the tax burden.

17 Prior to World War II, taxes were such that on the average we only had to work about two and a half months each year to pay our total Federal, state, and local tax bill. Today we have to work about five months to pay that bill.

18 Some say shift the tax burden to business and industry, but business doesn't pay taxes. Oh, don't get the wrong idea, business is being taxed—so much so that we are being priced out of the world market. But business must pass its costs of operation, and that includes taxes, onto the customer in the price of the product. Only people pay taxes—all the taxes.

19 Government first uses business in a kind of sneaky way to help collect the taxes. They are hidden in the price and we aren't aware of how much tax we actually pay. Today, this once great industrial giant of ours has the lowest rate of gain in productivity of virtually all the industrial nations with whom we must compete in the world market. We can't even hold our own market here in America against foreign automobiles, steel, and a number of other products.

20 Japanese production of automobiles is almost twice as great per worker as it is in America. Japanese steelworkers out-produce their American counterparts by about 25 percent.

21 This isn't because they are better workers. I'll match the American working man or woman against anyone in the world. But we have to give them the modern tools and equipment that workers in the other industrial nations have.

22 We invented the assembly line and mass production, but punitive tax policies and excessive and unnecessary regulations plus Government borrowing have stifled our ability to update plant and equipment. When capital investment is made it is too often for some unproductive alterations demanded by Government to meet various of its regulations.

23 Excessive taxation of individuals has robbed us of incentive and made overtime unprofitable.

24 We once produced about 40 percent of the world's steel. We now produce 19 percent.

25 We were once the greatest producer of automobiles, producing more than all the rest of the world combined. That is no longer true, and in addition, the big three, the major auto companies, in our land have sustained tremendous losses in the past year and have been forced to lay off thousands of workers.

26 All of you who are working know that even with cost-of-living pay raises you can't keep up with inflation. In our progressive tax system as you increase the number of dollars you earn you find yourself moved up into higher tax brackets, paying a higher tax rate just for trying to hold your own. The result? Your standard of living is going down.

27 Over the past decades we've talked of curtailing Government spending so that we can then lower the tax burden. Sometimes we've even taken a run at doing that. But there were always those who told us taxes couldn't be cut until spending was reduced. Well, we can lecture our children about extravagance until we run out of voice and breath. Or we can cure their extravagance simply by reducing their allowance.

28 It is time to recognize that we have come to a turning point. We are threatened with an economic calamity of tremendous proportions and the old business as usual treatment can't save us.

29 Together, we must chart a different course. We must increase productivity. That means making it possible for industry to modernize and make use of the technology which we ourselves invented; that means putting Americans back to work. And that means above all bringing Government spending back within Government revenues, which is the only way, together with increased productivity, that we can reduce and, yes, eliminate inflation.

30 In the past we've tried to fight inflation one year and then, when unemployment increased, turn the next year to fighting unemployment with more deficit spending as a pump primer. So again, up goes inflation. It hasn't worked. We don't have to choose between inflation and unemployment—they go hand in hand. It's time to try something different and that's what we're going to do.

31 I've already placed a freeze on hiring replacements for those who retire or leave Government service. I have ordered cut in Government travel, the number of consultants to the Government, and the buying of office equipment and other items. I have put a freeze on pending regulations and set up a task force under Vice President Bush to review regulations with an eye toward getting rid of as many as possible. I have decontrolled oil, which should result in more domestic production and less dependence on foreign oil. And I am eliminating the ineffective wage and price program of the Council on Wage and Price Stability.

32 But it will take more, much more, and we must realize there is no quick fix. At the same time, however, we cannot delay in implementing an economic program aimed at both reducing tax rates to stimulate productivity and reducing the growth in Government spending to reduce unemployment and inflation.

33 On Feb. 18 I will present in detail an economic program to Congress, embodying the features I have just stated. It will propose budget cuts in virtually every department of Government. It is my belief that these actual budget cuts will only be part of the savings. As our Cabinet Secretaries take charge of their departments, they will search out areas of waste, extravagance and costly administrative overhead which could yield additional and substantial reductions.

34 At the same time we are doing this, we must go forward with a tax relief package. I shall ask for a 10 percent reduction across the board in the personal income tax rates for each of the next three years. Proposals will also be submitted for accelerated depreciation allowances for business to provide necessary capital so as to create jobs.

35 Now here again, in saying this, I know that language, as I said earlier, can get in the way of a clear understanding of what our program is intended to do. Budget cuts can sound as if we are going to reduce Government spending to a lower level than was spent the year before.

36 This is not the case. The budgets will increase as our population increases and each year we'll see spending increases to match that growth. Government revenues will increase as the economy grows, but the burden will be lighter for each individual because the economic base will have been expanded by reason of the reduced rates.

37 Let me show you a chart I've had drawn to illustrate how this can be. Here you see two trend lines. The bottom line shows the increase in tax revenues. The red line on top is the increase in Government spending. Both lines turn upward reflecting the giant tax increase already built into the system for this year 1981, and the increases in spending built into the '81 and '82 budgets and on into the future.

38 As you can see, the spending line rises at a steeper slant than the revenue line. That gap between those lines illustrates the increasing deficits we've been running, including this year's $80 billion deficit.

39 Now, in the second chart, the lines represent the positive effects when Congress accepts our economic program. Both lines continue to rise allowing for necessary growth but the gap narrows as spending cuts continue

over the next few years, until finally the two lines come together meaning a balanced budget.

40 I am confident that my Administration can achieve that. At that point, tax revenues, in spite of rate reductions, will be increasing faster than spending, which means we can look forward to further reductions in the tax rates.

41 In all of this we will of course work closely with the Federal Reserve System toward the objective of a stable monetary policy.

42 Our spending cuts will not be at the expense of the truly needy. We will, however, seek to eliminate benefits to those who are not really qualified by reason of need.

43 As I've said before, on Feb. 18 I will present this economic package of budget reductions and tax reform to a joint session of Congress and to you in full detail.

44 Our basic system is sound. We can, with compassion, continue to meet our responsibility to those who through no fault of their own need our help. We can meet fully the other legitimate responsibilities of Government. We cannot continue any longer our wasteful ways at the expense of the workers of this land or our children.

45 Since 1960 our Government has spent $5.1 trillion; our debt has grown by $648 billion. Prices have exploded by 178 percent. How much better off are we for it all? We all know, we are very much worse off.

46 When we measure how harshly these years of inflation, lower productivity, and uncontrolled Government growth have affected our lives, we know we must act and act now.

47 We must not be timid.

48 We will restore the freedom of all men and women to excel and to create. We will unleash the energy and genius of the American people—traits which have never failed us.

49 To the Congress of the United States, I extend my hand in cooperation and I believe we can go forward in a bipartisan manner.

50 I have found a real willingness to cooperate on the part of Democrats and members of my own party.

51 To my colleagues in the executive branch of Government and to all Federal employees, I ask that we work in the spirit of service.

52 I urge those great institutions in America—business and labor—to be guided by the national interest and I'm confident they will. The only special interest we will serve is the interest of the people.

53 We can create the incentives which take advantage of the genius of our economic system—a system, as Walter Lippmann observed more than 40 years ago, which for the first time in history gave men "a way of producing wealth in which the good fortune of others multiplied their own."

54 Our aim is to increase our national wealth so all will have more, not just redistribute what we already have, which is just a sharing of scarcity. We can begin to reward hard work and risk-taking, by forcing this Government to live within its means.

55 Over the years we have let negative economic forces run out of control. We have stalled the judgment day. We no longer have that luxury. We are out of time.

56 And to you, my fellow citizens, let us join in a new determination to rebuild the foundations of our society, to work together to act responsibly. Let us do so with the most profound respect for that which must be preserved as well as with sensitive understanding and compassion for those who must be protected.

57 We can leave our children with an unrepayable massive debt and a shattered economy or we can leave them liberty in a land where every individual has the opportunity to be whatever God intended us to be. All it takes is a little common sense and recognition of our own ability. Together we can forge a new beginning for America.

58 Thank you and good night.

KEYNOTE ADDRESS TO NATIONAL URBAN LEAGUE

Vernon E. Jordan, Jr.

Vernon E. Jordan, President of the National Urban League, delivered this address at the National Urban League Annual Conference in Washington, D.C. on July 19, 1981. Having missed the previous Annual Conference because he was recovering from a would-be assassin's bullet, Jordan began his address with expressions of love and appreciation for his audience members who had served well in his absence. But the threat posed to League interests by President Reagan's economic policy led the speaker not to linger long with social amenities. Rather, he delivered a stinging attack on the Reagan Administration's lack of compassion for the poor.

Jordan begins his attack by belittling the ideology of radical conservatism embraced by the Reagan Administration. While praising President Reagan as a man, an interesting rhetorical strategy, he discredits the ideology that undergirds Reagan's economic policy by calling it "slogans" rather than ideas. In a series of passages beginning with the parallel words "Black People don't need to be told," Jordan makes the ideology of "Radical conservatism" appear simplistic if not silly.

Having belittled the ideology as a notion, Jordan moves to a direct attack on the economic policy that reflects the ideology. The Administration's economic program is viewed as taking from the poor to give to the rich. President Reagan is viewed as a man whose actions are vastly inconsistent with his words. What effect is achieved by juxtaposing Candidate Reagan's words to the Urban League with President Reagan's "Jelly Bean Budget?"

Jordan then details seven holes torn in the Black "safety net" by the new budget. In a speech rich with figurative language, this section uses plain language and short sentences. What effect does such plain talk have? Jordan then attacks common defenses of the budget. In a series of sentences beginning with the parallel form "we are told," he questions the rationales that the Administration has advanced as support for the budget. How effective is the speaker's use of irony in discrediting the justifications of the Reagan Administration?

In the second half of the speech, Jordan first scolds former supporters of Black and poor causes for deserting the movement. He then sets forth courses of action that must be pursued by the National Urban League in the light of economic policies of the Reagan Administration. As a policy speech, this address both attacks an Administration's policy and advocates a policy for NUL members. To what extent does the attack on one policy strengthen the endorsement of a second policy?

This speech is rich in figurative language. How often does the speaker use parallelism as a strategy for organizing ideas? To what effect? What different kinds of figures of speech are employed? To what effect?

This speech is reprinted by permission from *Vital Speeches of the Day*, August 15, 1981, pp. 659–663.

1   Last year's NUL Conference was the first in my decade in the Urban League that I did not attend personally. I saw the proceedings on video tape. I spoke to the Conference on audio tape. But all the while, I felt deeply deprived, for there can be no more vital experience than being among the people I love in this meeting of the Movement I love.

2   But last year's experience also renewed my appreciation of the strength of the Urban League. Few organizations could sail through a crisis such as we faced last spring and summer. Few could demonstrate the depth of skills and experience that we did.

3   Our Chairman, Coy Eklund, merits our deep appreciation for the way he helped our agency pull through. Coy, our dedicated trustees, and our 25,000 volunteers all provided encouragement and support far beyond the call of duty.

4   With their help, national and affiliate staff performed with the devotion to excellence and to results that typifies the Urban League. And John Jacob displayed a unique blend of grace under pressure, hard work, wisdom and leadership that won the admiration of everyone—in and out of our Movement. He deserves a special thanks from all of us for his superb job.

5   Thanks to your great efforts, the Urban League emerged from its crisis stronger than ever. So it is good to be here tonight, to salute you—not on tape, but in full, living color.

6 My first Urban League Conference address was in 1971. Then too, it dealt with a conservative Administration in Washington. But that Administration, while hostile to black people, was pragmatic. It had to be. There was still a strong national consensus that operated to preserve black gains. The Congress was a bulwark against attempts to dismantle important social programs. We had a two-party system then.

7 Today, there is another conservative Administration in Washington. But this time, much has changed.

8 This Administration is wedded to an ideology of radical conservatism. This Administration has introduced a new political vocabulary—"budget reconciliation," "truly needy," "supply side economics," and other phrases. But it has dropped from the political vocabulary the one word that makes government relevant to the governed, the one word that grants legitimacy to its laws—"compassion."

9 This is not mere semantics. The Administration's refusal to temper ideology with compassion makes it a clear and present danger to black people and to poor people.

10 Those are harsh words, but true ones. And they apply despite the obvious charm of the President. We must make a clear distinction between our political and ideological differences with President Reagan and our high personal regard for him. The President is a good man, a courageous man, and on a personal level, a compassionate man.

11 Not since Franklin Delano Roosevelt has America been led by so gifted a communicator. Not since Lyndon Johnson has it been led by so skillful a politician. And not since Herbert Hoover has it been led by a President willing to sacrifice millions of people on the altar of an outmoded ideology.

12 Yes, outmoded. The President claims to be bringing us new ideas and new policies. But they are actually a recycled version of ideas and policies that were buried in the Great Depression. And with good reason.

13 What are the new ideas the Administration is ramming down the throats of the nation? Get government off our backs. Give power and programs to the states. Federal programs have failed. Rely on the free enterprise system. Build more missiles.

14 Those are not ideas they are slogans. Like most slogans, they contain a grain of truth. And like most slogans, they oversimplify and distort. They reinforce the meanest instincts of selfishness. They cut society loose from its moral bearings.

15 Black people don't need to be told that government is on our backs because we know it has been by our side, helping to counterbalance the vicious racism that deprived us of our lives, our liberty, and our rights.

16 Black people don't need to be told that power and programs should go to the states, because we know the few, feeble programs that have helped us were those mandated by Washington. It was the state and local govern-ments that excluded us from everything from voting to paved streets. And it is they who will trample on our interests again if this Administration dumps the programs we need into block grants.

17 Black people don't need to be told federal programs have failed because we know many have succeeded. The Pentagon may be able to land helicopters in Iran, but the Food Stamp program has fed the hungry; social security has wiped out poverty for most older citizens; CETA has put the jobless to work, compensatory education programs have improved reading scores of disadvantaged youth, and Legal Services has given poor people access to the justice system.

18 Black people don't need to be told to rely on the free enterprise system. We believe in the free enterprise system. We want to be part of it. We want our fair share of it.

19 And we know that will not happen without a federal government that pushes the private sector into affirmative action programs. It will not happen without a federal government that has setasides for minority enter-prises and job and training programs for the disadvantaged.

20 Black people don't need to be lectured about the need for economic growth. When others were talking of "an era of limits," "less is more," and "small is beautiful," we were saying "bake a bigger pie." We want economic growth. We know that in this America we will not get our fair share unless there is more for everyone. But we also know that we will not get our fair share just because there is more. America has managed to push us from the table of prosperity in good times as in bad.

21 So it is not enough just to have growth. What we want to know is "economic growth for whom?" A rising tide lifts all boats" is no answer. A rising tide lifts only those boats in the water; our boats are in the drydock of America's economy. And we know we will be stranded on dry land, far from that rising tide, unless government steps in with the programs and protection that help launch us into the mainstream.

22 That will not happen with an economic program that gives to the wealthy in the vague hopes that some of it will trickle down to the poor. What little trickles down is soaked up long before it reaches us.

23 Let us cut through the rhetoric of a supply-side economics that supplies misery to the poor: this Administration's economic program amounts to a massive transfer of resources from the poor to the rich.

24 It takes money, programs, and opportunities from poor people and promises them in return an end to inflation and prosperity for all. It says to poor people: give up the little you have today and we promise you a lot more in the bye and bye. Well, black people aren't buying pie-in-the-sky economics.

25 Last year Candidate Reagan came to the Urban League's annual conference. He catalogued the many economic problems our nation faces. And he said: "let us make a compact among ourselves—a compact not to fight these problems on the backs of the poor."

26 But that is exactly what this jelly bean budget does!

27 Candidate Reagan said: "Think of how discouraging it must be for those who have always had less, to now be told that they must further reduce their standard of living."

28 But that is exactly what this jelly bean budget does!

29 Last month President Reagan said: "I do not intend to let America drift further toward economic segregation."

30 But that is exactly what this jelly bean budget does!

31 When we look at that budget, we say to the President, in the words of the Psalmist: "Thou hast showed thy people hard things: thou hast made us to drink the wine of astonishment."

32 A brief look at what happened to some of the major domestic programs will demonstrate that black people are the major victims of a budget that tears huge, gaping holes in our safety net:

33 —Social security. The minimum benefit—a measly $122 a month is eliminated. Who gets hurt? Poor black people who spent their working lives on their knees cleaning floors. Disability benefits are tightened. Who gets hurt? Workers who are injured or fall sick and can't work anymore—a disproportionate number of them black.

34 —Food Stamps. A million people will lose their food stamps, millions more will have their benefits reduced. Who gets hurt? The working poor. Over a third of all food stamp recipients are black.

35 —Public service jobs ended: CETA training cut back. Who gets hurt? Over a third of all CETA workers are black.

36 —Medicaid is capped. Poor people will suffer reductions in access to health care. Who gets hurt? Over a third of Medicaid recipients are black.

37 —Legal Services. The Administration wanted to kill it. But our compassionate Congress just cut its budget by two-thirds. Who gets hurt? People who can't afford a lawyer. Poor people. A third are black.

38 —Welfare is cut and a forced work program authorized in the hope that unpleasant make-work jobs will drive people off the rolls. Who gets hurt? Almost half the recipients are black children and black mothers. Who gets hurt most? Working mothers who get small welfare checks to supplement their low earnings.

39 —Education aid cut heavily. Who gets hurt? Disadvantaged children, over a third of them black.

40 Defenders of that budget will tell us black people are not being singled out. That's true. It's only poor people who are being victimized. And we are twelve percent of the population but a third of the poor—so we are the main victims.

41 We are told the nation can no longer afford to help the poor. But it can afford to throw one-and-a-half trillion dollars at the Pentagon over the next five years.

42 We are told social programs don't help poor people: they help the people in social service professions. Tell that to the families deprived of their food stamps, their welfare checks, their public service jobs.

43 We are told social programs breed dependency. Tell that to the working mothers who will have to quit their jobs or lose benefits. Tell it to young people in training programs who will lose their chance to learn and to earn their way out of poverty. Tell it to sick people whose public health clinics are shut down.

44 We are told that it's bad to look to government for special help— everyone should be treated the same. Tell that to the affluent who will get huge tax cuts on top of their loopholes. Tell it to the corporations on welfare. Tell it to the special interests who still get their subsidies while poor people lose their life-lines.

45 Last month the Congress rushed this jelly bean budget through. With no real debate, the programs that help the poor were cut to ribbons. With no real debate, years of slow, patient progress were swept out to sea by the rising ride of radical conservatism.

46 Never have so few taken so much from so many in so little time!

47 Where was the outcry against that outrage? Where were the Democrats? Where were the liberals? Where were the Congressmen who once fought for the programs that give poor people opportunities?

48 With some honorable exceptions, they were engaged in a last-ditch fight to cut the President's three-year tax cut back to two years. They were in a last-ditch fight to save benefits for the middle class and farm interests. Roovevelt led a Party concerned with the "ill-housed, ill-clad, ill-nourished." Today his successors are concerned with the upper-middle class.

49 Democrats and Republicans alike need some arithmetic lessons. They need to learn that poll results still show significant public support for social programs that work.

50 They need to learn that when they cut social programs whose beneficiaries are one-third to one-half black, the remainder are white. Whites make up half to two-thirds of the victims of the cuts.

51 And if they don't care about blacks and poor whites, they must remember that this is just the beginning. Tax cuts combined with massive increases in defense spending mean more budget cuts down the road. And when the poor have no more programs left to cut, the cuts will start reaching into the middle class constituency the Democrats are now courting.

52 One last word for the Democrats who take the black vote for granted—an opposition that does not oppose is not worthy of governing.

53 But the silence extends well beyond a passive Congress. When aid to the arts is cut, there are full-page newspaper ads of protest. There are petitions, and loud protest. When an aggressive foreign policy is implemented, there is the same. But where are the voices raised in behalf of poor people? Where are the churches, the universities, the other sectors of our society that once marched with us and supported us?

54 And where is the enlightened business community? Will they keep their silence as the price for their tax cuts? Will they choose short-term profits over the long-term social stability that ultimately is the surest guarantee of the free enterprise system? Will they silently pocket billions in tax cuts without speaking out on behalf of poor working people who lose their food stamps?

55 The silence is frightening because the real issue extends beyond the specific budget cuts. The real issue is the grand design of substituting charity for entitlements, local tyranny for federal protection, and unbridled, law-of-the-jungle capitalism for a balanced cooperation between the public and private sectors.

56 Thus, the real issue is the nature of our society. We of the National Urban League Movement believe there is no contradiction between equality and liberty; between economic growth and social justice, between a strong defense and healthy cities; between government assistance and individual opportunities. We believe that a moral society requires compassion for the poor, economic justice and racial equality.

57 We will play our part in the national dialogue about the future of the nation we love so much and for which we have sacrificed so much. We will do our part by following the Biblical mandate to "open thy mouth, judge righteously, and plead the cause of the poor and needy."

58 But a dialogue means listening to opposing views as well. We will listen. Tomorrow the Vice President will speak to us. Other high Administration officials will also present their case. We welcome them.

59 We want to hear them address issues of concern to black people and to all Americans. We want to hear them explain their program. We want to hear them give us their vision of America and of black people's role in its future.

60 I hope they go beyond the usual justifications for their program. We agree with them that inflation must be curbed. We agree with them that blacks do better when the economy is better. We agree with them that America must produce more and create more jobs in the private sector.

61 But what I hope they will tell us is: what are black and poor people supposed to do in the meantime?

62   Even the wildest optimist knows it will take years for the President's program to produce the prosperity he promises. What do we do until then? How do poor people survive without the basic programs they need until then? How do they take advantage of future opportunities when present training and education programs are cut, when despair replaced hope?

63   A true dialogue goes beyond simple slogans and partial truths. It cuts to the core of the issues. So if this Administration is serious about engaging in a frank, open dialogue with us, will it tell this Urban League Annual Conference how the black poor are to survive in the interim?

64   Will it tell us how its program will bring equality to black people, when we have had far higher unemployment and far lower income than whites, even when times were good?

65   Will it tell us what we are to say to our poor black constituents when we go home to our 116 cities where misery lies thick on the ground and the weeds of despair flourish?

66   The black community today feels itself under seige. It is victimized by the budget cuts. It is harassed by attacks on affirmative action. It is alarmed that state legislatures will redistrict our representatives out of the Congress and out of local offices. It is outraged by the Administration's tilt toward racist South Africa. It is threatened by block grants.

67   And it is burdened by events beyond the political arena: by growing racial insensitivity and rising anti-black attitudes; by the murders of black children in Atlanta and violence against blacks elsewhere; by the continued deterioration of black neighborhoods; by the flow of drugs and the increase of crime; and by the rise of the fanatics of the far right like the Klan and the Nazis.

68   High on our long list of concerns is the future of the Voting Rights Act. It expires next year. Voting is, in President Reagan's words, "the most sacred right of free men and women." That sacred right will be lost to millions of black and Hispanic people unless the President comes out forcefully in favor of extending the Voting Rights Act.

69   The fight for voting rights symbolizes the erosion of black gains. We are now fighting the fight we fought sixteen years ago. And in some ways, we are dealing with basic issues like better race relations that were issues of the 1950s. We moved far beyond that stage, and now we are thrust back to square one.

70   But the path of progress has always been crooked and twisted. It has always been marked by two steps forward and one step backward. We cannot give way to despair; rather we must mobilize the black community to protect its rights and to prepare for the next push forward on the hard, rocky road to equality.

71   In many ways, today's challenges are more difficult. The national consensus for racial justice has withered.

72   The complexities of today's racial, economic and political issues are such that there is no one grand strategy or leader to deliver us. We will have to draw on our immense resources of survival skills to get us through these hard times. And we will have to cultivate our bonds of unity to once again overcome.

73   In many ways, it is back to basics for black people. That means a recommitment to the slow, agonizing work of building community strengths and community institutions.

74   The progress we have achieved has been due to the institutions rooted in our communities and responsive to our needs. Throughout history, it has been our churches, our press, our colleges, our community organizations that have fought on our behalf.

75   So now is the time for us to shore up those institutions, to strengthen them and support them. We of the Urban League Movement know we cannot be fully effective unless other community institutions are strong. In effect, the civil rights movement is as strong as its weakest link, and each of us must cooperate and work together, while performing the roles and functions best suited to us.

76   Back to basics also means a recommitment to group progress. We reject completely the notion that individual progress is meaningful while half of our black brothers and sisters are mired in ghetto poverty. We reject completely the notion that a black person who has worked and clawed his way into the middle class has no responsibility to the black poor. And we reject just as completely the vile notion that a black person who has gained a toehold in America's middle class has anything to apologize for.

77   We are sick and tired of hard working black people having to apologize for sharing the American Dream of a decent standard of living; of having to apologize for not being poor; of having to apologize for aspiring and achieving, of being put on a guilt trip for trying to make it.

78   We will not allow ourselves to be held hostage to other people's ideas about what our proper place is. We know that if you are black in America, you are in trouble; you are not safe, you are always in danger of losing the little you have. We know what it is to be poor; most of us are the first generation to be educated and to wear a white collar to work. All of us are bound by ties of family and racial unity to all black people.

79   Back to basics also means a recommitment to excellence. There is no margin granted to black Americans—we've got to be better than others in order to get what other Americans take for granted. That spirit of excellence and accomplishment must be characteristic of all our institutions. That spirit must be transmitted to our young people. The spirit of excellence can be the spark that revitalizes our communities.

80 Back to basics also means political action. It's hard to break through the cynicism that grips people who have been subjected to brutalizing poverty and hopelessness. But the 1980s must be the decade of maximizing black political strength. We have the numbers to influence events, but in election after election we throw away half our power by not voting. So citizenship education and political involvement in all parties must be a major priority in the 1980s.

81 Back to basics also means building coalitions. We've got to reach across class and ethnic lines to win victories for all people. America's tragedy is the racism that drives a wedge between whites and blacks who have so much to gain by working together.

82 Back to basics also means devising new strategies, alternatives for a nation that thinks old ideas that led to the Great Depression are new ideas for an uncertain future; alternatives like the Urban League's income maintenance plan.

83 Back to basics also means challenging America's institutions. It means challenging the Administration and the Congress to discover compassion, to make their conservatism humane. It means challenging the private sector to live up to its job creation and affirmative action obligations. It means challenging the churches to practice the morality they preach. It means challenging weak-kneed liberals and hard-hearted conservatives wherever they may be found. It means reminding America's institutions that black people are Americans too, that our blood, sweat, and tears helped make this country what it is, and all we want is our fair share.

84 And back to basics means back to protesting our condition. Protest has been the basic response of black Americans, from the protest of the slave revolts to the protest of the March on Washington.

85 Now, when all about us is dark with despair, now is the time to raise high a fresh banner of protest. Now is the time to speak out loud and clear. Now is the time to tell the Administration that poor people can't live on a diet of jellybeans, to tell local officials they can't close our hospitals, to tell corporations they can't hire us last and fire us first, to tell the school boards they are failing their duty to our children, to tell all of America's institutions that they must root out the racism at the core of our national life.

86 It was a black preacher right here in Washington, D.C., Francis Grimke, who said many years ago:

> "It is our duty to keep up the agitation of our rights, not only for our sakes, but for the sake of the nation at large. It would not only be against our own interest not to do so, but it would be unpatriotic for us quietly to acquiesce in the present condition of things, for it is a wrong condition of things. If justice sleeps in this land, let it not be because we

have helped to lull it to sleep by our silence, our indifference; let it not be from lack of effort on our part to arouse it from its slumbers."

87   That is our duty, to our nation, to ourselves, to our children, and to our children's children. Let us then get back to the basic job of building new foundations for a new thrust for equality. Let us get back to the basic job of making America America again—this time for everyone!

A TIME FOR PEACE

Kenda Creasy

An undergraduate student at Miami University, Kenda Creasy represented her school and the state of Ohio at the 107th Annual Contest of the Interstate Oratorical Association in Denver, Colorado on May 2-3, 1980. After preliminary, semi-final, and final competition, Ms. Creasy was awarded first place.

In affirming the value of hospices as a means for dealing with the terminally ill, Creasy contrasts the hospice approach with the traditional approach according to three "basic facts of Life:" the limits of curative medicine, the isolation of institutions, and the psychological impact of death. With respect to each of these topics, she identifies the shortcomings of the present system and then discusses the superiority of hospices. By placing the two systems in juxtaposition, she dramatically illustrates the advantages of the hospice system over the traditional system.

After contrasting the two systems, Creasy relates hospices to the lives of her listeners in a very personal way. By so doing, she seems to demonstrate a genuine concern for the welfare of her audience members. What impact is such an expression of concern likely to have on an audience's perception of a speaker's credibility?

This speech both begins and ends with a reference to the well-known expression "to all things there is a season and a time to every purpose under heaven." Authors of speech textbooks often identify such a "reference to the introduction" as an effective concluding device in that it ties the speech together and provides "psychological closure." Does this method of closing affect you in the desired way?

This speech is printed by permission from *Winning Orations*, 1980, pp. 81-83.

1   "To all things there is a season; and a time to every purpose under heaven—a time to be born, and a time to die. . ."

2   Except today. Today modern medicine is better prepared to prolong life in all seasons. But for millions of Americans this year, it won't be enough.

They will be diagnosed as terminally ill—and once labeled terminal, our medical know-how no longer applies. According to the Department of Health, Education and Welfare, you and I stand a one in four chance of suddenly assuming unexpected responsibilities because someone in *our* family has been diagnosed as terminally ill. But we could have help—with hospices.

3 A hospice is an alternative method of terminal care comprised of a team of doctors, psychologists, clergy, and volunteers who, basically, make housecalls. A hospice's aim is to help people die with as little discomfort and as much serenity as possible, involving family and friends along the way, and usually taking place in the person's home. Hospices do not cure; instead, they make medical, psychological, and spiritual help available to both the patient AND his family, before and after the funeral. As one health analyst put it, "A hospice is really more of an idea than a place." Unfortunately, even though the hospice movement is supported by the American Medical Association and HEW, hospices in the United States are too unknown to have the impact they could have. So what can we do? Well, first we must compare hospices with our present ailing approach to terminal illness, and then see what we can do to remedy the problem. At least then we can stop sacrificing a quality of life for a quantity of days.

4 The traditional American approach to terminal illness ignores three basic facts of life: the limits of curative medicine, the isolation of institutions, and the psychological impact death has on both the patient and his family. The first problem is the inherent limits of a medical system designed to cure. Hospitals *maintain* life: everything from visiting hours to progress reports are designed for the temporary stay. But the terminal patient's stay is *not* temporary; he will not get well. *Time* magazine pointed out in June, 1978, "Imbued as the medical establishment is with the idea of fighting at all costs to prolong life, it is naturally geared to the hope of success rather than to the fact of failure." But as *Changing Times* explained in April, 1979, "When care designed to cure and rehabilitate is applied to a person who knows he has a terminal illness, it creates a feeling of isolation and despair, especially if he senses the staff is just going through the motions."

5 Hospices make no such false promises. Dr. James Cimino explains, "For the hospice patient, it is too late for cures. The operations, radiation, and chemotherapy have been tried elsewhere. They've been declared incurable and inoperable. The patient is entirely aware of his situation." Hospices provide two choices: either the person can go to the hospice or, more likely, the hospice will come to him, 24 hours a day, if necessary, with a team of doctors, psychologists, clergy, good neighbors, and volunteers. Treatment is palliative—that is, designed to ease pain and manage symptoms, such as nausea, but no heroic effort is made to cure the disease. The results? The person is comfortable, and his mind is clear.

6 Unfortunately, there is more to dying than just futile treatment of an illness. The second problem is institutionalization, which is more often easy than essential. Nearly 70% of terminally ill Americans spend their final year in a hospital or a nursing home—but at the moment, there is not much choice. For one thing, says John Abbott of Hospice, Inc., families doubt their own ability to care for a dying member, and find institutions more convenient. But in a hospice, he says, "When families ask, 'Can we care for our loved one?' we say, 'Yes you can—and we'll help you.' " The problem is, first you've got to find the hospice.

7 This summer, a family friend's grandmother spent the last six weeks of her life in the hospital begging to go home. The family was unable to find someone willing to provide round-the-clock painkillers to a ninety-three-year-old woman dying at home, and they called me to see if I knew of anyone. "The physical pain," they said, "doesn't hurt her half as much as not being home." Well, I didn't know of anyone—and two weeks later she died: in the hospital, by herself. To all things there is a season.

8 Had I known at that time that a hospice was located in Central Ohio, that expensive and futile hospitalization could have been avoided. And more importantly, a person who desperately wanted to be at home when she died could have been spared the trauma of an institution. Hospices in New Haven, Connecticut, allow 50% of terminally ill patients in that area to live at home—at a cost, incidentally, of about $25 a day, as opposed to $200 a day in a hospital. In those hospices which do provide residential facilities, rules are avoided, visiting hours are round-the-clock, and pets and personal effects are encouraged. Hospices allow that choice. Institutions do not.

9 But the third problem of terminal illness comes *after* the funeral, for in what psychologists call our "death-denying culture," we ignore the family and deny them the catharsis of knowing they have done everything that they can. The Comptroller General's Report to Congress found that, as a result of a dying person's illness, family suicides jumped significantly. Three sociologists' study of widows found that 24% developed reactive depression, 12% became emotionally unstable, and 4% turned to alcohol within the first year of their husbands' deaths. Two separate studies show, that parents stand a 70% chance of divorce within two years of the death of a child.

10 Susan Silver, of the National Hospice Organization, explains: "When a family is intimately involved with a dying member, there is much less guilt afterward. They witness the natural dying process, they give of themselves, and their grief is not so prolonged." Hospice personnel do everything from drafting wills to feeding pets to providing family counseling—including a follow-up after the funeral. Volunteers either help out within the households or are trained by the hospice professionals. One woman, after a hospice team had helped her cope with her mother's death, said, "When she died it was a victory for all of us. None of us felt any guilt."

11 Today we appreciate life more—and go to greater lengths to preserve it—than any society in human history. But the fact is, for some of us, modern medical miracles will fail. Terminal illness is not discriminating: heart disease has no season, sickle cell anemia has no cure. There is a cancer death every 80 seconds—and one out of every four people you've met this weekend will eventually have cancer. What if, when you call home tonight, you find out it has hit there as well? It does happen.

12 The hospice movement in the United States needs our support, and with three simple steps we can provide it. First, encourage federal, state, and local government efforts to enhance the hospice movement. For example, as some states have already done, Medicare and Medicaid must be expanded to include hospice care for the aged and the poor.

13 Second, protect yourself. Buy insurance that covers hospices as well as hospitalization. Blue Cross and Blue Shield already do that; but with incentive, other companies would follow suit.

14 And most importantly, you and I have got to provide the personal concern that sets hospice care apart in the first place. Tell your parents about hospices: if they become ill tomorrow, wouldn't you want them to know? Or what if they did know, but there was no hospice that was near enough to help? Many hospices begin through local churches or community organizations, with grants available from HEW; consider them for yours. And above all, when someone *you* care for is diagnosed as terminally ill—and it *will* happen—don't simply say, "Well, if there's anything I can do. . . ." Call him up, walk the dog, provide cassettes for last notes, help tie up school or business ends. The important thing to remember is that hospices are not places, they're people. But without the support of family and friends, hospice becomes just another empty room.

15 When Joseph Califano visited the New Haven hospice, he said: "I visited with the idea that hospice was about dying. I came away realizing it's about living." We can't give a dying person *more* time—for to all things there *is* a season. But with little effort and much compassion, we *can* give him back the time he has. . . . A time to cry, and a time to laugh; a time for love, and a time for peace.

CAMBODIA

Richard M. Nixon

President Nixon delivered this address over national television on April 30, 1970. He chose this moment to announce and defend a policy he already had decided upon—namely, to conduct joint American and South Vietnamese military action inside Cambodia. The speech, and the decision it announced, deflated much of the public optimism generated by his earlier announcement of additional American troop withdrawals. News commentators analyzed the speech widely. Protests, temporarily in a lull, again escalated on college campuses, sometimes leading to major disasters, especially at Kent State University.

As a defense of policy speech, it seeks to prove justifications for the actions. Search out this rationale and assess the degree of reasonableness with which President Nixon developed and supported these justifications. Consider, also, possible general characteristics of a "defense of policy" speech. In what ways are the opportunities and limitations different for such a speech compared to a speech seeking public support *before* adoption of a new policy?

As one means of attempting to demonstrate that a need existed to undertake *some kind* of action, observe how President Nixon contrasts in positive and negative terms the past American and North Vietnamese actions (paragraphs 8, 10, 13, 15, 45, 46). Evaluate Nixon's use in paragraphs 19-41 of the "this-or-nothing" approach to analyzing the options open to him. Is the first a *real* option if, indeed, a need exists to do *something?* Are there any major possible options he has omitted, such as use of *only* South Vietnamese troops but supported by American supplies and communications? Does he justify as reasonable the third choice as the best alternative? To help show that the military action undertaken is advantageous, the President attempts to link the policy to major audience values. At several points he seeks to justify the policy by claiming it will promote a "just peace" and will preserve America's reputation for courage, strength, freedom, and justice.

In paragraphs 64-69 and 73-75, Nixon seems consciously to attempt to bolster his personal credibility with the audience. Assess the effectiveness, relevance, and ethicality of his invocations of respected prior Presidents and his expression of personal sacrifice. Note, also, his attack in paragraph 56 on "mindless" student protests. How relevant is his condemnation to the central purpose of the speech? Does his use of the word "systematic" imply some kind of organized campaign or conspiracy?

This speech is reprinted by permission from *Vital Speeches of the Day,* May 15, 1970, pp. 450-52.

1   Good evening my fellow Americans. Ten days ago in my report to the nation on Vietnam I announced a decision to withdraw an additional 150,000 Americans from Vietnam over the next year. I said then that I was making that decision despite our concern over increased enemy activity in Laos, in Cambodia and in South Vietnam.

2   And at that time I warned that if I concluded that increased enemy activity in any of these areas endangered the lives of Americans remaining in Vietnam, I would not hesitate to take strong and effective measures to deal with that situation.

3   Despite that warning, North Vietnam has increased its military aggression in all these areas, and particularly in Cambodia.

4 After full consultation with the National Security Council, Ambassador Bunker, General Abrams and my other advisors, I have concluded that the actions of the enemy in the last 10 days clearly endanger the lives of Americans who are in Vietnam now and would constitute an unacceptable risk to those who will be there after withdrawal of another 150,000.

5 To protect our men who are in Vietnam, and to guarantee the continued success of our withdrawal and Vietnamization program, I have concluded that the time has come for action.

6 Tonight, I shall describe the actions of the enemy, the actions I have ordered to deal with that situation, and the reasons for my decision.

7 Cambodia—a small country of seven million people—has been a neutral nation since the Geneva Agreement of 1954, an agreement, incidentally, which was signed by the government of North Vietnam.

8 American policy since then has been to scrupulously respect the neutrality of the Cambodian people. We have maintained a skeleton diplomatic mission of fewer than 15 in Cambodia's capital, and that only since last August.

9 For the previous four years, from 1965 to 1969 we did not have any diplomatic mission whatever in Cambodia, and for the past five years we have provided no military assistance whatever and no economic assistance to Cambodia.

10 North Vietnam, however, has not respected that neutrality. For the past five years, as indicated on this map, as you see here, North Vietnam has occupied military sanctuaries all along the Cambodian frontier with South Vietnam. Some of these extend up to 20 miles into Cambodia.

11 The sanctuaries are in red, and as you note they are on both sides of the border.

12 They are used for hit-and-run attacks on American and South Vietnamese forces in South Vietnam. These Communist-occupied territories contain major base camps, training sites, logistics facilities, weapons and ammunition factories, airstrips and prisoner of war compounds.

13 And for five years neither the United States nor South Vietnam has moved against these enemy sanctuaries because we did not wish to violate the territory of a neutral nation.

14 Even after the Vietnamese Communists began to expand these sanctuaries four weeks ago, we counseled patience to our South Vietnamese allies and imposed restraints on our own commanders.

15 In contrast to our policy the enemy in the past two weeks has stepped up his guerrilla actions and he is concentrating his main force in these sanctuaries that you see in this map, where they are building up the large massive attacks on our forces and those of South Vietnam.

16 North Vietnam in the last two weeks has stripped away all pretense of respecting the sovereignty or the neutrality of Cambodia. Thousands of their soldiers are invading the country from the sanctuaries. They are encircling the capital of Pnompenh. Coming from these sanctuaries as you see here, they had moved into Cambodia and are encircling the capital.

17 Cambodia, as a result of this, has sent out a call to the United States, to a number of other nations, for assistance. Because if this enemy effort succeeds, Cambodia would become a vast enemy staging area and a springboard for attacks on South Vietnam along 600 miles of frontier: a refuge where enemy troops could return from combat without fear of retaliation.

18 North Vietnamese men and supplies could then be poured into that country, jeopardizing not only the lives of our men but the people of South Vietnam as well.

19 Now confronted with this situation we had three options:

20 First, we can do nothing. Now, the ultimate result of that course of action is clear. Unless we indulge in wishful thinking, the lives of Americans remaining in Vietnam after our next withdrawal of 150,000 would be gravely threatened.

21 Let us go to the map again.

22 Here is South Vietnam. Here is North Vietnam. North Vietnam already occupies this part of Laos. If North Vietnam also occupied this whole band in Cambodia or the entire country, it would mean that South Vietnam was completely outflanked and the forces of Americans in this area as well as the South Vietnamese would be in an untenable military position.

23 Our second choice is to provide massive military assistance to Cambodia itself and, unfortunately, while we deeply sympathize with the plight of seven million Cambodians whose country has been invaded, massive amounts of military assistance could not be rapidly and effectively utilized by this small Cambodian Army against the immediate trap.

24 With other nations we shall do our best to provide the small arms and other equipment which the Cambodian Army of 40,000 needs and can use for its defense.

25 But the aid we will provide will be limited for the purpose of enabling Cambodia to defend its neutrality and not for the purpose of making it an active belligerent on one side or the other.

26 Our third choice is to go to the heart of the trouble.

27 And that means cleaning out major North Vietnamese- and Vietcong-occupied territories, these sanctuaries which serve as bases for attacks on both Cambodia and American and South Vietnamese forces in South Vietnam.

28   Some of these, incidentally, are as close to Saigon as Baltimore is to Washington. This one, for example, is called the Parrot's Beak—it's only 33 miles from Saigon.

29   Now faced with these three options, this is the decision I have made. In cooperation with the armed forces of South Vietnam, attacks are being launched this week to clean out major enemy sanctuaries on the Cambodian-Vietnam border. A major responsibility for the ground operation is being assumed by South Vietnamese forces.

30   For example, the attacks in several areas, including the Parrot's Beak, that I referred to a moment ago, are exclusively South Vietnamese ground operations, under South Vietnamese command, with the United States providing air and logistical support.

31   There is one area however, immediately above the Parrot's Beak where I have concluded that a combined American and South Vietnamese operation is necessary.

32   And now, let me give you the reasons for my decision.

33   A majority of the American people, a majority of you listening to me are for the withdrawal of our forces from Vietnam. The action I have taken tonight is indispensable for the continuing success of that withdrawal program.

34   A majority of the American people want to end this war rather than to have it drag on interminably.

35   The action I have taken tonight will serve that purpose.

36   A majority of the American people want to keep the casualties of our brave men in Vietnam at an absolute minimum.

37   Tonight, American and South Vietnamese units will attack the headquarters for the entire Communist military operation in South Vietnam. This key control center has been occupied by the North Vietnamese and Vietcong for five years in blatant violation of Cambodia's neutrality.

38   This is not an invasion of Cambodia. The areas in which these attacks will be launched are completely occupied and controlled by North Vietnamese forces.

39   Our purpose is not to occupy the areas. Once enemy forces are driven out of these sanctuaries and once their military supplies are destroyed, we will withdraw.

40   These actions are in no way directed to security interests of any nation. Any government that chooses to use these actions as a pretext for harming relations with the United States will be doing so on its own responsibility and on its own initiative and we will draw the appropriate conclusions.

41   The action I take tonight is essential if we are to accomplish that goal.

42 We take this action not for the purpose of expanding the war into Cambodia but for the purpose of ending the war in Vietnam, and winning the just peace we all desire.

43 We have made and will continue to make every possible effort to end this war through negotiation at the conference table rather than through more fighting in the battlefield.

44 Lets look again at the record.

45 We stopped the bombing of North Vietnam. We have cut air operations by over 20 percent. We've announced the withdrawal of over 250,000 of our men. We've offered to withdraw all of our men if they will withdraw theirs. We've offered to negotiate all issues with only one condition: and that is that the future of South Vietnam be determined, not by North Vietnam, and not by the United States, but by the people of South Vietnam themselves.

46 The answer of the enemy has been intransigeance at the conference table, belligerence at Hanoi, massive military aggression in Laos and Cambodia and stepped-up attacks in South Vietnam designed to increase American casualties.

47 This attitude has become intolerable.

48 We will not react to this threat to American lives merely by plaintive diplomatic protests.

49 If we did, credibility of the United States would be destroyed in every area of the world where only the power of the United States deters aggression.

50 Tonight, I again warn the North Vietnamese that if they continue to escalate the fighting when the United States is withdrawing its forces, I shall meet my responsibility as commander and chief of our armed forces to take the action I consider necessary to defend the security of our American men.

51 The action I have announced tonight puts the leaders of North Vietnam on notice that we will be patient in working for peace. We will be conciliatory at the conference table, but we will not be humiliated. We will not be defeated.

52 We will not allow American men by the thousands to be killed by an enemy from privileged sanctuary.

53 The time came long ago to end this war through peaceful negotiations. We stand ready for those negotiations. We've made major efforts many of which must remain secret.

54 I say tonight all the offers and approaches made previously remain on the conference table whenever Hanoi is ready to negotiate seriously.

55 But if the enemy response to our most conciliatory offers for peaceful negotiation continues to be to increase its attacks and humiliate and defeat us, we shall react accordingly.

56 My fellow Americans, we live in an age of anarchy, both abroad and at home. We see mindless attacks on all the great institutions which have been created by free civilizations in the last 500 years. Even here in the United States, great universities are being systematically destroyed.

57 Small nations all over the world find themselves under attack from within and from without. If when the chips are down the world's most powerful nation—the United States of America—acts like a pitful, helpless giant, the forces of totalitarianism and anarchy will threaten free nations and free institutions throughout the world.

58 It is not our power but our will and character that is being tested tonight.

59 The question all Americans must ask and answer tonight is this:

60 Does the richest and strongest nation in the history of the world have the character to meet a direct challenge by a group which rejects every effort to win a just peace, ignores our warning, tramples on solemn agreements, violates the neutrality of an unarmed people and uses our prisoners as hostages?

61 If we fail to meet this challenge all other nations will be on notice that despite its overwhelming power the United States when a real crisis comes will be found wanting.

62 During my campaign for the Presidency, I pledged to bring Americans home from Vietnam. They are coming home. I promised to end this war. I shall keep that promise. I promised to win a just peace. I shall keep that promise.

63 We shall avoid a wider war, but we are also determined to put an end to this war.

64 In this room, Woodrow Wilson made the great decision which led to victory in World War I.

65 Franklin Roosevelt made the decisions which led to our victory in World War II.

66 Dwight D. Eisenhower made decisions which ended the war in Korea and avoided war in the Middle East.

67 John F. Kennedy in his finest hour made the great decision which removed Soviet nuclear missiles from Cuba and the western hemisphere.

68 I have noted that there's been a great deal of discussion with regard to this decision I have made. And I should point out that I do not contend that it is in the same magnitude as these decisions that I have just mentioned.

69 But between those decisions and this decision, there is a difference that is very fundamental. In those decisions the American people were not assailed by counsels of doubt and defeat from some of the most widely known opinion leaders of the nation.

70 I have noted, for example, that a Republican Senator has said that this action I have taken means that my party has lost all chance of winning the November elections, and others are saying today that this move against enemy sanctuaries will make me a one-term President.

71 No one is more aware than I am of the political consequences of the action I've taken. It is tempting to take the easy political path, to blame this war on previous Administrations, and to bring all of our men home immediately—regardless of the consequences, even though that would mean defeat for the United States; to desert 18-million South Vietnamese people who have put their trust in us; to expose them to the same slaughter and savagery which the leaders of North Vietnam inflicted on hundreds of thousands of North Vietnamese who chose freedom when the Communists took over North Vietnam in 1954.

72 To get peace at any price now, even though I know that a peace of humiliation for the United States would lead to a bigger war or surrender later.

73 I have rejected all political considerations in making this decision. Whether my party gains in November is nothing compared to the lives of 400,000 brave Americans fighting for our country and for the cause of peace and freedom in Vietnam.

74 Whether I may be a one-term President is insignificant compared to whether by our failure to act in this crisis the United States proves itself to be unworthy to lead the forces of freedom in this critical period in world history.

75 I would rather be a one-term President and do what I believe was right than to be a two-term President at the cost of seeing America become a second-rate power and to see this nation accept the first defeat in its proud 190-year history.

76 I realize in this war there are honest, deep differences in this country about whether we should have become involved, that there are differences to how the war should have been conducted.

77 But the decision I announce tonight transcends those differences, for the lives of American men are involved. The opportunity for a 150,000 Americans to come home in the next 12 months is involved. The future of 18-million people in South Vietnam and 7-million people in Cambodia is involved, the possibility of winning a just peace in Vietnam and in the Pacific is at stake.

78 It is customary to conclude a speech from the White House by asking support for the President of the United States.

79 Tonight, I depart from that precedent. What I ask is far more important. I ask for your support for our brave men fighting tonight halfway around the world, not for territory, not for glory but so that their younger brothers and their sons and your sons can have a chance to grow up in a world of peace and freedom, and justice.

80 Thank you, and good night.

VIETNAM VETERANS AGAINST THE WAR

John F. Kerry

On April 22, 1971, John Forbes Kerry delivered this formal statement as part of his testimony before the Foreign Relations Committee of the U.S. Senate. A Yale graduate and former Navy officer with combat experience in Vietnam, the twenty-seven year old Kerry received three Purple Hearts, a Bronze Star, and a Silver Star. As a spokesman for an organization called the Vietnam Veterans Against the War, he here argues for discontinuance of present American policy through immediate withdrawal from Vietnam.

Kerry blends a variety of rhetorical techniques and strategies to develop his argument. Analyze how well he employs the following kinds of support: value judgments, specific instances, rhetorical questions, and refutation. Also consider at what specific audience the speech seems aimed: the Foreign Relations Committee, the Congress, or the nation at large? Can you identify any concrete attempts at audience adaption?

This public testimony is reprinted from *Legislative Proposals Relating to the War in Southeast Asia: Hearings before the Committee on Foreign Relations, United States Senate, Ninety-Second Congress, First Session* (Washington, D.C.: U.S. Government Printing Office, 1971), pp. 180-85.

1 Thank you very much, Senator Fulbright, Senator Javits, Senator Symington, Senator Pell. I would like to say for the record, and also for the men behind me who are also wearing the uniforms and their medals, that my sitting here is really symbolic. I am not here as John Kerry. I am here as one member of the group of 1,000, which is a small representation of a very much larger group of veterans in this country, and were it possible for all of them to sit at this table they would be here and have the same kind of testimony.

2 I would simply like to speak in very general terms. I apologize if my statement is general because I received notification yesterday you would hear me and I am afraid because of the injunction I was up most of the night and haven't had a great deal of chance to prepare.

3   I would like to talk, representing all those veterans, and say that several months ago in Detroit, we had an investigation at which over 150 honorably discharged and many very highly decorated veterans testified to war crimes committed in Southeast Asia, not isolated incidents but crimes committed on a day-to-day basis with the full awareness of officers at all levels of command.

4   It is impossible to describe to you exactly what did happen in Detroit, the emotions in the room, the feelings of the men who were reliving their experiences in Vietnam, but they did. They relived the absolute horror of what this country, in a sense, made them do.

5   They told the stories at times they had personally raped, cut off ears, cut off heads, taped wires from portable telephones to human genitals and turned up the power, cut off limbs, blown up bodies, randomly shot at civilians, razed villages in fashion reminiscent of Genghis Khan, shot cattle and dogs for fun, poisoned food stocks, and generally ravaged the country-side of South Vietnam in addition to the normal ravage of war, and the normal and very particular ravaging which is done by the applied bombing power of this country.

6   We call this investigation the "Winter Soldier Investigation." The term "Winter Soldier" is a play on words of Thomas Paine in 1776 when he spoke of the Sunshine Patriot and summertime soldiers who deserted at Valley Forge because the going was rough.

7   We who have come here to Washington have come here because we feel we have to be winter soldiers now. We could come back to this country; we could be quiet; we could hold our silence; we could not tell what went on in Vietnam, but we feel because of what threatens this country, the fact that the crimes threaten it, not reds, and not redcoats but the crimes which we are committing that threaten it, that we have to speak out.

8   I would like to talk to you a little bit about what the result is of the feelings these men carry with them after coming back from Vietnam. The country doesn't know it yet, but it has created a monster, a monster in the form of millions of men who have been taught to deal and to trade in violence, and who are given the chance to die for the biggest nothing in history; men who have returned with a sense of anger and a sense of betrayal which no one has yet grasped.

9   As a veteran and one who feels this anger, I would like to talk about it. We are angry because we feel we have been used in the worst fashion by the administration of this country.

10   In 1970 at West Point, Vice President Agnew said "some glamorize the criminal misfits of society while our best men die in Asian rice paddies to preserve the freedom which most of those misfits abuse," and this was used as a rallying point for our effort in Vietnam.

11 But for us, as boys in Asia whom the country was supposed to support, his statement is a terrible distortion from which we can only draw a very deep sense of revulsion. Hence the anger of some of the men who are here in Washington today. It is a distortion because we in no way consider ourselves the best men of this country, because those he calls misfits were standing up for us in a way that nobody else in this country dared to, because so many who have died would have returned to this country to join the misfits in their efforts to ask for an immediate withdrawal from South Vietnam, because so many of those best men have returned as quadriplegics and amputees, and they lie forgotten in Veterans' Administration hospitals in this country which fly the flag which so many have chosen as their own personal symbol. And we cannot consider ourselves America's best men when we are ashamed of and hated what we were called on to do in Southeast Asia.

12 In our opinion, and from our experience, there is nothing in South Vietnam, nothing which could happen that realistically threatens the United States of America. And to attempt to justify the loss of one American life in Vietnam, Cambodia, or Laos by linking such loss to the preservation of freedom, which those misfits supposedly abuse, is to us the height of criminal hypocrisy, and it is that kind of hypocrisy which we feel has torn this country apart.

13 We are probably much more angry than that and I don't want to go into the foreign policy aspects because I am outclassed here. I know that all of you talk about every possible alternative of getting out of Vietnam. We understand that. We know you have considered the seriousness of the aspects to the utmost level and I am not going to try to dwell on that, but I want to relate to you the feeling that many of the men who have returned to this country express because we are probably angriest about all that we were told about Vietnam and about the mystical war against communism.

14 We found that not only was it a civil war, an effort by a people who had for years been seeking their liberation from any colonial influence whatsoever, but also we found that the Vietnamese whom we had enthusiastically molded after our own image were hard put to take up the fight against the threat we were supposedly saving them from.

15 We found most people didn't even know the difference between communism and democracy. They only wanted to work in rice paddies without helicopters strafing them and bombs with napalm burning their villages and tearing their country apart. They wanted everything to do with the war, particularly with this foreign presence of the United States of America, to leave them alone in peace, and they practiced the art of survival by siding with whichever military force was present at a particular time, be it Vietcong, North Vietnamese, or American.

16   We found also that all too often American men were dying in those rice paddies for want of support from their allies. We saw first hand how money from American taxes was used for a corrupt dictatorial regime. We saw that many people in this country had a one-sided idea of who was kept free by our flag, as blacks provided the highest percentage of casualties. We saw Vietnam ravaged equally by American bombs as well as by search and destroy missions, as well as by Vietcong terrorism, and yet we listened while this country tried to blame all of the havoc on the Vietcong.

17   We rationalized destroying villages in order to save them. We saw America lose her sense of morality as she accepted very coolly a My Lai and refused to give up the image of American soldiers who hand out chocolate bars and chewing gum.

18   We learned the meaning of free fire zones, shooting anything that moves, and we watched while America placed a cheapness on the lives of orientals.

19   We watched the U.S. falsification of body counts, in fact the glorification of body counts. We listened while month after month we were told the back of the enemy was about to break. We fought using weapons against "oriental human beings," with quotation marks around that. We fought using weapons against those people which I do not believe this country would dream of using were we fighting in the European theater or let us say a nonthird-world people theater, and so we watched while men charged up hills because a general said that hill has to be taken, and after losing one platoon or two platoons they marched away to leave the high for the reoccupation by the North Vietnamese because we watched pride allow the most unimportant of battles to be blown into extravaganzas, because we couldn't lose, and we couldn't retreat, and because it didn't matter how many American bodies were lost to prove that point. And so there were Hamburger Hills and Khe Sanhs and Hill 881's and Fire Base 6's and so many others.

20   Now we are told that the men who fought there must watch quietly while American lives are lost so that we can exercise the incredible arrogance of Vietnamizing the Vietnamese.

21   Each day—[Applause.] Each day to facilitate the process by which the United States washes her hands of Vietnam someone has to give up his life so that the United States doesn't have to admit something that the entire world already knows, so that we can't say that we have made a mistake. Someone has to die so that President Nixon won't be, and these are his words, "the first President to lose a war."

22   We are asking Americans to think about that because how do you ask a man to be the last man to die in Vietnam? How do you ask a man to be the last man to die for a mistake? But we are trying to do that, and we are

doing it with thousands of rationalizations, and if you read carefully the President's last speech to the people of this country, you can see that he says, and says clearly:

But the issue, gentlemen, the issue is communism, and the question is whether or not we will leave that country to the Communists or whether or not we will try to give it hope to be a free people.

23 But the point is they are not a free people now under us. They are not a free people, and we cannot fight communism all over the world, and I think we should have learned that lesson by now.

24 But the problem of veterans goes beyond this personal problem, because you think about a poster in this country with a picture of Uncle Sam and the picture says "I want you." And a young man comes out of high school and says, "That is fine. I am going to serve my country." And he goes to Vietnam and he shoots and he kills and he does his job or maybe he doesn't kill, maybe he just goes and he comes back, and when he gets back to this country he finds that he isn't really wanted, because the largest unemployment figure in the country—it varies depending on who you get it from, the VA Administration 15 percent, various other sources 22 percent. But the largest corps of unemployed in this country are veterans of this war, and of those veterans 33 percent of the unemployed are black. That means 1 out of every 10 of the Nation's unemployed is a veteran of Vietnam.

25 The hospitals across the country won't, or can't meet their demands. It is not a question of not trying. They don't have the appropriations. A man recently died after he had a tracheotomy in California, not because of the operation but because there weren't enough personnel to clean the mucous out of his tube and he suffocated to death.

26 Another young man just died in a New York VA hospital the other day. A friend of mine was lying in a bed two beds away and tried to help him, but he couldn't. He rang a bell and there was nobody there to service that man and so he died of convulsions.

27 I understand 57 percent of all those entering the VA hospitals talk about suicide. Some 27 percent have tried, and they try because they come back to this country and they have to face what they did in Vietnam, and then they come back and find the indifference of a country that doesn't really care, that doesn't really care.

28 Suddenly we are faced with a very sickening situation in this country, because there is no moral indignation and, if there is, it comes from people who are almost exhausted by their past indignations, and I know that many of them are sitting in front of me. The country seems to have lain down and shrugged off something as serious as Laos, just as we calmly shrugged off the loss of 700,000 lives in Pakistan, the so-called greatest disaster of all times.

29   But we are here as veterans to say we think we are in the midst of the greatest disaster of all times now because they are still dying over there, and not just Americans, Vietnamese, and we are rationalizing leaving that country so that those people can go on killing each other for years to come.

30   Americans seem to have accepted the idea that the war is winding down, at least for Americans, and they have also allowed the bodies which were once used by a President for statistics to prove that we were winning that war, to be used as evidence against a man who followed orders and who interpreted those orders no differently than hundreds of other men in Vietnam.

31   We veterans can only look with amazement on the fact that this country has been unable to see there is absolutely no difference between ground troops and a helicopter crew, and yet people have accepted a differentiation fed them by the administration.

32   No ground troops are in Laos, so it is all right to kill Laotians by remote control. But believe me the helicopter crews fill the same body bags and they wreak the same kind of damage on the Vietnamese and Laotian countryside as anybody else, and the President is talking about allowing that to go on for many years to come. One can only ask if we will really be satisfied only when the troops march into Hanoi.

33   We are asking here in Washington for some action, action from the Congress of the United States of America which has the power to raise and maintain armies, and which by the Constitution also has the power to declare war.

34   We have come here, not to the President, because we believe that this body can be responsive to the will of the people, and we believe that the will of the people says that we should be out of Vietnam now.

35   We are here in Washington also to say that the problem of this war is not just a question of war and diplomacy. It is part and parcel of everything that we are trying as human beings to communicate to people in this country, the question of racism, which is rampant in the military, and so many other questions also, the use of weapons, the hypocrisy in our taking umbrage in the Geneva Conventions and using that as justification for a continuation of this war, when we are more guilty than any other body of violations of those Geneva Conventions, in the useof free fire zones, harassment interdiction fire, search and destroy missions, the bombings, the torture of prisoners, the killing of prisoners, accepted policy by many units in South Vietnam. That is what we are trying to say. It is part and parcel of everything.

36   An American Indian friend of mine who lives in the Indian Nation of Alcatraz put it to me very succinctly. He told me how as a boy on

an Indian reservation he had watched television and he used to cheer the cowboys when they came in and shot the Indians, and then suddenly one day he stopped in Vietnam and he said "My God, I am doing to these people the very same thing that was done to my people." And he stopped. And that is what we are trying to say, that we think this thing has to end.

37 We are also here to ask, and we are here to ask vehemently, where are the leaders of our country? Where is the leadership? We are here to ask where are McNamara, Rostow, Bundy, Gilpatric and so many others. Where are they now that we, the men whom they sent off to war, have returned? These are commanders who have deserted their troops, and there is no more serious crime in the law of war. The Army says they never leave their wounded.

38 The Marines say they never leave even their dead. These men have left all the casualties and retreated behind a pious shield of public rectitude. They have left the real stuff of their reputations bleaching behind them in the sun in this country.

39 Finally, this administration has done us the ultimate dishonor. They have attempted to disown us and the sacrifice we made for this country. In their blindness and fear they have tried to deny that we are veterans or that we served in Nam. We do not need their testimony. Our own scars and stumps of limbs are witnesses enough for others and for ourselves.

40 We wish that a merciful God could wipe away our own memories of that service as easily as this administration has wiped their memories of us. But all that they have done and all that they can do by this denial is to make more clear than ever our own determination to undertake one last mission, to search out and destroy the last vestige of this barbaric war, to pacify our own hearts, to conquer the hate and the fear that have driven this country these last 10 years and more, and so when, in 30 years from now, our brothers go down the street without a leg, without an arm, or a face, and small boys ask why, we will be able to say "Vietnam" and not mean a desert, not a filthy obscene memory but mean instead the place where America finally turned and where soldiers like us helped it in the turning.

41 Thank you.

Chapter 8

SPEECHES THAT INTENSIFY SOCIAL COHESION

> *Social cohesion, any social order, rests on shared values, customs, and traditions which identify us in our roles as members of a society. We are disposed accordingly to empathy, cooperation, lawful behavior, and even altruistic acts. We understand each other, for we "speak the same language," that is, we share the same values, perceptions, identifications, ideals, reactions, and rules of action. A social order is both the effect and the source of shared values and beliefs.*
>
> Ernest van den Haag

THE NATURE AND IMPORTANCE OF SPEECHES THAT INTENSIFY SOCIAL COHESION

At the heart of an social order is a set of values that constitutes the basis for all social action. In recognition of the importance of values, Chapter 5 discussed the nature of speeches that seek to establish propositions of value. However, once values have been established, the perpetuation of social order demands that these values periodically be reaffirmed and intensified. A rhetorical critic, Ronald F. Reid, reminds us: "Building and maintaining social cohesion is an ever present need; for although individuals within society are obviously not all alike, they must transcend their differences if they are to function as a viable social unit."

There are numerous occasions in our society on which speeches that intensify social cohesion are given; church services, victory celebrations, awards convocations, retirement luncheons, funeral services, nominating conventions, fund-raising rallies, sales promotion meetings, and commencements are such occasions. At moments like these, speakers address audiences about the values that both share as members of a common group. The speeches given in such moments are noncontroversial for a specific audience. They do not urge adoption of new values or rejection of old values. Rather, they seek to reinforce and revitalize existing audience values. Speakers seek unity of spirit or a reenergizing of effort or commitment; they try to inspire, to kindle enthusiasm, or to deepen feelings of awe, respect, and devotion.

Among the types of speeches that intensify social cohesion are the following:

Sermons: A sermon articulates the tenets of a faith. It is designed to inspire stronger commitment to religious beliefs and values.

Eulogies: A eulogy pays tribute to the dead. It identifies, in the life of the departed, qualities which those who remain behind should value and emulate.

Dedication Speeches: A dedication speech marks the completion of a group project. It praises group achievement and stresses the importance of the object being dedicated to future group endeavors.

Commemorative Speeches: A commemorative speech marks the anniversary of an event. It demonstrates the significance of the event in the light of present group values, beliefs, and goals.

Commencement Speeches: A commencement speech signals the completion of a course of study. It praises those being graduated and speaks to the values which should be reflected in their future lives.

Keynote Speeches: A keynote speech serves as a preface to a meeting, conference, or convention. It stresses the social worth and importance of the work to be done by those assembled.

Welcoming Speeches: A speech of welcome extends a greeting to people who are to a group. It expresses satisfaction with the presence of new members or visitors and relates the values of the group to the values of those joining or visiting the group.

Farewell Speeches: A farewell speech is given by a person who is leaving a group. The speaker usually reflects on the quality of the experiences which were shared with the group and the emotions he or she is experiencing at the moment of departure.

Presentation Speeches: A presentation speech accompanies the presentation of an award to a group member. It specifies the qualities the award is meant to symbolize and justifies the presentation of the award to the person being honored.

Nomination Speeches: A nominating speech places the name of a person before a group of voters as a candidate for an elective office. It describes the requirements of the office (abilities, personal qualities, duties, problems to be faced), praises the virtues, accomplishments, and experience of the person being nominated, and depicts the success the group will have under the leadership of the nominee if he or she is elected.

Acceptance Speeches: An acceptance speech is given by the recipient of an award or honor. In accepting an award, a speaker is expected to express

                CONTEMPORARY AMERICAN SPEECHES

gratitude and to demonstrate the personal qualities the award is intended to symbolize.

Inaugural Address: An inaugural address is given by a person as he or she is about to assume a position of leadership in a group. The speaker normally acknowledges the passing of leadership, praises past group performance and achievements, and identifies the values and goals of future group activities.

Each of these types of speeches serves a different immediate purpose. However, all share the larger social purpose of intensifying social cohesion by paying tribute to the values of the group. By nature, the speech that intensifies social cohesion invites members to reaffirm their commitment to the values, customs, and traditions that are at the heart of group life.

Students often assign less importance to this form than to informative or persuasive communication. Drawing on their past experiences with ceremonial gatherings, they conclude that speeches that intensify social cohesion are often "flowery" and trite—given more to affected *or* artificial flourishes than to substantive issues. However, sociologist Robert Bellah warns against taking this speech form lightly. He observes:

> . . . we know enough about the function of ceremonial and ritual in various societies to make us suspicious of dismissing something as unimportant because it is "only a ritual." What people say on solemn occasions need not be taken at face value, but it is often indicative of deep-seated values and commitments that are not made explicit in the course of everyday life.[1]

Careful students will recognize that ceremonial speeches often capture the essence of a social fabric. Such speeches help to illuminate the central values that undergird group traditions, procedures, and goals. In fact, many of the greatest speeches of recorded history have sought to intensify social cohesion.

CRITERIA FOR EVALUATING SPEECHES THAT INTENSIFY SOCIAL COHESION

Although one could devise discrete criteria for the evaluation of each type of speech discussed in the previous section, each type may be meaningfully considered by applying criteria common to them all.

[1]Cited in Michael Novak, *Choosing Our King: Powerful Symbols in Presidential Politics* (New York: Macmillan, 1974), p. 142.

1. Has the speaker satisfied the ceremonial purpose(s) of the gathering?

Because speeches that intensify social cohesion are usually given at ceremonial gatherings, the first question to be asked is whether the speech has satisfied the ceremonial purpose. For example, when one attends a dedication ceremony, it is expected that the speaker will praise the object being dedicated. When one attends a commencement, it is expected that the graduating seniors will be appropriately honored and advised. A welcoming ceremony calls for a tribute to both the person being welcomed and the institution extending the welcome. A presentation ceremony calls for a speech in praise of the person being awarded a tribute.

Whenever the speaker prepares a speech designed to intensify social cohesion, the audience's expectations at that moment must be considered. The Christian minister who on Easter Sunday ignores the meaning of the resurrection, the commencement speaker who ignores the graduating seniors assembled, and the eulogist who ignores or condemns the life of the departed all err in their omissions by failing to meet the ceremonial demands of the occasion. What ever their personal reasons for speaking, speakers must conform to the particular expectations of their audiences on specific occasions if their speeches are to succeed.

2. Has the speaker selected group values worthy of perpetuation?

Although the ceremonial demands of the occasion strongly constrain the speaker's behavior when seeking to intensify social cohesion, the speaker should still be held responsible for the substantive worth of the message. Because speeches that intensify social cohesion attempt to strengthen group values, the speaker should be expected to identify values worthy of esteem and perpetuation by the audience.

In applying this criterion, the enlightened listener or reader will test the values selected by the speaker. Has the eulogist selected the finer values exemplified by a person's life? Has the inaugural speaker identified the most significant and worthy values as guides for future group action? Has the commencement speaker identified relevant and meaningful values for his audience of graduates? In evaluating Douglas MacArthur's speech "Farewell to the Cadets," reprinted later in this chapter, the reader should ask, "Are 'duty, honor, country' the finer values to which a soldier should subscribe in a free society?" In evaluating Martin Luther King's speech "I Have a Dream," also reprinted later, the reader should question whether the values of creative suffering and nonviolent resistance were those most relevant and wise for the black minority in a white America in 1963.

3. *Has the speaker given impelling expression to the values selected?*

Many critics have condemned speeches of this type because they tend to reexpress the commonplace values of our social order. For example, many critics have condemned the commencement speech as a genre. Such speeches, they claim, are seldom more than dull rearticulations of established truths. Born of truisms, these speeches are infrequently more than trite reexpressions of the public mind. Although such charges are too often justified, they are not inherent indictments of the speech form. Rather, they are criticisms made valid by speakers who are incapable of giving impelling expression and redefinition to the values that bind our society together.

Because speeches that intensify social cohesion must by definition treat shared values, the speaker must exercise special skill in giving new meaning and purpose to old values. Speakers have succeeded in accomplishing this difficult task. Through incisive analysis and amplification and through vivid and compelling language, gifted speakers can succeed in gaining renewed audience commitment to old values without seeming trite.

Through the process of analysis, speakers must determine the particular relevance of cherished values to contemporary events and problems. Through the process of amplification, speakers must select those anecdotes, comparisons, contrasts, descriptions, examples, restatements, and definitions that make their contemporary analyses come alive. In the process, they must also demonstrate that their analyses are appropriate to the emotions that the nature of the occasion naturally evokes—whether elation, hope, gratitude, affection, pride, sympathy, anger, hate, shame, remorse, or grief. Speakers must also select vivid and compelling language to clothe their ideas. Through such stylistic devices as metaphor, vivid imagery, alliteration, parallelism, antithesis, hyperbole, and personification, gifted speakers can find ways for language to give new excitement and meaning to old values.

CONCLUSION

Many situations call for speeches that urge audience recommitment to social values. Among the common types of speeches that intensify social cohesion are sermons, eulogies, dedication speeches, commemorative speeches, commencement speeches, keynote speeches, welcoming speeches, farewell speeches, presentation speeches, acceptance speeches, and inaugural speeches.

In evaluating speeches of this form, the critic must consider *whether the speaker has met the ceremonial purpose of the gathering, whether the speaker has selected group values worthy of perpetuation, and whether the speaker has given impelling expression to the values selected.*

For Further Reading

Allen, R. R., and McKerrow, Ray E. *The Pragmatics of Public Communication.* 2nd. ed. Kendall/Hunt Publishing Company, 1981. Chapter 7 examines ceremonial speaking and offers guidelines for building social cohesion.

Carlile, Clark S. *A Project Text for Public Speaking.* 4th ed. Harper and Row, 1981. Projects 22–28 involve a variety of speeches that aim primarily at social cohesion, including farewell, eulogy, dedication, anniversary, and nomination acceptance.

Culp, Ralph B. *Basic Types of Speeches.* Wm. C. Brown Company Publishers, 1968. Chapters 4–6 discuss a variety of speech types aiming at social cohesion.

Ehninger, Douglas, Alan Monroe, and Bruce Gronbeck. *Principles and Types of Speech Communication.* 8th ed. Scott, Foresman, 1978. Ch. 22 discusses varied types of speeches for ceremonial purposes, many of which seek social cohesion.

Ehninger, Douglas, Bruce Gronbeck, and Alan Monroe. *Principles of Speech Communication.* 8th brief ed. Scott, Foresman, 1980. Ch. 13 explores speaking for special ceremonial occasions.

King, Robert C. *Forms of Public Address.* Bobbs-Merrill, 1969. Chapters 3 and 4 examine speaking for cohesion on ceremonial and social occasions.

Perelman, Chaim, and L. Olbrechts-Tyteca. *The New Rhetoric.* Trans. John Wilkinson and Purcell Weaver. University of Notre Dame Press, 1969. pp. 47–54 discuss types of discourse that "establish a sense of communion centered around particular values recognized by the audience."

Reid, Ronald F. *The American Revolution and the Rhetoric of History.* Speech Communication Association, 1978. Ch. 3 analyzes ways in which present societal values are reinforced through appeals to noble Revolutionary forebearers and to noble Revolutionary principles.

Rosenfield, Lawrence W. "The Practical Celebration of Epideictic." In Eugene White, ed. *Rhetoric in Transition.* Pennsylvania State University Press, 1980, pp. 131–155. A scholarly reinterpretation of the nature and function of speeches in honor of excellence, speeches that acknowledge goodness, grace, and intrinsic excellence rather than merely praise achievements and accomplishments.

Rogge, Edward, and Ching, James C. *Advanced Public Speaking.* Holt, Rinehart, and Winston, 1966. Chapter 17 and 18 focus on speeches of introduction, welcome, presentation, tribute, eulogy, and farewell.

Walter, Otis M. *Speaking Intelligently.* Macmillan, 1976. Pages 185–92 examine the nature of discourse which seeks to intensify social cohesion and offer specific strategies for increasing group pride and identity.

Yeager, Willard H. *Effective Speaking for Every Occasion.* 2nd ed. Prentice-Hall, 1951. Chapters 4, 6, 8, and 9 discuss the following types of speeches: eulogies, nominations, commemorations, dedications, goodwill speeches, and inspirational speeches.

DEMOCRATIC CONVENTION KEYNOTE ADDRESS

Barbara Jordan

On July 12, 1976, Barbara Jordan, U.S. Congresswoman from Texas, delivered this nationally televised keynote address to the Democratic National Convention in New York City. A lawyer, Jordan was the first black woman elected to the Texas state senate. She came to national public prominence on July 25, 1974, with her eloquent and impassioned defense of the Constitution as a committee speaker during the televised hearings of the U.S. House of Representatives committee on President Nixon's impeachment. Her 21 minute speech at the 1976 Democratic convention followed a comparatively lackluster keynote speech by Sen. John Glenn, the astronaut hero. She was introduced via a film biography of her life and career and was greeted by the convention audience with a three minute standing ovation. In keeping with her reputation as an excellent public speaker, Jordan delivered the speech in a clear, forceful, and dramatic manner. A *New York Times* reporter (July 13, 1976, p. 24) describes the audience reaction: "Time and again, they interrupted her keynote speech with applause. And, after it was all over . . . she was brought back for a final curtain call and for the loudest ovation of all."

Clearly a political convention keynote address seeks to mold social cohesion. Typically the keynote speaker stresses the importance of the convention and the deliberations of the delegates, castigates the opposing party, praises the heritage, values, and policies of their own party, and exhorts the convention delegates and all party members to unite in a vigorous, successful campaign. A keynote speaker attempts to inspire and reenergize members by setting a theme, a tone, a *key note,* for the convention.

Throughout the speech Jordan develops the central theme of a people in search of a national community, in search of the common good. This note of cohesiveness is reflected in her choice of phrases: one nation; common spirit; common endeavor; common ties; each person do his or her part. Frequently she justifies a position or judgment as harmonious with the will or interests of "the people." She attributes to "the people" such values as common sense and generosity. (For an analysis of the socially cohesive function served by appeals to "the people" in political discourse, see Michael C. McGee, "In Search of 'The People'," *Quarterly Journal of Speech,* October 1975.)

In a major section of the speech, Jordan utilizes parallel phrasing (we believe, we are, we have) to outline the Democratic Party's concept of governing, its basic beliefs that reflect its view of human nature. She metaphorically ("bedrock") stresses the fundamental nature of these beliefs and claims that they are not negotiable. The beliefs have explicit or implicit values imbedded in them: equality (note the double antithetical phrasing of the first belief); opportunity; government of, by, and for the people; activity; innovativeness; adaptability; sacrifice for a good cause; optimism.

Note that Jordan frequently repeats words, rephrases ideas, and in vocal delivery overenunciates the pronunciation of words (gov-er-ning; hyp-o-crit-i-cal). She may have intentionally used such techniques of redundancy and emphasis to overcome the physical noise and listener inattention typical of political conventions. Some in the audience, most likely the television audience, may have felt that her attitude toward them was one of superiority, as if they were simpleminded folk who needed everything spelled out and overemphasized for comprehension.

In at least two ways, Jordan's address differs slightly from the expectations or traditions associated with political convention keynote speeches. First, she makes virtually no direct attacks on the Republicans. Her apparent attacks are implied. By metaphorically characterizing past Democratic mistakes as those "of the heart," she may be indirectly asserting calculating, devious mistakes by the Nixon Administration. By arguing that no President can veto the decision of the American people to forge a national community, she indirectly may be attacking President Ford's heavy use of the veto to block Congressional legislation.

In a second difference from tradition, she does criticize her own party, but in such a moderate way as to freshen the speech without weakening her praise of party principles or generating negative audience reaction. She admits the Democratic Party has made past mistakes, but they were in behalf of the common good and the Party was willing later to confess them. Metaphorically she underscores the point by saying that Party "deafness" to the will of the people was only temporary. Her warning that the Democratic Party at times has attempted to be "all things to all people" may be indirect criticism of Jimmy Carter who was faulted during the primaries for making that kind of appeal. As a final analytic consideration here, assess whether this warning against being "all things to all people" is to some degree inconsistent with her point earlier in the speech that the Democratic Party is an inclusive party ("Let everybody come.").

Reprinted by permission from *Vital Speeches of the Day,* August 15, 1976, pp. 645-46.

1 One hundred and forty-four years ago, members of the Democratic Party first met in convention to select a Presidential candidate. Since that time, Democrats have continued to convene once every four years and draft a party platform and nominate a Presidential candidate. And our meeting this week is a continuation of that tradition.

2 But there is something different about tonight. There is something special about tonight. What is different? What is special? I, Barbara Jordan, am a keynote speaker.

3 A lot of years passed since 1832, and during that time it would have been most unusual for any national political party to ask that a Barbara Jordan deliver a keynote address . . . but tonight here I am. And I feel that notwithstanding the past that my presence here is one additional bit of evidence that the American Dream need not forever be deferred.

4 Now that I have this grand distinction what in the world am I supposed to say?

5 I could easily spend this time praising the accomplishments of this party and attacking the Republicans but I don't choose to do that.

6 I could list the many problems which Americans have. I could list the problems which cause people to feel cynical, angry, frustrated: problems which include lack of integrity in government; the feeling that the individual no longer counts; the reality of material and spiritual poverty; the feeling that the grand American experiment is falling or has failed. I could recite these problems and then I could sit down and offer no solutions. But I don't choose to do that either.

7 The citizens of America expect more. They deserve and they want more than a recital of problems.

8 We are a people in a quandry about the present. We are a people in search of our future. We are a people in search of a national community.

9 We are a people trying not only to solve the problems of the present: unemployment, inflation . . . but we are attempting on a larger scale to fulfill the promise of America. We are attempting to fulfill our national purpose; to create and sustain a society in which all of us are equal.

10 Throughout our history, when people have looked for new ways to solve their problems, and to uphold the principles of this nation, many times they have turned to political parties. They have often turned to the Democratic Party.

11 What is it, what is it about the Democratic Party that makes it the instrument that people use when they search for ways to shape their future? Well I believe the answer to that question lies in our concept of governing. Our concept of governing is derived from our view of people. It is a concept deeply rooted in a set of beliefs firmly etched in the national conscience, of all of us.

12 Now what are these beliefs?

13 First, we believe in equality for all and privileges for none. This is a belief that each American regardless of background has equal standing in the public forum, all of us. Because we believe this idea so firmly, we are an inclusive rather than an exclusive party. Let everybody come.

14 I think it no accident that most of those emigrating to America in the 19th century identified with the Democratic Party. We are a heterogeneous party made up of Americans of diverse backgrounds.

15 We believe that the people are the source of all governmental power; that the authority of the people is to be extended, not restricted. This can be accomplished only by providing each citizen with every opportunity to participate in the management of the government. They must have that.

16 We believe that the government which represents the authority of all the people, not just one interest group, but all the people, has an obligation to actively, underscore actively, seek to remove those obstacles which would block individual achievement . . . obstacles emanating from race, sex, economic condition. The government must seek to remove them.

17 We are a party of innovation. We do not reject our traditions, but we are willing to adapt to changing circumstances, when change we must. We are willing to suffer the discomfort of change in order to achieve a better future.

18 We have a positive vision of the future founded on the belief that the gap between the promise and reality of America can one day be finally closed. We believe that.

19 This my friends, is the bedrock of our concept of governing. This is a part of the reason why Americans have turned to the Democratic Party. These are the foundations upon which a national community can be built.

20 Let's all understand that these guiding principles cannot be discarded for short-term political gains. They represent what this country is all about. They are indigenous to the American idea. And these are principles which are not negotiable.

21 In other times, I could stand here and give this kind of exposition on the beliefs of the Democratic Party and that would be enough. But today that is not enough. People want more. That is not sufficient reason for the majority of the people of this country to vote Democratic. We have made mistakes. In our haste to do all things for all people, we did not foresee the full consequences of our actions. And when the people raised their voices, we didn't hear. But our deafness was only a temporary condition, and not an irreversible condition.

22 Even as I stand here and admit that we have made mistakes I still believe that as the people of America sit in judgment on each party, they will recognize that our mistakes were mistakes of the heart. They'll recognize that.

23 And now we must look to the future. Let us heed the voice of the people and recognize their common sense. If we do not, we not only blaspheme our political heritage, we ignore the common ties that bind all Americans.

24 Many fear the future. Many are distrustful of their leaders, and believe that their voices are never heard. Many seek only to satisfy their private work wants. To satisfy private interests.

25 But this is the great danger America faces. That we will cease to be one nation and become instead a collection of interest groups: city against suburb, region against region, individual against individual. Each seeking to satisfy private wants.

26 If that happens, who then will speak for America?

27 Who then will speak for the common good?

28 This is the question which must be answered in 1976.

29 Are we to be one people bound together by common spirit sharing in a common endeavor or will we become a divided nation?

30 For all of its uncertainty, we cannot flee the future. We must not become the new puritans and reject our society. We must address and master the future together. It can be done if we restore the belief that we share a sense of national community, that we share a common national endeavor. It can be done.

31 There is no executive order; there is no law that can require the American people to form a national community. This we must do as individuals and if we do it as individuals, there is no President of the United States who can veto that decision.

32 As a first step, we must restore our belief in ourselves. We are a generous people so why can't we be generous with each other? We need to take to heart the words spoken by Thomas Jefferson:

33 Let us restore to social intercourse that harmony and that affection without which liberty and even life are but dreary things.

34 A nation is formed by the willingness of each of us to share in the responsibility for upholding the common good.

35 A government is invigorated when each of us is willing to participate in shaping the future of this nation.

36 In this election year we must define the common good and begin again to shape a common good and begin again to shape a common future. Let each person do his or her part. If one citizen is unwilling to participate, all of us are going to suffer. For the American idea, though it is shared by all of us, is realized in each one of us.

37 And now, what are those of us who are elected public officials supposed to do? We call ourselves public servants but I'll tell you this: we as public servants must set an example for the rest of the nation. It is hypocritical for the public official to admonish and exhort the people to uphold the common good if we are derelict in upholding the common good. More is required of public officials than slogans and handshakes and press releases. More is required. We must hold ourselves strictly accountable. We must provide the people with a vision of the future.

38   If we promise as public officials, we must deliver. If we as public officials propose, we must produce. If we say to the American people it is time for you to be sacrificial; sacrifice. If the public official says that we (public officials) must be the first to give. We must be. And again, if we make mistakes, we must be willing to admit them. We have to do that. What we have to do is strike a balance between the idea that government should do everything and the idea, the belief, that government ought to do nothing. Strike a balance.

39   Let there be no illusions about the difficulty of forming this kind of a national community. It's tough, difficult, not easy. But a spirit of harmony will survive in America only if each of us remembers that we share a common destiny. If each of us remembers when self-interest and bitterness seem to prevail, that we share a common destiny.

40   I have confidence that we can form this kind of national community.

41   I have confidence that the Democratic Party can lead the way. I have that confidence. We cannot improve on the system of government handed down to us by the founders of the Republic, there is no way to improve upon that. But what we can do is to find new ways to implement that system and realize our destiny.

42   Now, I began this speech by commenting to you on the uniqueness of a Barbara Jordan making the keynote address. Well I am going to close my speech by quoting a Republican President and I ask you that as you listen to these words of Abraham Lincoln, relate them to the concept of a national community in which every last one of us participates: "As I would not be a slave, so I would not be a master. This expresses my idea of Democracy. Whatever differs from this, to the extent of the difference is no Democracy."

REPUBLICAN NATIONAL CONVENTION
ACCEPTANCE SPEECH

Gerald R. Ford

On August 19, 1976, in Kansas City, Missouri, President Gerald Ford delivered this nationally televised acceptance of his party's nomination for the presidency. His 36 minute speech was preceded by a 15 minute film biography of Ford. In preparation for the speech, Ford read the acceptance speeches of all Democratic and Republican nominees since 1948, supervised the synthesis of drafts of the speech prepared by advisors and speechwriters, and for over a week practiced on videotape the delivery of the speech. According to *Newsweek* (August 30, 1976), "the result was a performance of rare polish and passion for a President noted for neither." Ford's confident, smooth, vigorous delivery was a strong point of the speech. He hoped to offset his reputation as a weak, disorganized, boring campaigner.

As an aid in evaluating Ford's speech, consider the applicability of the three questions we have suggested as critical guidelines for speeches aiming primarily at social cohesion. Has the speaker satisfied the ceremonial purpose(s) of the occasion? Has the speaker selected group values worthy of perpetuation? Has the speaker given impelling expression to the values selected? Among the ceremonial expectations an audience probably would have for a nomination acceptance speech by an incumbent President would be: (1) an expression of appreciation for the honor bestowed by the convention; (2) a plea for unity within the Party after a heated primary contest; (3) a plea for united support of all Americans, whether Republican, Democrat, or Independent; (4) emphasis on basic values all citizens can rally around; and (5) reassurance that the nominee can win.

To develop his image as a confident, vigorous candidate capable of success, Ford relies on varied strategies. In the introduction he provides a fresh twist on the stereotyped pledge to wage a coast-to-coast campaign by specifying the home states of his opponents, Walter Mondale and Jimmy Carter. Early in the speech he expresses his eagerness to debate Carter face-to-face. This offer to debate was a surprise last-minute addition to the speech and not included in the advance text released to the press. Throughout the speech Ford identifies himself with the fighting image ("Give 'em hell, Harry") of President Truman (a Democrat, but from Kansas City, Missouri area). Just as Truman in 1948 attacked the "do-nothing" Republican dominated 80th Congress, Ford attacks 22 years of Democratic majority rule in Congress and the inaction of the present "vote hungry, free spending" Democratic majority in Congress ("their own Congress won't act"). Toward the end of the address, Ford mentions Truman by name, pledges a fighting and winning effort, and shares Truman's suspicion of public opinion polls and political pundits as accurate election predictors.

Values honored by most Americans are reinforced through Ford's discussion of the accomplishments of his Administration and through his list of pledges for the next four years. Note that imbedded in this discussion and list are a number of traditional American values: economic progress, fiscal responsibility, peace, national and personal security, honesty, decency, openness, trust, fairness, equal opportunity, hard work.

In two major segments of the speech, he combines parallel structure and comparison to contrast the desirable and the undesirable. First, he emphasizes his stands, the Democratic Party platform positions, and the inaction of the Democratic Congress. Second, he looks at the domestic and foreign record of his two year Administration, describing the bleak situation when he took office and much improved circumstances now. One evaluative question to consider here is, how many of the causes of improvement actually were under control of the Ford Administration?

Metaphor is a major language resource utilized by Ford. To praise Ronald Reagan and to heal intra-Party wounds, he uses military and football metaphors. Ford takes the seemingly absolute stand that there "will be no embargoes" on farm products; he metaphorically stresses the point by assuring that farmers' bounty never will be used as a "pawn" in international diplomacy. Of interest is the fact that during the later campaign, Republican Vice Presidential nominee Robert Dole condemned Jimmy Carter for apparently taking such an absolute stance against embargoes. Evaluate the clarity, appropriateness, and freshness of other metaphorical images such as "mired," "shortchanged," and "truth is the glue."

In two sections Ford uses the stylistic device of antithesis to reinforce an indirect attack on Carter by contrasting positive traits to be associated with Ford and negative characteristics supposedly associated with Carter's image: progress, not platitudes; specifics, not smiles; performance, not promises (twice); experience, not expediency; real progress instead of mysterious plans. Alliteration as a stylistic device is the repetition of the same initial letter or sound, usually a consonant, in a series of words in proximity. Often this is used to make an idea more memorable or to associate several positive or negative ideas. Assess the functions apparently served by Ford's widespread use of alliteration. One example is: peace, preserved, prosperity, pride.

Ford clearly feels that the American voter is wary of political promises and he condemns various Democratic promises. To what degree might his audience, or you, consider his approximately 19 pledges (outlined through the parallel phrasing of "we will") as similar to or different from promises? Are they realistic, such as a balanced budget by 1978? Are they specific, such as an improved "quality" of life?

Finally, note how Ford places a positive interpretation on a statistical fact that during the campaign Democrats condemned as negative. While Democrats condemned his heavy use of the Presidential veto as out of tune with needed affirmative leadership, Ford sees his 45 vetos as a virtuous index of his commitment to being economical.

Reprinted by permission from *Vital Speeches of the Day,* September, 15, 1976, pp. 706-8.

1   Mr. Chairman, delegates and alternates to this Republican Convention: I am honored by your nomination, and I accept it with pride, with gratitude, and with a total will to win a great victory for the American people. We will wage a winning campaign in every region of this country,

from the snowy banks of Minnesota to the sandy plains of Georgia. We concede not a single State. We concede not a single vote.

2   This evening I am proud to stand before this great convention as the first incumbent President since Dwight D. Eisenhower who can tell the American People: America is at peace.

3   Tonight, I can tell you straightaway this Nation is sound, this Nation is secure, this Nation is on the march to full economic recovery and a better quality of life for all Americans.

4   And I will tell you one more thing. This year the issues are on our side. I am ready, I am eager to go before the American people and debate the real issues face to face with Jimmy Carter. The American people have a right to know firsthand exactly where both of us stand.

5   I am deeply grateful to those who stood with me in winning the nomination of the party whose cause I have served all of my adult life. I respect the convictions of those who want a change in Washington. I want a change, too. After 22 long years of majority misrule, let's change the United States Congress.

6   My gratitude tonight reaches far beyond this arena to countless friends whose confidence, hard work, and unselfish support have brought me to this moment. It would be unfair to single out anyone, but may I make an exception for my wonderful family—Mike, Jack, Steve and Susan, and especially my dear wife Betty.

7   We Republicans have had some tough competition. We not only preach the virtues of competition, we practice them. But tonight we come together not on a battlefield to conclude a cease-fire, but to join forces on a training field that has conditioned us all for the rugged contest ahead.

8   Let me say this from the bottom of my heart. After the scrimmages of the past few months, it really feels good to have Ron Reagan on the same side of the line.

9   To strengthen our championship lineup, the convention has wisely chosen one of the ablest Americans as our next Vice President, Senator Bob Dole of Kansas. With his help, with your help, with the help of millions of Americans who cherish peace, who want freedom preserved, prosperity shared, and pride in America, we will win this election.

10   I speak not of a Republican victory, but a victory for the American people. You at home listening tonight, you are the people who pay the taxes and obey the laws. You are the people who make our system work. You are the people who make America what it is. It is from your ranks that I come and on your side that I stand.

11   Something wonderful happened to this country of ours the past 2 years. We all came to realize it on the Fourth of July. Together, out of years

of turmoil and tragedy, wars and riots, assassinations and wrong-doing in high places, Americans recaptured the Spirit of 1776. We saw again the pioneer vision of our revolutionary founders and our immigrant ancestors. Their vision was of free men and free women enjoying limited government and unlimited opportunity.

12 The mandate I want in 1976 is to make this vision a reality, but it will take the voices and the votes of many more Americans who are not Republicans to make that mandate binding and my mission possible.

13 I have been called an unelected President, an accidental President. We may even hear that again from the other party, despite the fact that I was welcomed and endorsed by an overwhelming majority of their elected representatives in the Congress who certified my fitness to our highest office.

14 Having become Vice President and President without expecting or seeking either, I have a special feeling toward these high offices. To me, the Presidency and the Vice Presidency were not prizes to be won, but a duty to be done.

15 So, tonight, it is not the power and the glamor of the Presidency that leads me to ask for another 4 years. It is something every hard-working American will understand—the challenge of a job well begun, but far from finished.

16 Two years ago, on August 9, 1974, I placed my hand on the Bible, which Betty held, and took the same constitutional oath that was administered to George Washington. I had faith in our people, in our institutions, and in myself.

17 "My fellow Americans," I said, "our long national nightmare is over." It was an hour in our history that troubled our minds and tore at our hearts. Anger and hatred had risen to dangerous levels, dividing friends and families. The polarization of our political order had aroused unworthy passions of reprisal and revenge. Our governmental system was closer to stalemate than at any time since Abraham Lincoln took that same oath of office.

18 Our economy was in the throes of runaway inflation, taking us head-long into the worst recession since Franklin D. Roosevelt took the same oath. On that dark day I told my fellow countrymen, "I am acutely aware that you have not elected me as your President by your ballots, so I ask you to confirm me as your President with your prayers."

19 On a marble fireplace in the White House is carved a prayer which John Adams wrote. It concludes, "May none but honest and wise men ever rule under this roof." Since I have resided in that historic house, I have tried to live by that prayer. I faced many tough problems. I probably made some mistakes, but on balance, America and Americans have made an incredible comeback since August 1974. Nobody can honestly say otherwise. And the plain truth is that the great progress we have made at home and abroad was in spite of the majority who run the Congress of the United States.

20 For 2 years I have stood for all the people against a vote-hungry, free-spending congressional majority on Capitol Hill. Fifty-five times I vetoed extravagant and unwise legislation; 45 times I made those vetoes stick. Those vetoes have saved American taxpayers billions and billions of dollars. I am against the big tax spender and for the little taxpayer.

21 I called for a permanent tax cut, coupled with spending reductions, to stimulate the economy and relieve hard-pressed middle-income taxpayers. Your personal exemption must be raised from $750 to $1,000. The other party's platform talks about tax reform, but there is one big problem—their own Congress won't act.

22 I called for reasonable constitutional restrictions on court-ordered busing of schoolchildren, but the other party's platform concedes that busing should be a last resort. But there is the same problem—their own Congress won't act.

23 I called for a major overhaul of criminal laws to crack down on crime and illegal drugs. The other party's platform deplores America's $90 billion cost of crime. There is the problem again—their own Congress won't act.

24 The other party's platform talks about a strong defense. Now, here is the other side of the problem—their own Congress did act. They slashed $50 billion from our national defense needs in the last 10 years.

25 My friends, Washington is not the problem, their Congress is the problem.

26 You know, the President of the United States is not a magician who can wave a wand or sign a paper that will instantly end a war, cure a recession, or make bureaucracy disappear. A President has immense powers under the Constitution, but all of them ultimately come from the American people and their mandate to him.

27 That is why, tonight, I turn to the American people and ask not only for your prayers, but also for your strength and your support, for your voice and for your vote. I come before you with a 2-year record of performance, without your mandate. I offer you a 4-year pledge of greater performance with your mandate.

28 As Governor Al Smith used to say, "Let's look at the record." Two years ago, inflation was 12 percent. Sales were off. Plants were shut down. Thousands were being laid off every week. Fear of the future was throttling down our economy and threatening millions of families.

29 Let's look at the record since August 1974. Inflation has been cut in half. Payrolls are up. Profits are up. Production is up. Purchases are up. Since the recession was turned around almost 4 million of our fellow

Americans have found new jobs or got their old jobs back. This year, more men and women have jobs than ever before in the history of the United States. Confidence has returned and we are in the full surge of sound recovery to steady prosperity.

30   Two years ago America was mired in withdrawal from Southeast Asia. A decade of Congresses had shortchanged our global defenses and threatened our strategic posture. Mounting tension between Israel and the Arab nations made another war seem inevitable. The whole world watched and wondered where America was going. Did we in our domestic turmoil have the will, the stamina, and the unity to stand up for freedom?

31   Look at the record since August, 2 years ago. Today, America is at peace and seeks peace for all nations. Not a single American is at war anywhere on the face of this Earth tonight.

32   Our ties with Western Europe and Japan, economic as well as military, were never stronger. Our relations with Eastern Europe, the Soviet Union, and mainland China are firm, vigilant, and forward-looking. Policies I have initiated offer sound progress for the peoples of the Pacific, Africa, and Latin America. Israel and Egypt, both trusting the United States, have taken an historic step that promises an eventual just settlement for the whole Middle East.

33   The world now respects America's policy of peace through strength. The United States is again the confident leader of the free world. Nobody questions our dedication to peace, but nobody doubts our willingness to use our strength when our vital interests are at stake, and we will.

34   I called for an up-to-date, powerful Army, Navy, Air Force, and Marines that will keep America secure for decades. A strong military posture is always the best insurance for peace. But America's strength has never rested on arms alone. It is rooted in our mutual commitment of our citizens and leaders in the highest standards of ethics and morality and in the spiritual renewal which our Nation is undergoing right now.

35   Two years ago, people's confidence in their highest officials, to whom they had overwhelmingly entrusted power, had twice been shattered. Losing faith in the word of their elected leaders, Americans lost some of their own faith in themselves.

36   Again, let's look at the record since August 1974. From the start, my administration has been open, candid, forthright. While my entire public and private life was under searching examination for the Vice Presidency, I reaffirmed my life-long conviction that truth is the glue that holds government together—not only government but civilization, itself. I have demanded honesty, decency, and personal integrity from everybody in the executive branch of the Government. The House and Senate have the same duty.

37   The American people will not accept a double standard in the United States Congress. Those who make our laws today must not debase the reputation of our great legislative bodies that have given us such giants as Daniel Webster, Henry Clay, Sam Rayburn, and Robert A. Taft. Whether in the Nation's Capital, the State capital, or city hall, private morality and public trust must go together.

38   From August of 1974 to August of 1976, the record shows steady progress upward toward prosperity, peace, and public trust. My record is one of progress, not platitudes. My record is one of specifics, not smiles. My record is one of performance, not promises. It is a record I am proud to run on. It is a record the American people—Democrats, Independents, and Republicans alike—will support on November 2.

39   For the next 4 years I pledge to you that I will hold to the steady course we have begun. But I have no intention of standing on the record alone. We will continue winning the fight against inflation. We will go on reducing the dead weight and impudence of bureaucracy.

40   We will submit a balanced budget by 1978. We will improve the quality of life at work, at play, and in our homes and in our neighborhoods. We will not abandon our cities. We will encourage urban programs which assure safety in the streets, create healthy environments, and restore neighborhood pride.

41   We will return control of our children's education to parents and local school authorities. We will make sure that the party of Lincoln remains the party of equal rights. We will create a tax structure that is fair for all our citizens, one that preserves the continuity of the family home, the family farm, and the family business.

42   We will ensure the integrity of the social security system and improve Medicare so that our older citizens can enjoy the health and the happiness that they have earned. There is no reason they should have to go broke just to get well.

43   We will make sure that this rich Nation does not neglect citizens who are less fortunate, but provides for their needs with compassion and with dignity. We will reduce the growth and the cost of government and allow individual breadwinners and businesses to keep more of the money that they earn.

44   We will create a climate in which our economy will provide a meaningful job for everyone who wants to work and a decent standard of life for all Americans. We will ensure that all of our young people have a better chance in life than we had, an education they can use, and a career they can be proud of.

45   We will carry out a farm policy that assures a fair market price for the farmer, encourages full production, leads to record exports, and eases the hunger within the human family. We will never use the bounty of America's farmers as a pawn in international diplomacy. There will be no embargoes.

46 We will continue our strong leadership to bring peace, justice, and economic progress where there is turmoil, especially in the Middle East. We will build a safer and saner world through patient negotiations and dependable arms agreements which reduce the danger of conflict and horror of thermonuclear war. While I am President, we will not return to a collision course that could reduce civilization to ashes.

47 We will build an America where people feel rich in spirit as well as in worldly goods. We will build an America where people feel proud about themselves and about their country.

48 We will build on performance, not promises; experience, not expediency; real progress instead of mysterious plans to be revealed in some dim and distant future.

49 The American people are wise, wiser than our opponents think. They know who pays for every campaign promise. They are not afraid of the truth. We will tell them the truth.

50 From start to finish, our campaign will be credible; it will be responsible. We will come out fighting, and we will win. Yes, we have all seen the polls and the pundits who say our party is dead. I have heard that before. So did Harry Truman. I will tell you what I think. The only polls that count are the polls the American people go to on November 2.

51 And right now, I predict that the American people are going to say that night, "Jerry, you have done a good job, keep right on doing it."

52 As I try in my imagination to look into the homes where families are watching the end of this great convention, I can't tell which faces are Republicans, which are Democrats, and which are Independents. I cannot see their color or their creed. I see only Americans.

53 I see Americans who love their husbands, their wives, and their children. I see Americans who love their country for what it has been and what it must become. I see Americans who work hard, but who are willing to sacrifice all they have worked for to keep their children and their country free.

54 I see Americans who in their own quiet way pray for peace among nations and peace among themselves. We do love our neighbors, and we do forgive those who have trespassed against us.

55 I see a new generation that knows what is right and knows itself, a generation determined to preserve its ideals, its environment, our Nation, and the world.

56 My fellow Americans, I like what I see. I have no fear for the future of this great country. And as we go forward together, I promise you once more what I promised before: to uphold the Constitution, to do what is right as God gives me to see the right, and to do the very best that I can for America.

57 God helping me, I won't let you down. Thank you very much.

ADDRESS TO THE DEMOCRATIC NATIONAL CONVENTION

Edward M. Kennedy

Only a few hours after withdrawing his candidacy for the nomination for President, Ted Kennedy delivered this address to the delegates at the Democratic National Convention, August 12, 1980. For the most part, this speech easily could have served as his acceptance speech had he won the nomination instead of incumbent Jimmie Carter. In any case, weeks prior to the convention, Kennedy decided to address the delegates in behalf of his own party platform planks. In preparation, his speechwriters read memorable convention speeches, searched Reagan's record for vulnerable quotations, and wrote a fourteen page draft that Kennedy tested in part at delegate caucuses. A number of stylistic changes were contributed by Ted Sorensen, a former speechwriter for John F. Kennedy. According to *Newsweek* (August 25, 1980), this "barn-burner" address may have been "the best of his political career." "In one night, with one superb speech that was by turns graceful, rousing, poetic, and defiant, Kennedy transformed what was supposed to be a tearful last hurrah into a triumphant call to arms."

The speech fulfilled at least three major purposes for Ted Kennedy. First, he helped to unite a divided party following a tough primary campaign. He congratulates Carter as the nomination victor and he stresses his party's heritage of freely expressing differences of opinion prior to a united campaign effort. He soothes his disappointed supporters with direct words of praise for their efforts, praise cast in the form of an extended sailing metaphor. Following the speech his supporters responded with a 40 minute demonstration. To inspire united effort, he uses a quotation from Tennyson to stress dedication and persistence. Unity of effort and focus also is promoted by centering on Ronald Reagan as a target all Democrats must work together to defeat. Often using refrain and parallel structure to heighten the impact of a series of points, he shows how Reagan's own words seem to be inconsistent with Republican Party positions. And he denounces Reagan for abusing the heritage of Franklin D. Roosevelt.

In fulfilling a second purpose, Kennedy reinforces audience commitment to basic Democratic Party values and principles. He ties his "new hope" theme, reiterated at various points throughout the speech, to past Democratic themes such as the New Deal and the New Frontier. Use of parallel structure helps highlight Kennedy's vision of this new hope. He argues that although programs may change, old values and ideals will endure. Kennedy emphasizes such values as fairness, compassion, liberty, justice, and sharing of sacrifices. What other key values do you feel he stresses?

The speech helped Kennedy accomplish a third purpose, namely, keeping alive his personal hopes for future political candidacy. Note that at several points he explicitly reminds the audience of his legislative contributions on transportation and national health insurance. Both *U.S. News* (August 25, 1980) and *Newsweek* (August 25, 1980) agreed that this speech guaranteed Kennedy a continuing role as a potent political force.

Throughout Kennedy's address we find echos and adaptations of phrases previously used by noteworthy sources. To stress a commitment to fair housing for all ethnic groups, he utilizes the "house divided" idea made notable in a speech by Abraham Lincoln and originally found in the Bible (Mark, 3:25). Whereas F.D.R. said in 1936 that "this generation of Americans has a rendezvous with destiny," Kennedy observes that "each generation of Americans has a rendezvous with a different reality." In 1831 the anti-slavery publisher and agitator William Lloyd Garrison proclaimed: "I am in earnest—I will not equivocate—I will not excuse—I will not retreat a single inch; and I will be heard." Now Kennedy emphasizes personal and party support of the Equal Rights Amendment: "On this issue, we will not yield, we will not equivocate, we will not rationalize, explain, or excuse."

In addition to ones already noted, Kennedy puts to work a variety of language resources and stylistic devices to sharpen his points, make concepts clearer, and to make examples memorable. Consider what specific persuasive functions might be served by the following stylistic resources. Included in his uses of parallel structure are the following: let us pledge; to speak . . . to remember . . . to respond; and that nominee is no friend . . . ; I have listened . . . ; let us provide new hope. . . . Numerous usages of alliteration appear. Some alliterative phrases associate positive or desirable concepts: potential . . . Party . . . President; plainly, publicly, and persistently; power . . . possibilities . . . progress; carrying . . . cause . . . commitment . . . campaign. Other alliterations associate negative or undesirable concepts: prosperity . . . not be purchased by poisoning; reject . . . retreat . . . reaction; Detroit . . . debated . . . dared . . . doubt . . . dissent.

Consider to what extent Kennedy's use of metaphorical imagery might have been perceived by the audience as trite and dull, as familiar and comfortable, or as new and insightful. Note for example: heart . . . soul; awash with crocodile tears; scrap heap, unlock the doors; guiding star. Antithesis is a stylistic resource that Kennedy employs to contrast the undesirable with the desirable: long record . . . recent words; not . . . scapegoats . . . but; not to argue . . . but to affirm; not for smaller . . . or bigger . . . but better.

This speech is reprinted by permission from *Vital Speeches of the Day*, September 15, 1980, pp. 714-716.

1   Well, things worked out a little different than I thought, but let me tell you, I still love New York. My fellow Democrats and my fellow Americans: I have come here tonight not to argue for a candidacy, but to affirm a cause.

2   I am asking you to renew the commitment of the Democratic Party to economic justice. I am asking you to renew our commitment to a fair and lasting prosperity that can put America back to work.

This is the cause that brought me into the campaign and that sustained me for nine months, across a hundred thousand miles, in forty different states. We had our losses; but the pain of our defeats is far, far less than the pain of the people I have met. We have learned that it is important to take issues seriously, but never to take ourselves too seriously.

3 The serious issue before us tonight is the cause for which the Democratic Party has stood in its finest hours—the cause that keeps our party young—and makes it, in the second century of its age, the largest political party in this Republic and the longest lasting political party on this Planet.

4 Our cause has been, since the days of Thomas Jefferson, the cause of the common man—and the common woman. Our commitment has been, since the days of Andrew Jackson, to all those he called "the humble members of society—the farmers, mechanics, and laborers." On this foundation, we have defined our values, refined our policies, and refreshed our faith.

5 Now I take the unusual step of carrying the cause and the commitment of my campaign personally to our national convention. I speak out of a deep sense of urgency about the anguish and anxiety I have seen across America. I speak out of a deep belief in the ideals of the Democratic Party, and in the potential of that party and of a President to make a difference. I speak out of a deep trust in our capacity to proceed with boldness and a common vision that will feel and heal the suffering of our time—and the division of our party.

6 The economic plank of this platform on its face concerns only material things; but is also a moral issue that I raise tonight. It has taken many forms overy many years. In this campaign, and in this country that we seek to lead, the challenge in 1980 is to give our voice and our vote for these fundamental Democratic principles:

7 Let us pledge that we will never misuse unemployment, high interest rates, and human misery as false weapons against inflation.

8 Let us pledge that employment will be the first priority of our economic policy.

9 Let us pledge that there will be security for all who are now at work. Let us pledge that there will be jobs for all who are out of work—and we will not compromise on the issue of jobs.

10 These are not simplistic pledges. Simply put, they are the heart of our tradition; they have been the soul of our party across the generations. It is the glory and the greatness of our tradition to speak for those who have no voice, to remember those who are forgotten, to respond to the frustrations and fulfill the aspirations of all Americans seeking a better life in a better land.

11 We dare not forsake that tradition. We cannot let the great purposes of the Democratic Party become the bygone passages of history. We must not permit the Republicans to seize and run on the slogans of prosperity.

12 We heard the orators at their convention all trying to talk like Democrats. They proved that even Republican nominees can quote Franklin Roosevelt to their own purpose. The Grand Old Party thinks it has found a great new trick. But forty years ago, an earlier generation of Republicans attempted that same trick. And Franklin Roosevelt himself replied "Most

Republican leaders . . . have bitterly fought and blocked the forward surge of average men and women in their pursuit of happiness. Let us not be deluded that overnight those leaders have suddenly become the friends of average men and women. . . . You know, very few of us are that gullible."

13 And four years later, when the Republicans tried that trick again, Franklin Roosevelt asked: "Can the Old Guard pass itself off as the New Deal? I think not. We have all seen many marvelous stunts in the circus—but no performing elephant could turn a handspring without falling flat on its back."

14 The 1980 Republican convention was awash with crocodile tears for our economic distress but it is by their long record and not their recent words that you shall know them.

15 The same Republicans who are talking about the crisis of unemployment have nominated a man who once said—and I quote: "Unemployment insurance is a prepaid vacation plan for freeloaders." And that nominee is no friend of labor.

16 The same Republicans who are talking about the problems of the inner cities have nominated a man who said—and I quote: "I have included in my morning and evening prayers everyday the prayer that the federal government not bail out New York." And that nominee is no friend of this city and of our great urban centers.

17 The same Republicans who are talking about security for the elderly have nominated a man who said just four years ago that participation in Social Security "should be made voluntary." And that nominee is no friend of the senior citizen.

18 The same Republicans who are talking about preserving the environment have nominated a man who last year made the preposterous statement, and I quote: "Eighty percent of air pollution comes from plants and trees." And that nominee is no friend of the environment.

19 And the same Republicans who are invoking Franklin Roosevelt have nominated a man who said in 1976—and these are his exact words: "Fascism was really the basis of the New Deal." And that nominee, whose name is Ronald Reagan, has no right to quote Franklin Delano Roosevelt.

20 The great adventure which our opponents offer is a voyage into the past. Progress is our heritage, not theirs. What is right for us as Democrats is also the right way for Democrats to win.

21 The commitment I seek is not to outworn views, but to old values that will never wear out. Programs may sometimes become obsolete, but the ideal of fairness always endures. Circumstances may change, but the work of compassion must continue. It is surely correct that we cannot solve problems by throwing money at them; but it is also correct that we dare not throw our national problems onto a scrap heap of inattention and indifference. The poor

may be out of political fashion, but they are not without human needs. The middle-class may be angry, but they have not lost the dream that all Americans can advance together.

22 The demand of our people in 1980 is not for smaller government or bigger government, but for better government. Some say that government is always bad, and that spending for basic social programs is the root of our economic evils. But we reply: The present inflation and recession cost of our economy $200 billion a year. We reply: Inflation and unemployment are the biggest spenders of all.

23 The task of leadership in 1980 is not to parade scapegoats or to seek refuge in reaction but to match our power to the possibilities of progress.

24 While others talked of free enterprise, it was the Democratic Party that acted—and we ended excessive regulation in the airline and trucking industry. We restored competition to the marketplace. And I take some satisfaction that this deregulation was legislation that I sponsored and passed in the Congress of the United States.

25 As Democrats, we recognize that each generation of Americans has a rendezvous with a different reality. The answers of one generation become the questions of the next generation. But there is a guiding star in the American firmament. It is as old as the revolutionary belief that all people are created equal—and as clear as the contemporary condition of Liberty City and the South Bronx. Again and again, Democratic leaders have followed that star—and they have given new meaning to the old values of liberty and justice for all.

26 We are the party of the New Freedom, the New Deal, and the New Frontier. We have always been the party of hope. So this year, let us offer new hope—new hope to an America uncertain about the present, but unsurpassed in its potential for the future.

27 To all those who are idle in the cities and industries of America, let us provide new hope for the dignity of useful work. Democrats have always believed that a basic civil right of all Americans is the right to earn their own way. The party of the people must always be the party of full employment.

28 To all those who doubt the future of our economy, let us provide new hope for the reindustrialization of America. Let our vision reach beyond the next election or the next year to a new generation of prosperity. If we could rebuild Germany and Japan after World War II, then surely we can reindustrialize our own nation and revive our inner cities in the 1980s.

29 To all those who work hard for a living wage, let us provide new hope that the price of their employment shall not be an unsafe workplace and death at an earlier age.

30 To all those who inhabit our land, from California to the New York Island, from the Redwood Forest to the Gulfstream waters, let us provide new hope that prosperity shall not be purchased by poisoning the air, the rivers and the natural resources that are the greatest gift of this continent. We must insist that our children and grandchildren shall inherit a land which they can truly call America the beautiful.

31 To all those who seek the worth of their work and their savings taken by inflation, let us offer new hope for a stable economy. We must meet the pressures of the present by invoking the full power of government to master increasing prices. In candor, we must say that the federal budget can be balanced only by policies that bring us to a balanced prosperity of full employment and price restraint.

32 And to all those overburdened by an unfair tax structure, let us provide new hope for real tax reform. Instead of shutting down classrooms, let us shut off tax shelters.

33 Instead of cutting out school lunches, let us cut off tax subsidies for expensive business lunches that are nothing more than food stamps for the rich.

34 The tax cut of our Republican opponents takes the name of tax reform in vain. It is a wonderfully Republican idea that would redistribute income in the wrong direction. It is good news for any of you with incomes over $200,000 a year. For the few of you, it offers a pot of gold worth $14,000. But the Republican tax cut is bad news for middle income families. For the many of you, they plan a pittance of $200 a year. And that is not what the Democratic Party means when we say tax reform.

35 The vast majority of Americans cannot afford this panacea from a Republican nominee who has denounced the progressive income tax as the invention of Karl Marx. I am afraid he has confused Karl Marx with Theodore Roosevelt, the obscure Republican President who sought and fought for a tax system based on ability to pay. Theodore Roosevelt was not Karl Marx—and the Republican tax scheme is not tax reform.

36 Finally, we cannot have a fair prosperity in isolation from a fair society.

37 So I will continue to stand for national health insurance. We must not surrender to the relentless medical inflation that can bankrupt almost anyone—and that may soon break the budgets of government at every level.

38 Let us insist on real controls over what doctors and hospitals can charge. Let us resolve that the state of a family's health shall never depend on the size of a family's wealth.

39 The President, the Vice President, and the Members of Congress have a medical plan that meets their needs in full. Whenever Senators and Representatives catch a little cold, the Capitol physician will see them immediately, treat them promptly, and fill a prescription on the spot. We do not get a bill even if we ask for it. And when do you think was the last time a Member of Congress asked for a bill from the federal government?

40   I say again, as I have said before: if health insurance is good enough for the President, the Vice President, and the Congress of the United States, then it is good enough for all of you and for every family in America.

41   There were some who said we should be silent about our differences on issues during this convention. But the heritage of the Democratic Party has been a history of democracy. We fight hard because we care deeply about our principles and purposes. We did not flee this struggle. And we welcome this contrast with the empty and expedient spectacle last month in Detroit where no nomination was contested, no question was debated and no one dared to raise any doubt or dissent.

42   Democrats can be proud that we chose a different course—and a different platform.

We can be proud that our party stands for investment in safe energy instead of a nuclear future that may threaten the future itself. We must not permit the neighborhoods of America to be permanently shadowed by the fear of another Three Mile Island.

43   We can be proud that our party stands for a fair housing law to unlock the doors of discrimination once and for all. The American house will be divided against itself so long as there is prejudice against any American family buying or renting a home.

44   And we can be proud that our party stands plainly, publicly, and persistently for the ratification of the Equal Rights Amendment. Women hold their rightful place at our convention; and women must have their rightful place in the Constitution of the United States. On this issue, we will not yield, we will not equivocate, we will not rationalize, explain, or excuse. We will stand for E.R.A. and for the recognition at long last that our nation had not only founding fathers, but founding mothers as well.

45   A fair prosperity and a just society are within our vision and our grasp. We do not have every answer. There are questions not yet asked, waiting for us in the recesses of the future.

46   But of this much we can be certain, because it is the lesson of all our history:

47   Together a President and the people can make a difference. I have found that faith still alive wherever I have traveled across the land. So let us reject the counsel of retreat and the call to reaction. Let us go forward in the knowledge that history only helps those who help themselves.

48   There will be setbacks and sacrifices in the years ahead. But I am convinced that we as a people are ready to give something back to our country in return for all it has given us. Let this be our commitment: Whatever sacrifices must be made will be shared—and shared fairly. And let this be our confidence at the end of our journey and always before us shines that ideal of liberty and justice for all.

49 In closing, let me say a few words to all those I have met and all those who have supported me at this convention and across the country.

50 There were hard hours on our journey. Often we sailed against the wind, but always we kept our rudder true. There were so many of you who stayed the course and shared our hope. You gave your help; but even more, you gave your hearts. Because of you, this has been a happy campaign. You welcomed Joan and me and our family into your homes and neighborhoods, your churches, your campuses, and your union halls. When I think back on all the miles and all the months and all the memories, I think of you. I recall the poet's words, and I say: "What golden friends I had."

51 Among you, my golden friends across this land, I have listened and learned.

52 I have listened to Kenny Dubois, a glassblower in Charleston, West Virginia, who has ten children to support, but has lost his job after 35 years, just three years short of qualifying for his pension.

53 I have listened to the Trachta family, who farm in Iowa and who wonder whether they can pass the good life and the good earth on to their children.

54 I have listened to a grandmother in East Oakland, who no longer has a phone to call her grandchildren, because she gave it up to pay the rent on her small apartment.

55 I have listened to young workers out of work, to students without the tuition for college, and to families without the chance to own a home. I have seen the closed factories and the stalled assembly lines of Anderson, Indiana and South Gate, California. I have seen too many—far too many—idle men and women desperate to work. I have seen too many—far too many—working families desperate to protect the value of their wages from the ravages of inflation.

56 Yet I have also sensed a yearning for new hope among the people in every state where I have been. I felt it in their handshakes; I saw it in their faces. I shall never forget the mothers who carried children to our rallies. I shall always remember the elderly who have lived in an America of high purpose and who believe it can all happen again.

57 Tonight, in their name, I have come here to speak for them. For their sake, I ask you to stand with them. On their behalf, I ask you to restate and reaffirm the timeless truth of our party.

58 I congratulate President Carter on his victory here. I am confident that the Democratic Party will reunite on the basis of Democratic principles— and that together we will march toward a Democratic victory in 1980.

59 And someday, long after this convention, long after the signs come down, and the crowds stop cheering, and the bands stop playing, may it be said of our campaign that we kept the faith. May it be said of our party in 1980 that we found our faith again.

60 May it be said of us, both in dark passages and in bright days, in the words of Tennyson that my brothers quoted and loved—and that have special meaning for me now:

I am a part of all that I have met . . .
Tho much is taken, much abides . . .
That which we are, we are—
One equal temper of heroic hearts . . . strong in will
To strive, to seek, to find, and not to yield.

61 For me, a few hours ago, this campaign came to an end. For all those whose cares have been our concern, the work goes on, the cause endures, the hope still lives, and the dream shall never die.

FAREWELL TO THE CADETS

Douglas MacArthur

General Douglas MacArthur became a national hero during World War II as the Supreme Allied Commander in the Pacific. Perhaps his greatest moment was when he successfully returned to Manila after the Japanese early in the war had driven American forces from the Phillippines. Upon leaving Manila, MacArthur had vowed, "I shall return." At the close of the war, he commanded the Allied occupational forces in Japan, and his skillful supervision of the restoration of the Japanese nation was widely acclaimed, even by the Japanese. When President Truman ordered American forces into Korea in 1950 to stop the invasion of the South by the North, General MacArthur was again placed in command of the expedition. However, he became an outspoken critic of the administration's Korean policy, and, as a consequence, President Truman relieved General MacArthur of his command in 1951. MacArthur returned to America to a hero's welcome. He accepted an invitation to address a joint session of Congress, and his concluding remarks on the ballad of the "Old Soldier" captured the imagination of the American people. He died on April 5, 1964.

In leaving formal, active association with a group or position, persons sometimes deliver farewell speeches; at times the farewell is combined with an acceptance of an award from the group for outstanding service. In such a situation a critic could assess the ways in which the speaker satisfies various expectations probably held by audiences on such occasions. (1) Expression of gratitude for the award presented and/or for the cooperation and opportunities provided by the group. (2) Expression of sadness and other emotions on leaving the group or position. (3) Recollection of praiseworthy accomplishments or memorable events shared with the group.

(4) Praise for the group's values, principles, and goals, along with urging rededication to their continuation. (5) Discussion of the speaker's reasons for leaving; sometimes this even may mean discussion of disagreements or conflicts with superiors or others that led to the departure. (6) Description of the future in broad, sometimes vivid, outline if the group's values and efforts are perpetuated.

On May 12, 1962, General MacArthur, an honor graduate of the United States Military Academy at West Point, went there to receive the Sylvanus Thayer award for service to his nation. The Old Soldier, then 82, accepted the award and, despite failing health, made a moving and inspirational farewell speech to the cadets of the academy, an institution he had served earlier as superintendent. He sought to reinforce and defend the cadets' commitment to the values of "duty, honor, country," the motto inscribed on the academy coat of arms. Although MacArthur originally was gifted with an exceptionally rich and resonant voice, it was now hoarse and often faint. He spoke slowly and deliberately, gaining intensity with phrases such as "faint bugles blowing reveille" and "the strange, mournful mutter of the battlefield."

MacArthur had employed many of the key ideas and vivid phrases in this speech repeatedly in varied contexts in earlier speeches throughout his career. And parts of the two paragraphs (9, 25) were derived, without acknowledging the sources, from the previously published words of other people.[1] Although his powers of rhetorical invention might be criticized as being limited, an ability to combine rhetorical elements for moving impact nevertheless is reflected in this address.

As you analyze this speech, you should focus upon several important rhetorical factors. The first is credibility of source. MacArthur, a legendary war hero, doubtlessly enjoyed high ethos with the cadets. Moreover, the text of the speech reveals that MacArthur was fully aware of ethos factors. Second, MacArthur was a conscious speech stylist, a fact readily apparent in this address; imagery, metaphor, antithesis, parallelism, and elegance of language are pronounced. Do any of his images seem strained, or are any of his metaphors mixed? Third, note his strategy of linking "duty, honor, country" with desirable consequences (paragraphs 7-10) and with valiant men (11-18). And in paragraph 6 he promotes these values by asserting that blameworthy men consistently downgrade them. Finally, to what higher values does MacArthur relate "duty, honor, country" in order to defend the worth of the cadets' motto?

This speech was taken from a recording of the address and is printed by permission of the MacArthur Memorial Foundation.

1 As I was leaving the hotel this morning, a doorman asked me, "Where are you bound for, General?" And when I replied, "West Point," he remarked, "Beautiful place. Have you ever been there before?"

---

[1]Stephen Robb, "Pre-Inventional Criticism: The Speaking of Douglas MacArthur," in G.P. Mohrmann et al., eds., *Explorations in Rhetorical Criticism* (University Park: Pennsylvania State University Press, 1973), pp. 178-90.

2 No human being could fail to be deeply moved by such a tribute as this, coming from a profession I have served so long and a people I have loved so well.

3 It fills me with an emotion I cannot express. But this award is not intended primarily to honor a personality, but to symbolize a great moral code—the code of conduct and chivalry of those who guard this beloved land of culture and ancient descent. That is the animation of this medallion. For all eyes and for all time it is an expression of the ethics of the American soldier. That I should be integrated in this way with so noble an ideal arouses a sense of pride and yet of humility, which will be with me always.

4 Duty, honor, country: those three hallowed words reverently dicate what you want to be, what you can be, what you will be. They are your rallying points to build courage when courage seems to fail, to regain faith when there seems to be little cause for faith, to create hope when hope becomes forlorn.

5 Unhappily, I possess neither that eloquence of diction, that poetry of imagination, nor that brilliance of metaphor to tell you all that they mean.

6 The unbelievers will say they are but words, but a slogan, but a flamboyant phrase. Every pedant, every demagogue, every cynic, every hypocrite, every troublemaker, and, I am sorry to say, some others of an entirely different character, will try to downgrade them even to the extent of mockery and ridicule.

7 But these are some of the things they do. They build your basic character. They mold you for your future roles as the custodians of the nation's defense. They make you strong enough to know when you are weak and brave enough to face yourself when you are afraid.

8 They teach you to be proud and unbending in honest failure, but humble and gentle in success; not to substitute words for action; not to seek the path of comfort, but to face the stress and spur of difficulty and challenge; to learn to stand up in the storm, but to have compassion on those who fall; to master yourself before you seek to master others; to have a heart that is clean, a goal that is high; to learn to laugh, yet never forget how to weep; to reach into the future, yet never neglect the past; to be serious, yet never take yourself too seriously; to be modest so that you will remember the simplicity of true greatness, the open mind of true wisdom, the meekness of true strength.

9 They give you a temper of the will, a quality of the imagination, a vigor of the emotions, a freshness of the deep springs of life, a temperamental predominance of courage over timidity, of an appetite for adventure over love of ease.

10   They create in your heart the sense of wonder, the unfailing hope of what next, and the joy and inspiration of life. They teach you in this way to be an officer and a gentleman.

11   And what sort of soldiers are those you are to lead? Are they reliable? Are they brave? Are they capable of victory? Their story is known to all of you. It is the story of the American man-at-arms. My estimate of him was formed on the battlefields many, many years ago, and has never changed. I regarded him then, as I regard him now, as one of the world's noblest figures—not only as one of the finest military characters but also as one of the most stainless.

12   His name and fame are the birthright of every American citizen. In his youth and strength, his love and loyalty, he gave all that mortality can give. He needs no eulogy from me or from any other man. He has written his own history and written it in red on his enemy's breast.

13   But when I think of his patience under adversity, of his courage under fire, and his modesty in victory, I am filled with an emotion of admiration I cannot put into words. He belongs to history as furnishing one of the greatest examples of successful patriotism. He belongs to posterity as the instructor of future generations in the principles of liberty and freedom. He belongs to the present—to us—by his virtues and by his achievements.

14   In twenty campaigns, on a hundred battlefields, around a thousand campfires, I have witnessed that enduring fortitude, that patriotic self-abnegation, and that invincible determination which have carved his statue in the hearts of his people.

15   From one end of the world to the other, he has drained deep the chalice of courage. As I listened to those songs, in memory's eye I could see those staggering columns of the First World War, bending under soggy packs on many a weary march, from dripping dusk to drizzling dawn, slogging ankle-deep through the mire of shell-shocked roads; to form grimly for the attack, blue-lipped, covered with sludge and mud, chilled by the wind and rain, driving home to their objective, and, for many, to the judgment seat of God.

16   I do not know the dignity of their birth, but I do know the glory of their death. They died unquestioning, uncomplaining, with faith in their hearts, and on their lips the hope that we would go on to victory.

17   Always for them: duty, honor, country. Always their blood, and sweat, and tears, as we sought the way and the light and the truth. And 20 years after, on the other side of the globe, again the filth of murky foxholes, the stench of ghostly trenches, the slime of dripping dugouts, those boiling suns of relentless heat, those torrential rains of devastating storms, the loneliness and utter desolation of jungle trails, the bitterness of long separation from those they loved and cherished, the deadly pestilence of tropical disease, the horror of stricken areas of war.

18 Their resolute and determined defense, their swift and sure attack, their indomitable purpose, their complete and decisive victory— always victory, always through the bloody haze of their last reverberating shot, the vision of gaunt, ghastly men, reverently following your password of duty, honor, country.

19 The code which those words perpetuate embraces the highest moral law and will stand the test of any ethics or philosophies ever promulgated for the uplift of mankind. Its requirements are for the things that are right and its restraints are from the things that are wrong. The soldier, above all other men, is required to practice the greatest act of religious training—sacrifice. In battle and in the face of danger and death he discloses those divine attributes which his Maker gave when he created man in his own image. No physical courage and no brute instinct can take the place of the divine help, which alone can sustain him. However horrible the incidents of war may be, the soldier who is called upon to offer and to give his life for his country is the noblest development of mankind.

20 You now face a new world, a world of change. The thrust into outer space of the satellite spheres and missiles marks a beginning of another epoch in the long story of mankind. In the five-or-more billions of years the scientists tell us it has taken to form the earth, in the three-or-more billion years of development of the human race, there has never been a more abrupt or staggering evolution.

21 We deal now, not with things of this world alone, but with the illimitable distances and as yet unfathomed mysteries of the universe. We are reaching out for a new and boundless frontier. We speak in strange terms of harnessing the cosmic energy; of making winds and tides work for us; of creating synthetic materials to supplement or even replace our old standard basics; to purify sea water for our drink; of mining ocean floors for new fields of wealth and food; of disease preventatives to expand life into the hundreds of years; of controlling the weather for a more equitable distribution of heat and cold, of rain and shine; of space ships to the moon; of the primary target in war no longer limited to the armed forces of an enemy, but instead to include his civil populations; of ultimate conflict between a united human race and the sinister forces of some other planetary galaxy; of such dreams and fantasies as to make life the most exciting of all times.

22 And through all this welter of change and development your mission remains fixed, determined, inviolable. It is to win our wars. Everything else in your professional career is but corollary to this vital dedication. All other public purposes, all other public projects, all other public needs, great or small, will find others for their accomplishments; but you are the ones who are trained to fight.

23   Yours is the profession of arms, the will to win, the sure knowledge that in war there is no substitute for victory, that if you lose the nation will be destroyed, that the very obsession of your public service must be duty, honor, country.

24   Others will debate the controversial issues, national and international, which divide men's minds. But serene, calm, aloof, you stand as the nation's war guardians, as its lifeguard from the raging tides of international conflict, as its gladiator in the arena of battle. For a century-and-a-half you have defended, guarded, and protected its hallowed traditions of liberty and freedom, of right and justice.

25   Let civilian voices argue the merits or demerits of our processes of government: whether our strength is being sapped by deficit financing indulged in too long; by federal paternalism grown too mighty; by power groups grown too arrogant; by politics grown too corrupt; by crime grown too rampant; by morals grown too low; by taxes grown too high; by extremists grown too violent; whether our personal liberties are as firm and complete as they should be.

26   These great national problems are not for your professional participation or military solution. Your guidepost stands out like a tenfold beacon in the night: duty, honor, country.

27   You are the leaven which binds together the entire fabric of our national system of defense. From your ranks come the great captains who hold the nation's destiny in their hands the moment the war tocsin sounds.

28   The long, gray line has never failed us. Were you to do so, a million ghosts in olive drab, in brown khaki, in blue and gray, would rise from their white crosses, thundering those magic words: duty, honor, country.

29   This does not mean that you are warmongers. On the contrary, the soldier above all other people prays for peace, for he must suffer and bear the deepest wounds and scars of war. But always in our ears ring the ominous words of Plato, that wisest of all philosophers: "Only the dead have seen the end of war."

30   The shadows are lengthening for me. The twilight is here. My days of old have vanished—tone and tints. They have gone glimmering through the dreams of things that were. Their memory is one of wondrous beauty watered by tears and coaxed and caressed by the smiles of yesterday. I listen vainly, but with thirsty ear, for the witching melody of faint bugles blowing reveille, of far drums beating the long roll.

31   In my dreams I hear again the crash of guns, the rattle of musketry, the strange, mournful mutter of the battlefield. But in the evening of my memory always I come back to West Point. Always there echoes and reechoes: duty, honor, country.

32 Today marks my final roll call with you. But I want you to know that when I cross the river, my last conscious thoughts will be of the Corps, and the Corps, and the Corps.

33 I bid you farewell.

THE TRADE UNION MOVEMENT

George Meany

At age 85, on November 15, 1979, George Meany delivered this farewell address to 1000 delegates at the 13th Biennial Convention of the AFL-CIO in Washington, D.C. The speech marked the end of 24 years of service as the first and only president of this labor union. According to *Newsweek* (November 26, 1979), although Meany was suffering from a number of physical ailments that made his body gaunt and his once ruddy face yellowish, and although he spoke seated in a wheelchair, nevertheless he "managed to look and sound like a bulldog."

In our headnote introducing Douglas MacArthur's speech to the West Point cadets, we outlined six general expectations that audiences typically have for a farewell speech. This framework could be used as one perspective for evaluating Meany's address. For example, at a number of points he recounts the praiseworthy past and present accomplishments of united union efforts (par. 8-9, 16-19). Also, he urges rededication to the union's praiseworthy values, principles, and goals (6, 12, 14, 25-28). Note how he uses metaphorical imagery to sharpen vividness as he exhorts rededication (6, 14, 27). Quite naturally, he stresses the fundamental union value of unity (4, 20, 22). The unity appeal is reinforced with a metaphor familiar to union members (21).

Meany depicts the bright and honorable future to be had if the union's values and past efforts are perpetuated (10-11). In the conclusion of the speech (29-34), with his voice breaking with emotion, Meany expresses gratitude for the high honor of serving as their leader and for the cooperation and opportunities provided by the union.

This speech is reprinted with permission from *Vital Speeches of the Day*, January 1, 1980, pp. 164-166.

1 Today is the last time I will have the honor of opening a convention of the AFL-CIO. By coincidence it is also an historic anniversary for the American trade union movement.

2 Ninety-eight years ago on this day—in Pittsburgh, Pennsylvania— 107 trade unionists established the first, continuing national trade union center in this country. The AFL-CIO is its direct descendant.

3 On November 15, 1881 the Federation of Organized Trades and Labor Unions was born for one simple reason—the unions of that day knew—as we know—that in unity there is strength.

4 Of course, there were many trade unions, assemblies and councils in many cities, even national and international unions in existence in 1881. They had already made many important gains. But the founders of this great movement knew that much more could be accomplished through a combination of all those organizations.

5 So they organized and adopted a charter to "promote the general welfare of the industrial classes and secure that justice which isolated and separated trade and labor unions can never fully command."

6 Each succeeding generation of trade unions has given that charter life and breath. It has been a torch handed down from generation to generation—sometimes flickering, but never dimmed. It is now our responsibility—individually and collectively—to preserve that charter, to give it life and meaning in our time and to pass it, intact and shining, to those who follow us; to carry that torch high, with pride, with honor.

7 Despite what some of my friends in the media may believe, I did not attend that convention in 1881. But I have read the proceedings and I believe Gompers, Foster, Leffingwell and all the courageous founders of our movement would look with favor upon the stewardship of their successors.

8 Examine, if you will, their first platform. They determined to fight for compulsory free public education, an end to child labor, achievement of the 8-hour day, protection against garnishment, apprenticeship laws, payment of wages in legal tender, repeal of conspiracy laws, creation of a national bureau of labor statistics, workers' compensation, use of the ballot to elect friendly legislators. The trade union movement has achieved all these and more.

9 With equal vision, succeeding generations have extended the platform. They sought social security, unemployment insurance, civil rights, health care for the elderly and the poverty-stricken, minimum wage, occupational safety and health, pensions, a national labor relations act, food stamps, and much much more. And they achieved those goals as well.

10 And true to our mission to expand the frontiers of human progress, this generation of trade unionists has an agenda of platform items as yet unfulfilled—national health insurance, full employment, equal rights for women, labor law reform, to name but a few. And we recognize the constant need to refine and improve and protect those programs already enacted.

11 Labor's agenda and labor's platform are the issues of human concern. Labor's goals are economic and social justice and because human beings are fallible, achieving those goals requires ever new horizons and commands all of our energy.

12   To achieve those goals, the labor movement cannot be content with defending the status quo, or reliving past glories. We must constantly look to the future, develop new leadership, adapt policies to changing conditions and new technologies—but—always, always—with unswerving loyalty to the mission of the trade union movement as the instrument for improving and enhancing the working and living conditions of those who work for wages.

13   Two years from today I expect the AFL-CIO will be celebrating, in some form or other, the centennial of the American labor movement.

14   Because I know so well the calibre of the leaders of this movement, I am sure they will not be content to say smugly, "We've come a long way." Rather, I am confident, they will use that centennial as a launching pad for new campaigns to improve further the conditions of work and life in this land. For the quest for social and economic justice is never ending.

15   As I leave this office, I am happy and proud to report that the instrument workers created 98 years ago is alive and well and ready to do battle with any foe who would destroy it.

16   It is growing. Despite the combined effects of technology, unfair international trade policies and continued high unemployment—which have created particular problems in construction, manufacturing and transportation—the traditional bases of organized labor—more workers are covered by collective bargaining agreements today than ever before in this nation's history.

17   Despite the fact that the labor laws of this nation have been sharply tilted away from protecting the rights of workers to organize and bargain collectively, the movement is growing.

18   Indeed, I am confident that the labor movement is about to embark on another period of significant growth and expansion. The growth in unionization among public workers is continuing at a strong pace—and there are significant organizing breakthroughs by unions in the service trades. White collar and professional workers are seeking organization. Farm workers are proving their strength against the most oppressive tactics used by any employers anywhere in the nation.

19   The Executive Council report for the past two years clearly demonstrates the good health of this federation. Last year in Missouri we resoundingly defeated a so-called right-to-work referendum, despite a multi-million dollar campaign waged by our enemies and despite every prediction from every politician that with all the strikes in Missouri, we couldn't win, well, we won by 300,000 votes. This year in the Congress our combined legislative operations blocked every attempt to destroy or weaken the Davis-Bacon Act. Our civil rights efforts have resulted in strengthened and renewed bonds of cooperation with the major minority and women's organizations. Our combined organizing efforts have made major breakthroughs in areas of the country traditionally hostile to unions. Our state federations blocked efforts in state legislatures to force a constitutional convention that would impose a government-busting balanced budget requirement. Every one of our headquarters departments has made continuing, provable advancements and I am proud of the record established by the department directors and their hardworking staffs.

20 Yes, the unity in the federation itself is unmatched in our history. Without exception our affiliates are involved in the activities and programs of the federation. The 24 years of merger have proven, once again, that in unity there is strength, that all workers share common interests, needs and expectations—regardless of their craft, the color of the collar they wear or any other artificial distinction.

21 This federation is the house of labor. It is well-built—ready to stand and to shelter workers long beyond the lifetime of everyone in this hall. And there are plenty of rooms in the house of labor to accommodate all organizations of workers.

22 Today the American trade union movement is vital, dynamic, growing. It is strong and unified.

23 But it needs to continue to grow, to consolidate its strength. And, I predict with certainty, it will.

24 Workers face tough days ahead. The national economy is a mess. America's energy problems are growing while the oil companies reap outrageous profits; inflation is unchecked and family budgets are wrecked; the recession is at hand and, in the bellweather housing industry, the depression is already here, yet the banks raise interest rates to the highest level in the nation's history. The shifting, changing economic policies established by the administration have, without exception, failed because they were ill-advised, ill-considered, ineffective and inequitable.

25 Obviously there is need, at this time of economic crisis, for all elements in society to demonstrate their responsibility. We in the AFL-CIO have already done so.

26 For the national accord, recently reached between the administration and the AFL-CIO, is a demonstration of labor's willingness to shoulder its share of responsibility on a broad range of national concerns. It is an accord we would have willingly negotiated with the administration a year ago, but there was no real willingness on the part of the administration to treat us as a concerned partner at that time. We intend to do our share—and more—to help develop an economic policy that is fair and workable—that divides the burden of sacrifice equally.

27 We have the integrity to live up to our end of the bargain. We also have the courage to blow the whistle if the administration fails to fulfill the obligations it has undertaken.

28 We look for deeds, not rhetoric; programs, not promises. The whole history of this movement is that our word is our bond. We shall keep our word. We expect others to keep theirs.

29 Now the time has come for me to thank you and the members you represent for the highest honor that could be paid any human being—the honor of leading this great organization of workers who have built this nation. It has been both a humbling and a tremendously rewarding experience.

30 It has given me the opportunity of knowing and working with the members of the Executive Council—past and present. Each has made significant contributions to the work of the federation. Their counsel has been wise; their support outstanding; their friendship rich and warm.

31 The officers of each affiliate and constitutional department and all of the state and local central bodies have carried out the programs and made this federation a testament to the foresight of those who gathered in Pittsburgh 98 years ago.

32 To my assistant and to the staff of the federation—both in the headquarters and the field—goes my gratitude of a job well done.

33 To you—the delegates to this convention—the representatives of the workers of America—goes my sincere appreciation for this opportunity to serve.

34 And to my God go my prayers—prayers of thanks for granting me more than one man's share of happiness and rewards, and prayers for His continued blessing on this nation and on this movement and on each of you.

35 Thank you.

I HAVE A DREAM

Martin Luther King, Jr.

Late in August 1963, more than 200,000 Negroes and whites held a peaceful demonstration in the nation's capital to focus attention on Negro demands for equality in jobs and civil rights. The marchers assembled at the Washington Monument on the morning of the 28th and filed in two columns down to the Lincoln Memorial. A little later, 10 civil-rights leaders met with President Kennedy at the White House and subsequently returned to the Lincoln Memorial, where each of them addressed the assembled throng. As measured by crowd reaction, this speech by Martin Luther King was the high point of the day. In the months prior to his assassination in April, 1968, King broadened his advocacy to include the rights of poor people of all races and ethnic groups and to condemn continued American involvement in the Vietnam War.

One way to assess this speech would be to apply the criteria suggested at the start of this chapter for evaluating speeches that itensify social cohesion. Has the speech satisfied the ceremonial purpose(s) of the gathering? Has the speaker selected group values worthy of perpetuation? Has the speaker given impelling expression to the values selected? Or this speech might be examined as a particular type of social cohesion speech, namely a *rally speech* that arouses enthusiasm for tasks ahead through uplifting sagging spirits and through deepening of commitments. Rally speeches occur on various occasions, such as keynote addresses at political and professional conventions, sales promotion speeches at meetings of company sales personnel, and speeches to civic action groups. Speakers at rallies typically might utilize some combination of the following approaches. (1) Stress the importance, the value, of the work the group has been doing. (2) Promote group self-confidence by praising their past success, dedication and sacrifice and by praising their basic values, principles and goals. (3) Outline the tasks, opportunities, and challenges ahead. (4) Use vivid imagery and emotionally stimulating language to paint word pictures of the better future achievable through united, sustained group effort.

In this speech, King urges rededication to the black non-violent civil rights movement and reinforces values central to his view of that movement: courage, faith, hope, freedom, justice, equality, non-violence, sacrifice, dignity, and discipline. He sees these values as rooted in the traditional American Dream. Early in the speech, King balances pleas for non-violence and for cooperation between blacks and whites with a strong sense of urgency to achieve results. Perhaps to blunt the charges of gradualism and over-moderation made by some black leaders such as Malcom X, King stresses the "fierce urgency of now."

King's audience on this occasion would have attributed to him a very high level of ethos, a very positive degree of speaker credibility. His followers saw him as an expert, trustworthy, dynamic leader of their movement. In the speech and setting themselves, echos of Abraham Lincoln further reinforce his high ethos with this particular audience. As the Lincoln Memorial provides the physical setting, echos of the Gettysburg Address come through the structure of the speech (past, present, future) and in paragraphs one and seven.

King utilizes varied language resources to lend power, motivation, and inspiration to his message. Consider where, for what possible functions, and how effectively he uses such stylistic devices as repetition, parallelism, and refrain. Consider especially the "I have a dream" and "Let freedom ring" passages. In the same manner, examine his use of antithetical phrasing, including "meeting physical force with soul force," "heat of oppression . . . oasis of freedom and justice," and "jangling discords . . . beautiful symphony." How appropriate to the occasion and to King as a Southern Baptist minister was his frequent use of imagery, paraphrases, and direct quotations from the Bible? Finally, assess his heavy use of metaphors throughout the speech. Would the audience probably experience them as natural to the topic, as artificial, as fresh and stimulating, as trite and dull, or as familiar and reassuring? What functions might have been served by particular metaphors? Note especially the early extended metaphor (figurative analogy) of cashing a check.

1 I am happy to join with you today in what will go down in history as the greatest demonstration for freedom in the history of our nation.

2 Five score years ago, a great American, in whose symbolic shadow we stand today, signed the Emancipation Proclamation. This momentous decree came as a great beacon light of hope to millions of Negro slaves, who had been seared in the flames of withering injustice. It came as a joyous daybreak to end the long night of their captivity.

3 But one hundred years later, the Negro is still not free. One hundred years later, the life of the Negro is still sadly crippled by the manacles of segregation and the chains of discrimination. One hundred years later, the Negro lives on a lonely island of poverty in the midst of a vast ocean of material prosperity. One hundred years later, the Negro is still languished in the corners of American society and finds himself an exile in his own land. So we have come here today to dramatize a shameful condition.

4 In a sense we've come to our nation's Capitol to cash a check. When the architects of our republic wrote the magnificent words of the Constitution and the Declaration of Independence, they were signing a promissory note to which every American was to fall heir. This note was a promise that all men— yes, black men as well as white men—would be guaranteed the unalienable rights of life, liberty, and the pursuit of happiness.

5 It is obvious today that America has defaulted on this promissory note insofar as her citizens of color are concerned. Instead of honoring this sacred obligation, America has given the Negro people a bad check; a check which has come back marked "insufficient funds." But we refuse to believe that the bank of justice is bankrupt. We refuse to believe that there are insufficient funds in the great vaults of opportunity of this nation. So we've come to cash this check—a check that will give us upon demand the riches of freedom and the security of justice. We have also come to this hallowed spot to remind America of the fierce urgency of *now*. This is no time to engage in the luxury of cooling off or to take the tranquilizing drug of gradualism. *Now is the time* to make real the promises of Democracy. *Now is the time* to rise from the dark and desolate valley of segregation to the sunlight of racial justice. *Now is the time* to lift our nation from the quicksands of racial injustice to the solid rock of brotherhood. *Now is the time* to make justice a reality for all of God's children.

6 It would be fatal for the nation to overlook the urgency of the moment. This sweltering summer of the Negro's legitimate discontent will not pass until there is an invigorating autumn of freedom and equality. Nineteen sixty-three is not an end, but a beginning. Those who hope that the Negro needed to blow off steam and will now be content will have a rude awakening

if the nation returns to business as usual. There will be neither rest nor tranquility in America until the Negro is granted his citizenship rights. The whirlwinds of revolt will continue to shake the foundations of our nation until the bright day of justice emerges.

7 But there is something that I must say to my people who stand on the warm threshold which leads into the palace of justice. In the process of gaining our rightful place we must not be guilty of wrongful deeds. Let us not seek to satisfy our thirst for freedom by drinking from the cup of bitterness and hatred.

8 We must forever conduct our struggle on the high plane of dignity and discipline. We must not allow our creative protest to degenerate into physical violence. Again and again we must rise to the majestic heights of meeting physical force with soul force. The marvelous new militancy which has engulfed the Negro community must not lead us to a distrust of all white people, for many of our white brothers, as evidenced by their presence here today, have come to realize that their destiny is tied up with our destiny. And they have come to realize that their freedom is inextricably bound to our freedom. We cannot walk alone.

9 And as we walk we must make the pledge that we shall always march ahead. We cannot turn back. There are those who ask the devotees of civil rights, "When will you be satisfied?" We can never be satisfied as long as the Negro is the victim of the unspeakable horrors of police brutality. We can never be satisfied as long as our bodies, heavy with the fatigue of travel, cannot gain lodging in the motels of the highways and the hotels of the cities. We cannot be satisfied as long as the Negro's basic mobility is from a smaller ghetto to a larger one. We can never be satisfied as long as our children are stripped of their selfhood and robbed of their dignity by signs stating "For Whites Only." We cannot be satisfied as long as a Negro in Mississippi cannot vote and a Negro in New York believes he has nothing for which to vote. No, no, we are not satisfied, and we will not be satisfied until justice rolls down like waters and righteousness like a mighty stream.

10 I am not unmindful that some of you have come here out of great trials and tribulations. Some of you have come fresh from narrow jail cells. Some of you have come from areas where your quest for freedom left you battered by the storms of persecution and staggered by the winds of police brutality. You have been the veterans of creative suffering. Continue to work with the faith that unearned suffering is redemptive.

11 Go back to Mississippi, go back to Alabama, go back to South Carolina, go back to Georgia, go back to Louisiana, go back to the slums and ghettos of our Northern cities knowing that somehow this situation can and will be changed. Let us not wallow in the valley of despair.

12 I say to you today, my friends, so even though we face the difficulties of today and tomorrow, I still have a dream. It is a dream deeply rooted in the American dream

13 I have a dream that one day this nation will rise up and live out the true meaning of its creed: "We hold these truths to be self-evident; that all men are created equal."

14 I have a dream that one day on the red hills of Georgia the sons of former slaves and the sons of former slaveowners will be able to sit down together at the table of brotherhood; I have a dream—

15 That one day even the state of Mississippi, a state sweltering with the heat of injustice, sweltering with the heat of oppression, will be transformed into an oasis of freedom and justice; I have a dream—

16 That my four little children will one day live in a nation where they will not be judged by the color of their skin but by the content of their character; I have a dream today.

17 I have a dream that one day down in Alabama, with its vicious racists, with its governor having his lips dripping with the words of interposition and nullification, one day right there in Alabama little black boys and black girls will be able to join hands with little white boys and white girls as sisters and brothers; I have a dream today.

18 I have a dream that one day every valley shall be exalted, every hill and mountain shall be made low, and rough places will be made plane and crooked places will be made straight, and the glory of the Lord shall be revealed, and all flesh shall see it together.

19 This is our hope. This is the faith that I go back to the South with. With this faith we will be able to hew out of the mountain of despair a stone of hope. With this faith we will be able to transform the jangling discords of our nation into a beautiful symphony of brotherhood. With this faith we will be able to work together, to pray together, to struggle together, to go to jail together, to stand up for freedom together, knowing that we will be free one day.

20 This will be the day. . . . This will be the day when all of God's children will be able to sing with new meaning. "My country 'tis of thee, sweet land of liberty, of thee I sing. Land where my fathers died, land of the pilgrim's pride, from every mountainside, let freedom ring," and if America is to be a great nation—this must become true.

21 So let freedom ring—from the prodigious hilltops of New Hampshire, let freedom ring; from the mighty mountains of New York, let freedom ring—from the heightening Alleghenies of Pennsylvania!

22 Let freedom ring from the snowcapped Rockies of Colorado!

23 Let freedom ring from the curvaceous slopes of California!

24 But not only that; let freedom ring from Stone Mountain of Georgia!

25 Let freedom ring from Lookout Mountain of Tennessee!

26 Let freedom ring from every hill and molehill of Mississippi. From every mountainside, let freedom ring, and when this happens. . . .

27 When we allow freedom to ring, when we let it ring from every village and every hamlet, from every state and every city, we will be able to speed up that day when all of God's children, black men and white men, Jews and Gentiles, Protestants and Catholics, will be able to join hands and sing in the words of the old Negro spiritual, "Free at last! free at last! thank God almighty, we are free at last!"

INAUGURAL ADDRESS

John F. Kennedy

On January 20, 1961, the late John Fitzgerald Kennedy delivered his Presidential inaugural address to a large outdoor audience before the nation's Capitol on a cold, clear day. In contrast to his rapid-fire delivery during the campaign, Kennedy spoke slowly, giving careful emphasis to special phrases and the cadence of his prose.

An inaugural address by an American President typically reflects some now-traditional expectations and characteristics. Multiple audiences are addressed directly or indirectly: the inaugural crowd, Americans everywhere, world heads-of-state, and the people of the world. One major function is to set the general tone of the new administration. On social, economic, and military matters domestically and internationally, the President usually outlines in broad strokes some intended stances. But advocacy of specific, detailed policies and programs is not expected and abstract language may be more acceptable here than in other kinds of political discourse. A second major function is to promote social cohesion. The President seeks to heal the wounds and antagonisms of the recent political campaign, to urge reenergized commitment to central societal values and goals, and to promote a feeling of national unity. In an inaugural address, the President frequently will cite or adapt the words and wisdom of revered past Presidents and leaders. And such a speech may praise noble elements of America's heritage and applaud America's destiny. Both the introductions and conclusions of inaugural addresses typically call upon the blessings of God.

Kennedy's address demonstrates that effective style is not bombast or artificial ornament. Perhaps the most important stylistic quality of his speech is his sentence construction. Observe that his sentence length varies widely and that he employs many abstract and few concrete words. Is abstractness perhaps a natural quality of an inaugural address? What role do antithesis, parallelism, rhythm, and energy and movement play in this speech? Kennedy utilizes numerous metaphors, some rather hackneyed, but some fresh and subtle. Can you identify metaphors of each type?

The passage most frequently quoted from this speech is "Ask not what your country can do for you—ask what you can do for your country." Examine the context in which this sentence is used. Does it appear to be a natural outgrowth from the flow of ideas in the speech? Notice also phrases that echo passages in speeches by Abraham Lincoln (paragraphs 6 and 22) and by Franklin D. Roosevelt (10 and 25). Kennedy uses Biblical allusions (19 and 23) and images reflecting his Navy days in the South Pacific (20).

The text of this speech was taken from a recording of the address.

1 *Vice President Johnson, Mr. Speaker, Mr. Chief Justice, President Eisenhower, Vice President Nixon, President Truman, Reverend Clergy, Fellow Citizens:* We observe today not a victory of party but a celebration of freedom—symbolizing an end as well as a beginning—signifying renewal as well as change. For I have sworn before you and Almighty God the same solemn oath our forebears prescribed nearly a century and three quarters ago.

2 The world is very different now. For man holds in his mortal hands the power to abolish all forms of human poverty and all forms of human life. And yet the same revolutionary beliefs for which our forebears fought are still at issue around the globe—the belief that the rights of man come not from the generosity of the state but from the hand of God.

3 We dare not forget today that we are the heirs of that first revolution. Let the word go forth from this time and place, to friend and foe alike, that the torch has been passed to a new generation of Americans—born in this century, tempered by war, disciplined by a hard and bitter peace, proud of our ancient heritage—and unwilling to witness or permit the slow undoing of those human rights to which this nation has always been committed, and to which we are committed today, at home and around the world.

4 Let every nation know, whether it wishes us well or ill, that we shall pay any price, bear any burden, meet any hardship, support any friend or oppose any foe to assure the survival and the success of liberty.

5 This much we pledge—and more.

6 To those old allies whose cultural and spiritual origins we share, we pledge the loyalty of faithful friends. United, there is little we cannot do in a host of cooperative ventures. Divided, there is little we can do—for we dare not meet a powerful challenge at odds and split asunder.

7 To those new states whom we welcome to the ranks of the free, we pledge our word that one form of colonial control shall not have passed away merely to be replaced by a far more iron tyranny. We shall not always expect to find them supporting our view.

8 But we shall always hope to find them strongly supporting their own freedom—and to remember that, in the past, those who foolishly sought power by riding the back of the tiger ended up inside.

9 To those people in the huts and villages of half the globe struggling to break the bonds of mass misery, we pledge our best efforts to help them help themselves, for whatever period is required—not because the Communists may be doing it, not because we seek their votes, but because it is right. If a free society cannot help the many who are poor, it cannot save the few who are rich.

10 To our sister republics south of our border, we offer a special pledge—to convert our good words into good deeds—in a new alliance for progress—to assist free men and free governments in casting off the chains of poverty. But this peaceful revolution of hope cannot become the prey of hostile powers. Let all our neighbors know that we shall join with them to oppose aggression or subversion anywhere in the Americas. And let every other power know that this hemisphere intends to remain the master of its own house.

11 To that world assembly of sovereign states, the United Nations, our last best hope in an age where the instruments of war have far outpaced the instruments of peace, we renew our pledge of support—to prevent it from becoming merely a forum for invective—to strengthen its shield of the new and the weak—and to enlarge the area in which its writ may run.

12 Finally, to those nations who would make themselves our adversary, we offer not a pledge but a request: That both sides begin anew the quest for peace, before the dark powers of destruction unleashed by science engulf all humanity in planned or accidental self-destruction.

13 We dare not tempt them with weakness. For only when our arms are sufficient beyond doubt can we be certain beyond doubt that they will never be employed.

14 But neither can two great and powerful groups of nations take comfort from our present course—both sides overburdened by the cost of modern weapons, both rightly alarmed by the steady spread of the deadly atom, yet both racing to alter that uncertain balance of terror that stays the hand of mankind's final war.

15 So let us begin anew—remembering on both sides that civility is not a sign of weakness, and sincerity is always subject to proof. Let us never negotiate out of fear. But let us never fear to negotiate.

16 Let both sides explore what problems unite us instead of belaboring those problems which divide us.

17 Let both sides, for the first time, formulate serious and precise proposals for the inspection and control of arms—and bring the absolute power to destroy other nations under the absolute control of all nations.

18   Let both sides seek to invoke the wonders of science instead of its terrors. Together let us explore the stars, conquer the deserts, eradicate disease, tap the ocean depths and encourage the arts and commerce.

19   Let both sides unite to heed in all corners of the earth the command of Isaiah—to "undo the heavy burdens . . . [and] let the oppressed go free."

20   And if a beachhead of cooperation may push back the jungle of suspicion, let both sides join in creating a new endeavor: not a new balance of power, but a new world of law, where the strong are just and the weak secure and the peace preserved.

21   All this will not be finished in the first one hundred days. Nor will it be finished in the first one thousand days, nor in the life of this administration, nor even perhaps in our lifetime on this planet. But let us begin.

22   In your hands, my fellow citizens, more than mine, will rest the final success or failure of our course. Since this country was founded, each generation of Americans has been summoned to give testimony to its national loyalty. The graves of young Americans who answered the call to service surround the globe.

23   Now the trumpet summons us again—not as a call to bear arms, though arms we need—not as a call to battle, though embattled we are—but a call to bear the burden of a long twilight struggle, year in and year out, "rejoicing in hope, patient in tribulation"—a struggle against the common enemies of man: Tyranny, poverty, disease and war itself.

24   Can we forge against these enemies a grand and global alliance, North and South, East and West, that can assure a more fruitful life for all mankind? Will you join in that historic effort?

25   In the long history of the world, only a few generations have been granted the role of defending freedom in its hour of maximum danger.

26   I do not shrink from this responsibility—I welcome it. I do not believe that any of us would exchange places with any other people or any other generation. The energy, the faith, the devotion which we bring to this endeavor will light our country and all who serve it—and the glow from that fire can truly light the world.

27   And so, my fellow Americans: Ask not what your country can do for you—ask what you can do for your country.

28   My fellow citizens of the world: Ask not what America will do for you, but what together we can do for the freedom of man.

29   Finally, whether you are citizens of America or citizens of the world, ask of us here the same high standards of strength and sacrifice which we ask of you. With a good conscience our only sure reward, with history the final judge of our deeds, let us go forth to lead the land we love, asking His blessing and His help, but knowing that here on earth God's work must truly be our own.

INAUGURAL ADDRESS

Ronald Reagan

On January 20, 1981, Ronald Reagan delivered this twenty-minute Presidential inaugural address. According to the *New York Times* (January 20, 1981), Reagan started preparation for the speech with about 50 pages of ideas, notes, and memoranda assembled from various advisors, wrote a preliminary draft and a final draft himself, and created his own structure and phraseology. Political analyst James Reston (*New York Times*, January 21, 1981) praised Reagan for having the "gift of speech" and for presenting one of the "best inaugural speeches in recent memory."

William Safire, a political commentator and former speechwriter for President Nixon, rated the speech a 7 on a scale of 10, with Lincoln's two inaugurals and Woodrow Wilson's first meriting 10, John Kennedy's a 9, and Jimmie Carter's a 4. Safire graded the address on six elements and explained each of his judgments: structure (C); slogans (B); word choice (B); sensitivity to minorities (A); tone, or attitude toward audiences (B+ or A−); capitalization on physical setting (A). You may wish to read Safire's entire column (*New York Times*, January 22, 1981, Sec. A, p. 27) and decide to what extent you agree with Safire's evaluations. Also you could assess this speech in light of the traditional Presidential inaugural characteristics described in our introductory headnote for John Kennedy's Inaugural Address.

Clearly one of Reagan's aims is promotion of social cohesion. In varied ways he seeks to promote a spirit of national unity growing out of his overwhelming victory over President Carter. Note such uniting phrases as "all must share" and "all of us together . . . must bear the burden." Reagan also seeks to renew and reinforce audience commitment to a number of fundamental American values: determination, courage, strength, faith, hope, equality, compassion, fair play, freedom, dignity. Finally, he emphasizes the physical scene of the speech on the West Portico of the Capitol Building to stress a heritage common to all Americans (par. 67–82).

Reagan employs echos and paraphrases of speeches by previous noted Americans. To underscore the need for immediate action, in paragraph 15 Reagan captures the urgency of Franklin D. Roosevelt's words at an earlier time of economic crisis: "This nation asks for action, and action now." In echoing Lincoln, Reagan speaks of "government for, by, and of the people." A sense of realism as to the amount of time and effort needed to solve our problems appears in paragraph 17. Compare his language there to paragraph 21 in John Kennedy's inaugural. In justifying the need for military strength as the best guarantee that military force never actually will be used (par. 61), Reagan again echos Kennedy's inaugural (par. 13). What other similarities can you find between these two inaugural addresses?

As part of your analysis, consider some of the language resources and stylistic devices Reagan uses. In paragraphs 23-24 he lists examples to help us visualize the nature of "we the people." To help us visualize the consequences of the economic problems facing us, he employs vivid active verbs: distort, penalize, crush, threaten, shatter. Antithetical phrasing functions to stress the proper role of Government (35) and to preach the non-inevitability of national decline (39). Assess the quality of metaphorical imagery used by Reagan, such as beacon of hope, remove roadblocks, and reawaken the industrial giant. Finally, Reagan depicts the average American citizen as a true hero (41-44). To what degree is this comparison valid, appropriate, artificial, or strained?

This speech is reprinted by permission from *Vital Speeches of the Day,* February 15, 1981, pp. 258-260.

1   Thank you. Senator Hatfield, Mr. Chief Justice, Mr. President, Vice President Bush, Vice President Mondale, Senator Baker, Speaker O'Neill, Reverend Moomaw, and my fellow citizens:

2   To a few of us here today this is a solemn and most momentous occasion. And, yet, in the history of our nation it is a commonplace occurrence.

3   The orderly transfer of authority as called for in the Constitution routinely takes place as it has for almost two centuries and few of us stop to think how unique we really are:

4   In the eyes of many in the world, this every-four-year ceremony we accept as normal is nothing less than a miracle.

5   Mr. President, I want our fellow citizens to know how much you did to carry on this tradition.

6   By your gracious cooperation in the transition process you have shown a watching world that we are a united people pledged to maintaining a political system which guarantees individual liberty to a greater degree than any other. And I thank you and your people for all your help in maintaining the continuity which is the bulwark of our republic.

7   The business of our nation goes forward.

8   These United States are confronted with an economic affliction of great proportions.

9   We suffer from the longest and one of the worst sustained inflations in our national history. It distorts our economic decisions, penalizes thrift and crushes the struggling young and the fixed-income elderly alike. It threatens to shatter the lives of millions of our people.

10   Idle industries have cast workers into unemployment, human misery and personal indignity.

11 Those who do work are denied a fair return for their labor by a tax system which penalizes successful achievement and keeps us from maintaining full productivity.

12 But great as our tax burden is, it has not kept pace with public spending. For decades we have piled deficit upon deficit, mortgaging our future and our children's future for the temporary convenience of the present.

13 To continue this long trend is to guarantee tremendous social, cultural, political and economic upheaval.

14 You and I, as individuals, can, by borrowing, live beyond our means but for only a limited period of time. Why then should we think that collectively, as a nation, we are not bound by that same limitation?

15 We must act today in order to preserve tomorrow. And let there be no misunderstanding—we're going to begin to act beginnng today.

16 The economic ills we suffer have come upon us over several decades.

17 They will not go away in days, weeks or months, but they will go away. They will go away because we as Americans have the capacity now, as we have had in the past, to do whatever needs to be done to preserve this last and greatest bastion of freedom.

18 In this present crisis, government is not the solution to our problem; government is the problem.

19 From time to time we've been tempted to believe that society has become too complex to be managed by self-rule, that government by an elite group is superior to government for, by and of the people.

20 But if no one among us is capable of governing himself, then who among us has the capacity to govern someone else?

21 All of us together—in and out of government—must bear the burden. The solutions we week must be equitable with no one group singled out to pay a higher price.

22 We hear much of special interest groups. Well our concern must be for a special interest group that has been too long neglected.

23 It knows no sectional boundaries, or ethnic and racial divisions and it crosses political party lines. It is made up of men and women who raise our food, patrol our streets, man our mines and factories, teach our children, keep our homes and heal us when we're sick.

24 Professionals, industrialist, shopkeepers, clerks, cabbies and truck drivers. They are, in short, "We the people." This breed called Americans.

25 Well, this Administration's objective will be a healthy, vigorous, growing economy that provides equal opportunities for all Americans with no barriers born of bigotry or discrimination.

26 Putting America back to work means putting all Americans back to work. Ending inflation means freeing all Americans from the terror of runaway living costs.

27   All must share in the productive work of this "new beginning," and all must share in the bounty of a revived economy.

28   With the idealism and fair play which are the core of our system and our strength, we can have a strong, prosperous America at peace with itself and the world.

29   So as we begin, let us take inventory.

30   We are a nation that has a government—not the other way around. And this makes us special among the nations of the earth.

31   Our Government has no power except that granted it by the people. It is time to check and reverse the growth of government which shows signs of having grown beyond the consent of the governed.

32   It is my intention to curb the size and influence of the Federal establishment and to demand recognition of the distinction between the powers granted to the Federal Government and those reserved to the states or to the people.

33   All of us—all of us need to be reminded that the Federal Government did not create the states; the states created the Federal Government.

34   Now, so there will be no misunderstanding, it's not my intention to do away with government.

35   It is rather to make it work—work with us, not over us; to stand by our side, not ride on our back. Government can and must provide opportunity, not smother it; foster productivity, not stifle it.

36   If we look to the answer as to why for so many years we achieved so much, prospered as no other people on earth, it was because here in this land we unleashed the energy and individual genius of man to a greater extent than has ever been done before.

37   Freedom and the dignity of the individual have been more available and assured here than in any other place on earth. The price for this freedom at times has been high, but we have never been unwilling to pay that price.

38   It is no coincidence that our present troubles parallel and are proportionate to the intervention and intrusion in our lives that result from unnecessary and excessive growth of Government.

39   It is time for us to realize that we are too great a nation to limit ourselves to small dreams. We're not, as some would have us believe, doomed to an inevitable decline. I do not believe in a fate that will fall on us no matter what we do. I do believe in a fate that will fall on us if we do nothing.

40   So, with all the creative energy at our command let us begin an era of national renewal. Let us renew our determination, our courage and our strength. And let us renew our faith and our hope. We have every right to dream heroic dreams.

41   Those who say that we're in a time when there are no heroes—they just don't know where to look. You can see heroes every day going in and out of factory gates. Others, a handful in number, produce enough food to feed all of us and then the world beyond.

42   You meet heroes across a counter—and they're on both sides of that counter. There are entrepreneurs with faith in themselves and faith in an idea who create new jobs, new wealth and opportunity.

43   There are individuals and families whose taxes support the Government and whose voluntary gifts support church, charity, culture, art and education. Their patriotism is quiet but deep. Their values sustain our national life.

44   Now, I have used the words "they" and "their" in speaking of these heroes. I could say "you" and "your" because I'm addressing the heroes of whom I speak—you, the citizens of this blessed land.

45   Your dreams, your hopes, your goals are going to be the dreams, the hopes and the goals of this Administration, so help me God.

46   We shall reflect the compassion that is so much a part of your makeup.

47   How can we love our country and not love our countrymen? And loving them reach out a hand when they fall, heal them when they're sick and provide opportunity to make them self-sufficient so they will be equal in fact and not just in theory?

48   Can we solve the problems confronting us? Well the answer is a unequivocal and emphatic yes.

49   To paraphrase Winston Churchill, I did not take the oath I've just taken with the intention of presiding over the dissolution of the world's strongest economy.

50   In the days ahead I will propose removing the roadblocks that have slowed our economy and reduced productivity.

51   Steps will be taken aimed at restoring the balance between the various levels of government. Progress may be slow—measured in inches and feet, not miles—but we will progress.

52   It is time to reawaken this industrial giant, to get government back within its means and to lighten our punitive tax burden.

53   And these will be our first priorities, and on these principles there will be no compromise.

54   On the eve of our struggle for independence a man who might've been one of the greatest among the Founding Fathers, Dr. Joseph Warren, president of Massachusetts Congress, said to his fellow Americans, "Our country is in danger, but not to be despaired of. On you depend the fortunes of America. You are to decide the important question upon which rest the happiness and the liberty of millions yet unborn. Act worthy of yourselves."

55   Well I believe we the Americans of today are ready to act worthy of ourselves, ready to do what must be done to insure happiness and liberty for ourselves, our children and our children's children.

56 And as we renew ourselves here in our own land we will be seen as having greater strength throughout the world. We will again be the exemplar of freedom and a beacon of hope for those who do not now have freedom.

57 To those neighbors and allies who share our freedom, we will strengthen our historic ties and assure them of our support and firm commitment.

58 We will match loyalty with loyalty. We will strive for mutually beneficial relations. We will not use our friendship to impose on their sovereignty, for our own sovereignty is not for sale.

59 As for the enemies of freedom, those who are potential adversaries, they will be reminded that peace is the highest aspiration of the American people. We will negotiate for it, sacrifice for it; we will not surrender for it—now or ever.

60 Our forbearance should never be misunderstood. Our reluctance for conflict should not be misjudged as a failure of will.

61 When action is required to preserve our national security, we will act. We will maintain sufficient strength to prevail if need be, knowing that if we do we have the best chance of never having to use that strength.

62 Above all we must realize that no arsenal or no weapon in the arsenals of the world is so formidable as the will and moral courage of free men and women.

63 It is a weapon our adversaries in today's world do not have.

64 It is a weapon that we as Americans do have.

65 Let that be understood by those who practice terrorism and prey upon their neighbors.

66 I am told that tens of thousands of prayer meetings are being held on this day; for that I am deeply grateful. We are a nation under God, and I believe God intended for us to be free. It would be fitting and good, I think, if on each inaugural day in future years it should be declared a day of prayer.

67 This is the first time in our history that this ceremony has been held, as you've been told, on this West Front of the Capitol.

68 Standing here, one faces a magnificent vista, opening up on this city's special beauty and history.

69 At the end of this open mall are those shrines to the giants on whose shoulders we stand.

70 Directly in front of me, the monument to a monumental man. George Washington, father of our country. A man of humility who came to greatness reluctantly. He led America out of revolutionary victory into infant nationhood.

71 Off to one side, the stately memorial to Thomas Jefferson. The Declaration of Independence flames with his eloquence.

72   And then beyond the Reflecting Pool, the dignified columns of the Lincoln Memorial. Whoever would understand in his heart the meaning of America will find it in the life of Abraham Lincoln.

73   Beyond those moments, monuments to heroism is the Potomac River, and on the far shore the sloping hills of Arlington National Cemetery with its row upon row of simple white markers bearing crosses or Stars of David. They add up to only a tiny fraction of the price that has been paid for our freedom.

74   Each one of those markers is a monument to the kind of hero I spoke of earlier.

75   Their lives ended in places called Belleau Wood, the Argonne, Omaha Beach, Salerno and halfway around the world on Guadalcanal, Tarawa, Pork Chop Hill, the Chosin Reservoir, and in a hundred rice paddies and jungles of a place called Vietnam.

76   Under such a marker lies a young man, Martin Treptow, who left his job in a small town barber shop in 1917 to go to France with the famed Rainbow Division.

77   There, on the Western front, he was killed trying to carry a message between battalions under heavy artillery fire.

78   We are told that on his body was found a diary.

79   On the flyleaf under the heading, "My Pledge," he had written these words:

80   "America must win this war. Therefore I will work, I will save, I will sacrifice, I will endure, I will fight cheerfully and do my utmost, as if the issue of the whole struggle depended on me alone."

81   The crisis we are facing today does not require of us the kind of sacrifice that Martin Treptow and so many thousands of others were called upon to make.

82   It does require, however, our best effort, and our willingness to believe in ourselves and to believe in our capacity to perform great deeds; to believe that together with God's help we can and will resolve the problems which now confront us.

83   And after all, why shouldn't we believe that? We are Americans.

84   God bless you and thank you. Thank you very much.

SIR WINSTON CHURCHILL

Adlai E. Stevenson II

Sir Winston Churchill, statesman, author, and Prime Minister of Great Britain during World War II, died in January 1965 after a long and brilliant career. Through his leadership and his rhetorical brilliance, he managed to pull his nation through the dark days of the war. History will doubtlessly rank Churchill as one of the most eloquent orators of all time. It was therefore appropriate that Adlai E. Stevenson II, an excellent orator himself, should deliver the eulogy at the memorial services for Sir Winston Churchill at the National Cathedral in Washington, D.C., on January 28, 1956. Stevenson's distinguished career included his being Governor of Illinois, Ambassador to the United Nations, and twice the Democratic nominee for President of the United States. During his lifetime, Stevenson was called upon to deliver eulogies for other notables such as John F. Kennedy, Eleanor Roosevelt, and Dag Hammarskjold, the former Secretary General of the United Nations.

Speeches of tribute, such as testimonials for living persons and eulogies for the dead, typically reflect now rather traditional rhetorical resources to praise accomplishments and acknowledge virtues. The speaker may remind us that the person being paid tribute possesses various qualities of character, such as courage, justice, wisdom, temperance, concern for others, faith, charity, generosity, courtesy, dedication, honesty, industriousness, or humility. The speaker could describe qualities of the person's accomplishments: bravery; extreme difficulty; acknowledgment of excellence by others; personal harm incurred; a "first"; the "best"; the unexpected; the "only"; frequency of achievement; a "last" time ever. Immediate and long-term influences could be stressed, perhaps by describing the "debts" that society owes the person and how we can continue to "repay" that indebtedness through our attitudes and actions, how we can carry on the person's values and commitments. Speakers frequently emphasize the praiseworthy values, ideals, motives, and life goals held by the person. Among the kinds of rhetorical supporting materials typically used in speeches of tribute are factual examples, testimony from notables, experts, or literary sources, narration of incidents, comparison to other persons, Biblical quotations or allusions, and quotations or paraphrases of the person's own words.

By summarizing and slightly modifying the extensive research of Kathleen Jamieson, we can describe four characteristic functions of eulogies in European-American cultures.[1] First, by publicly confirming the person's death, the eulogy helps us overcome our temporary denial of the reality of the death; we overcome our initial reaction of "I just don't believe it." Second, the uneasy realization of our own eventual death is lessened by descriptions of ways in which the deceased "lives on" in history, in heaven, through good works, through followers, or through the person's family. Third, a recounting of the life and virtues of the person *in the past tense* allows

---

[1]Kathleen M. Jamieson, *Critical Anthology of Public Speeches* (Chicago: Science Research Associates, 1978), pp. 40–41.

us to reorient our own relationship with the deceased from present to past and from physical encounter to memory. Finally, by expressing community solidarity and social cohesion, the eulogy reassures us that our community or group will survive the death. To promote such social cohesion, audiences expect that the eulogist will not "speak ill of the dead," although some eulogists may mention modest "faults" in order to "humanize" the person. Sometimes the eulogist provides a rationale for the death so that we do not feel the death was in vain or due to pure chance. Such reasons might include God's will, fulfillment of destiny, evil conditions in society, or even a conspiratorial plot.

One study of four eulogies delivered by Adlai Stevenson concludes that he seemed well aware of three major purposes of the eulogistic form: (1) to express appropriate personal and audience grief; (2) to deepen appreciation and respect for the deceased; and (3) to give the audience strength for the present and inspiration for the future.[2]

Stevenson does not try to give any sort of biographical sketch of Churchill but tries to capture the true essence of the man—those factors that made Churchill great. He praises Churchill as the embodiment of courage, eloquence, and humor. These are values acknowledged by the audience and only need reinforcement. Lessons for the future are extracted from the example of Churchill's life. Numerous quotations from Churchill himself illustrate the characteristics praised. In summary fashion, the second-to-the-last paragraph catalogues Churchill's accomplishments and virtues. Stevenson stimulates in his audience the pleasurable emotions of gratitude and hope. And an intense sense of loss is metaphorically stated: "There is a lonesome place against the sky."

The text of this speech was taken from a tape recording of the address. The text also appears in the *London Times,* January 29, 1965, p. 15, and in the *Washington Post,* January 29, 1965, p. A5.

1   Today we meet in sadness to mourn one of the world's greatest citizens. Sir Winston Churchill is dead. The voice that led nations, raised armies, inspired victories and blew fresh courage into the hearts of men is silenced. We shall hear no longer the remembered eloquence and wit, the old courage and defiance, the robust serenity of indomitable faith. Our world is thus poorer, our political dialogue is diminished and the sources of public inspiration run more thinly for all of us. There is a lonesome place against the sky.

2   So we are right to mourn. Yet, in contemplating the life and the spirit of Winston Churchill, regrets for the past seem singularly insufficient. One rather feels a sense of thankfulness and of encouragement that throughout so long a life, such a full measure of power, virtuosity, mastery and zest played over our human scene.

[2]Paul C. Brownlow and Beth Davis, " 'A Certainty of Honor': The Eulogies of Adlai Stevenson," *Central States Speech Journal,* 25(Fall 1974), 217–24.

3   Contemplating this completed career, we feel a sense of enlargement and exhilaration. Like the grandeur and the power of the masterpieces of art and music, Churchill's life uplifts our hearts and fills us with fresh revelation of the scale and the reach of human achievement. We may be sad; but we rejoice as well, as all must rejoice when they "now praise famous men" and see in their lives the full splendor of our human estate.

4   And regrets for the past are insufficient for another reason. Churchill, the historian, felt the continuity of past and present, the contribution which mighty men and great events make to future experience; history's "flickering flame" lights up the past and sends its gleams into the future. So to the truth of Santayana's dictum, "Those who will not learn from the past are destined to repeat it," Churchill's whole life was witness. It was his lonely voice that in the Thirties warned Britain and Europe of the follies of playing all over again the tragedy of disbelief and of unpreparedness. And in the time of Britain's greatest trial he mobilized the English language to inspire his people to historic valor. It was his voice again that helped assemble the great coalition that has kept peace steady throughout the last decades.

5   "We cannot say the past is past without surrendering the future," he once said. So today the "past" of his life and his achievements are a guide and light to the future. And we can only properly mourn and celebrate this mighty man by heeding him as a living influence in the unfolding dramas of our time.

6   What does he tell us of this obscure future whose outlines we but dimly perceive? First, I believe, he would have us reaffirm his serene faith in human freedom and dignity. The love of freedom was not for him an abstract thing but a deep conviction that the uniqueness of man demands a society that gives his capacities full scope. It was, if you like, an aristocratic sense of the fullness and the value of life. But he was a profound democrat, and the cornerstone of his political faith, inherited from his beloved father, was the simple maxim "Trust the people." Throughout his long career, he sustained his profound concern for the well-being of his fellow citizens.

7   Instinctively, profoundly, the people trusted him, the peer's son. He could lead them in war because he had respected them in peace. He could call for their greatest sacrifices for he knew how to express their deepest dignity—citizens of equal value and responsibility in a free and democratic state.

8   His crucial part in the founding of the United Nations expressed his conviction that the Atlantic Charter so audaciously proclaimed by Roosevelt and Churchill at the height of Hitler's victories would have to be protected by institutions embodying the ideal of the rule of law and international co-operation.

9 For him, humanity, its freedom, its survival, towered above pettier interests—national rivalries, old enmities, the bitter disputes of race and creed. His words "In victory—magnanimity; in peace—good will" were more than slogans. His determination to continue in politics after his defeat in 1945 and to toil on in the 1950's to the limit of health and of endurance sprange from his belief that he could still "bring nearer that lasting peace which the masses of people of every race and in every land so fervently desire." The great soldier and strategist was first of all a man of peace—and for perhaps the most simple reason—his respect, his faith, his compassion for the family of man.

10 His career saw headlong success and headlong catastrophe. He was at the height. He was flung to the depths. He saw his worst prophecies realized, his worst forebodings surpassed. Yet throughout it all his zest for living, galantry of spirit, wry humor and compassion for human frailty took all grimness out of his fortitude and all pomposity out of his dedication.

11 Churchill's sense of the incomparable value and worth of human existence never faltered, for the robust courage with which he lived to the very full never faltered. In the darkest hour, the land could still be bright, and for him hopes were not deceivers. It was forever fear that was the dupe. Victory at last would always lie with life and faith, for Churchill saw beyond the repeated miseries of human frailty the larger vision of mankind's "upward ascent towards his distant goal."

12 He used to say that he was half American and all English. But we put that right when the Congress made him an honorary citizen of his mother's native land and we shall always claim a part of him. I remember once years ago during a long visit at his country house he talked proudly of his American Revolutionary ancestors and happily of his boyhood visits to the United States. As I took my leave I said I was going back to London to speak to the English Speaking Union and asked if he had any message for them. "Yes," he said, "tell them that you bring greetings from an English Speaking Union." And I think that perhaps it was to the relations of the United Kingdom and the United States that he made his finest contribution of all.

13 In the last analysis, all the zest and life and confidence of this incomparable man sprang, I believe, not only from the rich endowment of his nature, but also from a profound and simple faith in God. In the prime of his powers, confronted with the apocalyptic risks of annihilation, he said serenely: "I do not believe that God has despaired of his children." And in old age, as the honors and excitements faded, his resignation had a touching simplicity: "Only faith," he said, "in a life after death in a brighter world where dear ones will meet again—only that and the measured tramp of time can give consolation."

14 The great aristocrat, the beloved leader, the profound historian, the gifted painter, the superb politician, the lord of language, the orator, the wit—yes, and the dedicated bricklayer—behind all of them was the man of simple faith, steadfast in defeat, generous in victory, resigned in age, trusting in a loving providence and committing his achievements and his triumphs to a higher power.

15 Like the patriarchs of old, he waited on God's judgment and it could be said of him—as of the immortals that went before him—that God "magnified him in the fear of his enemies and with his words he made prodigies to cease. He glorified him in the sight of kings and gave him commandments in the sight of his people. He showed him his Glory and sanctified him in his faith. . . ."

Index of Rhetorical Principles

The first numbers after a term indicate page numbers; the numbers in parentheses specify paragraphs within the speeches.

Amplification

comparison: 37 (4); 86–87 (18); 96–97 (13); 147 (6); 158 (12); 164 (15); 315 (28).

contrast: 60 (6–7); 61 (9–10); 62 (12); 63 (17); 64 (18–19); 75 (13); 76–77 (17); 81 (5–6); 82 (13); 97 (14); 162 (10); 167 (31); 195–196 (26–27); 199 (43); 201 (52–53); 202 (60); 313 (14–15).

definition: 44–45 (38); 61 (9–10); 63 (17); 65 (22); 74 (13); 81 (5); 81–82 (8–10); 85 (10); 117 (15); 119 (35,39,41); 168 (35); 239 (10); 243 (23); 289 (3); 309 (3).

enumeration: 40–41 (18–21); 53–54 (50); 73 (9); 84 (4); 89–90 (37–41); 90 (43); 96 (10); 153–154 (31); 274 (9–12); 275 (16–17); 295–296 (31); 359 (21); 362 (8–10).

example: 39 (10); 42 (28); 45 (42); 52 (40); 54–55 (54–60); 63 (14); 64–65 (20); 77–78 (19); 79 (21); 90–91 (46); 99 (23); 239–240 (11–12).

historical account: 38 (7); 94–95 (5–6); 95–96 (7–9); 99–100 (27); 162 (7).

illustration: 46 (44–47); 71–72 (7); 83 (15); 83 (16); 116–117 (1–8); 121 (58–63); 148 (7); 159 (17); 201 (52); 201–202 (57); 216–217 (30–31); 217 (33); 241 (16).

personal recollection or illustration: 49 (10); 65 (21); 67 (25); 70–71 (4–5); 72–73 (8); 75–76 (15); 76 (16); 77 (18); 78–79 (20); 79 (22); 82–83 (14); 147 (6); 172 (4–7); 384 (12).

quotation: 37 (5); 38 (9); 39 (10); 39 (11); 40 (14); 41 (23); 43 (32); 45 (39); 53 (42); 55–56 (68); 62–63 (13); 81 (5); 81 (7); 82 (13); 97–98 (17); 98 (22); 159 (18); 378 (54); 383 (5); 384 (9,11,13).

repetition: 53 (47); 67 (25); 71 (5); 84 (2–3); 166 (27); 224 (35); 323 (27); 336 (16); 377 (33).

restatement: 42 (24).

statistics: 49 (8); 49 (13); 50 (24); 52 (34–36).

summary: 191 (6); 198 (37); 200 (48); 201 (53).

visual aid: 292–293 (7); 296–297 (37–39); 313 (10–12); 314 (21–22).

vivid description: 73–74 (10); 129–130 (17–20); 132 (34–35); 379–380 (68–73).

Interest Factors

allusion: 49 (12); 69 (3); 87 (22); 97 (15); 152 (18); 157 (7–8); 222 (10–11); 237 (2); 248 (1); 256–257 (6); 285 (37).

challenge: 164 (16); 235 (16).

conflict: 55 (67); 58–59 (2–3); 85 (6); 111 (3–5); 156 (1); 167 (32); 168 (37); 363 (15).

dialogue: 70–71 (5); 71–72 (7); 75 (14); 76 (16); 77 (18); 78–79 (20); 79–80 (23); 251 (22).

familiarity: 244 (27).

formula: 72–73 (8).

humor: 71–72 (7); 76–77 (17); 77–78 (19); 118 (22); 146 (3–4); 146–147 (5–6); 148 (8); 152 (20); 179 (7); 181 (13); 237 (2–3); 241–242 (17–19); 244 (27).

immediacy: 48 (4); 115 (39); 164 (18).

poetry: 355 (60).

proximity: 82 (10); 164 (18).

rhetorical question: 39 (13); 40 (18); 52 (41); 63 (16); 64 (18); 71–72 (7); 85 (7); 117 (16); 118 (30–31); 122 (74); 129 (14); 146–147 (5–6); 149 (9–10); 152 (17–18); 163 (11); 165 (25); 166 (27); 200 (49–50); 203 (62); 226 (54); 227 (61–62); 227 (66–67); 235 (20); 256–257 (5–8); 259 (21); 303 (47); 304 (53–54); 305 (62–65); 322 (22); 337 (26–29); 358 (11).

sarcasm: 50 (18); 51 (28); 55–56 (68); 70–71 (5); 115 (40); 117 (11–13); 118 (21); 118 (24–28); 147 (6); 187–188 (32); 303 (48); 322 (21).

story: 218 (43); 237 (1); 258–259 (15–16); 259 (18–19); 380 (76–80).

Organization

conclusions:

challenge: 57 (76); 189 (38).

startling statement: 80 (1); 124 (1).

statement of subject or purpose: 59–60 (5); 68–69 (1); 94 (4); 111 (8); 117 (14); 151 (9); 171 (3); 222 (12); 229 (3); 233 (6); 239 (8); 256 (4); 282 (20–21).

suspense: 84 (1); 288 (1).

patterns of development:

contrast: Reed speech, 150ff.

problem-solution: Harris speech, 279ff.; Creasy speech, 308ff.

scenarios-forces influencing choice: Cornish speech, 84ff.

thematic development: MacArthur speech, 356ff.; King, "Dream," 367ff.

trends-evaluation: Porter speech, 36ff.

topical: Baruch speech, 48ff.; King, "Civil Disobedience," 58ff.; Weisensel speech, 80ff.; Golub speech, 228ff.; Michener speech, 272ff.

summary (internal): 39 (12); 40 (17); 82 (11); 120–121 (53–57); 201 (55).

transition: 39 (13); 40 (18); 41 (22); 50 (16); 81 (5); 81 (7); 82 (12); 85 (11); 223 (25); 230 (8); 235 (16); 243 (24); 310 (6,9); 315 (32).

Stylistic Tactics

alliteration: 62 (13); 135 (47); 226 (57); 345 (38); 351 (23); 353 (44); 360 (31); 364 (24).

animation: 50 (22–24); 53 (44); Rowe speech, 68ff.; Alda speech, 145ff.; 222–223 (16–20); Jones speech 256ff.; Jordan speech, 299ff.; Kerry speech, 319ff.; King, "Dream," 366ff.

antithesis: 195 (22); 357 (8); 372 (15); 373 (27–28).

climax: 360–361 (30–33); 365 (32–35); 369–370 (21–27); 384–385 (14–15).

hyberbole: 48 (1); 147 (6).

imagery: 67 (25); 358 (15,17); 360 (28); 360–361 (30–33); King, "Dream," 366ff.

irony: 70–71 (5); 83 (16); 155 (33); 164 (18).

language (colorful): 45 (39); 135 (46); 182 (14).

loaded words: 74 (12); 127 (2); 147–148 (7); 152 (12); 153 (30–31); 257 (7–11); 305 (66).

empirical studies: 124 (3); 124–125 (4); 157 (10); 222 (14); 230 (8); 235 (21); 250–251 (19); 287 (56).

percentages: 121 (65); 152 (19); 323 (24,27).

personal illustration: 241–242 (17–18); 242–243 (21); 249 (11); 251 (26); 252 (33); 258 (12–14); 260 (23–24); 262 (32); 277–278 (33–34); 324–325 (36).

refutation: 275 (19); 302 (25–30); 314 (20–26); 320–321 (10–11).

specific instances/examples: 112 (14); 113 (20–21); 113 (24); 113–114 (28–29); 115 (37–39); 122 (66); 122–123 (76–77); 124 (3); 125–126 (8); 128 (9); 129 (15); 130–131 (25–26); 133 (38); 149 (7); 151 (11); 153 (26); 158–159 (16); 163 (11–12); 165–166 (25–26); 178–179 (4); 192–193 (12); 193 (15); 196 (29); 197 (35–36); 198 (40); 213 (11–14); 215 (23); 216 (26); 225–226 (50); 229 (4); 231 (9); 234 (9,11,13); 234–235 (14); 241–242 (17–18); 242–243 (21); 243 (23); 245–246 (31); 249–250 (12); 257 (10); 280–281 (8); 283 (23); 284 (31–33); 289 (5); 290 (13); 301 (17); 302 (33–39); 310 (7,10); 320 (5); 323 (25–26); 363–364 (19).

statistics: 113 (23); 128–129 (12–13); 178 (3); 194 (19); 222 (13); 225 (44); 230 (8); 292 (3–7); 293 (8–9); 297 (45); 310 (8–9).

testimony/quotation: 112 (15); 113 (22); 114 (30); 125 (7); 126 (9); 128 (10–11); 130 (21–22); 131–132 (29–31); 133 (36–37); 154 (32); 157 (9); 158 (12,14); 180 (10–11); 180–181 (12); 183 (20); 184 (22–24); 184–185 (25–27); 187 (31); 188–189 (36); 193–194 (17); 194–195 (21); 197 (34); 199 (45); 214 (16); 224 (30–31); 226 (51); 229 (5–6); 230 (7); 234 (10); 254 (44); 261 (29); 262–263 (35–39); 282 (19); 283 (24); 284 (34); 285 (42); 289 (6); 290 (11); 297 (53); 309 (4–5); 310 (10); 349–350 (12–13); 350 (15–19).

transcendence: 174–175 (32–35); 175–176 (38–51).